The First-Year Teacher's
Survival Guide

Ready-to-Use Strategies, Tools & Activities for Meeting the Challenges of Each School Day

THIRD EDITION

JULIA G. THOMPSON

JOSSEY-BASS™
A Wiley Brand

Library of Congress Cataloging-in-Publication Data has been applied for and is on file with the Library of Congress.
ISBN 978-1-118-45028-4 (paper); ISBN 978-1-118-64734-9 (ebk.); ISBN 978-1-118-64741-7 (ebk.)

THIRD EDITION

PB Printing   10 9 8 7 6

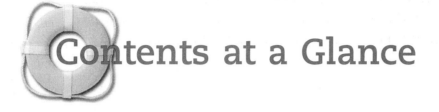

Contents at a Glance

I. Assume Your Professional Responsibilities

Section One: Know What It Means to Be a Twenty-First-Century
Educator 1
Section Two: Develop the Practical Skills You'll Need to Manage a
Classroom 35
Section Three: Collaborate with Others in Your School and
Community 73

II. Establish a Learning Community

Section Four: Begin a Successful School Term 107
Section Five: Develop Positive Classroom Relationships 139

III. Promote Student Achievement

Section Six: Control Class Time 175
Section Seven: Manage Your Classroom 201
Section Eight: Motivate Students to Succeed 221

IV. Design and Deliver Effective Instruction

Section Nine: Choose Appropriate Instructional Strategies and
Resources 259
Section Ten: Design Effective Instruction 279
Section Eleven: Deliver Engaging Instruction 303
Section Twelve: Meet the Needs of All of Your Students 331
Section Thirteen: Assess Your Students' Progress 365
Section Fourteen: Level the Playing Field by Covering Basic Skills 401

V. Maintain an Orderly Environment

Section Fifteen: Prevent Discipline Problems.. 427
Section Sixteen: Manage Discipline Problems... 447
Section Seventeen: Learn to Solve Classroom Problems... 483

Contents

Contents at a Glance v
DVD Contents xv
About the Author xix
Acknowledgments... xxi
About This Survival Guide xxiii

I. Assume Your Professional Responsibilities

Section One: Know What It Means to Be a Twenty-First-Century Educator... 1

The Challenges of Our Changing Profession 2
You Can Manage Your Professional Challenges Successfully............................... 3
Professionalism: The Powerful Force Underlying Everything We Do 4
Your Professional Responsibilities 5
Developing a Reflective Practice 9
Teacher Worksheet 1.1: Template for Professional Self-Reflection.................... 11
Teacher Worksheet 1.2: Characteristics of Successful Teachers......................... 12
Teacher Worksheet 1.3: Learning from Exemplary Teachers 13
Learning from Role Models and Mentors.. 14
Seeking Feedback on Your Professional Performance... 15
Teacher Worksheet 1.4: Making the Most of Peer Observations........................ 16
Using the Evaluation Process to Improve Your Teaching Skills......................... 17
Teacher Worksheet 1.5: How Observers Will Evaluate You 19
Teacher Worksheet 1.6: Data Tracking Sheet 22
Maintaining Sustained Professional Growth.. 25
Teacher Worksheet 1.7: Are You in Charge of Your Career?............................. 26
Teacher Worksheet 1.8: Track Your Professional Goals..................................... 30
Learning to Manage Your Stress.. 31
Best Practices Checklist... 32
Time to Reflect: What It Means to Be a Twenty-First-Century Educator........... 33

Section Two: Develop the Practical Skills You'll Need to Manage a Classroom 35

Arrange Your Own Work Area 35
Become an Efficient Teacher 42
Teacher Worksheet 2.1: Meet Your Classroom Priorities 44
Teacher Worksheet 2.2: Teacher's Daily To-Do List 47
Teacher Worksheet 2.3: Checklist of a Teacher's Weekly Reminders 49
General Tips for Managing School Papers 50
How to Organize and Manage Student Information 53
How to Grade Papers Quickly 54
Tips for Managing Electronic Files 56
Tips for Managing E-Mail 56
How to Maintain Your Class Web Page 57
How to Save Paper 58
Optimize Your Use of the Photocopier 59
Prepare Your Classroom for Students 59
How to Protect School Resources 66
How to Request Repairs 67
Classroom Safety Issues 67
Best Practices Checklist 70
Time to Reflect: Develop the Practical Skills You'll Need to Manage a Classroom 71

Section Three: Collaborate with Others in Your School and Community 73

Your School Community: A Network of Teams 73
Communities of Practice 74
Where Do You Fit in as a New Teacher? 75
Building Trust: The Importance of a Reputation for Integrity 76
Strategies for Effective Collaboration 77
Social Media Guidelines 80
The Importance of Perfect Attendance 81
The Support Staff 82
The Chain of Command 82
Collaborate Successfully with Administrators 83
Working Well with Parents and Guardians 84
What Parents and Guardians Expect from You 85
Prevent Miscommunication with a Transparent Classroom 86
Teacher Worksheet 3.1: How Effective Are You at Creating a Transparent Classroom? 89
The Importance of Keeping Contact Records 90
Teacher Worksheet 3.2: Contact Documentation Form 91
Be Positive with Parents and Guardians 92
Take Care to Interact Professionally 93
Class Newsletters 96

Conduct Successful Conferences with Parents and Guardians 97

Best Practices Checklist...104

Time to Reflect: Collaborate with Others in Your School and Community.......................104

II. Establish a Learning Community

Section Four: Begin a Successful School Term 107

The First Day Is Important...107

Overcome Those First-Day Jitters 108

What to Do on the First Day: Your Priorities..109

First-Day-of-School Welcome Packet 111

Parent or Guardian Worksheet 4.1: Inventory: Please Tell Me About Your Child..........113

Activities for the First Day 115

Teacher Worksheet 4.1: Planning Template for the First Day of School 117

Teacher Worksheet 4.2: Checklist for the First Day...119

Student Information Records 120

Student Worksheet 4.1: Student Information Form...121

Learn Your Students' Names Quickly 123

How to Get to Know Your Students 123

Student Worksheet 4.2: Inventory for Elementary Students...127

Student Worksheet 4.3: Inventory for Middle School Students...129

Student Worksheet 4.4: Inventory for High School Students...131

Create a Positive Group Identity 133

What You Can Expect During the First Week 135

Mistakes to Avoid at the Start of School 136

Best Practices Checklist...137

Time to Reflect: Begin a Successful School Term...138

Section Five: Develop Positive Classroom Relationships............................ 139

Develop a Positive Relationship with Students...139

Teacher Worksheet 5.1: How Appropriate Are Your Relationships with Students?.......142

Teacher Worksheet 5.2: Are You a Good Role Model? 149

Help Students Learn to Relate Well to Each Other 157

Teacher Worksheet 5.3: Checklist of Social Skills All Students Should Master 167

Best Practices Checklist...173

Time to Reflect: Develop Positive Classroom Relationships 174

III. Promote Student Achievement

Section Six: Control Class Time 175

You Control the Time Your Students Have with You 175

How Teachers Waste Time 176

Teacher Worksheet 6.1: How Well Do You Use Class Time?..177

Principles of Effective Classroom Time Management...179

Raise Your Students' Awareness of Class Time 180

How to Handle Interruptions 181

Pacing Instruction 182

The First Ten Minutes of Class..183

Teacher Worksheet 6.2: Plans for Starting Class Effectively...186

Productive Transitions 187

How to Handle Requests to Leave the Classroom..191

Teacher Worksheet 6.3: Student Sign-Out Sheet 195

The Last Ten Minutes of Class..196

Teacher Worksheet 6.4: Plans for Ending Class Effectively...198

How to Use Any Time Left at the End of Class 199

Best Practices Checklist..199

Time to Reflect: Control Class Time..200

Section Seven: Manage Your Classroom... 201

A Well-Managed Classroom..201

How to Focus Your Class on Good Behavior..202

The Importance of Clear Expectations...203

Procedures, Policies, Rules: When to Apply Each One 203

Policies You Will Need to Develop...204

Teacher Worksheet 7.1: Planning for Classroom Policies..205

Establish Procedures..209

Teacher Worksheet 7.2: Where to Find Help with Establishing Procedures 210

Suggestions for Establishing Three Necessary Procedures 211

Teach and Enforce School Rules 212

Creating Classroom Rules 213

Teacher Worksheet 7.3: Checklist to Determine If Your Rules Will Be Successful 215

Teaching Classroom Rules 216

Enforcing Classroom Rules...217

Enlisting Student Support for Class Rules...218

Positive or Negative Consequences? 218

Best Practices Checklist..219

Time to Reflect: Manage Your Classroom 219

Section Eight: Motivate Students to Succeed.. 221

The Self-Fulfilling Prophecy 221

Be Positive If You Want Positive Results 222

Lay a Solid Foundation..223

Motivate Your Students with a Variety of Methods..223

Extrinsic Motivation 226

Make Sure Intrinsic Motivation Is a Classroom Constant 228

Make Success Attainable...231

Teach Your Students to Follow Directions...232

Purposeful Learning...235

Teacher Worksheet 8.1: Assignment Checklist..237

Take a Goal-Oriented Approach to Learning...238

Student Worksheet 8.1: Setting and Achieving SMART Goals........................239

Make Success Visible..241

Teach Students to Track Their Own Mastery of Material 241

Student Worksheet 8.2: Progress Tracking Chart..243

How to Survive the Homework Debate..244

Teacher Worksheet 8.2: Plan Successful Homework Assignments 248

Student Worksheet 8.3: Missing Homework Explanation Form.......................252

Student Worksheet 8.4: Class Log Page...256

Best Practices Checklist...257

Time to Reflect: Motivate Students to Succeed 257

IV. Design and Deliver Effective Instruction

Section Nine: Choose Appropriate Instructional Strategies and Resources 259

Take Advantage of the Advances in Educational Research................................259

Why Small, Strategic Steps Are the Keys to Success..260

Overview of Just a Few of the Instructional Options Teachers Have................260

Classroom Technology Resources to Aid Your Instructional Practices.............267

Useful Web Sites for Educators 273

"There's an App for That!"..274

Best Practices Checklist...275

Time to Reflect: Choose Appropriate Instructional Strategies and Resources................276

Section Ten: Design Effective Instruction 279

The Benefits of Careful Planning...279

Backward Design: Think Big, but Start Small...280

Cover the Curriculum or Teach Your Students?...280

How Prepared Should You Be? 281

Common Planning Problems...281

How to Find the Time to Plan...282

Your State's Standards 283

The Common Core State Standards Initiative..283

Assess Your Students' Prior Knowledge...285

How to Begin Planning Instruction 286

Teacher Worksheet 10.1: Format for a Course Overview.................................288

Teacher Worksheet 10.2: Format for a Unit Plan 290

What to Include in Your Plans...291

Teacher Worksheet 10.3: Easy-to-Use Format for Daily Lesson Plans 294
Successful Learning for Nontraditional Schedules 295
How to Adjust a Lesson 296
Always Have a Backup Plan 296
Free Online Resources for Lesson Plans 298
Best Practices Checklist 300
Time to Reflect: Design Effective Instruction 301

Section Eleven: Deliver Engaging Instruction 303

Guidelines for Improving Your Classroom Charisma 303
Pitfalls That Plague Too Many Teachers 304
Improve Your Oral Presentations 305
How to Make a Point Students Will Remember 310
How to Help Students Stay on Track During a Lecture 311
Conduct Class Discussions That Engage Every Student 312
The Power of Play: Using Toys to Capture Attention 314
Games Your Students Will Enjoy 315
Use Graphic Organizers to Engage Students 318
Two Simple Techniques: Learning Cubes and Colored Dot Labels 320
Providing Models, Examples, and Samples 326
How to Make Seatwork Appealing 327
Best Practices Checklist 328
Time to Reflect: Deliver Engaging Instruction 328

Section Twelve: Meet the Needs of All of Your Students 331

Differentiated Instruction to Support All Learners 331
Teacher Worksheet 12.1: Individualized Instruction Worksheet 335
Teacher Worksheet 12.2: A Planning Tool for Differentiation 338
Students Who May Need Special Care 346
Best Practices Checklist 362
Time to Reflect: Meet the Needs of All of Your Students 363

Section Thirteen: Assess Your Students' Progress 365

Data-Driven Instruction: Summative and Formative Assessments 365
How to Use Formative Assessments 366
Teacher Worksheet 13.1: Tracking Formative Assessment Data 368
Student Worksheet 13.1: Assignment Reflection 376
The Two Most Common Written Assessments: Tests and Quizzes 377
Create Useful Objective Questions 379
How to Grade Objective Questions Quickly 381
Conduct Rules for Quizzes and Tests 381
What to Do If Many of Your Students Fail a Test or Quiz 382
Types of Authentic Assessments 383

Keeping Track of Grades 388

Student Worksheet 13.2: Grade Tracking Form for Student Success..................................391

How to Personalize a Grade Report 392

What You Should Do When Students Challenge Grades 392

What to Do When You Suspect a Student of Cheating...393

How to Manage Cyber Cheating 393

Extra Credit Dilemmas and Solutions..395

Success with Standardized Tests 395

Best Practices Checklist 399

Time to Reflect: Assess Your Students' Progress 399

Section Fourteen: Level the Playing Field by Covering Basic Skills............. 401

Media Literacy Skills..402

Listening Skills...404

Speaking Skills..405

Writing Skills 406

Vocabulary Acquisition Skills..407

Critical Thinking Skills 412

Reading Skills 417

Best Practices Checklist..424

Time to Reflect: Level the Playing Field by Covering Basic Skills 425

V. Maintain an Orderly Environment

Section Fifteen: Prevent Discipline Problems... 427

Punishment Is Not the Way to Prevent Problems 427

Self-Discipline Is the Key...428

Be Aware of the Causes of Most Discipline Problems...429

Easily Avoidable Mistakes Many Teachers Make 429

Teacher Worksheet 15.1: How Effective Are You at Preventing Discipline Problems?.......431

Your Role in Preventing Discipline Problems..432

Teacher Worksheet 15.2: Preventing or Minimizing Discipline Problems 433

Be Positive: Nothing Creates Success Like Success 434

Become a Consistent Teacher...434

Become a Fair Teacher..435

Withitness: One of the Most Valuable Prevention Techniques..436

Teacher Worksheet 15.3: What Is Your Level of Withitness?..437

A Crucial Step in Preventing Discipline Problems: Monitoring..438

How Students Can Get Help Quickly...439

Earn Your Students' Respect 440

An Unexpected Tip: Be a Good Listener 440

Early Intervention Strategies 441

When You Should Act 442

Harness the Power of Positive Peer Pressure 443

Best Practices Checklist 444

Time to Reflect: Prevent Discipline Problems 444

Section Sixteen: Manage Discipline Problems 447

Myths About Discipline 448

Control Your Anxiety with Proactive Strategies 448

Behaviors You Should Not Accept 449

What Do Your Supervisors Expect from You? 451

Respond Instead of Just Reacting 451

Teacher Worksheet 16.1: Classroom Management Techniques to Avoid 454

How to Avoid a Lawsuit: A Teacher's Legal Responsibilities 455

Teacher Worksheet 16.2: Behavior Incident Report 458

Due Process Procedures 459

Cultivate Grace Under Pressure 459

Great Advice: Don't Take It Personally 460

You May Be the Troublemaker 461

Think Before You Act 462

Don't Give Up on Your Difficult Students 463

How to Deal with a Difficult Class 463

How to Cope with a Student's Chronic Misbehavior 465

How to Hold Successful Conferences with Students Who Have Misbehaved 465

Put Detentions to Good Use 467

Manage Referrals to an Administrator with Confidence 469

Handling Four Common Types of Student Misbehavior 472

Best Practices Checklist 480

Time to Reflect: Manage Discipline Problems 481

Section Seventeen: Learn to Solve Classroom Problems 483

Questions to Consider When You Are Trying to Solve Classroom Problems 484

Take a Problem-Solving Approach 484

Teacher Worksheet 17.1: Work Through Classroom Problems 486

Problems Associated with Individual Students 487

Problems Associated with Enforcing School Policies or Rules 493

Problems Associated with Behavior During Instruction 497

Problems Associated with Students' Relationship with Their Teacher 501

Best Practices Checklist 503

Time to Reflect: Learn to Solve Classroom Problems 504

A Final Word 505

Index 507

How to Use the DVD 529

 DVD Contents

The DVD in the back of this book contains downloadable versions of worksheets and templates along with videos of the author discussing key topics. It also provides several bonus articles that will help you survive and thrive as a new teacher!

Section One: Know What It Means to Be a Twenty-First-Century Educator

Bonus Sections:

Lesson Study
Learning to Manage Your Stress

Teacher Worksheet B.1: Lesson Study Observation
Teacher Worksheet B.2: How Well Do You Currently Manage Your Stress Level?
Teacher Worksheet 1.1: Template for Professional Self-Reflection
Teacher Worksheet 1.2: Characteristics of Successful Teachers
Teacher Worksheet 1.3: Learning from Exemplary Teachers
Teacher Worksheet 1.4: Making the Most of Peer Observations
Teacher Worksheet 1.5: How Observers Will Evaluate You
Teacher Worksheet 1.6: Data Tracking Sheet
Teacher Worksheet 1.7: Are You in Charge of Your Career?
Teacher Worksheet 1.8: Track Your Professional Goals

Section Two: Develop the Practical Skills You'll Need to Manage a Classroom

Bonus Section:

Three Special Classroom Situations: Shared Classrooms, Portable Classrooms, and Overcrowded Classrooms

Teacher Worksheet 2.1: Meet Your Classroom Priorities
Teacher Worksheet 2.2: Teacher's Daily To-Do List
Teacher Worksheet 2.3: Checklist of a Teacher's Weekly Reminders

Section Three: Collaborate with Others in Your School and Community

Bonus Sections:

What to Do When You Have to Miss School

How to Have a Successful Open House

Connecting Your Students to Their Community and to the World

Teacher Worksheet 3.1: How Effective Are You at Creating a Transparent Classroom?

Teacher Worksheet 3.2: Contact Documentation Form

Section Four: Begin a Successful School Term

Parent or Guardian Worksheet 4.1: Inventory: Please Tell Me About Your Child

Teacher Worksheet 4.1: Planning Template for the First Day of School

Teacher Worksheet 4.2: Checklist for the First Day

Student Worksheet 4.1: Student Information Form

Student Worksheet 4.2: Inventory for Elementary Students

Student Worksheet 4.3: Inventory for Middle School Students

Student Worksheet 4.4: Inventory for High School Students

Section Five: Develop Positive Classroom Relationships

Bonus Sections:

Students Working in Collaborative Groups

Learning Partners: Pairing Students for Maximum Learning

Teacher Worksheet 5.1: How Appropriate Are Your Relationships with Students?

Teacher Worksheet 5.2: Are You a Good Role Model?

Teacher Worksheet 5.3: Checklist of Social Skills All Students Should Master

Section Six: Control Class Time

Teacher Worksheet 6.1: How Well Do You Use Class Time?

Teacher Worksheet 6.2: Plans for Starting Class Effectively

Teacher Worksheet 6.3: Student Sign-Out Sheet

Teacher Worksheet 6.4: Plans for Ending Class Effectively

Section Seven: Manage Your Classroom

Teacher Worksheet 7.1: Planning for Classroom Policies

Teacher Worksheet 7.2: Where to Find Help with Establishing Procedures

Teacher Worksheet 7.3: Checklist to Determine If Your Rules Will Be Successful

Section Eight: Motivate Students to Succeed

Bonus Sections:

Teaching Your Students Habits and Attitudes for Success
Focused Instructional Practices to Improve Student Work Habits

Teacher Worksheet 8.1: Assignment Checklist
Student Worksheet 8.1: Setting and Achieving SMART Goals
Student Worksheet 8.2: Progress Tracking Chart
Teacher Worksheet 8.2: Plan Successful Homework Assignments
Student Worksheet 8.3: Missing Homework Explanation Form
Student Worksheet 8.4: Class Log Page

Section Nine: Choose Appropriate Instructional Strategies and Resources

No DVD Content

Section Ten: Design Effective Instruction

Teacher Worksheet 10.1: Format for a Course Overview
Teacher Worksheet 10.2: Format for a Unit Plan
Teacher Worksheet 10.3: Easy-to-Use Format for Daily Lesson Plans

Section Eleven: Deliver Engaging Instruction

No DVD Content

Section Twelve: Meet the Needs of All of Your Students

Teacher Worksheet 12.1: Individualized Instruction Worksheet
Teacher Worksheet 12.2: A Planning Tool for Differentiation

Section Thirteen: Assess Your Students' Progress

Teacher Worksheet 13.1: Tracking Formative Assessment Data
Student Worksheet 13.1: Assignment Reflection
Student Worksheet 13.2: Grade Tracking Form for Student Success

Section Fourteen: Level the Playing Field by Covering Basic Skills

No DVD Content

Section Fifteen: Prevent Discipline Problems

Teacher Worksheet 15.1: How Effective Are You at Preventing Discipline Problems?

Teacher Worksheet 15.2: Preventing or Minimizing Discipline Problems

Teacher Worksheet 15.3: What Is Your Level of Withitness?

Section Sixteen: Manage Discipline Problems

Teacher Worksheet 16.1: Classroom Management Techniques to Avoid

Teacher Worksheet 16.2: Behavior Incident Report

Section Seventeen: Learn to Solve Classroom Problems

Teacher Worksheet 17.1: Work Through Classroom Problems

Videos

The Character Traits of Successful Teachers

Projecting Professionalism

Working Well With Colleagues and Administrators

Working Well With Parents

Showing Students That You Care

Acting Appropriately With Students

Minimizing Misbehavior

Increasing Positive Behavior

Cultivating Your Charisma as an Educator

The Importance of High Expectations

These materials are also available online at www.wiley.com/go/fyt3e. The password is the last five digits of this book's ISBN, which are 50284.

About the Author

Julia G. Thompson received her BA in English from Virginia Polytechnic Institute and State University in Blacksburg. She has been a teacher in the public schools of Virginia, Arizona, and North Carolina for more than thirty-five years. Thompson has taught a variety of courses, including freshman composition at Virginia Tech, English in all of the secondary grades, mining, geography, reading, home economics, math, civics, Arizona history, physical education, special education, graduation equivalency preparation, and employment skills. Her students have been diverse in ethnicity as well as in age, ranging from seventh graders to adults. Thompson currently teaches in Fairfax County, Virginia, where she is an active speaker and consultant. Author of *Discipline Survival Guide for the Secondary Teacher, The First-Year Teacher's Checklist,* and *The First-Year Teacher's Survival Guide Professional Development Training Kit,* Thompson also provides advice on a variety of subjects through her Web site, www.juliagthompson.com; on her blog, http://juliagthompson.blogspot.com; and on Twitter at https://twitter.com/TeacherAdvice.

For Phil, with gratitude, love, and admiration

Acknowledgments

I am grateful to my editor, Marjorie McAneny, for her encouragement, patience, and perceptive insights during the preparation of this book.

Thank you to the faculty, staff, and students of Windsor High School in Isle of Wight County, Virginia, for their continuing encouragement—something every teacher needs.

Special thanks to the following thoughtful teachers who offered their wise counsel, and who could remember what it's like to be a first-year teacher:

Dawn Carroll

Janice Dabroski

Bob Foley

Edward Gardner

Charlene Herrala

Matt Kissling

Jane Lankford

Stephanie Stock Mahoney

Debbie McManaway

Christina L. Myren

Carole Platt

Erin Sager

Luann Scott

Kathleen Stankiewicz

Kay Stephenson

Sarah Walski

Thanks, too, to these insightful novice teachers who took the time to share what it's like to be a first-year teacher in the twenty-first century:

Melinda Conner

Joshua Culver

Alanna Dougherty

Megan Kelly

Kristin Reagan

Jared Sronce

About This Survival Guide

This is the book that I needed as a first-year teacher. I knew a great deal about the content I was expected to teach, but I did not know very much at all about the children who would be occupying the desks in my new classroom. I did not know how to set up a grade book or administer a test or grade papers. I did not know what to do when a student talked back, told me a lie, or stopped paying attention to my carefully planned lesson. Worst of all, I did not even know where to begin to look for the answers that I needed then.

If you are like me, there is a great deal about our profession that intrigues you. You may feel uncertain at times about what to do, but you also feel pretty terrific when things go as planned. It's a great feeling to look around your classroom and realize that everyone is *learning*.

You know what you and your students are supposed to achieve, but you are not always sure how to proceed. Some days increase your confidence in your teaching skills, whereas others test your dedication.

Almost everyone begins a teaching career with the same emotions. Many veteran teachers also suffered through the tough days when they didn't know what to do and gloried in the days when they were able to engage every student in the magic of learning. The daily barrage of pressures on first-year teachers can be so exhausting and defeating that some eventually choose another career that is not as difficult but also not nearly as rewarding.

However, the first years of your teaching career can be immensely satisfying ones. Every day is a new opportunity to make a difference in a child's life. Your first years as a teacher can be years of dynamic professional growth and personal fulfillment as you achieve your own dreams while helping your students achieve theirs.

Helping you enjoy success in the first years of your career is the goal of *The First-Year Teacher's Survival Guide.* The suggestions and strategies in these pages can help you develop into a skillful classroom teacher who remains enthusiastic about the possibilities in every student. For instance, in this book you'll find

- Resources that can help you collaborate with other professional educators in classrooms around the globe
- Methods of reflecting on your current teaching skills and establishing goals for your professional life
- Suggestions for learning to work well with others as a member of a community of practice
- Guidance with the responsibility of translating the theories you learned as a student into successful classroom practice
- Assistance in identifying your professional responsibilities and establishing priorities to accomplish them
- Strategies for managing your school day so that you can find a successful balance between your personal and professional lives
- Efficient ways to manage paperwork and complete other routine tasks so that you can focus on teaching
- Motivational strategies designed to help you involve every student in meaningful, engaging learning activities
- Inspiration, insight, and practical advice from successful veteran and first-year teachers
- A wide variety of innovative and time-tested classroom management activities, strategies, and techniques to help you create a positive learning environment

This award-winning book gives beginning educators everything they need to survive and thrive in the classroom. The third edition covers new material, including

- How to collaborate with colleagues in a professional learning community
- How to access information and resources about timely topics, such as data-driven instruction, value-added assessment, and action research
- How to find teacher freebies and create a productive classroom environment on a budget
- How to use digital tools to design and deliver innovative, engaging, relevant lessons
- How to help students prepare for standardized tests, become media literate, and develop into socially responsible citizens
- How to reach students through educational games, toys, and hands-on activities
- How to help students learn to assume responsibility for their learning and become self-disciplined learners
- How to handle "homework push-back" from parents and guardians*

---

*As a classroom teacher, you will find that some of your students will live with one or more biological or adoptive parents, whereas others will live with one or more guardians. Throughout this book, you will find the use of "parents or guardians" or "parents and guardians" to indicate this relationship.

- How to fulfill your legal responsibilities and protect yourself from lawsuits
- How to reach out to students who need special care
- How to solve many behavior problems that all teachers face

The First-Year Teacher's Survival Guide was written to help K–12 teachers meet the challenges that each school day brings. In these pages, you will find the answers to the most common how-to questions that many first-year teachers have:

Section One	How can I become a successful educator in the twenty-first century?
Section Two	How can I fulfill the practical responsibilities inherent in my new profession?
Section Three	How can I develop successful collaborative relationships with my colleagues and with the families of my students?
Section Four	How can I organize my time, tasks, and classroom to begin a successful school term?
Section Five	How can I foster positive classroom relationships with my students as well as help them learn to relate well to each other?
Section Six	How can I use class time so that my students are on task from the start to the finish of class?
Section Seven	How can I establish a well-managed classroom?
Section Eight	How can I motivate my students to succeed?
Section Nine	How can I choose the best instructional options and equipment available to me?
Section Ten	How can I design lessons that will meet the needs of my students?
Section Eleven	How can I deliver instruction that will fully engage my students in learning?
Section Twelve	How can I meet the needs of all of my students through differentiated instruction?
Section Thirteen	How can I assess my students' progress throughout the school year?
Section Fourteen	How can I make sure that my students have acquired the appropriate basic skills that they need to be successful in my class?
Section Fifteen	How can I prevent discipline problems from disrupting the positive learning environment that I want to establish?
Section Sixteen	How can I successfully manage discipline problems once they occur?
Section Seventeen	How can I successfully manage the common problems that can happen in any classroom?

The First-Year Teacher's Survival Guide is meant to be a working resource, full of classroom-tested knowledge for you. What is the most effective way to use this book? The answers to this question are as varied as the teachers who use it.

- Browse through this guide section by section, gathering ideas to enrich your classes and strengthen your teaching skills. This method allows you to pick and choose from the practical advice and activities you'll find included here.

- When you have become familiar with the format and contents, use this book as a desktop resource. You can use the table of contents or the index to quickly look up solutions to specific problems that are of immediate concern.

- Work through a section at a time, learning, applying, practicing, and adapting the information as you go. Although you can't learn how to be an excellent teacher all at once, you can benefit from this systematic approach.

- When you have had a discouraging day, look over the practical advice from experienced educators, who offer strategies and insights to help you keep your troubles in perspective and solve the day's problems.

- If you are in a hurry (and what teacher isn't?), skim through the checklist of best practices at the end of each section to see how you can add to your repertoire of teaching skills.

- Finally, check out the bonus material on the DVD that accompanies this guide. There you will find the worksheets included in this book in an electronic format that will make it easy for you to download and print them for use in your class. In addition, you will find more information about some of the topics introduced in this book, but covered in more depth there.

However you choose to use this book (and the bonus material), it was designed to be an interactive experience. Use a pencil to fill in the assessments, set your goals, and scribble notes as you read each section. Highlight. Underline. Annotate information about the links and resources. Dog-ear the pages. Print out the worksheets on the DVD. Place bookmarks in the sections that appeal to you. As you go through the process of learning the intricacies of your new profession, refer to this book when you need assistance with the daily problems that can rob even the most stalwart educator of confidence.

The ultimate goal of the information in these pages is to help you become the self-assured and knowledgeable educator that you dreamed of being when you chose your new career. From the first day of school to the last day, you can be one of the greatest assets that our world can have—an effective teacher.

With patience and practice, you can realize your professional dreams. Millions of others have done it; you can, too. Your first years as a teacher can set you squarely on the path to achieving the satisfaction that only a career in education can bring.

Best wishes for a gratifying and enjoyable first year!

Julia G. Thompson

For more information on how you can have a successful first year, visit www.juliagthompson.com, juliagthompson.blogspot.com, or https://twitter.com/TeacherAdvice.

Staff Developers Take Note!
Do you want to use *The First-Year Teacher's Survival Guide* to train your new teachers? Each section ends with a set of questions that can be used to reflect and discuss in a group setting, and you can access a free downloadable guide for staff development facilitators at www.wiley.com/go/fyt3e.

The First-Year Teacher's
Survival Guide

SECTION ONE

Know What It Means to Be a Twenty-First-Century Educator

More than three million dedicated professionals. That's how many teachers will report to work on the first day of school this year in the United States. More than three million of us will unite in a profoundly significant undertaking—the education of a nation.

As a new teacher, you will contribute your unique insights, energy, skills, and knowledge to the efforts of your three million–plus colleagues. Understandably, there is no one profile that could define the American teacher. Our differences span not just geography and educational experiences but also age groups, lifestyles, ethnicities, and cultures.

Although each classroom is as unique as the teacher who leads it, we American educators at work in the twenty-first century do share some remarkable similarities. One of the most significant is that we share an idealistic sense of purpose. We know that what we do is important because we make a difference in the lives of our students. In fact, we are committed to the success of all learners in our classes. This common purpose is perhaps the single most important tie that binds us to each other, to our profession, and to our students.

Another similarity that we share is one that is very different from the experiences of teachers in the past. No longer do we have to make decisions that affect the welfare of an entire classroom without being able to talk them over with other educators. Instead, as a new teacher, you will find yourself involved with collaborative groups that will allow you to grow professionally as you solve problems in your classroom and in your school. Effective teamwork skills that make it easier to work productively with colleagues play a more important role than ever before in the lives of today's educators.

As teachers in the twenty-first century, we also have access to an ever-growing amount of information derived from academic research conducted to determine the factors that influence how students learn. We can use such information to design differentiated instruction that will appeal to the learning needs of all students. Tailoring lessons to match individual learning style preferences and needs is easier than ever.

Another defining trait of today's teachers is that they routinely use self-reflection to improve their teaching expertise. Although self-reflection has long been a key component of effective teaching, this practice plays a particularly large role for twenty-first-century teachers. Taking time to methodically reflect on the various aspects of their professional responsibilities and on their own effectiveness is one of the most important methods that teachers today can use to refine their skills and add to their knowledge.

Teachers in the twenty-first century also rely on technology to enhance their instructional practices. Although recognizing that nothing can replace the importance of a strong classroom leader, modern teachers know that integrating appropriate technology resources allows students to perform at their best and to participate competitively in today's global classrooms. We also use the technology resources available to us to network with other educators, research material for instruction, connect our students to students in faraway classrooms, access lesson plans, and offer engaging instruction.

Finally, to be a successful teacher in the twenty-first century means to be forward thinking. Whereas other professions tend to focus on events in the present or even in the past, we teachers know that what we do today in our classrooms affects the future. Whereas other adults may look at our students and just see young faces or childish behavior, we teachers see the future in our classes. Even though we may spend our days working in the here and now, our hearts are with our students in the future.

As a teacher, you will never be rich, even if your district has the good sense to pay you well. You will be rewarded repeatedly, however, because you will help students achieve their dreams, and, in doing so, you will achieve your own.

Welcome to your new profession.

The Challenges of Our Changing Profession

As a new teacher, you are entering the field of education at one of the most challenging times in history. New mandates, high expectations, low pay, diverse populations, overcrowded classes . . . it's not easy being a teacher. It is no secret that education has become one of the most intensely scrutinized professions in the world. Sometimes it seems as if everyone has an opinion about what is wrong with schools and how we should go about fixing them.

Because schools are designed to serve the various global, national, and local cultures that bond us all, they reflect the problems and demands of our daily lives. Such momentous issues as budget woes, rising illiteracy rates, and student discipline problems are just some of the many ever-changing challenges with which today's school personnel must contend. Some of these challenges may be easier to manage than others, but all of them will have an impact on your professional life.

In these challenging times, you will have the opportunity to make a positive difference in the lives of your students. Although it is exciting to think of the powerful influence you can have on your students, it is just as unnerving to accept the responsibilities that accompany that importance. Countless studies indicate that teachers are the most significant factor in any student's schooling. Although you may be tempted to think peer pressure or a student's home environment have more influence than you do, keep in mind that it is teachers who inspire students to believe they can achieve their goals and dreams, who teach students to read, to write, and to think. We show students how to be good citizens, how to become lifelong learners, and how to believe in themselves.

It's important to realize that despite the many challenges in every classroom, good teachers manage to turn those challenges into positive opportunities for growth. As a new teacher, you will be able to add your skills and your knowledge to the efforts of the dedicated community of educators who will be working with you to solve these momentous issues.

You Can Manage Your Professional Challenges Successfully

Given the purpose of your work and the diverse personalities, needs, and backgrounds of your students, problems are inevitable. Some will be simple to resolve, others will take longer, and still others may not have workable solutions. If you are like most new teachers, you may already be concerned about how well you will manage these problems. Will you be able to keep them small and manageable, or will they morph into insomnia-inducing stress?

On the days when your life as a teacher seems beset with serious problems, take comfort in knowing that you are not alone. All teachers experience professional challenges. First-year teachers, experienced teachers, teachers at every grade level and every ability level have to cope with various types of problems, no matter how ideal their school situation.

Anytime you feel overwhelmed, remember that all teachers have had to deal with what you are going through. In fact, here are some of the most common challenges that all teachers experience:

- Stacks of tedious paperwork
- Fatigue and burnout
- Difficulty in connecting with parents and guardians

One day in the cafeteria, I noticed a young man who was not his usual fun self. I walked by, stopped, and asked him quietly if everything was all right. He said yes, but I knew it wasn't. I told him he knew where I was if he needed me, then moved on. The next morning, I found a note on my desk, all folded, teen-style. In the note, this young man thanked me for asking him if he was okay. He said he had been struggling with some very hard news and was really thinking of doing something stupid, but I had made him rethink his decision. I was awed at the power. As teachers, we never, ever know the full extent of our effect on those lives entrusted to us. We must truly exercise caution in how we interact with young people. I carry that note, now almost thirty years old, in my wallet every day of my life, to remind me of this moment. The good news: this young man is now a productive member of our community with a lovely wife (who was also my student) and three great children. What greater reward could any teacher desire?

Luann Scott, 37 years' experience

- A culture or generation gap with students
- Not enough equipment or materials
- Students with overwhelming family problems
- Uncertainty about the right course of action to take

If some of these problems seem all too familiar, take heart. Remember that the sure sign of a great teacher is not the absence of problems, but the ability to generate and implement innovative and effective solutions to an array of classroom challenges. So critical is this ability, in fact, that the last section of this book, Section Seventeen, is devoted to helping you solve some of the most common problems you will have to face as a new teacher. With a positive attitude, a professional approach, a bit of creativity, and plenty of practice, you will soon be able to solve the problems that you will encounter at school.

Professionalism: The Powerful Force Underlying Everything We Do

Although many educators use the term *professionalism* when referring to excellent teaching practices, reaching a common consensus about the definition of the term is not as easy. We tend to recognize it when we see it in action, but may not be able to articulate exactly what it means. Simply put, though, professionalism means being the very best teacher that you can be every day. When you choose to conduct yourself in a professional manner, you send the message that you are in control of your classroom and yourself.

It is not always easy to be an educator, especially when you are just starting out, but resolving to be guided by the principles of professionalism is a sound decision with far-reaching effects. By behaving in a professional manner, you will earn the respect of your students, their families, and your colleagues. You will be able to enjoy your school days instead of struggling with the unpleasant consequences brought about by poor decisions.

If you want to be highly regarded as an educator, keep in mind that such regard does not come about by accident. Choosing to act in a professional manner is a deliberate decision made by every excellent teacher. You, too, can begin your new occupation in a positive way by allowing your career decisions to be guided by the three most basic principles of professionalism:

Principle One: Commit yourself to maintaining high standards of professional performance. When you make the decision to set and achieve high standards of professional performance, you will find yourself working to develop the persona of a competent professional educator. You will hone your skills and increase your base of knowledge about pedagogy as well as about the subject or subjects you teach. You will also find that high standards of professional performance mean that you will learn to work successfully as part of a collaborative team dedicated to the welfare of all students in your care.

Principle Two: Commit yourself to establishing a productive, positive classroom environment. A productive, positive classroom environment is crucial to the success of your students. In this type of classroom, you will establish vital and appropriate connections with and among your students so that the emotional climate of the class is one that is centered on learning and not on strife. You will also find that using proactive classroom management strategies to encourage self-discipline is key to the long-term success of your students.

Principle Three: Commit yourself to actively promoting student achievement and learning. When you focus on actively promoting student achievement and learning, you will use class time and space to create a productive, student-centered environment. You will be able to take a prescriptive approach to differentiating instruction—whereby you create individualized instruction for your students after determining their strengths and weaknesses as learners—because your decisions will be informed by data. You will design and deliver appropriate, dynamic instruction designed to meet the needs of all learners in your class.

Your Professional Responsibilities

Education is a complex undertaking. It differs from many professions in the multitude and variety of daily tasks that teachers must accomplish. As a teacher, you not only have to master the art of interacting effectively with others at all times but also face an extensive array of other responsibilities.

One of your most difficult tasks as a new teacher is learning how to manage all of your duties in a proficient manner. To accomplish this, you should first focus on your three most important professional responsibilities: creating a culture of high performance, using action research to inform classroom decisions, and becoming a highly qualified and highly effective teacher.

PROFESSIONAL RESPONSIBILITY ONE: CREATE A CULTURE OF HIGH PERFORMANCE

One of the fundamental outcomes of education reform efforts at local, state, and national levels involves an important shift in the expectations that school districts have for teacher performance. As a twenty-first-century educator, you will be expected not just to maintain a well-managed classroom with well-behaved students but also to create a culture of high performance for your students. All teachers, no matter what subject matter they teach or the age and ability levels of their students, are expected to create this culture in their classes.

Although creating such a culture seems to be a difficult task at first, this shift in expectations can make your life as a teacher much more rewarding as you watch your students master the material they are expected to learn. How will you know when you have created the productive culture of high performance that you want for your students? Here are some of the distinctive hallmarks of a classroom in which there is a culture of high performance:

- The classroom is student centered, with students taking ownership of their learning and responsibility for their success.
- Students are fully engaged in meaningful, respectful, and appropriate learning tasks.
- The overall focus of the work is goal oriented and purposeful.
- The teacher uses current research findings and best practices to inform instructional decisions.
- Students move forward in their learning, mastering the assigned material and then moving on to the next topic under study. Students learn what they are supposed to learn.
- The teacher makes instructional decisions based on a thoughtful analysis of available data.

Creating a culture of high performance is not a task that can be done in a day or two, but rather requires consistent and sustained effort. It begins with the expectations that you have for your students. Set high goals and expectations for them; make sure that these expectations and goals are ones that students perceive as achievable.

Next, all students should know the goals and expectations that you have for them. Be very clear so that students know what they need to do to be successful and how to proceed to meet the expectations you have for them. Students in a classroom where there is a culture of high performance know the specifics of what they are supposed to achieve, and, most important, they commit themselves to reaching their learning goals.

Knowledgeable teachers have found that it is impossible to create a culture of high performance without encouraging teamwork. Students who work together learn to support each other. Those successful teachers also focus on the connection between practice and effort and students' ability to meet high expectations. Take time to promote this connection whenever possible to reinforce the validity of the work that you ask of students.

Finally, in a classroom where there is a culture of high performance, the students and teacher take time to acknowledge their triumphs and celebrate their successes. The culture of this type of classroom is overwhelmingly positive and conducive to creating more success.

PROFESSIONAL RESPONSIBILITY TWO: USE ACTION RESEARCH TO INFORM CLASSROOM DECISIONS

The term *action research* is one that has been part of the glossary of education terms for many years, but it has assumed new prominence with the recent emphasis on site-based decision making. Action research is simply the research that educators do as they go about testing new strategies and ideas, analyzing the resulting data, and then deciding how to implement their findings. It differs from scholarly or theoretical research in that it is solution oriented and controlled by the members of a school community themselves.

Using the procedures in the action research process is a productive and systematic way to make decisions about such diverse topics as the most appropriate teaching methods, how best to deliver content, or the best ways to motivate students to achieve. In addition, teachers have found that when they undertake collaborative action research projects, the benefits are even greater than when they work alone.

In fact, at any given time in a school there may be many different types of action research projects under way: individual teachers may be investigating ideas for their classroom, collaborative groups of teachers may be testing ideas that affect their grade-level or professional learning teams, and the entire school community may be involved in a large-scale exploration of a topic of interest to all. To begin the procedures in the action research process in your own classroom practice, follow these proven techniques for successful action research:

- **Step One**: Determine an issue or problem that you want to investigate. It can be as simple as asking why your students don't always complete their homework assignments or as elaborate as helping your students learn to use effective reading practices.

- **Step Two**: Formulate a potential solution and apply it to the problem. The solution that you apply should be something that you believe has the potential to resolve the issue or problem. Once you have determined a possible solution, systematically put it into practice.

- **Step Three**: Collect data. Depending on the problem or issue that you are investigating, the data can be examples of student work, standardized test scores, formative assessment results, or products of any other method that allows you to test the effectiveness of your possible solution.

- **Step Four**: Analyze the data you have collected. Your analysis will indicate if you should continue the implementation of your possible solution or if you should formulate another one based on what you have learned from your original data collection and analysis.

One of the greatest benefits of the emphasis on the role that teachers play in action research is that it allows us to make the changes that we determine to be necessary in a school. As a classroom teacher, you will benefit greatly when you become involved in an action research project. You will be able to be methodical in the way you assess the effectiveness of new ideas; assume responsibility for your classroom decisions; contribute in a meaningful way to the culture of your school; and increase your own knowledge, skills, and confidence as an educator.

PROFESSIONAL RESPONSIBILITY THREE: BECOME A HIGHLY QUALIFIED AND HIGHLY EFFECTIVE TEACHER

On January 8, 2002, No Child Left Behind (NCLB) was officially enacted by Congress, thus becoming a critical aspect of the reform movements that have characterized the field of education in this century. One of the crucial hallmarks of this legislation is the requirement that all teachers be highly qualified. To be considered highly qualified, all teachers have to meet three important provisions: they must have earned at least a bachelor's degree from a four-year institution of higher learning, they must hold a teaching certificate from the state in which they intend to practice, and they must demonstrate competence in the core academic subject or subjects they will teach.

Since the enactment of this important legislation, other reforms in education policy have been proposed and enacted. NCLB has been extended as well as altered to make it more flexible in allowing more school districts to continue to meet its goals. In addition to this aspect of the reform of NCLB, reformers recognize that although being highly qualified is a worthwhile goal, it is not enough for a teacher to just be highly qualified if students are to succeed. Teachers today are also expected to be highly effective.

The impact of this change in the way reformers view teachers has been significant for all teachers. We are expected to help our students rise to achieve high performance standards, as evidenced by a variety of standardized tests. Highly effective teachers make sure that their students learn what they are supposed to learn, increase their knowledge, and improve their skills from the first day of school until the last day.

As a novice teacher, you may find it difficult at first to become a highly effective educator. However, there are many ways to ensure that you have the necessary skills and knowledge to make sound decisions that will have a positive influence on your students. No one begins his or her first year as a highly effective teacher. Work steadily and with purpose in small, strategic steps:

- Take advantage of as many professional development opportunities as you can.
- Talk over problems with colleagues when the problems are still small.
- Make a point of using best practices to design and deliver instruction.
- Take advantage of local, state, and national resources as often as possible.
- Network with other teachers who are also working to be highly effective educators.
- Be thoroughly familiar with the curriculum that you are expected to cover, and have at least a general idea of the content in the grades that precede and follow yours.
- Be aware of the learning needs and styles of your students so that you can offer remediation and enrichment when necessary.

In addition to these steps, there are several other ways you can work to become a competent and highly effective teacher: develop a reflective practice, find role models and mentors, seek feedback on your professional performance, use the evaluation process to improve your teaching skills, maintain sustained professional growth, and learn to manage your stress. As you read ahead, you will learn more about how these steps can assist you in your efforts to become a competent and highly effective teacher.

> Enjoy this time. Teaching can be a lot of fun when you connect with a student. Do not expect instant payback. You are laying the foundation for years to come, both in and out of school.
>
> *Edward Gardner, 36 years' experience*

Developing a Reflective Practice

Highly effective teachers soon realize that no one is a natural teacher. Teaching is a deliberate act. As educators, we cannot just rush through the hurly-burly of a school day paying cursory attention to what we are expected to accomplish and then hope to be successful. Reflecting on our teaching should be part of every aspect of our professional lives. Such reflection needs to systematic, methodical, and purposeful.

There are different ways to reflect on your teaching practice. You can gather information about your performance from a variety of sources, such as by asking colleagues to observe you, surveying your students, joining staff discussion groups, or even videotaping yourself. Examining the information that you gather in these ways will allow you to assess your strengths as well as your weaknesses. You will be able to discern trends and patterns in your teaching as you seek to improve your skills.

One very common and useful method of maintaining a reflective teaching practice can also involve recording ideas and observations in a journal on a regular basis. Whether you choose to maintain a journal online, in a computer desktop folder, on paper, or even in an audio format, it is important to be diligent about recording regularly. The questions that follow can help you use the time you dedicate to reflecting on your teaching practice as efficiently as possible.

- Are my goals for lessons reasonable and appropriate?
- Are my students challenged to do their best?
- Do students learn what they are supposed to master? How can I ensure that they always do this?
- At what points in a lesson did I have to change strategies or activities? Why? How productive was this flexibility on my part?
- How can I offer remediation or enrichment activities to the students who need them?
- What data do I need to collect before moving on to the next unit of study? How can I gather this information?
- What can I do to improve my skills when it comes to collaborating with colleagues?

- What worked in today's lesson? What did not work?
- How do I want my students to interact with each other as a whole group?
- What can I do to help my students collaborate with each other in small groups?
- What is the most efficient way to _____?
- How can I integrate technology into my lessons?
- What problems did I have to manage today? How well did I manage those problems?
- Where can I learn more about how to _____?
- How well do I listen to my students? What can I do to make sure that I model good listening skills?
- Which students were off task? What caused them to be off task?
- When were my students on task? What can I do to make sure that continues?
- How did I show that I was enthusiastic about the subject matter?
- How effective were the motivational techniques I used? How can I modify them for future lessons?
- How can I foster an atmosphere of mutual respect and courtesy among my students?
- How well do I manage my classroom? What can I improve?
- What should I do to help my students become self-disciplined learners?
- How much progress am I making in improving my teaching knowledge or skills? What can I do to improve?
- How can I use my strengths as a teacher to full advantage in my classroom?
- What are my strengths as a classroom leader?

TEACHER WORKSHEET 1.1

Template for Professional Self-Reflection

Using a template such as this one will make reflecting on your classroom practices a manageable daily task.

Date: _____

1. What lessons did I learn today?

   _____
   _____
   _____
   _____

2. How can I improve the way I manage my class?

   _____
   _____
   _____
   _____

3. How can I improve the way that I handle my academic responsibilities?

   _____
   _____
   _____
   _____

4. What problems did I find solutions for today, and what problems do I still need to solve?

   _____
   _____
   _____
   _____

5. What successes did I have today, and how did I achieve them?

   _____
   _____
   _____
   _____

Characteristics of Successful Teachers

Pausing every now and then to look at how well you measure up against other successful teachers is a useful way to reflect on your teaching practice. Place a check mark in the blank beside each character trait you already possess. After you have made this quick self-assessment, look over the list again to determine how to develop other characteristics that will help you become a competent, successful teacher.

Successful teachers are

_____ Patient with their students, their colleagues, and themselves

_____ Able to let their students know they care about them

_____ Energetic and willing to work

_____ Able to engage children whose attention span is brief

_____ Optimistic that what they do today affects the future

_____ Successful at listening to students both in groups and individually

_____ Able to make quick decisions pertaining to a variety of issues all day long

_____ Enthusiastic about their subject matter and about their students

_____ Efficient at planning, organizing, and managing time

_____ Not afraid to ask for help

From *The First-Year Teacher's Survival Guide, 3rd Edition*, by Julia G. Thompson. Copyright © 2013 by John Wiley & Sons, Inc. Reproduced by permission.

TEACHER WORKSHEET 1.3

Learning from Exemplary Teachers

Read each statement carefully. In the space provided, first briefly record a time when you have observed the characteristic in action, as demonstrated by a successful teacher. Then briefly brainstorm how you can put what you have learned into practice in your own classroom.

1. Today's successful educators work well in collaboration with a variety of other members of a school community.

   _____

   _____

   _____

2. Successful teachers make a point of being efficient at planning, organizing, and managing their time.

   _____

   _____

   _____

3. Exemplary teachers are able to design and deliver engaging instruction that meets the needs of every learner.

   _____

   _____

   _____

4. Modern teachers who are successful use creative and innovative approaches to solve classroom problems.

   _____

   _____

   _____

5. Successful teachers in the twenty-first century are enthusiastic about their subject matter and even more enthusiastic about their students. They know that what happens in their classroom has a profound effect on the lives of students.

   _____

   _____

   _____

Learning from Role Models and Mentors

One of the most important ways to develop into a highly effective teacher is to find good role models and mentors. These helpful colleagues show us the best ways to fulfill the various requirements of our career. No matter how long you teach, you will be able to learn from those competent school allies who are generous with their time, energy, and knowledge.

TIPS FOR FINDING APPROPRIATE ROLE MODELS

We all have idealistic visions of the kind of teacher we want to be—forever calm, inspiring, able to reach every student with effortless ease. Who would not aspire to be Jaime Escalante in *Stand and Deliver,* or Mr. Holland in *Mr. Holland's Opus,* or even the tough Joe Clark in *Lean on Me*? Unfortunately, too often these idealistic visions of the perfect educator are unrealistic and potentially self-defeating.

Although it is possible to learn valuable lessons from our vision of the perfect teacher, it is much more valuable to find real-life role models much closer to our own classroom. If you look around your school, you'll find an organized teacher or two who can serve as role models when it comes to efficiency. You will find someone who is masterful at dealing with upset parents or who can make even the most disruptive student remain focused and on task.

Soon you will see that role models for just about every aspect of your school life are all around you. Your role models need not be unrealistic media superteachers to make a positive impact on your career. Everyday role models are everywhere if you take the time to look and learn.

TIPS FOR WORKING WELL WITH MENTORS

You will probably be assigned an official mentor, but just as there are role models nearby, you will also find many other mentoring opportunities. To find a mentor, begin by searching for competent teachers who have high standards for themselves and who are comfortable being observed by other teachers. An effective mentor is good humored, tactful, knowledgeable, and eager to share ideas with you. In short, look for a mentor who is enthusiastic about teaching, about students, and about helping you learn to be a better teacher.

What should you ask of a mentor? Although novice teachers will obviously have a wide range of needs, there are some common concerns that all teachers share. These usually can be divided into two levels of questions that you will discuss with your mentor.

The first is the practical level: the daily concerns that are so difficult to manage at first. Here are just a few of the day-to-day concerns that you can discuss with your mentor:

- How to handle planning and curriculum concerns
- How to use various educational software programs
- How to obtain materials and supplies
- How to work with parents and guardians

- How to find where equipment is stored
- How to group students successfully

The second level of questions that you should ask a mentor focuses on issues that are more complex. After you have settled into the school term and mastered the general information you need to manage a class, you will be able to expand your focus to the art of teaching. Some of the complex issues your mentor can discuss with you include these:

- Solving common classroom problems
- Helping students with special needs
- Increasing student motivation
- Designing differentiated instruction
- Handling diverse groups of students
- Evaluating students fairly
- Incorporating a variety of teaching strategies

> What do you do when it's a kid's birthday? Where do the cupcakes go? What is fair punishment for incomplete homework? How does the school file papers that go home? Endless small but important questions filled my first month, although I only realized that I needed answers to those when the issues arrived.
>
> *Christina L. Myren, 4 years' experience*

Seeking Feedback on Your Professional Performance

One of the most useful approaches you can take to develop into a highly effective teacher is to seek feedback on your professional performance from a variety of sources. In the past, teachers have done this informally, such as by watching their students' body language, looking at test scores, or paying attention to how often their students were off task.

With today's emphasis on using data to inform instructional decisions, however, classroom teachers now use a variety of sources to gather as much feedback as possible so that the conclusions they make about their skills are valid. To make sure that you have an accurate a view of your strengths and the areas in which you could improve, try these methods of obtaining feedback:

- Use an instrument, such as the free surveys at SurveyMonkey (www.surveymonkey .com), to solicit your students' opinions about classroom matters.
- Record or videotape yourself as you present a lesson.
- Ask colleagues to observe you for part of a lesson you teach. (See Teacher Worksheet 1.4 for help with this.)
- Use exit slips or reflection questions at the end of class to ask your students to comment on the day's lesson.
- Install a suggestion box so that students can offer advice and suggestions about classroom concerns.

Making the Most of Peer Observations

Use this worksheet to make peer observations as beneficial as possible. Ask a colleague to complete this worksheet while he or she observes you as you teach.

Observer name: _____ Date: _____

Planned class activities:

_____

_____

_____

Special observation requests:

_____

_____

Observed teacher's areas of concern noted in advance:

_____

_____

_____

Observer's response to the areas of concern noted in advance:

_____

_____

_____

Positive teacher actions observed:

_____

_____

_____

Positive student actions observed:

_____

_____

_____

Questions for the observed teacher:

_____

_____

_____

Suggestions for the observed teacher:

_____

_____

_____

From *The First-Year Teacher's Survival Guide, 3rd Edition*, by Julia G. Thompson. Copyright © 2013 by John Wiley & Sons, Inc. Reproduced by permission.

Using the Evaluation Process to Improve Your Teaching Skills

Evaluations can be of enormous benefit to you, or they can turn you into a nervous wreck; the difference is in your attitude. If you want to grow as a teacher, then adopt the attitude that your evaluators only offer you advice in areas in which you need to improve.

Remember this: no teacher is perfect. Every teacher has areas of performance that can be improved. One way to identify those areas is through evaluations. You can suffer through the process, or you can benefit from it. The choice is yours.

As a teacher, you can expect to be evaluated on a variety of criteria often during your career. The evaluation process has several components. First, you can expect one of your supervisors to discuss your goals and effectiveness with you in a preobservation conference. At this time, if you do not already have a copy of your district's evaluation form and the other district information related to it, you should obtain these items. This is a good time to mention any particular problems you are having and to solicit advice. You can also expect to discuss very specific goals for your school year with your administrator. You will be expected to collect data and other evidence throughout the rest of the year to track how well you have met your goals.

Sometime after your preobservation conference, your evaluator will make a planned classroom observation. At this point, the evaluator will be looking for your strengths and weaknesses as an educator.

After the observation, you will meet with your evaluator again. At this conference, the evaluator will talk with you about the lesson you taught as well as your strengths and weaknesses as a teacher.

There will be other observations during the course of the year. The number varies from school district to school district. Expect to have many informal visits from administrators over the course of your career, but especially during your first few years, when you are not a tenured teacher.

Near the end of the school year, you will have a final evaluation conference. This conference will involve more than just a discussion of the formal classroom observations you have had throughout the year; it will address your overall effectiveness as an educator. There should be no surprises in regard to your final evaluation. If your supervisors believe that you are not an effective teacher, you should certainly have received some indication of that before the final meeting.

HOW TO PREPARE FOR AN OBSERVATION

In many ways, informal visits by evaluators are much easier to get through than the planned, formal observations. You do not have time to worry about an unannounced visit, whereas knowing that an administrator is going to observe you in a few days gives you time to feel anxious. It is normal to feel nervous about being observed. In addition, taking the following steps can help you feel confident both before and during the observation:

- **Be proactive.** Make sure that you have a copy of the supervisor's observation form if there is not a copy in your faculty manual. In fact, you should do this as early in the term as you can. Study the form so that you know what the observer will be looking for as you teach.

- **Keep your lesson simple so that you can do it well.** The observer will want to see you interacting with your students, so do not plan a test or a video. Elaborate activities, such as a class skit or student debates, may not highlight your instructional skills very well.

- **Tell your students what is going to happen.** Tell them that there will be a visitor in the classroom and that you would appreciate their cooperation.

- **Write out your lesson plan, and collect extra copies of all handouts, textbooks, or materials needed for the lesson for the observer.** Select an unobtrusive place for your visitor, and place these materials there. Be ready to show your lesson plan book as well as your grade book.

- **Get control of your anxiety.** This is the most important step in your preparation. If you are ready and have a well-planned lesson, you do not have to worry. Expect to be nervous, but also expect to do well because you have prepared thoroughly. You can also use Teacher Worksheet 1.5 to help you prepare for an observation.

TEACHER WORKSHEET 1.5

How Observers Will Evaluate You

During a classroom observation, your observers will make notes on a form that has been approved by your school district. Although these forms vary from district to district, certain items are common to most of them. You can be proactive in how you prepare for an observation by looking at yourself as an evaluator does. Choose a particular class session in which to evaluate your own teaching. Rate your performance on each of these positive qualities by circling the number that best fits your assessment of your own skills. Use this scale:

    1 = I had no problems in this area.

    2 = I had a few problems in this area.

    3 = I really need to work on this skill.

1	2	3	I followed the district's curriculum.
1	2	3	I had objectives for the lesson.
1	2	3	I delivered accurate and appropriate information.
1	2	3	I showed a depth of understanding of the material.
1	2	3	I made use of all available class time.
1	2	3	I kept all of my students on task.
1	2	3	I allowed time for transitions between activities.
1	2	3	I used a variety of teaching strategies.
1	2	3	I demonstrated effective questioning skills.
1	2	3	I had an assessment instrument for the lesson.
1	2	3	I motivated my students to succeed.
1	2	3	I established the relevance of the lesson.
1	2	3	I provided timely feedback.
1	2	3	I monitored my students effectively.
1	2	3	I encouraged and assisted students.
1	2	3	I interacted in a positive way with my students.
1	2	3	I maintained an orderly classroom.
1	2	3	I minimized disruptions.
1	2	3	I incorporated critical thinking activities into the assignment.
1	2	3	I had classroom rules posted.
1	2	3	I enforced classroom rules.
1	2	3	I made sure that procedures for routine tasks were in place.
1	2	3	I delivered clear instructions.
1	2	3	I projected a professional image.

TURNING CRITICISM INTO A POSITIVE EXPERIENCE

One of the most difficult aspects of being observed and evaluated is hearing negative things about your teaching performance. Veteran teachers will tell you that although it is not easy to have a supervisor discuss the problems with your performance, such criticism can be very conducive to professional growth. With a professional, open-minded attitude, you will find that discussing your teaching performance during the evaluation conference can be a valuable way to improve your teaching skills. Here are some suggestions to make an evaluation conference a positive and productive experience:

- Go into your evaluation conference with paper, a pen, and an open mind. Be prepared to hear negative as well as positive comments about your performance.

- Listen objectively. Most of the criticism will probably cover issues you have already started to address yourself. If you find yourself becoming defensive, stop and make an effort to remain objective and open minded.

- Listen more than you speak. Ask for advice and suggestions for improvement, then listen carefully, write them down, and follow them.

- After the conference, when you have had an opportunity to correct some of your weaknesses, keep the administrator updated on your progress in following his or her suggestions.

THE IMPACT OF VALUE-ADDED ASSESSMENTS ON THE EVALUATION PROCESS

The term *value-added assessment* refers to the way that evaluators assess the performance of a specific teacher by comparing current standardized test scores with past test scores for that teacher's students. In many cases, student test scores of one teacher are also compared with the scores of other students on the same grade level or in the same content area. The intended result of these comparisons is to determine the contributions to student achievement made by each teacher in a single year.

Although the intent of value-added assessment is to provide a reasonable and objective method of assessing teacher effectiveness, the practice is controversial. Some of the problems with the use of value-added assessments can include, for example, missing past test scores, past test scores that are not comparable to present ones, or even test scores that could be skewed by various factors.

Controversial as this method of assessment may be, many school districts today use value-added assessments as a major part of a teacher's evaluation process. The implications of this are significant for all teachers. There are several actions that you can take to avoid being adversely affected by a value-added assessment:

- Look at your students both as individuals and as part of an entire group. Although you may design instruction for the group, keep in mind that it is individual students whose test scores will be compared.

- Learn as much as you can about your students as quickly as possible. Gather base-line data at the start of the term so that you will be aware of your students' past test scores and other helpful information. You can adapt Teacher Worksheet 1.6 to help you track data.

- Take care to learn about your students' learning style preferences and to use that information to differentiate instruction as much as possible as often as possible.

- Assess your students' strengths and weaknesses in terms of their knowledge and skill level at the beginning of each unit of study. Use that early assessment to guide you as you differentiate instruction for the unit.

- Make sure to maintain accurate records of your students' subject matter mastery. This will allow you to correct gaps in knowledge or skills as necessary.

- Be aware of the populations in your class, such as the children of poverty, students who are reluctant to learn, and students who do not speak English as a first language, who are at the highest risk for poor performance on standardized tests. This knowledge will enable you to intervene early to help them succeed.

- Teach the academic vocabulary and test-taking skills that are appropriate for your students. Offer practice sessions so that your students will not be intimidated by unfamiliar test procedures.

- Don't hesitate to ask early in the school term for assistance for those students who may be struggling. Involve support personnel as well as adult and peer tutors to help those students.

- Don't teach to the test. Instead, research shows that those teachers whose lessons cover broad concepts and require higher-level thinking skills tend to have students with higher test scores than those teachers who just cover the basic material on the test.

TEACHER WORKSHEET 1.6

Data Tracking Sheet

You can use this worksheet as a convenient way to record and analyze the data that you will gather about your students during the school year. Keeping the data that you collect in a brief form such as this one will allow you to quickly review your students' strengths, weaknesses, and instructional needs.

Student name: _____ Date of birth: _____

I. Work Samples

Use this space to record samples of the work that you collect from your students.

Sample 1: _____ Date: _____
Sample 2: _____ Date: _____
Sample 3: _____ Date: _____
Sample 4: _____ Date: _____
Sample 5: _____ Date: _____

II. Previous Test Scores

Use this space to record and analyze the data that you gather from any standardized tests your students may have taken before entering your class.

Test 1: _____ Date administered: _____ Score: _____
District projected test score: _____
Difference between previous and projected scores: _____
Analysis of score:

_____
_____

Actions to take based on analysis of score:

_____
_____

Test 2: _____ Date administered: _____ Score: _____
District projected test score: _____
Difference between previous and projected scores: _____

From *The First-Year Teacher's Survival Guide*, 3rd *Edition*, by Julia G. Thompson. Copyright © 2013 by John Wiley & Sons, Inc. Reproduced by permission.

Analysis of score:

_____

_____

Actions to take based on analysis of score:

_____

_____

Test 3: _____   Date administered: _____   Score: _____

District projected test score: _____

Difference between previous and projected scores: _____

Analysis of score:

_____

_____

Actions to take based on analysis of score:

_____

_____

III. Unit Tests

Use this space to record the data that you collect as you teach various units throughout the school year.

Unit	Pretest score	Posttest score
Unit 1: _____	Pretest score: _____	Posttest score: _____
Unit 2: _____	Pretest score: _____	Posttest score: _____
Unit 3: _____	Pretest score: _____	Posttest score: _____
Unit 4: _____	Pretest score: _____	Posttest score: _____
Unit 5: _____	Pretest score: _____	Posttest score: _____
Unit 6: _____	Pretest score: _____	Posttest score: _____
Unit 7: _____	Pretest score: _____	Posttest score: _____
Unit 8: _____	Pretest score: _____	Posttest score: _____
Unit 9: _____	Pretest score: _____	Posttest score: _____
Unit 10: _____	Pretest score: _____	Posttest score: _____

WHAT TO DO IF YOUR EVALUATION IS POOR

Almost every thoughtful evaluator will offer recommendations on how you can correct weaknesses in your teaching performance, but there is a difference between those constructive recommendations and an evaluation that indicates that your classroom performance is not acceptable according to your school district's standards.

If you receive a poor evaluation, it is very likely that your first priority will be to deal with the overwhelming emotions of anger, frustration, shock, and despair that will accompany the news of your evaluation. Although such emotions are understandable, the best course of action for you to take is to master these feelings quickly so that you can respond in a professional manner.

Next, you should strive to be as objective and proactive as possible in dealing with the situation. Ask yourself these questions:

- Am I clear about exactly what my noted areas of weakness are and what I am expected to do to remediate them?
- To whom in my school and in my district can I turn for assistance?
- What immediate changes can I make to improve my teaching performance?
- How can I contact my local education association representative for guidance?
- How can I learn more about my district's evaluation and firing policies?
- What long-term plans should I make to ensure that I have remediated the areas of poor performance indicated?
- How can I attend professional development workshops or classes to improve my performance?

You should also keep in mind that your poor performance evaluation is not a topic that should be the subject of gossip at school or, even worse, among your students or their families. Do not vent indiscriminately or discuss your evaluation with anyone other than trusted colleagues and friends. Keep in mind that you want to solve this problem, not spread the news.

Even though your evaluation may be a poor one, employees are still expected to sign the evaluation. If you want to write a letter to rebut or explain any part of evaluation, you should feel free to do so and to ask that it be added to your personnel file along with the evaluation itself. Refusing to sign the evaluation can be regarded as an insubordinate act on your part.

Finally, you should learn about your legal rights as an employee of your school district. Contact your local education association representative as well as your district's human relations office to learn as much as you can about how to manage your situation most effectively.

Maintaining Sustained Professional Growth

One of the most important differences between teachers who enjoy their first years as educators and teachers who continue to struggle with stress is a constructive decision that successful teachers make to enhance their professional development through a self-planned program of sustained professional growth.

As a classroom teacher, you will become a lifelong learner just by the very nature of the profession. It is simply impossible to be a good teacher and not want to know more about the content you are teaching or about the best methods to instruct your students. Becoming a teacher who is actively involved in a program of sustained professional growth is one of the wisest decisions you can make as a novice educator. Setting and working to achieve professional goals, attending conferences, learning though reading professional journals, investigating the National Board for Professional Teaching Standards, joining professional organizations, and keeping a professional portfolio are all steps you can take to ensure that you are involved in a program of sustained professional growth. You can use Teacher Worksheet 1.7 to assess your current state of professional growth and to make plans to grow as a professional educator.

> Remember that in a twenty-day working month, fifteen days will be average. Three will be tops, but you will have two bad days. The longer you teach, the more days that are tops you will have.
>
> *Edward Gardner, 36 years' experience*

SET AND WORK TO ACHIEVE PROFESSIONAL GOALS

Setting professional goals not only will give you direction and purpose as you begin to focus on the larger issues involved in developing into an effective educator but also will provide you with valuable baseline data so that you can chart a clear path for career success year after year. Goals tend to energize and motivate those of us who set them because they allow us to focus on what's important and thus to prioritize our efforts.

Experienced teachers also know that it's important to set SMART goals (goals that are specific, measurable, attainable, relevant, and timely) because they are easier to achieve than vague ones. Many teachers find that writing down their professional goals makes it easier to assess their achievements throughout the school year and to track the professional skills they know they want to improve. You can use Teacher Worksheet 1.8 to record your goals and track your progress.

Are You in Charge of Your Career?

Place a check mark beside each statement that applies to your professional growth at this point in your career.

1. _____ I have a well-thought-out plan for developing my skills as an educator.

2. _____ I have at least three colleagues I can rely on for support and guidance in addition to my official mentor.

3. _____ I have made a point of networking with local and online education groups that are appropriate for my teaching position.

4. _____ I have created a set of manageable and achievable career goals for this year and for the future.

5. _____ I frequently read materials that will keep me informed about current issues, trends, and techniques in education.

6. _____ I have joined professional organizations related to my teaching assignment. If possible, I also plan to attend a conference this year.

7. _____ I take advantage of professional development opportunities, such as workshops, Webinars, online courses, and seminars offered by my school district.

8. _____ I maintain a professional portfolio so I will be able to measure my own growth as a teacher as the year progresses.

9. _____ I have an organized method of maintaining my professional records: my teaching license, evaluations, letters of recommendation, and so on.

10. _____ I have a plan to observe other teachers as often as I can. I will ask them to observe me to offer their insights about my teaching performance, also.

From *The First-Year Teacher's Survival Guide, 3rd Edition*, by Julia G. Thompson. Copyright © 2013 by John Wiley & Sons, Inc. Reproduced by permission.

ATTEND CONFERENCES

As a first-year teacher, you may not believe that attending a professional conference is a good use of your time when you have so much work to do that you struggle not to be overwhelmed. However, conferences provide opportunities to learn new strategies and network with other professionals. If your school district gives you a chance to attend a conference, accept the offer.

LEARN THROUGH READING PROFESSIONAL JOURNALS

Just as attending conferences can help you develop professional expertise, so can reading professional journals. Through such reading, you can learn a great deal about the interests you share with others in your field. Subscribing to one of these journals will enrich your teaching experience in many ways:

- *Education Week* (www.edweek.com). This weekly periodical is devoted to up-to-the-minute news and commentary about topics related to education.
- *Educational Leadership* (www.ascd.org). This journal is the voice of the Association for Supervision and Curriculum Development and a useful resource for teachers at all grade levels. Here you can find professional resources for your classroom as well as for addressing schoolwide issues.
- *Instructor* (www.scholastic.com). This widely read magazine devoted to K–8 concerns offers practical support through a variety of timely articles.
- *Learning* (www.learningmagazine.com). This is another supportive resource for teachers of younger students, offering practical advice on a wide range of topics.
- *Phi Delta Kappan* (www.pdkintl.org). This journal, published by Phi Delta Kappa International, a professional association for teachers, addresses issues of policy and serves as a forum for debates on controversial subjects.

INVESTIGATE THE NATIONAL BOARD FOR PROFESSIONAL TEACHING STANDARDS

As a first-year teacher, you may not yet be eligible to work toward national certification, but it is a positive choice for all teachers to make as early in their career as they can. As you work to improve your overall teaching skills, you will also learn how to teach the material in your state and district standards effectively. You can learn more at the Web site of the National Board for Professional Teaching Standards (www.nbpts.org).

JOIN PROFESSIONAL ORGANIZATIONS

One of the best ways to acclimate yourself to your new profession is to join an organization just for education professionals. Joining a professional association is a way to stay abreast of the latest developments and trends in education. Through collaboration and networking, you learn from other teachers with shared interests and concerns. Here are some of the professional organizations for teachers:

- **American Federation of Teachers (AFT) (www.aft.org).** The AFT is a teachers' union allied with the American Federation of Labor and Congress of Industrial Organizations. With 1.3 million members, the AFT has been a strong voice supporting classroom teachers for decades.
- **Association for Supervision and Curriculum Development (www.ascd.org).** This is a nonpartisan, nonprofit national and international organization for educators at all grade levels.
- **Coalition of Essential Schools (www.essentialschools.org).** This organization provides professional development and networking opportunities, conducts research, and serves as a policy advocate for public education.
- **National Association for the Education of Young Children (www.naeyc.org).** This is the nation's largest organization for early childhood educators. Its focus is to provide support and resources for the educators of young children.
- **National Education Association (NEA) (www.nea.org).** With over three million members, the NEA is the largest organization for public school teachers in the United States. It provides strong national support for educators at all grade levels.
- **National High School Association (www.nhsa.net).** This nonprofit association is dedicated to improving the professional knowledge of high school educators.
- **Association for Middle Level Education (AMLE) (www.amle.org).** With over thirty thousand members, AMLE is the largest national education association committed to the educational needs of young adolescents.

CREATE A PROFESSIONAL PORTFOLIO

Creating a professional portfolio serves two purposes. As a tool to showcase you to prospective employers, a portfolio can reveal a great deal of useful information about you and your teaching experiences. Another valuable result of the creation and maintenance of a professional portfolio is the opportunity it gives you to reflect on your teaching experiences and philosophy.

Most professional portfolios contain materials that can be grouped into two parts: (1) evidence or artifacts from your career and (2) your reflections on various aspects of your teaching experiences. Here are some of the items you can include:

Artifacts

- Formal observations
- Student ratings of your class

- Representative lesson plans—usually a week's worth
- A videotape or audio recording of a lesson
- Lists of committees you've served on
- Lists of extracurricular work and activities
- Annotated samples of student work
- Letters of recommendation
- Awards or honors
- Evidence from professional development workshops or courses
- An explanation of your teaching responsibilities

Reflections

- Sample pages from a journal recording your reflections on your teaching practice
- Annotated lesson plans

Track Your Professional Goals

In this template, you can record your goals as a teacher, and then record your progress for each semester of a school term.

Goal	Semester One Progress	Semester Two Progress
Sample: Hold a weekly Friday ceremony as a recap of the week's learning (for five minutes at the end of class).		
1.		
2.		
3.		
4.		
5.		
6.		
7.		
8.		
9.		
10.		

Learning to Manage Your Stress

An important part of becoming an effective teacher is learning to manage stress. Teachers who learn to manage their stress level enjoy school and find its challenges stimulating. Teachers who do not are the ones who burn out and leave the profession. Unfortunately, the cost of burnout goes far beyond the unhappy and stressed-out teacher; whole classrooms of students are also negatively affected.

For more detailed information about how you can learn to manage the stressful parts of your school day, consult the bonus material on the DVD that accompanies this book.

Because being teachers means that our daily responsibilities begin early and seem never to end, it is not always easy to leave the demands of school at school. Because we are in the business of changing lives, we feel the weight of those responsibilities long after we have left the building. One of the occupational hazards all successful teachers face is that it is all too easy to take home not just papers and plans to be made but also our worries about our school days.

Successful teachers who want a long-term career in education learn how to juggle the demands of being in a classroom all day long and still maintain a satisfactory personal life. The key? Finding a balance between the challenges of a new career and such personal needs as maintaining friendships, meeting family responsibilities, and pursuing other endeavors that bring fulfillment and joy to human life.

To learn how to be one of those successful teachers who seem to have found the right balance between their personal and professional lives, consider putting some of these suggestions into practice:

> We all have different ways of handling stress, and I think that finding something that suits your personality and interests is key. For me, I noticed that my stress level was taking a toll on me physically. What I did to try to manage my stress and improve my health was to focus on a healthy diet and lifestyle.
>
> *Alanna Dougherty, first-year teacher*

- **Make time for yourself.** This may seem obvious, but school and worries about students can consume your life unless you make an effort to take care of yourself. Eat well. Exercise. Count your blessings. Plan enjoyable activities. Your students will not thrive if their teacher is exhausted and burned out. Take good care of yourself if you want to be able to spend your days focused on caring for your students.

- **Work efficiently while you are at school.** Prioritize the tasks that you must accomplish and work steadily at them. Use your planning time and any spare moment to their fullest advantage. The more you accomplish at school, the less you will have to do at home, and soon your stress level will diminish to the point at which you will easily be able to manage the demands of your professional workload.

- **Focus on the tasks at hand.** Too often teachers find it easy to second-guess their decisions or to replay troublesome scenarios from the day. Instead of endlessly rehashing what went wrong, focus on productive tasks, such as designing the plans you need to create or coming up with motivational activities to spark your students' interest.

- **Set boundaries.** No one expects you to be on call twenty-four hours a day. For example, it is not wise to give out your personal phone number. Although there will be many after-school demands on your time, learn to gently refuse those that will be too demanding or unproductive.

- **Keep your career worries in perspective.** When something goes wrong, ask yourself if you will still be affected by it in a year, in a few months, or even in a week. Try to focus on the big picture instead of allowing nagging small issues to rob you of your peace of mind.

- **Always have something to look forward to.** Make a point of planning a weekend excursion or an outing with family and friends or even setting aside time to work on a hobby. Looking forward to something pleasant in the future will help you maintain your equanimity in the present.

- **Don't forget that your new profession is only one part of your life.** If you find that you are spending too much time at school or worrying about school after you have left for the day, then take steps to manage that school-induced stress. Your new career, no matter how exciting it may be at times, should be only one part of a rewarding and busy life.

> I try to manage my stress by doing what I need to do for school, but always leaving time to do something outside of teaching in the evening. It is important that I try to maintain a balance that allows me to be a teacher, but also who I am as an individual outside of the classroom.
>
> *Kristin Reagan, first-year teacher*

Best Practices Checklist

1. Determine your personal strengths as an educator and use them as a foundation for future success.

2. Begin the process of becoming a lifelong learner by learning as much as you can as quickly as you can about your new profession.

3. Take charge of your career! Develop a plan for professional growth and set SMART goals to provide focus and direction.

4. Develop the communication and teamwork skills necessary to become a skillful collaborator at school. Learning to work well with others will be a key to your success as an educator.

5. Become a researcher as well as a teacher. Use the action research process to solve classroom and school problems.

6. Strive to create a culture of high performance in your classroom. Use a variety of thoughtfully planned strategies to achieve this.

7. Establish a procedure to develop a reflective teaching practice. Make reflection a regular part of your school day.

8. Actively seek the best role models and mentors who can guide you to be the most competent teacher possible.

9. Begin preparing for your final evaluation as soon as you can. Track student data and solicit feedback about your performance from a variety of sources.

10. Begin early in taking the necessary steps to start managing stress and finding a balance between your work and personal lives.

Time to Reflect
What It Means to Be a Twenty-First-Century Educator

Use the information in this section to guide your thinking as you reflect on these questions. They are designed to encourage you to think more deeply about the issues in the text or to discuss those issues with colleagues.

1. What are some of the challenges you can anticipate as a twenty-first-century teacher? Where can you get help with them? What are some of the rewards you can anticipate as you begin your new career?

2. Which individuals come to mind when you think of the term *professionalism*? What can you learn about how to conduct your own professional life from these people?

3. What actions can you take to commit yourself to actively promoting the success of your students? Where can you find help with this?

4. What steps can you take to grow professionally during your first year as a teacher? How will you use self-reflection and action research to become the best teacher you can be?

5. What plans can you make to be proactive in managing your stress and in finding a balance between your personal and professional lives?

SECTION TWO

Develop the Practical Skills You'll Need to Manage a Classroom

If you were to browse for images of teachers on just about any search engine, you would find pictures that are remarkably similar: smiling adults delivering a lecture while writing on a chalkboard or interacting with children of all ages. These iconic illustrations may be accurate, but they only reveal the part of our profession that is most visible. Being a successful teacher involves a great deal of difficult background work so that we can manage our classroom, handle our heavy workload, and focus on what's most important—teaching.

This behind-the-scenes work requires all of us as teachers to develop practical workplace skills so that we can focus our attention on the activities depicted in the iconic images of us. Those of us who are highly effective learn quickly that it is necessary to take an organized and methodical approach to our daily tasks. The most important practical skills you need to manage your classroom proficiently are learning to arrange your own work area so that you can be productive, becoming efficient at managing your daily tasks, and making sure that your classroom is arranged so that your students can thrive.

Arrange Your Own Work Area

Your personal work area may determine whether you will be comfortable in your classroom or not. Because you will be spending so many of your daylight hours in your classroom, your personal work area should be comfortable as well as businesslike. The area you designate as your work area may include a lockable drawer, your desk and chair, a coat cabinet, a bookshelf, or some other space that is solely for your use and not for your students to access.

YOUR DESK AREA

Your desk area is an important part of your personal space in your classroom. Here are some suggestions for making sure that it functions well for you:

- Keep the top of your desk as free of clutter as you can. Although the items on your desk can reflect your personality, you should keep them businesslike as an example for your students and to make it easier for you to get your work done. Here are some of the things you should have on top of your desk:
  - Trays for folders and papers
  - A calendar (Even if you rely on an electronic calendar, a paper version will come in handy.)
  - Pens and pencils
  - Notepads
  - A stapler (Label it "Teacher Use.")
  - Paper clips

- You will probably be issued a laptop or other type of computer. Be sure to leave room on your desk for it and to arrange the cords and cables that accompany it.

- Because your desk is a space allotted for your personal use, you should discourage students from taking items from it. Set up a student work center at a spot near the door. In this area, place a stapler (labeled "Student Use"), a hole punch, a trash can, a recycled paper bin, and a tray for collecting student papers.

- Do not place scissors, knives, liquid paper, tacks, markers, glue, or any sharp object on the top of your desk. If an item could harm a student or be used as a weapon, it should be stored inside your desk.

- You will need a safe place to store and lock away your personal belongings. Experienced teachers seldom have credit cards or much cash at school.

- One mistake that many teachers make is putting their desk at the front of the classroom, right in front of the board. If your desk is at the back of the room instead, you can easily monitor your students' activity from there. You can have personal conferences with students without having the entire class as an audience, and you will not block students' view of the board.

- If possible, your file cabinet and other personal storage areas should be set up near your desk, so that you can quickly find what you need.

Getting acclimated to all of the demands of a teacher's day, like schedules, grades, meetings, parent-student relationships, and getting to know how everyone on your team works, was very demanding. It changed me in such a way that I understand my role as a teacher. It has made me a better communicator, and I am more organized.

Joshua Culver, first-year teacher

SUPPLIES YOU WILL NEED

You will need more than just red pens and a grade book to provide dynamic and engaging instruction. Unfortunately, many schools do not provide teachers with enough money to pay for the supplies they need. Teachers everywhere have learned to adjust to a tough economy by recycling, asking parents and guardians or businesses for help, and making good use of the supplies they have.

Some teachers have been able to obtain supplies by asking for donations or creating wish lists on such sites as Craigslist (www.craigslist.org), the National Teacher Registry (www.nationalteacherregistry.com), and Teacher Wish Lists (www.teacherwishlists.com).

Another way that many teachers can obtain school supplies is by searching for freebies online. Here is just a small sampling of the many sites you can search for items that could benefit you and your students:

- **Print-A-Poster.com (http://print-a-poster.com).** Here teachers can download and print free posters on a wide variety of topics.

- **Block Posters (www.blockposters.com).** At this site, teachers can upload their own photos and in just a few clicks transform them into posters of any size at no cost.

- **Federal Resources for Educational Excellence (http://free.ed.gov).** You can access more than 1,600 federal teaching and learning resources, such as documents, photos, and videos organized by subject: art, history, language arts, math, science, and more.

- **Abcteach (www.abcteach.com).** Search here for free pre-K–8 materials and creative activities including printable worksheets, interactive activities, and much more.

- **SchoolExpress (www.schoolexpress.com).** This site offers thousands of free worksheets, games, and awards of various types.

- **About.com Freebies (http://freebies.about.com).** Use "teacher freebies" as a search term to access hundreds of different types of freebies that teachers and students can use.

The following are two lists of some of the supplies you may find useful as you go though the school year. Included in these lists are plenty of recycled, free, and found items.

Basic Items That All Teachers Need

- Pens—blue and black
- Colored pens for grading
- Pencils
- File folders

- Labels
- A hole punch
- A calculator
- Transparent tape
- A flash drive or other memory storage device
- An easy-to-find key ring
- Rubber bands
- A pencil sharpener
- Staplers (one for students and one for you)
- Paper clips of all sizes
- Scissors
- Three-ring binders
- Stackable trays
- Board erasers
- Reward stickers
- Mints

Useful Items That May Come in Handy

- Colored pencils
- Baby food jars
- Wallpaper samples
- Plastic tubs
- Duct tape
- Boxes, especially cereal boxes and shoe boxes
- Pieces of cardboard
- Display boards from old science fair projects
- Newspapers
- Poster mounting putty
- Fabric remnants
- Plastic tablecloths
- Glue
- Printer cartridges
- Blank note cards
- Get-well cards
- Thank-you notes

- Envelopes
- A personal first aid kit
- A needle and thread
- Packing peanuts
- Store samples
- Yarn
- Dental floss
- Fishing line
- Safety pins
- Restaurant menus
- Discarded books from libraries
- Garage sale furniture
- Cotton from pill bottles
- Board games and puzzles
- Wrapping paper
- Old clothes, hats, and sunglasses

If You Spend Twenty-Five Dollars on Your Classroom Supplies

Although there are many ways to find free, reusable, gently used, recycled, or inexpensive materials for your classroom, it is not always easy to know how to allocate the money that you may have available to you. Although every classroom is different, if you are not sure where to begin and you have twenty-five dollars to spend, you would be wise to focus your spending on these items:

- Bulletin board materials
- Storage containers
- Organizers for your paperwork
- Organizers for student papers
- A stapler
- Pencils, markers, and pens
- Crayons
- Scissors for your use

If You Spend Fifty Dollars on Your Classroom Supplies

If you have a bit more money to spend on your classroom, then you should purchase the items in the twenty-five-dollar budget and then choose which of these would be appropriate for your classroom:

- Extra lighting
- Poster board
- Colored paper for student use
- Colored pencils or markers
- Shelving
- A rug, a beanbag chair, and pillows

ORGANIZING YOUR PAPER FILE STORAGE

You will need to set up a filing system for the paperwork you must deal with each day. If you have a system in place before the term begins, you will save yourself much frustration and time later. Setting up a file cabinet is not a difficult task, but it does require planning and effort.

Step One: Once you have a file cabinet, clean it out and lubricate any stuck drawers.

Step Two: Go searching for file folders. Begin your search by letting it be known that you can use any folders that anyone in your building is about to toss out.

Step Three: If your school has allotted money for you to spend on supplies, be sure to spend some of it on materials for your file cabinet. Purchase hanging file frames and hanging files for as many drawers as your budget permits. In addition to hanging files, you will need file folders, labels, and permanent markers.

Step Four: Set aside one file drawer for student business. Here you will keep student information, progress reports, report cards, copies of parent correspondence, and other paperwork related to students. You should be able to lock this drawer to protect confidential records.

Step Five: Set aside another file drawer for general business. Here you will store information for substitutes, hall passes, detention forms, and other general paperwork.

Step Six: In the other drawers, file such materials as unit plans, handouts, tests, and paperwork related to your curriculum either in alphabetical order or in the order that you will cover them.

Step Seven: After you have completed the basic steps in setting up your filing system, implement the following refinements, which will make your system much more efficient and easy to use:

- Label the front of each drawer in large, bold letters so you can tell at a glance what is inside.

- File materials according to subject. Make a special effort to maintain orderly files. Neatness counts!

- Label everything. If you can color-code your labels, it will be even easier to find what you need quickly.
- Stagger the tabbed labels on hanging files and the file folders within them so that you can see what is in the file drawer at a glance.
- Do not stuff a file drawer so full that it is almost impossible to move files around.

THE DOS AND DON'TS OF YOUR SCHOOL COMPUTER

One of the most pleasant moments of any orientation program for new teachers is the issuance of school computers. No matter what type of computer you are issued, it is exciting to be connected to the other employees in your district and to have access to the same resources that are available to them. Being issued a school computer also means that new teachers have to adopt a professional approach to the way they use this ubiquitous tool. After years of working on personally owned computers, many new teachers are not always sure which behaviors are acceptable and which ones are not, even though they may have signed a document outlining their district's acceptable use policies. To make sure that your use of your school computer is as professional as possible, be guided by these lists of dos and don'ts.

School Computer Dos

- Do remain aware that the computer is the property of your school district.
- Do be cautious, conservative, and professional when using your school computer.
- Do transport your computer in the case or bag that was issued with it if it is portable.
- Do periodically go through your files to keep them organized and up to date.
- Do back up your work to an external drive on a regular basis.
- Do follow your school's protocol for saving to a school network.
- Do use bookmarks to keep your topics easy to find in a hurry.
- Do use your computer only for school business.
- Do create passwords for your various school accounts that are logical and easy to recall, and that can be updated periodically.
- Do respect the intellectual property rights of others.
- Do make sure to lock a portable computer in a secure place if you don't take it home each day.
- Do keep your virus protection updated.
- Do report problems with your computer as quickly as you can.
- Do remember to take your computer to school each day, if it is portable.

School Computer Don'ts

- Don't download any software program without permission—preferably in writing.
- Don't have food or drink near your computer. Spills can be costly.
- Don't forget that your e-mail account may be monitored by district personnel.
- Don't leave your computer unattended if you have to leave your classroom.
- Don't allow students to use your computer.
- Don't use other teachers' accounts without their permission.
- Don't visit sites with content such as pornography or extreme political views that could indicate that you are not a good school employee.
- Don't decorate your computer or your computer's case with stickers, images, or anything that has not been approved by your school district.
- Don't open suspicious attachments that could infect your computer.
- Don't share your passwords with others.
- Don't conduct personal business on your school computer.

> Embrace the technology that is meant to make your job easier and more efficient. Nearly every school system is using an online system for Individualized Education Programs (IEPs), so don't let poor keyboarding skills slow you down. Learn the programs, and hone those typing skills.
>
> *Charlene Herrala, 31 years' experience*

Become an Efficient Teacher

Being an efficient teacher is only common sense. As a teacher, your school days are packed with tasks and responsibilities that you have to accomplish quickly. Efficiently managing the routine chores that make up your day allows you time to focus on your students and their needs.

HOW TO PRIORITIZE TASKS

Whether you are a novice teacher or an experienced classroom veteran, it is easy to be overwhelmed by the bewildering amount of work that needs to be accomplished each school day. Unfortunately for all classroom teachers, not only does most of it need to be done right away but also it needs to be done well so that our students can make the progress in their learning that we want for them.

With this type of workplace pressure, it is crucial to prioritize your tasks so you can accomplish everything you need to do; move forward in meeting your goals; reduce your own stress level; and, most important, be the teacher your students need you to be.

Efficiency experts advise those who are seeking to prioritize workplace tasks to first determine which tasks are most important. Whereas our daily tasks will change during the course of the year, our priorities will not. In the list that follows, you will find the ten most important priorities that all of us, no matter what we teach, must carefully attend to as teachers. You can also use Teacher Worksheet 2.1 to help you accomplish your own classroom tasks while meeting these priorities.

- **Provide an orderly and safe environment in which courtesy is the order of the day.** Successful classroom management requires consistent effort on your part. It does not happen by chance.

- **Accept your role as classroom leader.** You are the primary positive force in your classroom. When you accept responsibility for what happens in your class, all of your students benefit.

- **Quickly develop and maintain a positive relationship with every learner.** This is a sure way to a successful school year for students and teachers alike.

- **Become thoroughly familiar with the content you are teaching.** You must be the authority on this material in the classroom. If you do not know the material, then your students cannot learn.

- **Establish clear objectives for your students' learning.** Clear objectives focus your instruction and allow your students to concentrate on what is essential for mastery in each lesson.

- **Recognize and address the diverse needs of students in each of your classes.** Your teaching should take into account your students' skill levels, readiness, ability levels, preferred learning styles, and previous knowledge.

- **Develop interesting, innovative strategies for teaching the material your students need to know.** You should include a variety of activities to meet the needs of every student every day.

- **Provide appropriate, helpful, and timely feedback.** Make it your goal to return graded papers to your students within three days and to provide helpful rather than critical comments.

- **Maintain accurate records so your instructional decisions can be driven by relevant data.** It makes good sense to analyze and then use the various types of data available to you to inform your instructional practices.

- **Work in collaboration with other educators, your students, and their parents or guardians.** Teamwork is vital in creating a productive and successful learning environment for your students.

Keep two files pinned to the computer desktop. The first is titled "To Do." Keep a daily list of the things you need to get done in the next day or two. The second is titled "Next Year." Take time to record your thoughts about what you would like to do differently next year for each unit.

Bob Foley, 2+ years' experience

Meet Your Classroom Priorities

Use this list of classroom priorities to make sure that your classroom is well organized and efficiently managed, noting down your strategies for meeting each priority.

Week of _____

1. Provide an orderly and safe environment in which courtesy is the order of the day.

   _____

   _____

2. Accept your role as classroom leader.

   _____

   _____

3. Quickly develop and maintain a positive relationship with every learner.

   _____

   _____

4. Become thoroughly familiar with the content you are teaching.

   _____

   _____

5. Establish clear objectives for your students' learning.

   _____

   _____

6. Recognize and address the diverse needs of students in each of your classes.

   _____

   _____

7. Develop interesting, innovative strategies for teaching the material your students need to know.

   _____

   _____

8. Provide appropriate, helpful, and timely feedback.

   _____

   _____

9. Maintain accurate records so your instructional decisions can be driven by relevant data.

   _____

   _____

10. Work in collaboration with other educators, your students, and their parents or guardians.

   _____

   _____

From *The First-Year Teacher's Survival Guide, 3rd Edition*, by Julia G. Thompson. Copyright © 2013 by John Wiley & Sons, Inc. Reproduced by permission.

HOW TO MAXIMIZE YOUR TIME WHILE YOU ARE AT SCHOOL

It only makes sense to use your time at school as efficiently as you can, not only so you can accomplish everything you need to do but also so you can maintain the necessary balance between your personal and professional lives. In addition to heeding the items in the lists that follow, you can use the lists in Teacher Worksheets 2.2 and 2.3 to help you organize your time.

- When you have complicated tasks, divide them into smaller pieces with specific deadlines for each one.
- Write yourself reminders. Teachers have too much to do to keep everything straight without reminders. Set reminders on your phone or send yourself reminder e-mails when you have important deadlines if handwritten ones don't work as well for you.
- If a task will take less than three minutes, do it right away.
- Use your calendar as a planner. Record tasks, appointments, and other information you'll need to remember as you plan your workdays. Don't just plan for the day, but for the week, for the month, for the semester, and for the year.
- Refuse politely when someone asks you to give time you cannot spare.
- Stay organized and keep your work area free of clutter.
- Remember to use your biological clock whenever you can. If you are not a morning person, don't set aside time in the morning to accomplish detailed work. Do it later instead.
- Follow the old business rule: touch each sheet of paper only once.
- Keep your keys in the same location each day.
- Deal efficiently with mail. Act immediately on items that require a written response. Throw away or recycle junk mail. File catalogues for later use.
- Set up equipment early in case there are problems.
- Don't arrive too early or too late to meetings or duty assignments.
- Delegate as much as you can. Even very young students can accomplish many routine tasks, such as putting up posters or keeping the supply area clean.
- Have an up-to-date set of emergency lesson plans ready—just in case.
- Maintain order in your classroom to avoid having to spend time dealing with behavior problems.
- While students are working on an opening exercise, walk around the room and check homework assignments individually. This will allow you to grade efficiently and also assess student needs.

Further, you should learn to use small blocks of time wisely. You will be surprised at how much you can accomplish in a short amount of time. Here are just a few things that you can accomplish in just a few minutes if you stay focused:

In fifteen minutes, you can

- Grade the objective portion of a set of test papers
- Update your class Web page or blog
- Create a review sheet
- Answer e-mail
- Create warm-up exercises for the entire week

In ten minutes, you can

- Call students' parents or guardians
- Write a lesson plan
- Grade some essay questions
- Average grades and post them
- Check homework papers

In five minutes, you can

- Create a dynamic closing exercise
- Write a positive note, and send it home with a student
- Use the hole punch on a set of papers
- Write a positive comment on at least five papers
- Review key points in a lesson with a brief multimedia presentation

In three minutes, you can

- Record grades
- Drill your students with PowerPoint games
- Put stickers on a set of papers
- Praise a class for good behavior
- Have students write an evaluation of the day's lesson

In one minute, you can

- Erase the board
- Display an image related to the day's lesson
- Have students tidy the room
- Recognize the student of the day or week
- Write an inspirational message on the board

> When you get hired, you have all these great ideas for the students and you want to do them all. I realized very quickly that implementing a few things at a time well is better than trying to do everything and struggling to get through it.
>
> *Jared Sronce, first-year teacher*

TEACHER WORKSHEET 2.2

Teacher's Daily To-Do List

Here are some of the tasks that many teachers have to manage successfully each day. Use this list to plan how to manage your daily responsibilities.

Date: _____

Phone calls concerning students:

Student	Parent or Guardian	Phone Number	Reason

Other phone calls or contacts:

_____

_____

Conferences:

Student	What	When	Where	Outcome

Other meetings:

_____

_____

_____

(continued on next page)

(continued from previous page)

After-school or extra duty responsibilities:

_____

_____

_____

_____

Items to duplicate:

_____

_____

_____

Lesson plans or projects to complete:

_____

_____

_____

Notes, reminders, and errands:

_____

_____

_____

TEACHER WORKSHEET 2.3

Checklist of a Teacher's Weekly Reminders

Although not every teacher's weekly reminder list will be the same, there are some tasks that almost every teacher should consider doing on a weekly basis. Use this checklist to assess how well you are doing each week. The more items you can check off, the more productive you will be.

1. _____ Plan active, fun-filled learning experiences for your students.
2. _____ Look ahead and design lesson plans as far in advance as you can.
3. _____ Find relevant online materials to include in lessons.
4. _____ Plan how you will provide remedial instruction.
5. _____ Plan how you will enrich instruction.
6. _____ Use formative assessments to check your students' progress at least twice.
7. _____ Run off materials for upcoming lessons.
8. _____ Return graded papers so that students have timely feedback.
9. _____ Record all grades for the week.
10. _____ Send home progress reports.
11. _____ Send a positive note home with at least five students.
12. _____ Hold a recap session so that students can review the week's learning.
13. _____ Celebrate student successes.
14. _____ Tidy the classroom and ready it for the next week's activities.
15. _____ Update your class Web page.
16. _____ File handouts and other materials that are no longer needed.
17. _____ Reflect on your effectiveness as a teacher.
18. _____ Collect data on a classroom issue and decide how to use this information effectively.
19. _____ Teach or reinforce at least one study skill.
20. _____ Make sure your classroom policies are as transparent as possible.

General Tips for Managing School Papers

One of the most stressful aspects of a teaching career is the heavy load of paperwork. Like many other professionals, teachers have to document progress, write plans, and keep accurate records. And like other professionals, teachers complain about the proliferation of their stacks of paperwork.

In the last few decades, the amount of paper all professional educators have to deal with has multiplied. During the course of just one school year, the average teacher will have to handle more than ten thousand student papers. When you consider the additional notices, directives, printouts, purchase orders, letters, forms, catalogues, and publications a teacher receives each day, the amount of paperwork is staggering.

You can learn to stay ahead of paperwork by creating your own system for managing those stacks. For any sheet of paper you receive, you have three choices: act on it, file it, or discard it. Get in the habit of acting quickly and you will never have to face towering piles of papers.

In addition to deciding how you will react to each type of document, you will also have to decide how to organize your paperwork. Just stuffing your paperwork into a desk drawer or file cabinet will only work for a day or so. Efficient teachers soon develop their own system for keeping papers organized so that they can quickly find each one. When you begin to plan how you will manage your paperwork, consider all of the options you have for storage:

- Bins
- Folders
- Expandable folders
- Trays of various sorts
- Boxes
- File drawers
- Binders
- Individual student folders
- Electronic folders

> Bringing home piles of marking every night expecting to get it done just doesn't work. Instead, I set small deadlines for myself like marking ten assignments every day after school until they are all marked. Then I leave for the day, guilt-free, instead of dragging home a big briefcase full of assignments that always seem far too overwhelming to tackle when I'm exhausted from the workday.
>
> *Alanna Dougherty, first-year teacher*

DOCUMENTS YOU NEED TO MANAGE

Although specific paperwork is unique to each teacher, there are some important documents that all teachers have in common. Here, briefly, are some of the documents that you will have to manage efficiently:

Grading

- Your grade book
- Student papers to be graded

- Graded student papers
- Sample student papers to assess long-term progress

Professional Business

- Your teaching portfolio items
- Your faculty handbook
- Your parent or guardian conference notes and log
- Teachers' meeting notes
- Your reflections

Instructional Concerns

- State and district curriculum guidelines
- Unit plans
- Daily plans
- Copies of the syllabi for each grading period
- Reference materials for future lessons
- Strategies and activities you would like to incorporate into lessons
- Ideas for motivating students
- Extra handouts for students
- Makeup work for students
- Tests, quizzes, and other assessments
- Handouts for the current unit of study

Classroom Routines

- Blank templates for routine business, such as hall passes, lunch counts, or notes home
- Rewards or certificates
- Bulletin board ideas or materials
- Exit or entrance slips and topics

Student Information

- Student contact information
- Student inventories
- Student assessment data

> My biggest challenge as a first-year teacher was attempting to manage the influx of papers that crossed my desk every day. It felt like I was swimming in papers during the first few weeks of school. Staying organized is a battle that I am still working on managing, and it seems entirely plausible that I will continue to do so for many years to come.
>
> *Kristin Reagan, first-year teacher*

- Confidential student information
- Attendance data

Confidential Documents to Be Kept in a Secure Location

- All documents (including e-mails and conference notes) related to a student's IEP
- 504 Plan forms
- All documents related to student health issues
- Discipline referrals

WHAT TO KEEP AND WHAT TO DISCARD

During a year when so much of your work experience is new, having difficulty with something as seemingly uncomplicated as knowing which documents to keep and which to discard can be frustrating. Although some of these documents will be in paper format, if you can store work electronically it will save paper and space as well as make it easier for you to access documents quickly. The types of documents teachers need to manage may vary widely depending on the grade or grades they teach, but you can adapt these lists to help you make decisions about the materials and papers you should keep:

Documents to Keep Until the Start of the Next School Year

These documents are generally the ones that you need to store for future reference. Many times teachers have even been asked to produce such documents as attendance records or parent or guardian contact logs to justify an end-of-course grade.

- Save your grades for each grading period as well as the end of the year.
- Keep all attendance data records.
- Keep all parent or guardian contact logs.
- Keep all accident reports.
- Keep all discipline referrals, detention notices, and student behavior contracts.
- If you have sent home papers for parents or guardians to sign, keep them on file. This practice applies to progress reports, informal notes, grade sheets, and any other signed papers. Keep the documents you have collected in each student's individual folder.
- Don't throw away any information about curriculum guidelines in your state and local district. Keep it handy, and refer to it often.
- Don't throw away course calendars and syllabus information.

- Maintain a file of old tests and quizzes to draw from in future terms.
- If you give examinations, you should keep not only a master copy and a key but also student copies. If a grade is challenged, you will need to produce the test paper.
- Save copies of each handout that you want to reuse in the future.
- Keep your lesson plans. Annotated unit plans will be particularly useful when you begin to plan new units in future years.
- Keep all papers related to your own professional observations and evaluations.
- Save your personal reflections or discussion group notes to review in the future.
- Set up your teaching portfolio (see Section One) and save the items to be included in it.
- Be sure to hang on to any complimentary notes you have received. They will help remind you why you are a teacher on tough days.
- Save e-mails about students who require special consideration because of such concerns as illness, family problems, or learning disabilities.

Documents You Can Safely Discard at the End of Each Semester

These documents are generally ones to which you will not need to refer in the future. Although they may have served a valuable purpose during the semester, saving too many documents will only add clutter to your paper and electronic files, making them hard to manage.

- Dispose of meeting notes or reminders that you have already acted on.
- Clear out routine e-mails about school business or daily tasks.
- Remove archived electronic and paper files that you no longer find relevant for lesson planning.
- Discard student classwork or homework papers that you may have saved instead of sending them home with students.

How to Organize and Manage Student Information

In addition to the many other documents you will have to keep track of, the information about your students that comes to you from a variety of sources throughout the term is something you also have to manage. Although there are a number of ways to manage this information, many teachers have found that the following simple approach works well because it is easy to maintain:

Step One: Set aside space in a lockable desk or file drawer.

Step Two: Create a folder for each student, and arrange the folders alphabetically.

Step Three: Promptly file every piece of information you receive about a student. Date each item. Place new papers behind other items in a file folder so you don't have to shuffle through all of them to find a particular one.

Step Four: To stay organized, make a point of filing papers daily.

How to Grade Papers Quickly

Although all professionals may have to cope with heavy loads of paperwork, the largest and most stressful part of a teacher's paperwork is unique: student papers that require grading. Planning will make this part of your school day much easier. Student papers should follow a consistent path:

- **Step One**: Have students place them in a designated area.
- **Step Two**: Move them to a color-coded folder to be graded.
- **Step Three**: Grade them.
- **Step Four**: Record the grades.
- **Step Five**: File the papers or return them to students.

In addition to having a consistent path for managing student papers, there are many other ways you can grade papers quickly. To reduce the time and energy you have to spend on this chore and still offer productive feedback to students, consider the suggestions that follow.

SUGGESTIONS FOR GRADING IN GENERAL

- Stagger due dates if you teach more than one class.
- Offer incentives for turning in work before a deadline.
- Don't grade everything your students produce. Some teachers find it easier to grade only part of an assignment—spot-checking for patterns of errors. Still others ask students to submit an example of their best work in a series of assignments.
- Compile a list of the most common mistakes you find your students making. Spend time teaching and reteaching this material so that students are less inclined to make these errors.
- Create very specific checklists or rubrics that guide students as they complete assignments. This allows students to know what they have to do to succeed.
- Do not try to grade stacks and stacks of papers in one sitting. Divide the work into smaller batches and tackle these in a systematic manner.
- Time yourself as you grade to see how you can be more efficient and focused.
- Reward yourself when you have finished grading an onerous set of papers. This will encourage you to stay on task.

- Don't focus only on the errors that your students have made. Use a highlighter to point out the parts of their assignments that they did particularly well. Students not only appreciate the kindness in this action but also learn a great deal more from your positive comments than from a sea of red ink.

SUGGESTIONS FOR GRADING LONGER ASSIGNMENTS, ESSAYS, AND PROJECTS

- Don't mark every possible error in a writing assignment. Marking all errors tends to overwhelm and dishearten students. Instead, decide on a few errors that you want to focus on as you design the assignment. Focus on helping students with those errors and you will see improvements more quickly.

- Create a method of correcting student work that is simple for your students to understand, and then use it consistently. Using the same proofreading marks on every assignment, for example, will make it easy for students to understand their mistakes. Post these marks online and on the board, and make sure each student has a copy.

- Spend time at the start of an assignment making sure students understand the directions and the expectations you have of them. This time spent at the start of an assignment will reduce the amount of time you will have to spend finding errors later.

- Before students turn in essays or projects, take time to confer with them and to offer opportunities for peer editing.

- When you make assignments with more than one part, consider grading each part separately. For example, instead of grading all of the parts of an essay at once, have students turn in their outline to be graded first. Then, you could evaluate each student's rough draft and offer suggestions before grading the final essay. This practice does spread an assignment over several days, but the successful student results and reduced stress for you are worth it.

- When you write margin comments, be sure to point out what students did well, what they need to improve, and what they have improved. Encourage them to continue to work hard in the future.

SUGGESTIONS FOR GRADING QUIZZES AND TESTS

- When you grade quizzes and tests, grade the same page on every quiz or test in the stack before moving on to the next page.

- Make the answer sheets that your students use for quizzes and tests easy to grade. Allow plenty of white space and room for students to write so that you can read their responses quickly.

Tips for Managing Electronic Files

Failing to create a workable system for managing your electronic files can cost you hours of frustrated searching for lost documents. With just a bit of planning, you can design a scheme for managing your electronic files so that they are quick and easy to access.

- Use a consistent method for naming files that will make it easy for you to understand what each file contains without having to open it. Many teachers find that it is helpful also to include a date in the file name. For example, "Ch 2 Quiz 2014" is an excellent title, whereas "Ch 2" is not.

- Group like things together in folders. For example, place all videos related to a unit of study in a folder labeled in such a way that you can quickly find the video you need. Many teachers tend use to use such labels as "Presentations," "Enrichment Activities," "Remediation Activities," "Quizzes," "Tests," "Formative Assessments," and "Review Work" when they organize their materials.

- Place files in folders as you work on them. If you create folders for each unit at the start of the unit, you will find it easy to avoid having to sort through a messy display of unorganized files.

- Be selective about what you save electronically, just as you would be with paper copies. Periodically purge your folders of files that you no longer find useful. Clutter just makes it difficult to find files when you need them.

Tips for Managing E-Mail

Most teachers will admit to having mixed feelings about school e-mail. On the plus side, e-mailing is an efficient and quick way to communicate with parents or guardians, students, and colleagues. On the minus side, angry e-mails from colleagues and parents or guardians can ruin any teacher's day. Checking and responding to e-mails often consume far too much of a busy teacher's time. Also, as professionals, we know that an e-mail cannot convey our tone effectively, and so sometimes we send confusing messages with the potential to create or exacerbate unpleasant situations.

It is important that all of your correspondence be as professional and clear as possible. To avoid unpleasantness and to create a positive relationship with those with whom you correspond, try these tips for making sure that your e-mails reflect your professionalism:

- If you are considering sending an e-mail about a discipline incident or similar concern, make a phone call instead. Not only is it more courteous but also you are far more likely to resolve the problem.

- Be very careful about forwarding any messages that may embarrass the original sender.

- When you write the subject line, take care to be as clear as possible so that the receiver can prioritize the e-mail and so that it can be retrieved easily later.

- Protect the privacy of your students by not mentioning them by name in e-mails to colleagues about sensitive issues.

- Make a time management plan detailing how you will check and respond to e-mails during the school day. Many teachers only check e-mails at established intervals to avoid being distracted from their teaching duties.

- Keep in mind that your colleagues often receive dozens of e-mails each day. Make it easy for them to read and understand ones from you.

- Be careful before you decide to "reply all" to group e-mails, avoid being too casual with your greeting or jargon, and be aware that attempts at humor can often be misread.

- Adopt a systematic approach to how you manage your e-mail folders. Create a system that allows you to retrieve e-mails quickly when needed. Many teachers group e-mails that they need to archive into folders with reasonably limited categories, such as meeting notes, special projects, or specific students.

- When you create your e-mail signature, remember that it should reflect your status as a school employee. If you include a quotation or motto, it should reflect your pride in your school and your profession rather than make a statement about your personal philosophy about life.

How to Maintain Your Class Web Page

With a class Web page, you can keep students and their parents or guardians informed about what is happening in your classroom; connect students through blogs, wikis, and discussion boards; and build a sense of community.

Your class Web page is an opportunity to present yourself as a caring and capable professional. The tone of the information you post on your class Web page should be positive and supportive, and should convey your enthusiasm about your subject matter and your students. Take care to write carefully and to proofread your work before posting. You should also make sure to update it regularly. Students and their parents and guardians will complain if your page is hard to follow or if the information is out of date.

There are thousands of teacher pages on the Web for you to search through to get ideas about what to include on your own page. You can also consider posting these items:

- Your contact information
- Policies, rules, and procedures
- Homework assignments
- Information about class activities

- Class notes
- Handouts
- Skills covered each grading period
- Remediation or enrichment activities
- Links to helpful sites
- Useful resources for students
- Class blogs, wikis, or discussion boards
- Photographs and displays of students and their work

Here are two helpful sites for teachers who want to establish a basic classroom Web page that allows effective communication with students and their parents or guardians.

- **Classroom Tripod (www.tripod.lycos.com).** At Classroom Tripod, you can build a basic Web page, share photos, and maintain a class blog.
- **School Notes (http://schoolnotes.com).** At School Notes, you can post classroom notes and resources with ease. School Notes offers examples of teacher Web pages to use as examples as well as user-friendly directions and suggestions.

How to Save Paper

One of the most costly expenses in many schools is paper. From construction paper to photocopy paper, the cost of those sheets can mount up quickly. Instead of being part of the problem, you can choose to be part of the solution by making an effort to save paper. Here are some tips for you and your students:

- Cut paper use in half by asking students to use both sides of a sheet. If you use both sides when you photocopy and also allow your students to write on both sides, you not only will save paper but also will encourage good environmental stewardship in your students.
- If you can present material electronically or in another way that enhances learning and does not require paper, try to do so.
- If it is appropriate to the situation, allow students to share handouts.
- Make it a class project to devise ways to save paper. When your students become involved, you are on the way to successfully conserving paper.
- If an assignment is a brief one, have students tear a sheet in half and share.
- Ask students to reuse paper whenever they can, and model the same responsible behavior.
- Keep scrap paper on hand for students to use as needed.

Optimize Your Use of the Photocopier

Few things can annoy an entire school staff more than a broken photocopier. Because so many people depend on a copier, the professional etiquette surrounding this important piece of machinery is clear-cut:

- Never make others wait unnecessarily while you run off hundreds of copies. If you do so, expect the line behind you to become an angry mob.

- If you need to adjust your master copy, step away from the copier to work so that others can use it.

- Be generous in allowing people with only a few copies to go before you in line if you have many copies to make.

- Take care not to be the cause of a copier breakdown. Use the correct paper or transparency type. Remove all staples, tape, and paper clips from paper you insert into the feeder. Be careful not to make the situation worse when clearing paper jams.

- Try to avoid peak photocopying times: before the term begins, in the morning before class begins, at the end of the day, and right before exams or standardized tests.

- Don't violate copyright laws. Not only do you put yourself at risk for legal action but you set a bad example for your students as well.

- If paper or the number of copies you can make is limited, be careful to use the amount that you are allotted wisely. Plan ahead to make sure you will have enough when you really need to copy.

Prepare Your Classroom for Students

Preparing your classroom for your new students is an enjoyable and worthwhile task. Creating an inviting, safe, and welcoming place where students can comfortably work together is worth all of the hard work and energy it takes to complete such tasks as shoving furniture, creating seating charts, and decorating bulletin boards.

CHECKLIST FOR THE START OF SCHOOL

Because there are so many tasks that all teachers must complete in the few weeks and days before the beginning of a school term, it is very easy to be overwhelmed. If you were hired some months before the start of a new term, you have an advantage over teachers who are not as lucky.

If you were offered your position just a few weeks or even a few days before the beginning of school, you will have much to do to catch up. Either way, the timeline that follows will help you prioritize your responsibilities and avoid being overwhelmed with too much to do in too little time:

A Month Before the Term Begins

- Hit the back-to-school sales for supplies.
- Make sure that your wardrobe reflects your professional status.
- Order any supplies your district allows.
- Gather the other supplies you may need.
- Begin searching the Internet for information about the subject or subjects you will teach.
- Pick up or download your district's calendar for the school year.
- Pick up or download your state and district curriculum guides.
- Pick up teachers' editions and supplementary materials.
- Begin reading and studying the course materials.
- Create your professional goals.

Three Weeks Before the Term Begins

- Create a course overview for the year.
- Join at least one professional organization. (See Section One for suggestions.)
- Decide on the resources you will need for each unit of study.
- Create unit plans.

Two Weeks Before the Term Begins

- Create syllabi or planners for your students.
- Make sure that the equipment in your room works well.
- Brainstorm a list of classroom management strategies and solutions to possible problems. (See Section Seven for further information.)
- Create your class rules and procedures. (See Section Seven for further information.)
- Put together information for substitute teachers, in case you need them.
- Put your classroom in order.
- Set up your desk and files.

One Week Before the Term Begins

- Obtain the school forms you will need.
- Work with a mentor to get answers to your procedural questions.
- Make sure you are prepared for emergency drills (discussed later in this section).
- Create a daily routine for attendance, lunch counts, and other student business.
- Write a letter to introduce yourself to parents and guardians. (See Section Four for a sample letter.)

- Investigate the Web site you will use to set up your class Web page.
- Write out your first three weeks of daily lesson plans. (See Section Ten for tips on writing lesson plans.)
- Study your class rosters to learn your students' names.
- Create a seating chart.
- Familiarize yourself with the software programs you will be expected to use during the school year.

The Day Before School Starts

- Finish any last-minute tasks.
- Ask any last-minute questions.
- Exercise, eat well, and get enough rest.
- Make a plan to manage your work-related stress.

> Managing all of the different aspects of being a new teacher can be a challenge, and it is stressful. I try to minimize stress by using my planning periods to get as much done as humanly possible. Getting to work early on particularly busy days is helpful to feel prepared for the day.
>
> *Kristin Reagan, first-year teacher*

MAKING YOUR CLASSROOM INVITING ON A BUDGET

Your students will thrive in an environment in which you take their needs seriously and in which they feel valued. When you create a classroom that invites students to join in a learning community, you are reaching out to your students in a tangible way. An inviting classroom sends a clear message to your students that they are important to you—that you approve of them.

Fortunately, it is not necessary to spend a great deal of your own money to make your classroom an attractive, comfortable, and productive learning environment. One of the best choices for a teacher who wants to create an inviting classroom is to make the classroom reflect the interests and concerns of the students, not those of the teacher. Too often, teachers make the mistake of decorating their classroom beautifully, but with items that appeal to their own tastes instead of their students'.

With creativity and careful planning, it is possible to create a welcoming classroom on a budget. Here are some suggestions that will help you get started:

Think outside the box! Go beyond those four blank walls and decorate the entire classroom with items that will enhance your students' school day. Use fishing line or dental floss to hang items from the ceiling, tape messages and reminders to the floor, or use the ceiling to remind students of important facts. You can use the space on the front of your desk, the back of the door, or the sides of file cabinets. Hang a clothesline under the chalkboard, and pin papers to it. Purchase inexpensive cork squares, and pin student work to them. Your students will delight in your efforts to make this room different from the ordinary classroom box.

Decorate your classroom with student work. Students feel a sense of ownership and pride in a classroom where their work is displayed. Be sure to display everyone's work. If you hang only the best work, students might feel that you are playing favorites, which, of course, would be harmful to the class environment. You can display all sorts of student work, not just creative projects or A papers. Have students list facts on bright note cards, and then post them near the door as a review. Post drawings, notes, graphic organizers (learning tools noted for their nonlinguistic appeal, such as cluster maps and Venn diagrams)—anything that shows how much you value your students' efforts. Students will enjoy seeing a changing display of things they have created far more than a purchased poster.

Set aside an area for class business. You can keep your students informed and involved by posting such items as assignments, due dates, school announcements, and other shared business. Your students should participate in keeping this area up to date, if they are old enough to do so.

Set aside an area for tracking progress. If you have class competitions, students should see the results displayed. For example, if you want to improve the way your students complete homework assignments, create poster-size bar graphs to record each day's results. Making progress visible is a powerful way to keep students on the right path.

Set aside an area for motivation. Have students bring in inspiring posters or display ones they make themselves. Students could illustrate words of wisdom from the Internet, books they have read, or song lyrics. Consider using a giant graphic of brainstormed mottoes for success to remind students how much you care about their future.

Create areas where students can work with enrichment and remediation materials. Learning centers are not just for young students. Use trays, baskets, large envelopes, or rolling carts to store materials for students to use after they have finished their assignments. In this area, you could include a variety of items that interest your students:

- Books
- Magazines
- Board games
- Pen-and-paper puzzles
- Jigsaw puzzles
- Flash cards
- Art supplies
- Bingo boards
- Reusable plastic bags
- Recycled cans (Be sure there are no sharp edges.)
- Plastic jugs or bottles (Ask in the cafeteria for large ones.)
- Shoe boxes
- Tissue boxes
- Margarine tubs
- Cereal boxes

- Ice cream tubs
- Sturdy trash bags

Use bulletin boards to send positive messages to your students. Take advantage of this space to welcome your students all year long. Try these simple tricks to make the bulletin boards in your classroom effective connection builders:

- Use inexpensive fabric or wrapping paper as a background. Staple it into place at the start of the term and you will not have to replace it the rest of the year.
- Borders can be as simple as strips of construction paper, or they can be more creative. Cut out borders from old newspapers, comics, magazines, wrapping paper, or even maps.
- Go three-dimensional. Consider using stuffed animals; objects made of craft foam; or other items students love, such as balloons.
- Many Web sites have great tips for using the bulletin boards in your room to connect with your students. Use the following sites to search for good ideas to adapt for your students:
  - **Kathy Schrock's Guide to Everything (www.schrockguide.net/bulletin-boards.html).** Here teachers can find a comprehensive list of sites, images, and books devoted to bulletin boards.
  - **Teacher's Corner (www.theteacherscorner.net).** This award-winning site offers many seasonally themed bulletin board ideas as well as bulletin board ideas of general interest.

TRAFFIC FLOW CONSIDERATIONS

Traffic flow in a classroom is more important than many novice teachers realize. For example, if you place your trash can near the door, the stapler on your desk at the back of the room, and a tray to collect completed work near the front, students will wander all over your room after a test just to throw away scrap paper, staple their work, and turn in their test.

Carefully consider the routine activities your students will perform before you set up your room, so that you can minimize distractions and interruptions. Some of these routine activities could include

- Entering class
- Checking posted material
- Checking the calendar
- Checking the clock
- Using hand sanitizer

- Working on the board
- Passing in papers
- Speaking with you privately
- Using a computer
- Picking up supplies
- Disposing of trash
- Sharpening a pencil
- Using a stapler

VARIOUS TYPES OF SEATING ARRANGEMENTS

Arranging student desks so that your students can focus on their work is important for their success. You will probably change the arrangement of desks several times during the term to allow your students to work in groups of various sizes. To arrange student desks for an optimum effect, keep these pointers in mind:

- Arrange desks such that you can see every student's face. Every student should also be able to see you with no difficulty.
- Retain the ability to move freely around the room. You should be able to walk behind every row of desks.
- Keep desks away from attractive graffiti spots, such as bulletin boards, window ledges, or walls.
- Avoid placing desks near distractions, such as a pencil sharpener or a computer monitor with an interesting screen.

Three Common Student Desk Arrangements

Although there seems to be an endless number of ways to arrange student desks, there are three common ones that many teachers find particularly effective in helping students stay on task all class long.

Traditional Rows

Many teachers begin the year with desks in traditional rows. This sends the message that you want your students to focus their attention on you and not on each other. Traditional rows at the start of the year also make it very easy for you to learn your students' names. The traditional row configuration makes it easy for you to see every student and for the students to see you as you work from the front of the classroom. Many teachers who routinely use other desk arrangements often move their students into traditional rows for testing to reduce the possibility of cheating.

Whole-Group Horseshoe

In this configuration, the students on the two sides of the horseshoe face each other while the students seated in the connecting row at the back of the horseshoe face the front of the classroom. This arrangement is well suited for class discussions because it encourages students to talk with each other.

Pairs or Triads

Seating students in permanent pairs or triads makes it very easy for them to work together on a daily basis. This configuration facilitates the formation of collaborative study groups because students grow to depend on and support their group partners. It is ideal for allowing students to be able to work together as well as getting them to focus on you when appropriate.

Why You Need Seating Charts (and How to Create Them)

No matter how old your students are, seating charts are necessary. Seating charts solve many problems and prevent many more. If you use a seating chart, here's how you and your students will benefit:

- Students from the same neighborhood will not sit next to each other, avoiding what might have been an obvious ethnic separation.
- Timid students will have the same seating opportunities that aggressive ones do.
- Students will not argue with each other over which desk belongs to whom.
- Unmotivated students can be moved from the back of the room to a place where you can more easily engage them in lessons or offer assistance.
- Easily distracted students can be seated in a place where it will be easier for them to stay on task.
- Students with special needs can sit in a location where their needs can be met with a minimum of fuss.
- Students with medical problems can be accommodated as necessary.
- Taller students will not block the view of smaller ones.
- Students will receive a clear message that you are the person in charge of the class.

Begin the school year with a preliminary seating chart that will make it easier for you to learn your students' names. In a few days, after you get to know your students, you should make up a permanent seating chart for each class based on other factors. Here's how:

Step One: Begin by drawing a diagram of your room in which each desk is represented by a rectangle.

Step Two: Using your class roster, pencil the names of your students on your diagram. Begin with the students who must sit in a certain area of the room due to medical issues or the terms of their IEP or 504 Plan.

Step Three: After you have considered students with special needs, move on to the students who misbehave in their current seat. Place them where they can focus on you and their work rather than on having fun with their classmates.

Step Four: Finally, move the rest of your students. Do your best to find each student a seat that will be comfortable for his or her size and temperament.

How to Protect School Resources

There are many reasons to protect the resources available to you at your school. In today's uncertain economic atmosphere, it only makes sense to behave as if repairs and replacements to supplies and equipment are not feasible. When you do make an effort to take good care of school resources, you also present yourself in a professional manner. Finally, if you act as a classroom role model, your students will notice your efforts and follow your lead. Here are some easy ways to protect the school resources in your class:

- Prevent vandalism by being alert. Clean stray marks from desks, and move desks away from walls and other areas where students will be tempted to deface school property.

- Enlist your students' help in keeping the room tidy. If you keep simple cleaning supplies, such as paper towels and a broom, on hand, it will be easy to delegate cleaning chores.

- At the end of class, allow time for students to dispose of trash and straighten up their work area. When a classroom is neat, students will tend to take pride in keeping it tidy.

- Survey your classroom for the areas that are most easily damaged and plan how you can protect them. Window blinds, electronic equipment, books, and student desks are good places to begin your survey.

- If students are allowed to eat in your classroom, create procedures for disposing of trash, wiping up spills, or dealing with other mishaps.

- Arrange electric cords with student safety in mind. If students were to stumble, they could cause equipment to topple and possibly injure themselves.

- Get help from other staff members when you are attempting to move heavy objects, such as room dividers or bookcases. This will help keep you safe from injury as well.

- Take care to turn the LCD projector off when you are not using it. One of the most expensive repairs is replacing bulbs in LCD projectors.
- Be careful to keep remote controls secure. The replacement of remote controls represents another unnecessary expense.
- Because cables and cords seem to abound in today's wired classrooms and are often expensive to replace, keep them with their corresponding equipment. Consider labeling them as well.
- When you are not in your classroom, turn off the lights and electronic equipment.
- Make sure to secure equipment that is easy to steal, close windows, and lock the door as you leave your classroom at the end of the day.

How to Request Repairs

Follow these five quick tips when you need to request repairs to classroom equipment:

- Be as reasonable as possible in the types of repairs you request. Tight budgets make some repair requests impossible to fulfill.
- Unless student safety is an issue, be patient. Some repairs may not be treated as high-priority items when ones that are more urgent are pending.
- Follow the chain of command. Speak first to the maintenance personnel assigned to your classroom. Not only is this courteous but also they may be able to expedite the repair.
- Follow your district's procedure for requesting repairs. This usually involves completing a form describing the needed repair. Before you submit the request, make a copy of the filled-out form for your own records.
- If you notice a repair that needs to be made, try to make the request while fixing the problem is still simple. For example, it is easier to fix a leaky faucet in a classroom sink than it is to replace furniture ruined by a flood.

Classroom Safety Issues

Maintaining classroom safety is one of the most important tasks that we have. After all, the well-being of a classroom full of students depends on our diligence. It's a good idea for you, as a new teacher, to learn about school safety by following your district's safety procedures, observing other teachers, asking questions, and using common sense. Follow these suggestions to make your classroom secure for you and for your students:

- Check classroom windows and screens to be sure they are in good working condition.

- Check all outlets. When you do plug in equipment, make sure all electrical cords are secure.

- Keep your classroom as clean as you can to reduce the spread of contagious diseases.

- Use only cleaning supplies that meet your school's policies and are not harmful to students.

- If possible, teach with your door closed. You will minimize disruptions from outside your classroom.

- Don't keep matches, sharp scissors, or other potentially harmful items where your students can take them.

- Discourage your students from taking such items as staplers from your desk. Instead, provide materials just for their use in another part of the room and teach students to respect your property.

- If your classroom is not in use, keep it locked. No room should be left unattended.

- Make it easy for students to move about. Space desks carefully, and don't block the exits to your classroom.

- Stabilize all bookcases and other tall pieces of equipment so they can't tip over. Make sure all objects on them are also placed securely.

- Keep all of your personal belongings, confidential documents, and any money that you collect during the day securely locked out of sight.

- Never give a student keys to your classroom or car.

- Learn your school's procedures for such emergencies as fire drills, disaster drills, or intruders in the building.

- When students say that they are feeling unwell, take the matter seriously.

- Don't use hard candy as a reward or treat. It is too easy for students to choke on it.

- Never leave your students unsupervised.

- Report suspected weapons or potential acts of violence immediately.

- Be aware of the procedures you are to follow to assist your students who have a chronic illness.

- If you suspect that a student has been abused, act at once.

- Make your classroom as orderly as possible. Teach and enforce your rules and procedures on a daily basis until everyone understands what you expect of them.

- Monitor your students at all times. Be especially careful when they are working together in activities that require lots of movement.

- Take a stand against bullying in your classroom. Make it easy for students to talk to you if they are the victims of bullies.

- When students leave the room with a hall pass, be alert to when they return. You are responsible for their safety.
- Make it clear that you will not tolerate racial, cultural, or other prejudices.

FIRE, DISASTER, AND INTRUDER DRILLS

As much as we would like to believe that schools are safe for all students all the time, the reality is that schools are not always as safe as we want them to be. For this reason, you will have to learn how to successfully manage the various types of emergency drills that will happen periodically throughout the school year. By taking these drills seriously, familiarizing yourself with the procedures you are to implement, and training your students in how to handle themselves in a drill, you will help your students be prepared in case an emergency does threaten them. Here are three key ideas to remember when dealing with fire, disaster, and intruder drills:

- Your district will have a policy for managing various types of drills. Become as familiar with each procedure as you can.
- You should post evacuation maps in your classroom and make sure that students know what to do in case of a drill well in advance of the first one.
- When a drill occurs, you should take it seriously and make it clear to your students that you expect the same from them.

HEALTH CONCERNS

One of the most practical workplace skills you can develop is to monitor and protect your students' health. This can range from something as simple as having hand sanitizer available to educating yourself about a student's chronic illness. In the list that follows, you will find some of the practical techniques you can use to keep your students as healthy as possible.

- When a student's parents or guardians or the school nurse informs you of a health issue with a student, listen carefully and take care to keep the student safe.
- Provide hand sanitizer if it is appropriate for your students.
- Keep adhesive bandages on hand for small cuts or scratches. Your school's clinic will probably supply you with these at the start of the year.
- Keep desktops and keyboards clean. Using disinfectant wipes or sprays is an easy way to keep desks as germ-free as possible.
- Encourage students to wash their hands frequently and to cover their mouth when they sneeze or cough.

Many first-year teachers face additional challenges in the classroom. You may find yourself sharing a classroom, in a portable classroom, or in a seriously overcrowded class. If you do, you can check out ways to manage each one of these situations in the bonus material included on the DVD that accompanies this book.

Assigned seating is critical. At the start of the year, I allow a couple of days of open seating. I carefully observe who sits where and next to whom. I then use those observations to assign new seats. Students who work well together stay together; others get moved around.

Bob Foley, 2+ years' experience

- Provide tissues for students with a cold or allergies. Your school's clinic is a good place to find these.

- If you notice that several students seem to have a cold or another contagious illness, consider delaying group work or arranging desks so that students do not sit too close together.

- Be careful about having screenless open windows. Some students may be allergic to stings from the insects that fly in.

Best Practices Checklist

1. Take a professional approach to the technology you use for school business. Be sure to follow your district's policies and guidelines when using your school computer.

2. Work at being efficient and organized. Use planners, to-do lists, and other methods to organize your work life.

3. Spend time planning how you will create and maintain a system for managing the various documents that will come your way.

4. Learn to grade papers efficiently so that you have time for all of your other duties. Remember this veteran teacher tip: not every student paper has to be fully graded.

5. Return graded papers as promptly as possible so that students can benefit from your feedback. Develop time management strategies that will enable you to do this regularly.

6. Delegate as many tasks as you can to involve students in an appropriate manner. For example, peer review of a work in progress is acceptable. Allowing students to grade a final product is not.

7. Devise an orderly system for storing and maintaining electronic files. Be sure to purge your files periodically.

8. Keep problems as small as possible by enlisting help from parents and guardians when you can. It's often better to call home with a problem than it is to send an e-mail.

9. Share the responsibility and engage students at the same time; encourage your students to become responsible school citizens by enlisting their cooperation in protecting school resources.

10. Keep your students safe. Pay attention to the arrangement of your room, emergency information, and student health concerns.

Time to Reflect
Develop the Practical Skills You'll Need to Manage a Classroom

Use the information in this section to guide your thinking as you reflect on these questions. They are designed to encourage you to think more deeply about the issues in the text or to discuss those issues with colleagues.

1. What skills do you currently possess when it comes to being an efficient teacher? How can you capitalize on your strengths, and how can you overcome your weaknesses?

2. Have you been able to obtain all of the supplies you and your students will need for the term? What can you do to make sure that you will have everything?

3. A well-organized classroom is crucial to beginning a new term successfully. What plans can you make to organize your room and the materials and supplies you will need to use all year? What do you still need to accomplish? How can your colleagues help you?

4. Correctly organizing your file cabinet and your electronic files is a necessary chore that you will benefit from all year. What techniques have you employed to make sure your system is efficient and easy to use?

5. What have you done to make sure your classroom is a safe and inviting place for your students? How can your colleagues help you with this?

SECTION THREE

Collaborate with Others in Your School and Community

For most of us, it will come as no surprise to learn that the reason many employees are fired is not poor job performance but the inability to work well with others. It is also no surprise that schools are much more complex than many organizations—extending far beyond the boundaries of the school yard. Each school is an ever-changing mixture of clerks, custodians, technical assistants, nurses, counselors, coaches, media personnel, paraprofessionals, and police liaison officers as well as teachers, students, and students' families.

One of the most important challenges for twenty-first century teachers is learning to work well with all members of their school community. As a new teacher, you will have to work closely with two groups in particular: your faculty colleagues and the parents or guardians of your students. Collaborative groups in schools make the workload easier and tasks more pleasant only if all of the group members have the skills to work well together. Just what does it take to collaborate well with others? Teachers who collaborate effectively treat all people in their work community with courtesy, listen to others' opinions before making decisions, commit themselves to the good of their school, and are quick to celebrate the hard work and success of their colleagues and their students. As you begin forming your own collaborative groups with coworkers, students, and students' families, you will find that your school life will be much richer for the experience.

Your School Community: A Network of Teams

If you were to create a diagram of the various teams in your school, you would probably need several oversize sheets of paper and plenty of time. The overlapping nature of teams in a twenty-first-century school necessitates a very different method of working with students than we had even a few years ago.

> The camaraderie among teachers is wonderful and replenishes me when I am exhausted and overwhelmed.
>
> *Melinda Conner, first-year teacher*

You can expect to belong to several different teams even at the very start of your career. Some of these may be dedicated to grade-level concerns, content-specific issues, procedure or policymaking, or various types of literacy instruction.

The implication for a first-year teacher is that you are supported by a community of teams. You will have many opportunities to collaborate with others with a sense of unified purpose. The overlapping circles of collaboration that make up a modern school will allow you to grow and develop as a teacher, confident that you are making sound decisions because you have had the opportunity to consult others.

Communities of Practice

Although the term *communities of practice* was coined fairly recently by anthropologists Jean Lave and Etienne Wenger in their 1991 landmark book, *Situated Learning: Legitimate Peripheral Participation* (published by Cambridge University Press), it refers to a learning phenomenon that has existed since antiquity—individuals working together for a common purpose. The purpose can cover a wide range of activities—from solving problems or determining best practices to something as broad as learning new information. In the broadest sense, a community of practice includes the various teams within a school and even beyond its boundaries, stretching to include the school's surrounding community and global concerns that can affect students and staff members.

One of the most important communities of practice to which many new teachers have the opportunity to belong is a professional learning community (PLC). As a member of a PLC, you will have the opportunity to collaborate with other teachers in your school, all working toward a goal, such as raising student achievement or improving teaching methods. A successful PLC begins with a purpose that is clearly defined and supported by the group's members.

In addition, successful collaboration in a PLC is based on deliberate norms established by the group itself. Some of these norms can include such items as who will record the minutes of each meeting; what format the agenda that the group will use will be and who will be able to maintain it; the dates, times, and places of meetings; and who will serve as the group's leader.

Another important community of practice to which many teachers have chosen to belong is a professional learning network (PLN). A PLN is an interactive online community through which teachers from around the globe can join in debates, share ideas, and learn from each other regardless of geographic location. Wikis; RSS feeds; social media sites such as Twitter, Facebook, and LinkedIn; and social bookmarking sites, such as Delicious or Diigo, can offer plenty of opportunities for any teacher who wants to join an online team of other educators with similar concerns or interests.

Here are just a few of the most well-known sites that you may want to explore:

- **Educator's PLN (http://edupln.ning.com).** At this award-winning site, thousands of educators share ideas about a variety of topics. You can join in discussions of various topics, read blogs, listen to podcasts, and learn from videos.
- **edWeb.net (www.edweb.net).** This social networking site for teachers makes it easy to share new ideas, learn more about various topics, and be connected to other educators with similar interests.
- **Twitter (https://twitter.com).** There are many PLN opportunities available to teachers who want to use Twitter to connect to other educators. After setting up your account, begin searching for other educators and education groups. You will soon find it easy to be connected with a group that appeals to your interests.
- **AllThingsPLC (www.allthingsplc .info).** At this site, maintained by leading experts in the field, teachers will find excellent resources, articles, blogs, videos, and much more helpful information.

> I realized that everyone has his or her own strengths and weaknesses. The more diverse a team and its personalities are, the stronger the team as a whole. These differences also allowed me to find my own strengths within the group.
>
> *Christina L. Myren, 4 years' experience*

Where Do You Fit in as a New Teacher?

As a new teacher, you will find that it is sometimes very tempting to jump in immediately and offer suggestions about problems that you notice at your new school. Even though your ideas may be sound ones and you may be completely correct in your assessment of the issues, if you have not yet established your reputation as a serious professional, it is likely that your suggestions will fall on deaf ears.

Until you have had the opportunity to get to know your colleagues and let them get to know you as a dedicated and knowledgeable collaborator, a wise course of action is to take note of things that you would like to improve, but delay acting on them until you have a team of coworkers behind you all the way. Fitting in at a new school takes time and patience and commitment to the well-being of everyone at that school. If you focus on your primary responsibility—your students—it will not be long before your coworkers will begin to trust your judgment and take what you have to offer with the seriousness it deserves.

> The support of my team members exceeded my expectations in the best way possible. I was amazed at how many teachers recognized it was my first year teaching and willingly reached out to help me and send resources my way. What an impact that makes!
>
> *Christina L. Myren, 4 years' experience*

Building Trust: The Importance of a Reputation for Integrity

One of the most important facets of your professional reputation—one that you should establish as quickly as possible—is your reputation for integrity. One of the distinguishing hallmarks of our profession is that no matter where we are, we are still teachers. As a teacher, you are expected to uphold the values of your community—to live up to the high standards that your students, colleagues, and community have for its professional educators.

The rewards of this reputation are significant. Teachers with a spotless reputation are the ones on whom other staff members can rely for help with both big and small tasks. Collaboration with your colleagues as well as with the parents and guardians of your students will be much easier. You will find yourself working in a supportive environment with others who value your contributions and who trust you to do the right thing. Here are some of the large and small ways that you can begin to establish your professional reputation:

- Keep your promises. Because this is so important, be very careful not to make promises you cannot keep. It is very easy to become caught up in the enthusiasm of a moment and agree to something you may regret later. Take your time, and ease into your new responsibilities.

- Do not purchase alcohol, tobacco products, or other very personal items in a place where you could run into your students, their family members, or unsympathetic colleagues.

- Avoid sharing too much information about your personal life at work. Before you reveal anything about your personal life, ask yourself, "Would I be comfortable revealing this if a school board member were in the room?"

- Do not make personal phone calls or send personal e-mail messages while you are at school. The phone calls may be overheard, and school e-mail is not private.

- If you decide to date a staff member, keep your relationship as private as possible. Your students should have absolutely no idea that you are involved with a fellow staff member.

- Do not talk about students when you are not at school. When you do this, you violate their privacy and your professional ethics.

- Refuse to talk about other staff members in an unpleasant way. In a social setting, it is not acceptable for you to discuss the failings of other staff members. People who do not work at your school should not be privy to the disagreeable quirks of your coworkers.

- Be especially careful to model honest behavior in regard to copyright laws and in giving credit to sources that you use for your work. Your students learn more from your example than you can ever realize.

- Don't rehash a disagreeable incident. When something unpleasant happens at school, it is tempting to discuss it. Discussing your school's problems around people who are not involved is not acceptable. You will only spread ill will about your school if you do so.

Strategies for Effective Collaboration

Because education is such an incredibly complex undertaking in the twenty-first century, successful collaboration is a crucial part of any school setting. As the school year progresses, you will see that it is personally satisfying to work with others for the greater good of the school. You need support from your colleagues for several reasons. For example:

- You will save time when you share ideas and materials for such routine tasks as planning lessons, decorating bulletin boards, or devising efficient classroom procedures.
- Guidance from your peers can increase your self-confidence.

Here are some useful suggestions for being the best team member you can be:

- Be an active listener as you consider others' viewpoints. Stop trying to talk, and instead really listen to your colleagues. Be especially careful to allow speakers to finish before you respond.
- Seek clarification during meetings if you are not sure of what has been said. Ask intelligent questions to avoid misunderstanding.
- Be aware of your body language. Make an effort to appear calm and engaged when others are speaking.
- Familiarize yourself with the goals of your school's improvement plan. What can you do to help achieve them?
- Learn to work well with all staff members, not just the faculty. Student success is everyone's responsibility.
- Be dependable. Honor your commitments and be honest about your abilities, time constraints, and skills.
- Have good attendance and be on time to school and meetings.
- Be positive. Negativity makes any undertaking harder to accomplish. Begin by focusing on the accomplishments and strengths of your colleagues.
- Be straightforward with what you have to say. Talking in generalities or around a subject will confuse and irritate others.
- Be patient. When something goes wrong, don't assign blame.
- Be proud of your school and let that pride show.

HOW TO HANDLE PROFESSIONAL DISAGREEMENTS

One of the most stressful parts of a school day can occur if you find yourself in a disagreement with a colleague. Because of the need for productive collaboration in twenty-first-century schools, it is important to learn how to handle professional disagreements. If you find yourself in a conflict, try these suggestions to resolve it:

- Instead of just reacting, respond by taking a problem-solving approach to try to work out a resolution. Deciding to resolve a problem instead of just letting it fester by ignoring it or by lashing out in anger is a productive and professional approach. Talk privately, but candidly, with the other person. Ask, "What can we do to change this?"

- Think about how you may have contributed to the problem instead of blaming the other person. Make sure that you are not overreacting or misreading the situation. In the hurried pace of a school day, it is very easy to misread another's intentions or reactions.

- Refuse to act in kind if the other person has been rude or uncooperative. Try to be as open minded, respectful, and tolerant as possible.

- If you are involved in a curriculum dispute, refer to your state's guidelines and standards. All instruction must satisfy those requirements, even if you have colleagues who think differently. Curriculum issues constitute a frequent area of disagreement.

- Resist the urge to vent about the conflict with colleagues. Limit its negative impact by involving as few people as possible.

WHAT YOUR COWORKERS EXPECT FROM YOU

Your colleagues expect you to

- Be courteous and cooperative
- Share ideas in meetings as well as listen carefully to the ideas of others
- Work toward shared goals
- Be understanding and supportive
- Conduct yourself with professionalism
- Work for the good of everyone in your school
- Clean up after yourself
- Focus on school business while you are at school
- Be on time for everything
- Keep your promises

- Value their experience
- Be willing to do your share of extra duties
- Communicate openly and professionally
- Be interested in others but not gossip
- Admit when you're not sure of something
- Have a sense of fun
- Be open to new ideas
- Keep trying to improve

> Go observe the teachers in your building. A lot can be gained from watching an experienced teacher, especially a great one.
>
> *Debbie McManaway, 19 years' experience*

WORKING WELL WITH DIFFICULT COLLEAGUES

People in all professions have to learn to deal with difficult colleagues, and teachers are no exception. Some colleagues may be so difficult to get along with that you find it very challenging to work with them. Just as in any other profession, difficult colleagues can come in many forms—ranging from those who grouch constantly or make offhand rude comments to backstabbers or incessantly negative complainers.

No matter how difficult a colleague can be, however, to be a successful professional and part of an effective team, you need to work well with everyone. The best guideline to follow in trying to work well with difficult colleagues is to recognize that you share a common goal: the education of the children entrusted to your care. If you keep this common goal in mind, you have little choice but to work well together because the alternative could result in failure for students and for you. The following tips will help you learn to work well with colleagues you find difficult:

- Be clear about your professional beliefs and responsibilities. This will lend you confidence and make it harder for others to intimidate you.
- Don't rush to judgment. For example, when you meet someone at the start of the term, you are probably meeting a harried, stressed colleague with too much to do. Be patient, and wait until you know the person better before making a judgment.
- Look for the good traits in your colleagues. Although everyone has irritating personality quirks, each person also has appealing characteristics. Be on the lookout for these positive traits in every person you work with.
- Pick your battles. Save your time and energy for the important issues at school instead of worrying about the less important ones. If you can ignore a coworker's behavior without harming students or the school program, make the effort to do so.
- Because school can be extremely stressful at times, don't be surprised to see normally serene coworkers lose their cool under pressure.

- If you find yourself persistently annoyed with a colleague, remind yourself that he or she is not likely to change. Instead, if you can make an effort to change your attitude, you will find it easier to work with annoying coworkers.

- Do not gossip about a person you find difficult. If you are unsure of the best course of action to take with a difficult person, ask a close colleague or a mentor for advice.

- When dealing with a colleague who is a bully, use the same technique you probably learned in grade school: stand up for yourself. Do not try to argue with a bully; just make your point firmly. When you have to do this, be professional in your approach. It is often better to act sooner rather than later when ill feelings have had an opportunity to build.

- Sometimes, when you need to collaborate closely on a potentially contentious matter, agree to disagree. Not all solutions are simple ones.

- Remember that negative people are that way for many reasons. Their chief harm is that they encourage you to be negative, too. Negative attitudes spread quickly. Because it is almost impossible to cheer people up who are determined to be negative, associate with upbeat people who are focused on learning to be outstanding teachers instead.

> Keep your fresh innocence alive. Don't fall victim to the negativity of those who no longer seem to be able to find a bit of good in the world.
>
> *Dawn Carroll, 17 years' experience*

Don't be one of the difficult people in your school! Listen more than you talk, and be as tolerant of others as you can. Your reputation for working well with others will make it easier for you to do this as time goes by.

Social Media Guidelines

As teachers, many of us feel frustrated by the current nebulous relationship between social media and education. On the one hand, social media offers unprecedented opportunities to connect with our students in positive ways. The prospective power of social media is intriguing for those of us who recognize how important and engaging it is to our students. On the other hand, teachers have been fired for indiscreet private postings or even tags that followed them into their professional lives.

At present, and probably for a few years into the future, the educational use of social media and the tools that deliver it to our students rest in a murky limbo. As school districts struggle to develop policies that will allow students and teachers to take full advantage of the benefits of social media in their professional lives, wise teachers are cautious about how they use it at school. Before you jump into using social media professionally, consider following these guidelines to make sound decisions for yourself and your students:

- Educate yourself about your school district's policies in regard to how social media can and can't be used by school employees and students. Follow those policies.

- Keep the distinction between your personal accounts and your professional ones very clear. Protect your own privacy by limiting access to your personal online information and communication. Do not allow students to friend you, for example, on an account that you use for your personal communication with friends and family members.

- If you do communicate with students online, be sure to use school accounts instead of personal ones. Using a school e-mail address will offer you protection because you have no expectation of privacy there and so can't easily be accused of inappropriate behavior that you did not commit. You should assume that your school e-mail account is monitored by district personnel.

- Use this as a quick guide: if a comment would be inappropriate in a classroom setting, it is also inappropriate online. Be careful about what you say to students online and be clear about the tone and subjects that you find acceptable from them in return.

- Avoid just browsing students' accounts, even when you have access to them. For example, if students in your class have to tweet a comment on Twitter for homework, don't scrutinize your students' other tweets or follow links that they may have posted.

- If you have a Web site or blog or contribute to wikis, chat rooms, electronic mailing lists, or other shared sites yourself, be aware that you are personally responsible for the content you produce. Be sensible—do not write about your students or your school district.

- Ask your friends to be mindful of any unflattering or potentially compromising photo in which you may be tagged. Remove any that you can find yourself. It is better to be cautious than to have to try to explain indiscreet behavior in your past.

The Importance of Perfect Attendance

Even though it may seem surprising that your absence from school could have a negative effect on your colleagues as well as on your students, a teacher's absence really does affect the entire school. Your colleagues may have to give up a planning period to cover for you or print and deliver your plans or even help the substitute teacher manage your students' behavior. Striving for perfect attendance is a worthwhile goal that will make it easier for you to be an effective teacher for your students and collaborator with your coworkers.

To learn more about how to successfully manage those times when you do have to miss school, including what to do, whom to inform, how to leave effective lesson plans, what information your substitute needs, and how to handle problems once you return, consult the bonus material in the DVD that accompanies this book.

The Support Staff

As a new teacher, you will have to learn many new faces and names as quickly as possible. Although it is sensible to learn the names of other faculty members first, it is a mistake to think that they are your only colleagues. A school community is composed of many different people in many different positions. Each of them deserves your cooperation and respect, because you all work toward the same goal: the good of the students in your school. You can do much to encourage a spirit of teamwork with your colleagues. Here is a brief list of just some of the actions that you can take right away to treat all staff members as colleagues:

- Learn the names of the support personnel in your school as quickly as possible. Greet each by name when you meet. Treat each person in the building with the same courtesy that you would like to receive.

- Develop professional relationships with other staff members. Learn the roles that various people play in your school and how they contribute to the overall picture. By doing this, you will be able to be supportive when they need your help.

- Encourage your students to respect the work of support personnel by modeling that respect yourself. Speak courteously to the cafeteria, clerical, custodial, and other staff. Make sure that your students leave their work area clean. Let them see you picking up trash in the hall.

- Never make a disparaging comment about the work of support staff members when you are with students. This courtesy means that you should go as far as avoiding making unkind remarks about the food served in the cafeteria, the media ordered by the school librarian, or the computer glitches that technicians can't solve quickly.

- Be as cooperative as possible. If a colleague requests that you hand in reports, grade sheets, attendance information, or other paperwork, respond promptly.

- Respect your colleagues' time, equipment, and other resources. For example, if the school secretary asks you not to tie up a phone line, respect that request, even though you may have a very important call to make.

The Chain of Command

To work well with your supervisors and other staff members, you must know and follow the chain of command at your school. Few things annoy other employees as much as a person who does not have enough respect for other employees to follow the chain of command when things are not going well.

Not following the chain of command may win you a momentary victory, but it will be a hollow one. For example, if you have requested certain repairs to your classroom and these repairs have not been made, you may be tempted to speak to the principal about this problem. If you do this instead of speaking with the custodian in charge of your classroom, you may have been unfair to that person. There may be a good reason for the incomplete repairs. As a rule of thumb, if you need additional assistance in solving a problem, it is a good idea to talk with a mentor instead of ignoring the chain of command.

Collaborate Successfully with Administrators

The supervisory staffs of your school district and of your school building depend on faculty members to make things run smoothly. Although it is only natural that there will be problems, it is up to you to work well with your supervisors. Having a positive relationship with the administrators at your school means that you will be less stressed, more productive, and happier at work.

There is a specific hierarchy of supervision at any school. It is likely that you report to a department head, lead teacher, or grade-level leader who serves as a liaison between staff members and administrators. Assistant principals make up the next level. At the top of the hierarchy in your school is the principal, who is the instructional leader of your building. At the district level, your supervisors may differ in their titles but will include curriculum coordinators and assistant superintendents who report to their supervisor, the superintendent of schools. The hierarchy does not end there. The school board supervises all employees, including the superintendent.

If you want to establish productive relationships with your supervisors, you will need to take positive action. Do not just hope that no one will notice you because you are a first-year teacher. In fact, you are particularly noticeable just because you are a first-year teacher!

Follow these suggestions to establish a positive working relationship with all of your supervisors:

- **Behave in a professional manner at all times.** This will win the support of administrators because it makes their job easier. In addition, if you maintain a solid reputation, it is easier for them to support you when you make mistakes and more likely that they will want to offer their support.

- **Take time to familiarize yourself with the information in your faculty manual or handbook.** This will help you avoid mistakes that may lead to negative interactions with your supervisors.

- **Remember that administrators are responsible for the entire school and you are responsible for only a very small part of it.** If you can maintain this point of view, you'll find it easier to understand some of the policies you might otherwise find confusing.

- **Think before you voice public criticism.** Accept the fact that although you are not always going to agree with the decisions and actions of the administrators with whom you work, public criticism of their actions might seriously damage your professional reputation.

- **Don't threaten to send your students to the office instead of resolving the problem through other more successful methods of discipline.** Maintain control of your classroom so that when you have to send a student out of class, the action will have meaning for students as well as administrators.

- **Remember to be professional in your dealings with administrators.** Always present a calm and competent image, not one of a furious teacher who lacks self-control. Regardless of your personal feelings toward a supervisor, always model respect.

- **When you make a mistake, be truthful in discussing it with your supervisors.** If you can do this before they find out the bad news from someone else, you should do so. Don't ever try to hide problems. Ask for help instead.

- **Be positive.** Sharing good news or taking a positive stance when problems occur will make it easier for an administrator to help you when you really need it. Constant complaints eventually fall on deaf ears.

- **Share your successes with your supervisors.** Help them create positive public relations for your school by letting them know about noteworthy news pertaining to your students.

Working Well with Parents and Guardians

All parents and guardians have the right to remain informed about their child's behavioral and academic progress. Not only is it their right but also you will find that your job is much easier when you make parents and guardians part of their child's success team. Because they want their child to be successful and look to you for assistance in achieving this success, parents and guardians can be enormously helpful.

Without a doubt, home support is a major influence on students' attitudes about school. When students know that the important adults in their lives present a united front, they are less likely to misbehave and more likely to strive for success.

It is your responsibility to reach out to your students' parents and guardians before they feel the need to reach out to you. Although reaching out makes extra demands on your time, it is time well spent. Always remember to treat parents and guardians with careful respect, even if you disagree with the way they express their concern for their child.

Follow these suggestions to create a strong connection with the significant adults in your students' lives:

- Be careful to make your first contact with your students' parents and guardians a positive one. A good example of how to make initial contact is sending home a letter with information about what they and their child can expect in the year ahead. (See Section Four for a sample letter.)

- If there is a crisis in a student's family, express your concern and offer assistance. For example, if there is a death in the family, send a note expressing condolences and offer to help the student catch up on missing work.

- Encourage parents and guardians to drop by your classroom often. They can do many things—volunteer or be guest speakers, for example.

- Some experienced teachers send out class newsletters or have a Web page for their classes. You might try this after you have adjusted to your teaching responsibilities.

- Take the time to make positive phone calls at the start of the term. Send home positive news as often as you can. Parents and guardians who hear good news will be more willing to work with you when a problem develops.

- Return phone calls to parents and guardians as soon as possible. Make it a rule to call back within twenty-four hours.

- Take the time to be a good listener when you talk with parents and guardians. Together, you can work out many problems while they are still small.

- When you talk with parents and guardians, realize that their own past negative experiences with school may affect their perception of you. Be as positive and professional as possible to help them overcome their negative feelings.

- Don't give out your home phone number. Keep your relationships businesslike. You have a right to protect your privacy at home.

- Notify parents and guardians as soon as you begin to notice a problem developing. Many parents and guardians complain that teachers wait too long to call.

- When you call parents and guardians at work, ask if they have a moment to talk instead of plunging in with an account of the problem. This small courtesy will enable them to focus on their conversation with you.

- Avoid becoming confrontational with parents and guardians, even when they are unpleasant and confrontational first. Continue to show your concern and caring.

- Never discuss another person's child with a parent or guardian. This violates the child's privacy and is unprofessional.

What Parents and Guardians Expect from You

When you are a novice teacher who is just beginning to work with the families of your students, you may find it hard to decipher what they expect from their child's teacher. Some may want you to be a tough disciplinarian, whereas others may expect you to assume an "anything goes" attitude. As confusing as these extremes can be, however, most parents and guardians are reasonable in their expectations. Parents and guardians expect you to

- Treat their child fairly
- Teach the material their child needs to succeed

> Every teacher needs to be able to communicate with parents and guardians with honesty, in a polite manner, and without condescension. Always document conferences, whether phone conferences or face-to-face conferences.
>
> *Charlene Herrala, 31 years' experience*

- Work with them for the good of their child
- Communicate with them early about problems
- Show that you value their child
- Keep their child safe from harm
- Act in a professional manner at all times
- Respect their rights and efforts as parents and guardians
- Agree to reasonable requests that benefit their child
- Make school a pleasant experience

Prevent Miscommunication with a Transparent Classroom

One of the easiest ways to prevent miscommunication and establish a positive relationship with the parents and guardians of your students is to make sure that your classroom is as transparent as possible. You can do this by providing easily accessible information about your students and their learning activities. A transparent classroom is one where your students, their families, your colleagues, and community members can all view what is taking place. A transparent classroom provides support while encouraging accountability for you and for your students.

When you create a transparent classroom, you are not just a teacher who grudgingly shares test dates or other routine information with your students' families. Instead, as a twenty-first-century teacher, you actively reach out to solicit participation and support from everyone concerned. With today's technology, making sure that everyone knows firsthand what is happening in your class is easier than ever. Your students' parents and guardians expect to be kept informed about these topics:

- Class policies, rules, and consequences
- Beginning-of-the-year information
- Homework and major assignments
- Tests and other assessments
- Grading concerns
- Due dates
- Field trips
- Special projects
- Resources to help students learn
- Positive things about their child

When teachers take the time to communicate directly with the parents and guardians of their students, the trouble that can follow miscommunication diminishes. One frequent complaint that parents and guardians have involves not being informed about homework assignments and important project due dates. Take extra care to make sure your homework policies are published in several different ways and that project due dates are announced well in advance. The parents and guardians of your students should not have to struggle to find out what their child's homework is and when work is due.

Some of the ways you can make sure students and their parents or guardians are aware of the expectations, rules, policies, procedures, and activities in your class include these low-tech options:

- Send positive notes home frequently.
- Maintain a daily class log or calendar.
- Use the bulletin board space in your room to post information.
- Photograph your students at work and display the photos.
- Publish a syllabus so that students and their families can plan ahead.
- Send home progress reports frequently.
- Return all phone calls promptly.
- Make sure parents and guardians know that they are welcome to visit your class.
- Invite parents or guardians to visit your class for special occasions, such as field trips and exhibits of student work.

Some methods that other teachers have found effective for creating a transparent classroom using technology resources include these options:

- Create slide shows of your students at work for parents and guardians to view at open house or other schoolwide meetings.
- Publish a class blog or have students maintain individual blogs as learning logs. An excellent free site for this is Edublogs (http://edublogs.org). At this site, over a million teachers and students around the globe maintain classroom blogs.
- Create videos of your students working and publish them on your class Web page. (See Section Two for more information about how to maintain a class Web page.)
- Have students create podcasts about what they are learning. There are hundreds of sites online to help teachers with classroom podcasts, but one of the easiest to use is the free site Podomatic (www.podomatic.com). Here teachers and students can create and publish podcasts and minicasts (photographs combined with an audio track) with ease.

> Being transparent is the best way to teach. Everything is out on the table, and there are no secrets.
>
> *Jared Sronce, first-year teacher*

One of the most important ways to create a transparent classroom is to hold a successful open house. An open house can be stressful for you as a teacher. You will have much to do in preparation, and you will be on display for several hours. Both of these can be exhausting when you must do them at night after you have already put in a long day. To learn more about how your open house experience can be positive and productive, consult the bonus material on the DVD included with this book. There you can learn a few general guidelines about how to proceed, what to include in your presentation to parents or guardians, and how to inspire confidence. There is also a timeline of tasks to help you manage your professional responsibilities.

TEACHER WORKSHEET 3.1

How Effective Are You at Creating a Transparent Classroom?

Place a check mark beside each of the statements in the following list that are true for you. Any statements that are not currently true for you are ones you should begin working on to create the transparent classroom that will benefit your students.

1. _____ I frequently send home notes, e-mails, and progress reports.

2. _____ I maintain a daily class log or calendar so that students know what happened in class while they were absent.

3. _____ I use the bulletin board space in my room to post information for students.

4. _____ I photograph students at work and display the photographs in my classroom.

5. _____ I publish a syllabus so that students and their families can plan ahead.

6. _____ I return all phone calls and answer e-mails within twenty-four hours.

7. _____ I make sure parents and guardians know that they are welcome to visit our class.

8. _____ I create slide shows, videos or other electronic presentations of my students at work for parents and guardians to view at open house or other schoolwide meetings.

9. _____ I invite parents or guardians to visit our class for special occasions, such as field trips and exhibits of student work.

10. _____ I maintain a class blog and Web page to keep students, parents, and guardians informed about my students' learning activities.

The Importance of Keeping Contact Records

By now you are probably convinced that you will spend all of your free hours at school documenting things you took for granted in your own student days. There are forms for just about every interaction you will have with your students, and you must complete each form accurately and promptly.

It is a sensible practice to keep accurate records of the times when you have contacted parents and guardians. Even the very best teacher could be asked to provide proof that he or she did all that could be done to help a particular student. Every year, there are countless cases in which frustrated parents and guardians sue teachers in an attempt to find a simple cause for a complex problem. Although it may be upsetting to think that this could happen to a dedicated teacher, it does happen.

Fortunately, you can protect yourself with just a few minutes of planning and paperwork. You can enhance your professional reputation by being able to provide documentation that you have contacted parents and guardians appropriately. Keeping a record of home contacts does not have to be time consuming. Use or modify Teacher Worksheet 3.2, and keep plenty of copies on hand so that you can complete one each time you contact a student's parents or guardians. Fill out the form, and file it in a folder or binder with the other paperwork for that student.

TEACHER WORKSHEET 3.2

Contact Documentation Form

Student name: _____

Parent or guardian name(s): _____

Phone number: _____

Date and time of contact: _____

Type of contact:

_____   Phone call

_____   E-mail

_____   Letter

_____   Detention notice

_____   Home visit

_____   Informal meeting

_____   Meeting with administrator

_____   Meeting with counselor

_____   Other: _____

Person(s) initiating the contact: _____

Topics discussed:

_____

_____

_____

_____

Steps parent(s) or guardian(s) will take:

_____

_____

_____

Steps teacher will take:

_____

_____

_____

Additional notes and reflections:

_____

_____

_____

_____

_____

_____

Be Positive with Parents and Guardians

There are many ways to make positive contact with the parents and guardians of your students. Although it may take time to follow through on these little actions, the benefits will compensate for the time you spend on them. Start with one or two of the ones you find easy to manage, and reach out from there.

- Call at the start of the term to relate a positive message.
- Send home positive updates as often as you can.
- Have parents and guardians sign papers with good grades as well as bad ones.
- Compliment parents and guardians to other people. Do not hesitate to let students know that you think highly of their parents or guardians.
- Make it a habit to thank parents and guardians of your students for their support whenever you see them.
- Call or e-mail parents and guardians with good news.
- If you have a school voice mail, record a positive message to parents and guardians.
- Send home a thank-you note after a conference.

One of the most effective ways to be positive with the parents and guardians of students at all grade levels is to send home positive messages as often as you can. Even the parents

---

Sample 3.1

Positive Message to Parents or Guardians

Although many formats can be used to notify parents and guardians of student achievements, it is best to keep your message simple. Adapt the format of this sample message for your own students:

To the Parents or Guardians of _____:

I am writing to let you know how pleased I am with your child's recent success in my class. You will be proud to know that

_____.

I know you are as proud of this effort and achievement as I am. Thank you for your support.

Sincerely,

and guardians of older secondary students will appreciate the effort you take to recognize their child's hard work and successes.

You can create your own "positive postal," or try one of these Web sites:

- **A to Z Teacher Stuff (www.atozteacherstuff.com/printables).** This teacher-created site is a good place to search for printable positive message templates for students of all ages. You can find thousands of online resources quickly and easily. This site provides numerous templates for students of all ages.

- **Teachnology (www.teach-nology.com/worksheets).** This Web portal offers a wide variety of free and easy-to-use resources, including printable templates. It also provides links to other sites focusing on best practices in education.

Take Care to Interact Professionally

Making an effort to work well with parents and guardians can create a team of allied adults whose purpose is to work together for the good of the students involved. Interacting professionally is important, and many areas of this delicate relationship may require special attention. In the paragraphs that follow, you will learn strategies to ensure that your interactions are as professional as possible. Interacting with your students and their families in a professional way in every situation is not always easy, but it will be worth the effort.

ASSIST PARENTS AND GUARDIANS WHO DO NOT SPEAK ENGLISH

At some point in your career, whether you teach in a small town or in a large city, you will have to communicate with parents or guardians whose primary language is not English. This situation can be awkward and confusing for everyone if you are not prepared to offer assistance. Although it is likely that your school district made efforts to provide such assistance when the student enrolled, it is up to you to find a way to communicate effectively if you cannot find an adult interpreter.

One solution is to have students translate for their parents or guardians. This is effective if the child is trustworthy and old enough to handle the task. Another solution is to involve an older sibling of the student if that person is dependable.

You can also use technology to help with this problem. Many Internet sites are available to assist you in translating what you need to communicate to parents or guardians. Some sites allow you to type in what you want to say, and it will be translated quickly into another language. Try visiting iLoveLanguages (www.ilovelanguages.com) the next time you need a translator. This site has a comprehensive catalogue of more than 1,900 language-related Internet resources. Click on the "Languages" tab at the top of the home page to find sites that can translate bits of text free of charge.

BE A GOOD LISTENER

To build positive relationships with your students' parents and guardians, it is important to develop good listening skills. Try these simple suggestions for improving your listening skills, and enjoy the benefits of improved communication:

- Stop talking. Allow the other person to speak without fear of interruption from you.

- Give nonverbal cues to indicate that you are paying attention. Nod your head, look the person in the eye, or lean forward in your seat. When appropriate, prompt the speaker by asking questions.

- Jot down notes so that later you will be able to recall what was discussed. Before you begin, tell the other person that you are going to take notes to help you recall the conversation.

- Make sure that you fully understand the other person by asking for clarification if you need it. Say, "I am not sure I understand what you are saying. Do you mean _____?" or "I think I hear you saying _____."

MAKE A GOOD IMPRESSION THROUGH EFFECTIVE CORRESPONDENCE

If you thought that your English teachers in high school were quick to catch your grammatical errors, you have not yet experienced the embarrassment of sending home a note with a misspelled word. With a bit of careful effort, you can spare yourself this humiliation.

When you send home a note or letter or send an e-mail message, it represents your effectiveness as a teacher. The correspondence you send home should be businesslike because it reflects your professional competence. Follow these suggestions for making a good impression with effective correspondence:

- Before going into detail in writing about an incident at school, consider phoning the parent or guardian instead. Often you can clear up confusion quickly with a friendly phone call.

- Make sure that what you write in a letter is accurate; verify the dates, times, and other details.

- Be brief, but not brusque. Cover your points quickly. Use bulleted lists or other businesslike writing techniques to make your letters easy to follow.

- Remember that appearance counts! Photocopy with clean edges and with enough ink or toner to make clean and clear copies. Avoid cute graphics or unusual fonts whenever you can. Use letterhead stationery when appropriate.

- Know that grammar and word usage matter a great deal in letters home. Have a colleague proofread your correspondence before you send it out.

- When you send home handwritten notes, write legibly. Use a pen with dark ink for readability, and take the time to proofread your work.

- Never give in to the temptation to fire off an angry e-mail or send a hasty note home. Cool off before you contact parents or guardians.

MAKE TELEPHONE CALLS WITH CONFIDENCE

Phoning parents or guardians when there is a problem is one of the unpleasant tasks teachers must do well. Even experienced teachers dread interacting with the occasional angry parent or guardian who makes phoning a student's home a negative and upsetting experience. However, as disagreeable as this task can be, phoning a parent or guardian is a necessary and often helpful action. There are several strategies you can adopt to make phoning home easier:

- To save time, use the contact information you collected from your students early in the term instead of searching database records that may not be as up to date.

- Plan what you want to say and what information the parent or guardian needs to know so that you can work together to solve the problem.

- Find a phone at school from which you can make the call with at least some privacy and in a place where you are not likely to be interrupted.

- Be sure to have a pen and the notes you have made about the situation with you.

- Don't hesitate to call a parent or guardian at work. However, be careful not to reveal too many details to the colleagues of the person you are calling. Protecting his or her privacy shows respect, making it more likely that this individual will be cooperative when you ask him or her for help.

- If you call while a parent or guardian is at work, begin the conversation by asking, "Do you have a few minutes right now?" so that this person can set his or her work aside long enough to listen.

- Remember that the purpose of the phone call is not to allow you to vent your frustration but rather to enable you to solve a problem by working with the parent or guardian.

- Begin with a positive statement about the student, and then say that you would like to enlist help in solving a problem: "I had a problem with Jim today, and I wonder if you could help me."

- Be very specific about the problem. Don't just say, "Jim is acting odd today." Try, "Jim laughed out loud at inappropriate moments six times today and fell asleep right before lunch."

- After detailing the problem, state what you have done to correct it. Again, be very specific, and give the result of your actions.

- Pay attention while the parent or guardian explains what he or she knows about the situation. Make sure to listen carefully and clarify any points you do not understand.

- Never lose sight of the fact that you and the parent or guardian are working together to solve the problem. A team approach is the best one to take.

- Finish the call with a positive statement, expressing your appreciation that a solution has been devised.

- Before you go on to your next task, document the call. Complete a contact documentation form (see Worksheet 3.2) so that you have a record of the conversation and what each party decided to do.

Class Newsletters

Class newsletters have played a strong role in classrooms for many years and are likely to remain prominent for many more years for those teachers who want to use them instead of or in addition to class blogs. Although they are most often used by teachers of younger students, newsletters are a valuable tool for all teachers who wish to connect with parents and guardians in a meaningful way.

Newsletters can serve many purposes—for example, keeping parents and guardians informed about what is happening in your class, informing parents and guardians of upcoming events, and including everyone in creating a caring learning environment.

Newsletters can be written entirely by a teacher, or they can be managed by students as an authentic writing activity. Either way, parents and guardians as well as students gain new insights as they communicate with each other and with you. To make sure that the newsletters you send home represent your professional best, try including some of these items:

- A message from you
- Student art and projects
- A review of the work covered in class since the previous newsletter
- A list of topics currently under study
- Information about standardized tests
- Student work samples
- Creative writing samples
- Student success stories
- Upcoming events, such as conferences or field trips
- A word of the week

- Ways that parents and guardians can help students study
- Links to articles that would be helpful for parents and guardians
- Links to community resources
- A survey of parents and guardians on a relevant topic
- An inspirational message
- A request for donations
- A note thanking parents and guardians for their support

Conduct Successful Conferences with Parents and Guardians

Although there are many different types of conferences a teacher can have with parents and guardians, the type of conference that produces high-level anxiety for everyone involved—students, parents and guardians, and teachers—is one in which there is a problem to be solved. Despite the anxiety they produce, face-to-face meetings can be a very effective way to solve problems.

Teachers who want to communicate well realize that parents and guardians want to be reassured that their child is thriving and can succeed in school. Even if that is not what is happening at the moment, parents and guardians want teachers to work with them to help their child. A strong connection with your students' parents and guardians is achievable if you make sure that your goals for conferences are clear. Here are five goals you should have for every conference:

- **Goal One**: Parents and guardians should see you as a friendly and knowledgeable teacher who has their child's best interests at heart.
- **Goal Two**: Parents and guardians should feel an atmosphere of cooperation and support when they are meeting with you.
- **Goal Three**: Parents and guardians should leave a conference with all their questions answered and all the points they wanted to discuss covered.
- **Goal Four**: You as well as parents and guardians should share a sense of mutual respect and an understanding of each other's problems and viewpoints.
- **Goal Five**: Workable solutions to any problems should be agreed on, and everyone involved should work together to help the student.

Conferences with parents and guardians are much more involved than a quick chat after school. Successful conferences require planning; attention to detail; and effort before, during, and after the meeting.

> Remember that every child, even the most challenging or disrespectful kid in class, is someone's pride and joy.
>
> *Melinda Conner, first-year teacher*

ACTIONS TO TAKE BEFORE A CONFERENCE

Once you have decided that there is a need for a conference, take the time not only to make careful plans but also to set up the area where the conference will be held. Use these guidelines to guarantee that the conferences you have this year are positive and productive:

- Make sure you have a clear purpose for the conference and a clear understanding of the outcome you would like.
- Plan the points you want to cover. Write them down.
- Gather samples of student work or other evidence you would like to use in the conference. Include progress reports and other information related to grades or behavior.
- Review cumulative records and report card information.
- Take notes on the student's strengths and weaknesses as well as any other special information you would like to present.
- Anticipate potential reactions and questions, and jot down notes about possible answers that you may be too nervous to recall in the conference.
- Create a seating arrangement that will be comfortable for adults. Arrange chairs around a table or desks large enough for adults in a circle. Do not plan to sit behind your desk.
- Make sure you provide a pen and paper for everyone.
- Plan to remain calm before, during, and after the conference. If you lose your cool, you will gain nothing.
- Make a neat "Do Not Disturb" sign; post it on your door so that you can meet without distractions.
- Meet the parents or guardians and escort them to your room.

ACTIONS TO TAKE DURING A CONFERENCE

During a conference, there are many actions you can take to ensure that it will be as productive and positive an experience as possible for everyone involved.

- Be prepared to begin promptly. Do not make parents or guardians wait while you shuffle papers.
- Begin by expressing your appreciation that the parents or guardians have come to the conference. Try to establish a tone of goodwill and friendly cooperation as quickly as you can.
- Use language that will make the parents or guardians comfortable. Do not use educational jargon.

- Begin with positive remarks about the child. Talk about the student's aptitude, special talents, improvements, and potential. Focus on strengths even if there is a serious problem. Never lose sight of the fact that the child is very important to his or her parents or guardians.

- Convey the attitude that the child's welfare is your primary concern.

- State any problems in simple, factual terms. Express your desire to work with the parents or guardians for a successful resolution.

- Discuss specific examples of a problem. Show examples of work that illustrates or give details about the student's behavior.

- Let the parents or guardians say what they need to say. It is always best to allow upset or angry parents or guardians to speak first. After the parents or guardians have had the opportunity to say everything they need to say, then—and only then—can they listen to what you have to say or begin to work on a solution to a problem.

- If you have discussed a problem before, let the parents or guardians know of any improvement.

- Be sure to state what you have done to try to correct problem situations.

- If you want to solve a problem, give your full attention throughout the entire conference. Your nonverbal language is crucial for success. Be friendly and attentive.

- Don't put the parents or guardians on the defensive by becoming angry or by asking personal questions.

- Don't try to outtalk the parents or guardians. You may make your point, but the parents or guardians will not listen to you. Do not give in to the temptation to interrupt.

- End the conference gracefully by recapping the points that you have covered.

- Determine what you will do to follow up on the conference and to keep in contact with the parents or guardians.

- Express appreciation again for their concern and the time they have spent with you in the conference.

ACTIONS TO TAKE AFTER A CONFERENCE

Immediately complete your notes and the documentary evidence of what was discussed and the agreed-on decisions. Spend enough time on this so that your records are complete. Should you need to refer to this material later, you may not remember details accurately if your notes are not thorough.

> Let the parents know that you are in this together and you have the student's interests at heart.
>
> *Jared Sronce, first-year teacher*

WHY SOME PARENTS AND GUARDIANS MAY NOT RELATE WELL TO YOU

As you gain experience, you will find that not all parents and guardians are supportive of you and the other teachers in your school. Although your first tendency may be to take this personally, there are many possible reasons for such negative attitudes:

- Some parents and guardians may have had unpleasant experiences in school themselves.
- Their child may have told them something objectionable (although probably exaggerated or false) about you.
- One of your lessons may have contained information they find inappropriate.
- You may not have presented yourself as professionally as possible when you first met them.
- You may have allowed a problem to escalate by not contacting them as quickly as you should have.
- They may be reacting out of their own frustration with their child's behavior, particularly if the problem is a long-standing one.
- They may disagree with you about the appropriate consequences of their child's behavior.
- They may feel embarrassment at their child's behavior or lack of success.
- Their child may have had unsympathetic or unsupportive teachers in the past.
- Previous teachers may have reacted negatively to their efforts to parent their child.
- Your uncertainty and lack of confidence may be obvious.
- They may want to protect their child from potential embarrassment or punishment.

> Recognize that parents and guardians can be your biggest allies. Whatever issues you may be having at school, chances are the parents have been dealing with the same thing for years.
>
> *Christina L. Myren, 4 years' experience*

HELICOPTER PARENTS OR GUARDIANS

The term *helicopter parent* is a fairly recent one that describes a style of rearing children by parents or guardians who "hover" over their child, second-guessing every decision made by his or her teachers. Although there can be extreme cases of excessive involvement, experienced teachers have learned to appreciate parents and guardians who involve themselves in their child's education. Many of us would gladly learn to work well with helicopter parents or guardians instead of dealing with uninvolved ones who appear to be indifferent to their child's scholastic success.

If you find yourself having to deal with helicopter parents or guardians, there are several actions you can take to ensure that the relationship you have with them is as beneficial as possible. Consider using some of the actions in the list that follows to ensure that the relationship you have with all parents or guardians is a constructive one.

- Adopt a positive attitude about your ability to cope successfully with this type of parent or guardian. Working together for the good of the student is an important enough endeavor to justify a special effort.

- Strive to keep the channels of communication open. Having a transparent classroom can allay many concerns that parents or guardians may have about your class. Communicate often and be explicit about your expectations. Make it apparent that you want to work together productively.

- Be very clear that you like and respect their child and acknowledge their rights as parents or guardians.

- Try to prevent situations in which helicopter parents or guardians can react anxiously by taking extra care to follow your school and district policies and best practices. If necessary, educate them about those policies and best practices.

- If you receive an unpleasant phone call or e-mail, don't forget that you are a professional and take care to respond in a professional way. Lashing out in frustration will only make the situation worse.

- Schedule a face-to-face conference and really listen. Their anxiety about their child may be relieved once they have had the opportunity to speak freely and have their concerns heard by a competent, caring professional.

- Although you should actively promote the importance of the student's taking appropriate individual responsibility for his or her own academic and behavioral success, try to accommodate as many requests as you sensibly can. Sometimes giving in on small issues may make it easier for you to refuse unrealistic requests when it comes to larger ones.

- Never stoop to putting the student in the middle of a battle between home and school or in a position in which he or she is made uncomfortable because of a disagreement between the significant adults in his or her life.

- Do not try to manage helicopter parents or guardians by yourself. Involve knowledgeable colleagues who may have had similar experiences and who may be willing to assist you. Counselors and administrators can

Teachers should remember that communication with parents or guardians is always about the student. Never make or allow a situation to turn personal. If you are having an issue with a parent or guardian, always request to meet with that person with an administrator present. Always e-mail and call parents or guardians back, and if you have to reply to a negative e-mail more than twice, request a meeting.

Joshua Culver, first-year teacher

also be invaluable sources of support when working with helicopter parents or guardians.

UNREASONABLE PARENTS OR GUARDIANS

Although almost every contact you will have with a parent or guardian will be pleasant and productive, on rare occasions you may have to deal with unreasonable requests or reactions. When this happens, the situation can be unnerving and perplexing.

First of all, it is not always easy to determine, especially when you are a new teacher, if parents or guardians are being unreasonable. For example, it is reasonable for them to request that you send home a daily behavior report in a student's planner or respond to a daily e-mail from home. These are reasonable requests because the student will have to take responsibility for giving you the planner, or the parent or guardian will have to take responsibility for remembering to send you an e-mail. It is unreasonable to expect you to remember to call home every day to report on a child's behavior or to remember to send a note home without being reminded or to initiate a daily e-mail. Other requests that could be considered unreasonable might include being asked to offer extra credit just to one student, exempt a student from a standardized test or important project, or change the weight of an assignment just for one child.

If a request or a reaction from a parent or guardian seems unreasonable to you, there are some actions you should take right away.

- Do not act alone. Delay responding until you have time to think and to consult others. As soon as you can, consult a mentor, team members, or an administrator for advice.

- Try to be as compassionate and understanding as possible. You, as well as this parent or guardian, want what is best for the student. That can only happen if you are all in agreement and can work together.

- When you discuss the situation with the parent or guardian, be clear about what is reasonable and what is not. Try to work out a compromise when you can.

- Accept the idea that you will probably not win the parent or guardian over to your side of the conflict. You should attempt to calm the situation and work with him or her to create reasonable accommodations instead.

UNCOOPERATIVE PARENTS OR GUARDIANS

No matter how hard you try, parents and guardians will not always be as cooperative as you would like. The best way to avoid this situation is to intervene early, follow procedures and rules, maintain accurate records, present yourself as a professional, and keep parents and guardians informed about their child's progress.

If you find yourself in a confrontation with a hostile parent or guardian, it is up to you to assume control of the situation. The following steps can help you manage meetings so that they result in productive outcomes instead of heated words:

- Listen to what the angry parent or guardian has to say, without trying to interrupt or correct him or her. Do not try to present your side of the disagreement until the parent or guardian has had an opportunity to express himself or herself.

- Show your interest by asking questions about specific details. A simple misunderstanding is often the cause of the problem.

- Make sure to restate the problem, so that the other person can be reassured that you do understand. Try, "I think you're saying _____."

- Explain the problem from your viewpoint as objectively as you can. Be specific about what was expected, what the child did that was not appropriate, and how you responded.

- Make it clear throughout the confrontation that you want to work with the parent or guardian for the child's welfare.

- Remain calm.

- Remember that it will only harm you in the eyes of the parent or guardian and your supervisors if you act on your natural desire to justify your actions in a loud tone or to return insults.

- Do not accept threats or abuse from the parent or guardian. If, after you have sincerely tried to resolve a problem, the parent or guardian remains upset, suggest calling in an administrator to help.

- If you suspect that a parent or guardian plans to contact an administrator, make the contact first. It is never wise to allow your supervisors to be surprised with bad news. Instead, see an administrator, present your point of view, and ask for assistance.

One of the most exciting ways to collaborate with others in your school and community is to consider the larger community to which your students belong. With this in mind, you can learn strategies to help you connect your students to the world outside their classroom. If you would like to learn how to involve them in real-life projects and activities in the community, how to get started with global learning projects, and how to encourage your students to join others in making the world a better place, check out the bonus material on the DVD that accompanies this book.

Best Practices Checklist

1. Learn to view yourself as a member of a series of school teams, working together in collaboration with your colleagues and the parents and guardians of your students.

2. Make a point of developing a reputation for integrity, competence, and cooperation. And don't forget that building trust takes time.

3. Be extremely cautious about how you use social media. Take extra care to follow school and district guidelines.

4. Try not to miss school, but prepare for unexpected absences as early in the year as possible. Having a binder prepared with the routine materials that a substitute teacher would need to teach your class will reduce the stress you may feel when you have to miss school.

5. Follow the chain of command. Be aware of the role each staff member plays in the success of students at your school.

6. Create and maintain a transparent classroom to ensure that all people involved—students, parents or guardians, and colleagues—have necessary information.

7. Take a positive approach when dealing with parents and guardians. Remember that everyone wants the best for students.

8. Take care that the interactions you have with the parents and guardians of your students are professional and courteous at all times.

9. When conferring with parents or guardians, focus on solving problems and creating solutions. Don't focus on trying to prove that you are correct.

10. If a conflict with a parent or guardian arises, delay action until you have had an opportunity to confer with colleagues so that your response can be constructive and professional.

Time to Reflect
Collaborate with Others in Your School and Community

Use the information in this section to guide your thinking as you reflect on these questions. They are designed to encourage you to think more deeply about the issues in the text or to discuss those issues with colleagues.

1. What skills do you already possess that make it easier for you to work with the various groups at your school? How can you enhance these skills to help you become a valued coworker to those around you?

2. Why does learning to work well with supervisors and colleagues affect a teacher's ability to maintain a productive classroom? Identify teachers at your school who work well with their colleagues and supervisors. What can you learn from them?

3. Brainstorm additional strategies that you can use to adapt to your school's culture. How can a reputation as a positive and trustworthy individual enhance your ability to do this?

4. Why should teachers take the initiative to establish positive relationships with the parents or guardians of their students? What can you do to create this bond with your students' families? What can you do to make sure that your classroom is as transparent as possible?

5. This section offers information that can assist you as you meet in conferences with the parents or guardians of your students. In addition to the suggestions concerning sensible ways to prevent or minimize conflicts with parents or guardians, what other techniques would be helpful? What are your current concerns about these conferences? What can you do to alleviate those concerns?

SECTION FOUR

Begin a Successful School Term

The first day of class is an exciting and stressful time for teachers everywhere. Although we look forward to meeting our new students, it is stressful to realize that the rest of the year hinges on how well we manage to get our students off to a good start.

It is no wonder that many first-year teachers sleep poorly at the beginning of a new term. They spend restless nights worrying whether they will ever be ready for school to begin, pondering what to teach on that first day, wondering whether their students will like them, and thinking about what to do if they don't.

Your first day of class with your new students is one that you will always remember. Every experience will be new and intense. If you are like other teachers, you will be exhausted at the end of the day. With careful planning and attention to detail, however, having a fantastic first day can be one of the most meaningful tasks you will accomplish all year.

The First Day Is Important

The first day of class can be an intimidating experience for students. They worry about many things on this day: if they will get lost trying to find the classroom, if they will have friendly classmates, if they will know what to do once class starts, if they will fit in, and if their teachers will be approachable, just to name a few of their worries.

The first day of class can be intimidating for teachers, too. Not only will you meet your students for the first time but also it is probably the busiest day of the year for any teacher. We have to get everyone settled in comfortably and adjusted to our class expectations while we manage the paperwork that helps us make sure that all students are where they are

> Be yourself. The students are nervous, you are nervous, everybody is nervous. Take the time to set up expectations for the students, but try to get to know them.
>
> *Jared Sronce, first-year teacher*

supposed to be. In addition to the anxiety-inducing requirements of the first day of the term, you'll have just one chance to get your students off to a good start. Make the day a great one for everyone!

Overcome Those First-Day Jitters

There are many things you can do to handle the jitters that beginning a new school term can cause in even the most self-assured teacher. To calm yourself, try an assortment of tips and techniques from this list:

- Accept the fact that you will feel nervous and excited on the first day of school. Many veteran teachers do, too. Denying your concerns will not help you deal successfully with them.

- Boost your confidence by dressing well. Teachers traditionally dress up a bit on the first day—even the ones who slouched around in jeans before school started.

- Pack a good lunch, and force yourself to eat it when lunchtime arrives. Avoid having too much caffeine at breakfast.

- Ride to work with a colleague, if you can. Carpooling on the first day will give you a chance to share your fears and provide mutual support.

- Pack your book bag the night before and leave it by the door so you can just grab it as you leave.

- Prepare a seating chart. One easy and effective way to do this is to assign a number to each student on the roster, then place a number on top of the desk or on the seat. As you greet students at the door, ask for their name, tell them their number, and direct them to find their seat. You will also match faces to names quickly in this way. To learn more about how to create seating charts, see Section Two.

- Look over the list of your students' names one last time the night before school starts. You will feel better if you can pronounce them correctly.

- Plan more work than you believe your students can possibly accomplish, then plan some more. It is truly terrifying to run out of work for your students on the very first day of school.

- Have extra supplies on hand so that every student can complete assignments with no trouble.

- Arrive early. You do not have to be so early that you help the custodians unlock the building, but you should be early enough that you do not feel rushed in finishing any last-minute chores.

Finally, you can comfort yourself with these two reminders:

- The chances of major disruptions are slim on the first day of class; students tend to be on their very best behavior during the first few days of school.

- The most stressful part of your day will probably be sometime in the first half hour of class, when you realize that your students are nervous, cooperative, pleasant, and depending on *you*.

> Act like you've done this a million times. Don't be nervous; just lay out how you want your class to run for the rest of the year.
>
> *Megan Kelly, first-year teacher*

What to Do on the First Day: Your Priorities

As you begin thinking about the first day of class, you should give thought to how to convince your students that you are the best teacher they will ever have. Your new students will be concerned that they will not have a good teacher or a good year. Your first-year jitters may be bad, but theirs are probably worse.

Because it is so important that the first day of school be an encouraging experience for your students, you must present yourself to your students in as positive a manner as possible. This will be easy for you if you focus your energy on the following six important priorities:

PRIORITY ONE: TAKE CHARGE OF YOUR CLASS

- Even if you are overcome with stage fright, you must conquer your personal feelings and pretend to be confident and self-assured. Sometimes, by pretending to be confident, you can begin to convince yourself that you are.

- Have a seating chart ready so that you can show students to their respective seats and get them started on their opening exercise at once. Have an assignment on the board, or give students a handout as they enter the room.

- Before the term begins, when you have made up your class rules and expectations, consider having a friend record you presenting them. You can really have fun with this if you film your presentation at the beach, on a boat, or even in your own backyard. When school starts, show the video and give your students a handout on the class expectations to fill in as they watch and listen.

PRIORITY TWO: CALM YOUR STUDENTS' FEARS

- Stand at the door of your classroom and welcome students to your class. Wear a bright name tag. Make sure to prominently display your name and room number so that students and their parents or guardians can be sure that they are in the right place.

- Look happy to see every student. Greet each one pleasantly, using his or her name if you can.

- Teach your first lesson as if it is the most important lesson you will teach all year. In many ways, it is. Your students should feel not only that they learned something interesting but also that they will continue to learn something in your class every day.

PRIORITY THREE: INTRODUCE YOURSELF

Because you want the first day of class to go well, and because you want to control the amount of wild speculation about you, the new teacher, you should introduce yourself. You should be comfortable telling your students the following information:

- How to spell your last name
- Your title (Mr., Ms., Mrs., Dr.)
- Where you went to college
- Where you grew up
- Why you are looking forward to working with them
- The positive things you have heard about them
- The positive things you have heard about the school
- What your favorite subject was in school
- Why you chose to be a teacher

PRIORITY FOUR: ENGAGE YOUR STUDENTS' MINDS

- Design fast-paced, interesting instruction that will appeal to students with a variety of learning styles and engage their critical thinking skills.
- Consider a lesson that will allow you to assess your students' readiness levels as well as give them an overview of the skills they will learn or the material they will cover during the term. Make sure that the lesson is one that encourages them to be active, and not just one that requires them to listen passively.
- Include a brief homework assignment to reinforce the day's work and to get students into the habit of doing homework for your class.

PRIORITY FIVE: BEGIN TO TEACH THE CLASS ROUTINES

- Teaching acceptable school behavior is part of what teachers do and is certainly part of what students expect from their teachers. For example, when it is time for students to turn in the day's written assignment, show them the procedure for passing in papers that you will expect them to follow.

- If students lack supplies to do the assignment, lend them what they need for class and gently remind them that they will need to have paper and a pencil in the future.
- Keep any reprimands very low key. Stick to gentle reminders instead.

PRIORITY SIX: BEGIN TO BUILD A CLASSROOM COMMUNITY

- Even on the first day of class, your students will view themselves as members of a classroom group. You can enhance this natural tendency by using inclusive words, such as *our* or *us*, when referring to the class.

- Ask for their help in such routine tasks as passing out materials, tidying the room at the end of an activity, or helping each other.

- Take time for at least one icebreaker so that students can get to know their classmates. You will find more information about icebreakers later in this section.

> Do something fun the first day of class. Rules need to be established, but should children do rules all day? If you teach secondary classes, think about what kids will be doing in other classrooms when you prepare your lessons for the first day of class.
>
> *Stephanie Stock Mahoney, 36 years' experience*

First-Day-of-School Welcome Packet

One of the best ways to get your students off to a good start is to provide each one with a folder containing the many papers he or she will need on the first day of school. Even though many older students may come to school prepared to manage the numerous documents they will receive on the first day, younger students will certainly benefit if you help them organize their papers in a folder. Here are some suggestions for how to make that first-day-of-school packet appealing and helpful for all students in your class, no matter their grade level.

TIPS FOR MANAGING PACKETS

- Because the folders you send home filled with the various first-day forms and documents can then be used all year to organize individual student information, encourage your students to personalize their folder before they return it. This will also provide you with insight into their interests and skills.

- Sadly, not all students will see their parents or guardians after school on the first day of class, yet there will probably be many forms for parents and guardians to sign. If you allow students to return forms during the first few days of school instead of the next day, you will reduce their anxiety about not being able to complete this seemingly simple task.

- One good way to guarantee that students will return all the papers that need to be signed is to offer a reward for those who do it within a few days.

- If you create a spreadsheet with a column for each form that needs to be returned and a row for each student, you will be able to check off the forms quickly as students return them.

WHAT YOU CAN INCLUDE IN STUDENT PACKETS

In addition to the various forms that your school will require you to send home, you should consider including these items:

- A student inventory of interests or even learning style preferences to learn more about each of your students

- A parent or guardian inventory, such as the one in Parent or Guardian Worksheet 4.1

- An independent assignment for students to begin as soon as they find their seat. This can be a form to complete, a puzzle, an inventory, or any other activity that will engage their attention while you assist other students.

- You should also include a letter to parents or guardians, such as the one in Sample 4.1, that
  - Tells a bit about your experience in education
  - Gives information about how they can contact you
  - Requests their support
  - Explains the kinds of work they can expect to see their child doing all year
  - Explains the grading scale
  - Describes the supplies their child will need for class
  - Explains your homework policy
  - States the positive expectations you have for the year ahead

PARENT OR GUARDIAN WORKSHEET 4.1

Inventory: Please Tell Me About Your Child

Please use the space here to tell me the information that I need to teach your child successfully. You should feel free to include past school experiences, medical issues, how your child learns best, or anything else that may help me be an effective teacher for your child.

_____

_____

_____

_____

_____

_____

_____

_____

_____

_____

_____

_____

_____

_____

_____

_____

_____

_____

_____

_____

_____

_____

_____

_____

_____

_____

_____

_____

_____

_____

Sample 4.1

Letter of Introduction to Parents or Guardians

Use this sample letter of introduction as a model of one that you can send home with your students at the start of the school year.

Dear Parents or Guardians,

Let me introduce myself. I am a graduate of _____ with a degree in _____, and I am looking forward to a new school term as your child's _____ teacher. This year will be an exciting time for all of us. We will study vocabulary, literature, writing, and study skills in preparation for the successful completion of the state's standardized tests next spring. I have planned many activities throughout the course of the year that are designed to help your child succeed academically, not just this year but also in the future.

Students and their parents or guardians are naturally curious about the amount and types of homework to be assigned this term. There will be homework assignments almost every night. You should expect to see your child spending twenty to thirty minutes reviewing, reading, working on projects, studying, or writing essays. A copy of the weekly schedule will be given to each student to keep in his or her binder as well as posted on the class Web page. In addition, students are expected to copy their assignments into their assignment notebook at the start of class each day.

When you have questions, please feel free to e-mail me at _____ or to call me at school. Our number is _____.

I am looking forward to working with my new students this year. I am also looking forward to meeting you and working with you to help your child succeed.

Best wishes,

_____

_____

Activities for the First Day

In addition to an overview of the day's lesson and class expectations, your first day of class can include many other activities to engage students in meaningful work. Using the planning template in Teacher Worksheet 4.1 and the checklist in Teacher Worksheet 4.2 will make it easier for you to ensure that the first day of school will be a productive and positive one for your students. When you are trying to decide just what you want your students to do on the first day, consider some of these activities:

- Fill out forms together. While you are explaining your class expectations, students can fill in the information on a handout instead of just listening passively.

- Photograph students on the first day of class. This is a good way to begin your class scrapbook.

- Show examples of the supplies students need.

- Pass out colorful paper, and ask students to write what they can contribute to make the class a better one for everyone. Display the papers in a giant collage.

- Issue textbooks, and have students skim through them, looking for items in a textbook treasure hunt.

- Have students work with a partner, telling that person one thing that they can do well and one thing that they would like to learn how to do. Have partners introduce each other to the class by sharing this information.

- Ask students to write you a brief note, telling you three things you need to know about them so that you can teach them well.

- Place a large sheet of paper on the wall. Hand students old newspapers or magazines, and have them tear out words and photos that describe their strengths and talents. Focus on what students have in common. Glue the photos and words in place to create an instant piece of art that will interest every student.

- Have students jot down what they already know about the subject you are teaching and then share this information with the class.

- Have students fill out one of the student inventories you'll find later on in this section.

- Give students handouts with questions, directing them to find out what they have in common with their classmates. Some possible areas to explore are hometowns, hobbies, favorite

> At the beginning of the school year, I write a letter to my students telling them about myself. I give this letter to them on the first day of school and invite them to read it and ask questions. Their first assignment is to write a letter back to me in which they tell me more about themselves. It gives my students an opportunity to be open with me in a safe environment. It also gives me the opportunity to learn things about them that I may not ever get to know otherwise.
>
> *Kathleen Stankiewicz, 10 years' experience*

movies, pets, vacations, and sports. Go beyond the obvious and include attitudes for success, goals, or other mental traits.

● Have older students create bookmarks with inspirational messages for younger students.

● Ask older students to recount a memory from their earlier first days of school.

● Put a quotation or unusual word related to the day's lesson on the board, and ask students to tell you what they think about it.

● Have students write exit slips explaining what they learned in class on their first day.

TEACHER WORKSHEET 4.1

Planning Template for the First Day of School

Although not all of these items may be applicable to your class and to your students, this template can give you some idea of how you will want to plan for your first day.

Opening exercise (Time allotted: _____):

_____

_____

Supplies, materials, books to be issued (Time allotted: _____):

_____

_____

Student information forms and inventories to be used (Time allotted: _____):

_____

_____

Rules, policies, procedures (Time allotted: _____):

_____

_____

Introduction of self (Time allotted: _____):

_____

_____

Welcome activity (Time allotted: _____):

_____

_____

Forms to be sent home (Time allotted: _____):

_____

_____

Fees to be collected (Time allotted: _____):

_____

_____

Icebreaker (Time allotted: _____):

_____

_____

Lesson (Time allotted: _____):
Teacher input:

_____

_____

_____

(continued on next page)

(continued from previous page)

Student activity:

_____

_____

_____

Closing (Time allotted: _____):

_____

_____

TEACHER WORKSHEET 4.2

Checklist for the First Day

In this checklist of the most important things you must accomplish on the first day, you will find reminders of the tasks you will have to manage.

1. _____ Stand at your classroom door to offer your assistance to those students who may need help in finding their new classrooms.

2. _____ Meet all students at the door and direct them to their assigned seat.

3. _____ Begin learning your students' names as quickly as you can.

4. _____ Introduce yourself to your students.

5. _____ Teach an exciting lesson guaranteed to make your students want to learn more.

6. _____ Begin building a classroom community among your students.

7. _____ Set about creating a positive identity for your class.

8. _____ Help your students get to know each other.

9. _____ Distribute the necessary forms and the welcome packet that your students must take home.

10. _____ Project an attitude of enthusiasm and positivity about the class, the year ahead, and your students.

11. _____ Begin gathering data about your students' readiness levels, learning styles, and knowledge of the material in the course.

12. _____ Begin teaching the rules, procedures, policies, and expectations for your class.

13. _____ Make every student feel comfortable and welcome.

14. _____ Assign an appropriate homework assignment to help students transition from vacation back to school.

Student Information Records

Ask students to provide you with up-to-date contact information as close to the first day of school as you can. Use a form such as the one in Student Worksheet 4.1. Even young students will be able to fill in many portions of this form. It is also a good idea to ask younger students to take the form home to have adults complete it.

You could also ask students to tell about their hobbies, favorite classes, strengths, weaknesses, goals, or dreams. You could ask them to describe a past success they have had in school or in another activity. You could even ask them to give you advice on how to be the best teacher they will ever have.

STUDENT WORKSHEET 4.1

Student Information Form

Your full name: _____

What you want me to call you: _____

Your home phone number: _____

Your cell phone number: _____

Your e-mail address: _____

Your birthday: _____

Your student number: _____

Your age: _____

Your brothers' and sisters' names and ages:

_____

_____

What are your goals for the future?

_____

_____

What hobbies do you have?

_____

_____

What sports interest you?

_____

_____

Names of your parent(s) or guardian(s):

_____

_____

Which parent or guardian would you like me to contact if I need to call home?

Mr., Mrs., Ms., Dr.: _____   First name: _____   Last name: _____

Please tell me the cell phone number, work phone number, and e-mail address of each of your parents or guardians.

Mother: _____

Cell phone: _____   Work phone: _____

E-mail address: _____

(continued on next page)

(continued from previous page)

Father: _____

Cell phone: _____ Work phone: _____

E-mail address: _____

Guardian: _____

Cell phone: _____ Work phone: _____

E-mail address: _____

Guardian: _____

Cell phone: _____ Work phone: _____

E-mail address: _____

What is your address (street address, city, zip code)?

_____

Learn Your Students' Names Quickly

Learning how to correctly pronounce and spell your students' names is one of the most important tasks you will have to master as the school term begins. Being able to call all of your students by name is an important step in getting to know them as people and in managing your class.

The depth of resentment that mispronouncing or misspelling a student's name can cause is often surprising to first-year teachers. Although teachers may think of it as a small mistake, students tend to view teachers who do not call them by the right name as uncaring and insensitive.

Learning all of your students' names on the first or second day of school is not very difficult. These quick tips will make it possible for you to go home on the first day of school confident that you know the students in your class well enough to get the term off to a good start:

- Put in some preliminary work! Organize your seating charts, study class rosters, and prepare name tag materials.
- Make sure that your students each sit in their assigned seat for the first few days so that you can more quickly associate names with faces.
- If you have students fill out a student information form, when you read what your students have written, mentally match their face to the information in front of you.
- While students are working on a first-day writing assignment, walk quietly around the room, checking the roster.
- Ask each student to say his or her name for you. Repeat it as you study the child's face.
- Mark pronunciation notes on your roll sheet. Also, make notes to help you match names to students. For example, you can write "big smile" or "very tall" next to a student's name. These little clues will help you when you are struggling to recall a name on the second day of school. Make sure that you pay attention to characteristics that are not likely to change, such as height or hair color.
- Take photos of your students in their assigned seats and then study the photos at home later to help you match names and faces.
- When you cannot recall a child's name, admit it, and ask for help. When you hear it again, write it down, repeat it, and try again until you can recall it.

How to Get to Know Your Students

Getting to know your students as quickly as you can is extremely important. Although getting to know each child will take time, there are many ways to obtain the background information you need.

One way to get information is to review your students' records. Be sure to follow the correct procedures and confidentiality regulations. You may want to jot quick notes on each student as you scan his or her folder.

When you make a positive phone call to a student's parent or guardian, you have a wonderful opportunity to ask about his or her child. Likewise, when you send home an introductory letter, you can add a section asking parents or guardians to tell you about their child.

You can also learn a great deal about your students from writing assignments in which students respond to classroom issues.

Your students' previous teachers may be another good source of information. One drawback of this method is that you may sometimes get information that is not completely objective and that may bias your view of a child. Ask for information about students from their previous teachers only if they strike you as fair-minded professionals. If you find yourself listening to unfair horror stories about how much a student misbehaved in previous years, you should politely excuse yourself from the conversation.

One of the best ways to get to know your students and to help them get to know each other is to use icebreakers. As you watch students interact with each other, you will learn a great deal about them. In addition, icebreakers will give your students an opportunity to learn to value each other's contributions to the class. Try these strategies to get your students off to a good start:

- Have students work in pairs or triads to fill out information forms on each other. Include questions that will cause them to learn interesting and unusual details about each other. For example, having students list their favorite performers or athletes or a pet peeve is a good conversation starter.

- Try playing a chaining game in which students try to recite everyone's last name without having to stop to think. You can even offer a small reward for the first student who is able to do this.

- Pass around a large calendar on which each student can record his or her birthday. Also consider having students mark their birthplace on a large map.

- Create a class newsletter during the first week of class. Have students share a variety of ideas as they interview each other for articles in the newsletter. You can include almost anything you and your students might enjoy—for example, cartoons, interviews with parents or guardians or administrators, advice, predictions, or tips for studying.

- Create a duty roster for the classroom tasks that students can manage well. Sharing tasks will encourage students to work together to take ownership of the class.

- Take photographs of your students and post them later in the week. Ask students to bring in photographs from when they were much younger, and post these, too.

- Have each student find a quotation about school success and bring it to class. Post the quotes around your classroom to inspire all of your students.

- Have students create a time capsule to commemorate their first day in your class. Have them write a brief description of the first day with you. Ask questions to elicit responses that reveal personal impressions, predictions, and reactions. Gather these and place them in a container that you will keep sealed until a future date when you will share its contents with students.

- Hand students half sheets of paper and ask them to write three interesting things about themselves without stating their name or obvious characteristics. Have students ball up the sheets before dropping them into a large container. Shake the container to scramble the balled-up sheets. Distribute them randomly to each student. Give students three minutes to try to match their classmates with the information.

- If you have received your class rosters early, use a Web site, such as Discovery Education (www.puzzlemaker.com), to create a puzzle from your students' names.

- Put students in pairs. Give each pair a blank Venn diagram; have them chart how they are alike and different. After the initial pairs have completed the diagram, each pair should then join another pair and create another Venn diagram that shows how the pairs are alike and different.

- Have each student create a time line of his or her life. If you let students use large sheets of bulletin board paper and bright markers, you will be able to decorate your classroom with work that students will find fascinating.

- Have students group themselves according to birthday, eye color, favorite sports team, favorite music, or other common interests.

- Create a blank bingo grid and make copies for all of your students. In addition, print out a list of your students' names and make copies for all students. Ask students to fill in the grids with each other's names in random order. Play several rounds of bingo, choosing names randomly, until your students know each other's names. A variation on this game is to place interests, hobbies, talents, or other positive student characteristics in the grids.

- Check out the Ice Breakers Web site (www.icebreakers.us). This informative and interesting site contains a lengthy list of icebreakers. Although most are for adults, teachers can adapt many of them to use with their students.

- Ask your students to list ten things they do well. You will be surprised at how difficult this is for many students; too often, students focus on their weaknesses, not on their strengths.

- Put students into small groups and hand each group a bag with several common objects in it. Relate these objects to your discipline, if possible. Ask students to combine these objects in a new way. They can then name their invention and create a marketing plan for it. The point of this exercise is not just for you to learn about your students but also to have them work together in a way that forces them to think creatively.

- Group students into teams to create a cartoon panel that illustrates a topic related to school success. They can use stick figures to tell the story or generate a story line that uses the members of the group as characters.

- Place students in pairs and have them interview each other. A twist that makes this assignment interesting is to give each student an object and ask what he or she has in common with it. When your students present their findings to the class, you will learn a lot about them as they reveal how they are like paper clips, bookmarks, tissue boxes, or other common classroom items.

- Ask students to write descriptive paragraphs about each other. Photocopy these paragraphs and bind them into booklets for all students. This will be the most intently read document that you will give your students all term.

- Put your students into pairs and have them determine ten things they have in common. Insist that they go beyond the obvious to discuss such topics as shared experiences, attitudes, or aspirations, or other appealing topics.

In addition to the preceding suggestions, student inventories, mentioned earlier, are a good way to learn information about your students that you do not have time to learn in any other way. Many teachers ask students to fill out an inventory during the first few days of school. Still others find that if they wait a few days, their students will feel secure enough to reveal more information. Whenever you decide to use an inventory, be sure to give your students plenty of time to answer thoughtfully. Student Worksheets 4.2, 4.3, and 4.4 provide three inventories that you can reproduce for your students.

STUDENT WORKSHEET 4.2

Inventory for Elementary Students

Student name: _____   Date: _____

My birthday is _____

My family members are

_____

_____

When I grow up I want to be

_____

_____

My favorite things to do at home are

_____

_____

My special friends are

_____

_____

My favorite things to do at school are

_____

_____

The subjects I do best in are

_____

_____

The subjects I need help in are

_____

_____

If I could change anything about school, it would be

_____

_____

This year I am looking forward to learning about

_____

_____

I like it when my teachers

_____

_____

(continued on next page)

(continued from previous page)

I would like to know more about

_____

_____

I am happiest when I am

_____

_____

From *The First-Year Teacher's Survival Guide, 3rd Edition*, by Julia G. Thompson. Copyright © 2013 by John Wiley & Sons, Inc. Reproduced by permission.

STUDENT WORKSHEET 4.3

Inventory for Middle School Students

Student name: _____ Date: _____

My birthday is _____

My family members are

_____

_____

When I grow up I want to be

_____

_____

My closest friends are

_____

_____

My favorite things to do are

_____

_____

Here are my favorites:

Radio station: _____ Magazine: _____

Sport: _____ Hobby: _____

Book: _____ Movie: _____

Music: _____ Video game: _____

One thing people don't know about me is

_____

_____

A skill I have is

_____

_____

A person I admire is _____ because

_____

Something I would like to learn to do better is

_____

_____

(continued on next page)

129

(continued from previous page)

I appreciate it when a teacher

_____

_____

My previous teachers would tell you this about me:

_____

_____

I am proud of myself when I

_____

_____

STUDENT WORKSHEET 4.4

Inventory for High School Students

Student name: _____   Date: _____

My birthday is _____

My family members are

_____

_____

After graduation I plan to

_____

_____

My greatest asset is

_____

_____

I am an expert on

_____

_____

One thing people don't know about me is

_____

_____

My teachers from last year will tell you that I am

_____

_____

I have trouble dealing with

_____

_____

My favorite class is

_____

_____

The most influential person in my life is _____ because

_____

_____

It was difficult for me to learn

_____

_____

(continued on next page)

(continued from previous page)

It was easy for me to learn

_____

_____

I want to know more about

_____

_____

Three words that describe my personality are

_____

_____

One lesson I had to learn the hard way is

_____

_____

Here are some more inventory items that you can use or adapt to learn more about your students. You can even use these as brief, informal writing assignments at the start or end of a class.

- I am optimistic about _____.
- I am pessimistic about _____.
- I spend my free time _____.
- If I could do anything right now, I would _____.
- If I had ten dollars, I would _____.
- When I do poorly on a test, I _____.
- I tried hard to learn _____.
- If I were five years older, I _____.
- I am most proud of _____.
- I respect these people:
- The hardest thing I ever did was _____.
- At home, I have these rules:
- If I were a teacher, I would _____.
- I would like to visit _____.
- Not many people know _____.
- I always laugh when _____.
- I wish teachers would _____.
- I deserve a trophy for _____.
- I feel needed when _____.
- Something I value in a friend is _____.
- I like to learn about _____.
- The best advice I've ever received is _____.
- My favorite day of the week is _____.

Create a Positive Group Identity

Unless you create a positive identity for your class, students may take your smallest correction of their misbehavior to mean that you think of them as troublesome. This will happen even more quickly if students in your class have struggled with school in the past. Once a group starts to think of itself in a negative way, it is almost impossible to change the group's self-perception into a positive one.

Sometimes students have been dragging this negativity around for years. If you can eliminate the negative image and give your class a positive self-image, you will all benefit. This is no easy task, however. What you must do is make a conscious effort to praise and reinforce your class's positive group attributes. Thus, you will promote the group's desirable behaviors and extinguish the group's negative ones.

Even difficult classes can have positive attributes. If a group is very talkative, for example, you can put a positive twist on it and praise the students for their sociability. To create a positive group image, you must find and reinforce positive attributes. Here's how:

- **Step One**: If you learn that your class has a negative self-image, let students know that you disagree with it.
- **Step Two**: Observe two things about your class: how your students interact with each other and with you and how they do their work. Find at least one positive attribute that you can reinforce.
- **Step Three**: Begin praising that positive attribute as often as you can. In a few days, you will notice that your students will accept it as truth and will start to bring it up themselves.

Think of a positive label or two for each class and use these labels frequently. Students in each of your classes should believe that their class has a special place in your heart. Here are a few positive labels your students should hear you use at the start of the year:

- Caring
- Motivated
- Intelligent
- Prepared
- Successful
- Friendly
- Polite
- Accurate
- Efficient
- Reasonable
- Adaptable
- Reflective
- Adventurous
- Energetic
- Creative
- Studious
- Realistic
- Cooperative
- Industrious
- Likable

- Helpful
- Dependable
- Ingenious
- Determined
- Thoughtful
- Punctual
- Curious
- Inventive
- Unique

What You Can Expect During the First Week

The first week of a school term is one that is filled with many changes and adjustments for teachers and students. Although this can be stressful, having some idea of what to expect will allow you to prepare and plan so that your first week can be a smooth one. Here are some of the things that you can expect and plan for during the first week of school:

- Students will have schedule changes. Even if you teach very young students in a small school, it is prudent to expect that students will be added to and removed from your class during the first week.
- Some students will have trouble finding their classrooms during the first week. This is a potentially embarrassing situation for any student that you can alleviate by standing at your classroom door and greeting students in the hall and as they enter your room.
- At least a few of your students will not have supplies on the first day of school or even at the end of the week.
- You can expect to be surprised at how much your students will have forgotten from previous years. The lack of social skills can be particularly distressing until you get them accustomed to school manners again.
- Anxious students will act out in various surprising ways until they can be assured that you are a good teacher with their best interests at heart.
- Your to-do list will be very, very long. All of the tasks on it will be important ones with short deadlines.
- You will have to reach out to soothe anxious parents or guardians who worry about their child's potential for success in your class.
- You will feel exhilarated and exhausted at the same time.
- You will have to work hard to keep up with your keys and other important belongings that you are too stressed or distracted to put away with mindful deliberation.

- You will have to make an effort to find time to eat, rest, exercise, and take care of your personal business during the first few weeks of school.

- Some of your colleagues will want to share unpleasant and unhelpful stories about your students. Avoid these sessions as tactfully as you can.

- You will find that it is hard to pace lessons correctly during the first few weeks of school because you are not familiar with your students and the way they work and learn.

- The administrators and other staff members at your school will have to adjust to last-minute changes in enrollment and teaching positions. You will have to pay attention to the many directions that will come your way with changes that affect the entire school.

- You will notice that your students will have wildly varying learning styles and levels of readiness.

- Your students will need your patient and persistent help in learning how to relate appropriately to each other and to you, and how to adjust themselves to the routines of the class.

- At the end of the day you fill find it almost impossible to recall what you taught or said earlier in the day. Make a detailed lesson plan and follow it carefully.

Mistakes to Avoid at the Start of School

Here are a few of the most common mistakes that well-prepared teachers can easily avoid at the start of the school term with just a bit of careful planning and thought:

- Allowing yourself to listen to colleagues who are stressed out and negative about school and their students

- Not making learning your students' names one of your chief priorities during the first few days of class

- Neglecting to plan too much for your students to do until you become familiar with the rate at which your students work

- Being less than enthusiastic about the year ahead, the material your students will study, the opportunities for fun and learning they will have, and your students themselves

- Failing to make every student feel valued and welcome in your class

- Not being professional and efficient in the way you approach the paperwork that you will have to deal with at the start of the year

- Passing up an opportunity to teach a lesson on the first day of class that will motivate students to want to return for more

- Being impatient after a few days when students still do not have the necessary supplies that will make it easy for them to do well in your class

- Not creating a seating chart and making sure that students each sit in their assigned place
- Overlooking the importance of getting enough sleep, eating healthful food, and exercising
- Underestimating the importance of making time for students to get to know each other and to form a positive classroom community
- Not maintaining a to-do list to manage the many chores that you need to handle at the start of the term
- Neglecting to make positive contact with each student's parents or guardians
- Expecting all students to have the same level of readiness for the material that they are required to learn in your class
- Allowing students to have downtime instead of engaging them in interesting and dynamic learning activities
- Ignoring the importance of establishing and teaching class rules, policies, procedures, and expectations
- Discounting the importance of making sure that each student has a positive attitude about your class and you at the end of the first few days of school

Best Practices Checklist

1. Recognize the importance of the first day of school and make plans to welcome all of your students with an engaging lesson designed to get them off to a great start in your class.

2. Make plans to cope successfully with your first-day-of-school jitters so that you can help your students with theirs.

3. Set your priorities for the first day of school and go about accomplishing them. Make careful plans. Then plan some more.

4. Help your students keep up with and organize all of the forms that have to go home during the first week of school with a welcome packet.

5. Plan interesting activities for the first day of school that are geared toward helping your students adjust to their new class and begin to look forward to the rest of the term.

6. On the first day, you should begin gently establishing the expectations for student behavior in your class.

7. Begin gathering information about students—basic contact information as well as inventories of their interests.

8. Make a point of learning your students' names as quickly as you can.

9. Make time to get to know your students and make sure that they have plenty of opportunities to get to know each other.

10. Help your students come to see themselves as successful learners by creating a positive group identity for the class as a whole.

Time to Reflect
Begin a Successful School Term

Use the information in this section to guide your thinking as you reflect on these questions. They are designed to encourage you to think more deeply about the issues in the text or to discuss those issues with colleagues.

1. What can you do to make sure the first day of school is productive for you and your students?

2. What would you like your students to say about your class at the end of the first day?

3. Complete this statement: "On the first day of school, I want _____." How can you make this happen?

4. Brainstorm a list of icebreakers with your colleagues. Can you use any of these with your new students?

5. What image do you want your students to have of themselves as a class? How will you make this happen?

SECTION FIVE

Develop Positive Classroom Relationships

Almost all school districts seem to deal with similar problems, such as low student achievement, overcrowded classes, and expensive school repairs. As unpleasant as these problems can be, very few teachers leave the profession because of them. Instead, you are far more likely to be affected by the stress caused by the fallout from poor classroom relationships than by any other problem.

Although classroom relationships are complex in nature, they can easily be grouped into two different types: the relationships that you have with your students, and the relationships that exist among your students. In this section, you will first be able to learn some basic strategies to help you establish positive relationships with your students. You will then learn how to help your students learn to relate well to each other.

Develop a Positive Relationship with Students

Many factors can negatively affect this relationship, but only you can make sure it is a viable one. As the adult in the classroom, you are in charge of ensuring that you have a positive relationship with every student. You will have to be the one who builds the bridge, who reaches out to your students, who inspires them to do their best. A successful relationship with your students will be just like the other meaningful relationships in your life; it will require patience, planning, work, and commitment.

FACILITATOR, GUIDE, COACH, LEARNING PARTNER

One of the most exciting shifts in educational philosophy in the twenty-first century involves a change in the role that teachers play in modern classrooms. With few exceptions, when you began your own schooling, most teachers were regarded as the "sage on the stage" who had all the knowledge and transmitted that knowledge to students.

In today's classrooms, however, teachers play a very different role—that of a "guide on the side." Today's teachers are expected to help students learn by encouraging them to think for themselves, solve problems, determine meaning based on what they already know, and be much more self-directed than those students of the past who were expected to be passive receptors of knowledge.

Being a teacher also involves making decisions about how you want your students to perceive you. Just as actors create characters when they are at work, you'll need to develop a persona for yourself as a teacher. If you can create a strong impression as a professional educator, your school life will be much easier. You will realize that when your students criticize you, they really do not know you at all. They are only reacting to your professional self—a person who has to set limits and correct mistakes.

When you begin thinking about the different ways you can create a strong image of yourself as a teacher and develop positive relationships with your students, if you first think of yourself as a facilitator, guide, coach, or learning partner, you'll find that it is easer to plan how to relate well to your students. After all, you will no longer be expected to stand at the front of the room and lecture; instead, you will have the opportunity to interact with your students as they engage in meaningful activities that you have designed to help them learn.

WHAT YOUR RELATIONSHIP WITH YOUR STUDENTS SHOULD BE

As a first-year teacher, you may struggle to determine the relationship you want to have with your students. How friendly should you be? What if your students don't like you? What if they won't listen to you? How strict is too strict?

As a teacher, you are responsible for just about anything that can happen in a class. You will determine the relationship you have with each student as well as the relationship you have with the class as a whole. This is a daunting responsibility, but it is also empowering. If the type of relationship you have with your class is under your control, then you can make it a strong bond. This will take deliberate planning on your part. You can use Teacher Worksheet 5.1 to self-assess the appropriateness of the way you interact with your students.

Inspiring teachers who have a positive relationship with their students have characteristics that you should develop as quickly as possible. Here are brief descriptions of a few of these characteristics:

- **You should show that you care about your students.** Your students want you to like them and to approve of them, even when they misbehave. Sometimes it is easy to lose sight of this when you have so many demands on your time. It is crucial that your students feel that they are important to you and that you care about their welfare. Get to know them as people as well as pupils you have to instruct. Do not be afraid to let your students know you are interested in how they think and feel.

- **You should have a thorough knowledge of your subject matter.** Knowing your subject matter may not seem to have much to do with developing a successful relationship with your students, but it does. If you are not prepared for class, you will focus on what you do not know instead of on what your students need to know. The worst result of a faulty or inadequate knowledge of your subject matter is that your students will lose respect for you and no longer trust your judgment. Be prepared for class each day.

- **You should take command of the class.** If you do not assume a leadership role in your class, others will. Often there will be a continuing struggle as students try to dominate each other. Although you should not be overbearing, you should be in command of the class. You can and should allow your students as many options and as strong a voice in the class as possible, but never lose sight of your role as the classroom leader. Your students won't.

- **You should act in a mature manner all of the time.** This does not mean that you cannot have fun with your students; however, if having fun with your students means indulging in playful insults, then you are not acting in a mature manner. Here are a few of the other immature behaviors that will destroy your relationship with your students:

  - Being sarcastic
  - Losing your temper
  - Being untruthful
  - Being unprepared for class
  - Ignoring students
  - Playing favorites

> Love every child. Your love may be the only love some children get. Remember that many if not most of the children you teach bring a lot of baggage to school that was never even close to being a part of your world growing up and that you don't understand. Teach them anyway.
>
> *Charlene Herrala, 31 years' experience*

- **You should maintain a certain emotional distance from your students.** Being a teacher is much more than being a friend to your students; they have peers for friends. You are a teacher and not a peer. The emotional distance you keep between yourself and your students will enable you to make choices based on what students need instead of what they want.

How Appropriate Are Your Relationships with Students?

No one wants to be accused of misconduct, but all teachers are vulnerable to allegations of improper relationships with students. To avoid this and to become an effective teacher instead, let the characteristics in the lists that follow guide your interactions with students.

As you read through the list of the characteristics of inappropriate relationships with students, place a check mark in the blank before any that you may be guilty of. Be sure to eliminate each of those behaviors as soon as possible.

Next, move to the second list. Place a check mark in the blank before any that already apply to your relationships with students. If an action does not apply to you at the moment, try to incorporate it into your future relationships with students.

In inappropriate relationships, the teacher

1. _____ Assumes a parental role
2. _____ Shares too much personal information
3. _____ Becomes hostile to certain students
4. _____ Connects with students inappropriately on social media
5. _____ Is alone with students
6. _____ Loses sight of the immaturity of a child
7. _____ Socializes with students
8. _____ Is popular for all the wrong reasons
9. _____ Allows students to invade personal space
10. _____ Tries to be the students' friend

In appropriate relationships, the teacher

1. _____ Serves as a friendly adult whose primary concern is a child's best interests
2. _____ Guides students as they learn to make good choices
3. _____ Protects students from harm
4. _____ Is familiar with students' social, academic, and behavioral circumstances
5. _____ Helps students develop insights into the world around them
6. _____ Provides encouragement as students work to achieve goals
7. _____ Makes students aware of strengths and helps them correct weaknesses
8. _____ Is able to say no in a firm and pleasant way
9. _____ Treats students with respectful courtesy and expects to be treated likewise
10. _____ Empowers students by having high expectations for success

WHAT STUDENTS EXPECT FROM THEIR TEACHERS

When you are trying to create the positive relationship that you know will help you transform the students in your class into avid and cooperative learners, it is only wise to take into account their own expectations for their teachers. If you were to poll your students, you would be likely to find that they want a teacher who

- Listens to all students
- Enjoys being in the classroom
- Knows the subject matter
- Is not too strict but is not a pushover, either
- Respects them as people as well as students
- Is understanding when appropriate
- Makes learning fun
- Returns papers promptly
- Helps them learn
- Doesn't allow harassment
- Explains the material well
- Treats everyone fairly
- Makes the classroom comfortable
- Doesn't ever embarrass them
- Does not give too much homework
- Helps them believe in themselves

HOW TO CONNECT: CLASSROOM IMMEDIACY

Classroom immediacy is a broad term that refers to the different ways that teachers can lessen the emotional distance between themselves and their students. Behaviors that create classroom immediacy tend to engender positive attitudes in students because students believe that their teachers like them. And it's only common sense that students will be much more willing to cooperate with those teachers who clearly like them and are interested in their welfare. Let your actions reveal that you are a teacher who is approachable and enthusiastic about your students. Although there are many, many different ways to relate well in a classroom, in the list that follows you will find forty ways to create a sense of immediacy and connectedness with your students that you can adapt to fit your needs.

- Don't forget that the class is about your students and not about you. Be careful not to overpower your students with your knowledge or authority. Instead, be gentle and inclusive in your approach.

- Smile. As simple as it may seem, this is one of the most important ways you can relate well to your students.

- Be polite. Good manners smooth the way for positive relationships.

- It may seem obvious, but take the time to tell your students what you like about them. Make it a point to compliment them whenever you can.

- Be relaxed. Take a few deep breaths and focus on your students. Stressed-out teachers tend to transmit that negativity to their students, who will in turn respond negatively.

- Be prepared for class. When you are prepared, you will not have to worry about what you do or don't know. Instead, you can just teach.

- Praise your students often when they do things well. "Catch 'em being good" is a tried-and-true philosophy to follow.

- Show that you have a sense of humor. Share a laugh with your students whenever you can.

- Have fun with your students. Instead of just giving them a ball to toss during a group assignment, join in the group and toss the ball yourself. Playing together will make it fun for everyone.

- Present yourself as a confident teacher who is in control of his or her own emotions.

- Always have a backup plan so that you can engage students in productive learning. (See Section Ten for backup plans.)

- Make frequent eye contact with everyone when you address the whole group.

- When you speak with students, lean toward them slightly. Let your body language indicate that you are interested and accessible.

- Greet your students courteously as they come into the classroom. At the end of class, stand at the door and speak to them as they leave.

- Vary your tone of voice as well as your speech tempo. Make it easy for students to want to listen to what you have to say.

- Laugh at yourself! When you show that you have a bit of self-awareness of your own foibles, you show students how to laugh at themselves, too.

- Be aware of the gestures you make. Do they indicate that you are open and friendly or the opposite?

- Model how to do routine tasks correctly so that they become manageable for students. You'll avoid conflicts this way.

- Take the time to reveal a bit about yourself. For example, a brief story about a silly mistake you made or how you learned a lesson the hard way will make you much more accessible and appealing to your students than if you are always right.

- Ask questions and wait expectantly for answers. Let your body language signal that you are interested in the responses that you may receive.

- Move around the classroom. Every part of the room should be part of your circuit. Be part of the crowd instead of staying in the front or at your desk.

- Use inclusive pronouns, such as *we, our,* or *us,* instead of ones that exclude students from ownership in their class.

- Get your students up and moving. Sitting at a desk day after day will not just bore them but also make the distance between teacher and students greater.

- Be careful to allow for a change of pace in lessons so that students can be alert, focused, and engaged.

- Find out your students' goals and dreams and help them work toward achieving them.

- Provide opportunities for students to share their opinions and beliefs with you and with each other.

- Be empathetic and sympathetic. Acknowledge it when a student is having a bad day. Offer to help when you can.

- Be the first one to admit it when you have made a mistake.

- Ask students to help you and to help each other.

- Use such real-world technology tools as cell phones or social media sites when appropriate. By encouraging students to use the tools with which they are already familiar, you acknowledge their importance to your students.

- When you point at a student, try doing so with your hand palm up instead of using a closed fist with your index finger extended.

- Take advantage of as many opportunities as you can to interact with your students on a one-on-one or personal level. Ask about their hobbies, their problems, their family . . . whatever it takes to connect.

- Be fair. Few things destroy a relationship between teacher and student faster than a student's suspicion that he or she is being treated unfairly.

- Keep disruptions to a minimum whenever you can so that the potential for relationship damage is also minimized. All students will judge your performance when you have to manage a misbehaving classmate.

- Be tactfully honest. Students know when they are being lied to, and those lies will destroy the relationship you may want to build.

- Show respect for all of your students as well as for students' families, neighborhoods, and cultures.

- Pay attention to the emotions behind your students' words. When you know your students well enough to be sensitive to their feelings, you will find it easier to relate well to them.

- Use your students' names frequently and with a gentle tone of voice.

> Let kids know that they are special to you and that time with them is special.
>
> *Carole Platt, 35 years' experience*

- Make it clear that you expect the best from your students and you will be highly likely to get it.

USING VERBAL IMMEDIACY TO CREATE POSITIVE RELATIONSHIPS WITH STUDENTS

The words you use when you speak with your students constitute one of the most important ways you have of creating a strong bond with them. Kind words spoken in a gentle voice make it much easier for your students to connect with you. If you say something unkind to a student, it will hurt even more than an insult from a peer because it is from someone the student should be able to count on. Using language to create verbal immediacy is one of the best approaches you can take to create a positive relationship with students. Simply put, verbal immediacy is the sum of all of the verbal interactions that you have with your students that draw them to you. Calling students by name, sharing classroom jokes, greeting them at the door, and even using a friendly voice all serve to create an atmosphere in which you and your students are connected in positive ways.

There are very few rules about how you should speak to your students. The age and maturity levels of your students will guide how you speak. For example, it is usually a serious offense for a teacher in an elementary classroom to tell students to shut up. In a high school classroom, this phrase is not as serious; it is merely rude. You should avoid using it, however, because there are more effective ways to ask students to stop talking.

The one language mistake you should never make is to swear when you are with your students. When you do this, you cross the line of what is acceptable and what is not. If you are ever tempted to swear around your students, remember that teachers have been fired for swearing at students.

If a word slips out, you should immediately apologize to your students, let them know that you are embarrassed, apologize again, and then continue with instruction. After your class is over, you should speak with a supervisor and explain your side of the situation as soon as you can, and certainly before your supervisor hears about it from an angry parent or guardian.

Although swear words are clearly not something you should say around students, there are other language issues to which you should also pay attention. Make sure your own words are ones that help your students and do not hurt them. Never make negative or insulting remarks about any student's

- Race
- Gender
- Religion
- Family
- Friends

- Nationality
- Clothing
- Neighborhood
- Body size
- Sexual orientation
- Disability
- Age
- Appearance

> Remember that in the eyes of the community, you are a professional all of the time, even away from school.
>
> *Edward Gardner, 36 years' experience*

You should also make a point of using "I" messages whenever you can. "I" messages are statements that use such words as *I, we, us,* or *our* instead of *you.* For example, instead of the harsh "You'd better pay attention," a teacher can say, "I'd like for you to pay attention now." "You're too noisy" becomes "We all need to be quiet so that everyone can hear," and "You're doing that all wrong!" can become "I think I can help you with that."

With these simple changes, the statements are no longer accusatory, harsh in tone, or insulting. The language points out a problem but does not put anyone on the defensive. "I" messages work because they state a problem without blaming the student. This, in turn, creates a focus on a solution and not on an error the child has made.

BEING A ROLE MODEL

We live in a society that values its role models. For several decades, however, social scientists have been concerned about the scarcity of positive role models for young people in the media. Today, all too many children lack the adult support and direction they need to keep themselves safe from harm.

Although media heroes may be scarce, for many of your students you will be a hero whether you want this responsibility or not. It is not always easy to have the right answer, to make the right decision, or to say the right thing, although your students expect all of these from you.

For many students, their teachers are the only people in their lives who routinely stress the importance of hard work and good character. Depending on the grade you teach, your tasks as a role model may include making sure that your students wash their hands properly, learn about the dangers of using drugs, or get their college applications in the mail on time.

Your actions will influence your students, even when you are not aware that you are having an influence. It can be an overwhelming responsibility, but you have chosen a profession with a profound impact. You can be a positive influence on your students when you

- Help students manage their anger appropriately
- Show your appreciation for other staff members
- Are patient with every student
- Dress professionally
- Stay organized
- Are prompt
- Show sympathy and concern
- Handle misbehavior professionally
- Have high expectations
- Can laugh at yourself
- Treat parents and guardians with respect
- Accept criticism well

You will be a negative influence on your students if you allow yourself to

- Smell like alcohol or tobacco
- Have bad breath, unpleasant body odor, or unkempt hair
- Wear distracting makeup, perfume, or jewelry
- Chew gum in front of your class
- Wear ill-fitting, dirty, and wrinkled clothing with missing buttons or broken zippers
- Violate the student dress code

TEACHER WORKSHEET 5.2

Are You a Good Role Model?

If a statement in the following list applies to you, place a +1 in the blank beside it. You should aim for a perfect score of 30. If you can't place a +1 in a blank, then that is an area in which you can improve.

1. _____ I get enough sleep during the weekdays so that I can be prepared for class.
2. _____ I make it a point to speak Standard English in front of my students.
3. _____ I control my temper.
4. _____ I treat everyone I meet at school fairly and with respect.
5. _____ I speak out against student substance abuse and risky behavior.
6. _____ I listen carefully when others speak.
7. _____ I model the courteous behavior I expect from my students.
8. _____ I promote the positive values of my community.
9. _____ I am always prepared for class.
10. _____ I make sure that my written work is neat and accurate.
11. _____ I am willing to laugh at myself.
12. _____ I am respectful of other cultures.
13. _____ I am able to control my reactions when students are inadvertently funny.
14. _____ I assume the role of the adult in the classroom.
15. _____ I reveal only appropriate information about my life outside of school.
16. _____ I make sure that my class prepares students for a positive future.
17. _____ I am a model of honest behavior.
18. _____ I am not afraid to admit when I have made a mistake.
19. _____ I dress appropriately for school.
20. _____ I have a good attendance record.
21. _____ I am a teacher who works to create a sense of classroom immediacy.
22. _____ I am interested in learning about my students' world—interests, hobbies, likes, dislikes, and so forth.
23. _____ I make it a point to be extremely polite to my students and their families.
24. _____ I am knowledgeable about my subject matter.
25. _____ I am flexible when necessary.
26. _____ I am calm in an emergency.
27. _____ I protect students from bullies.
28. _____ I work to prevent misbehavior from beginning in my class.
29. _____ I follow school rules and expect my students to do the same.
30. _____ I act like a teacher and not a pal.

HOW MUCH OF YOURSELF SHOULD YOU SHARE?

"Do you smoke?" "What kind of beer do you like?" "What's your real hair color?" It is only natural that your students will be curious about you. After the first few days of school, they will become comfortable enough around you to ask personal questions. Because they are young, your students will not always know what is appropriate to ask and what is not.

Although you should not answer every personal question your students ask, you do need to handle them with tact. Your responses to personal questions will help determine the type of relationship you will have with your students and their families.

In general, your students will only know what you tell them about yourself. To help you determine whether information you are tempted to reveal is appropriate for students to know, ask yourself whether you would be comfortable revealing this information if an administrator or a student's parents or guardians were present. Because the answer to this question is sometimes going to be negative, be prepared with appropriate responses to possible student questions so that you are not taken by surprise. Here are a few other pointers to help you reveal only what you want your students to know:

Plan how you will answer student questions. It is not easy to deflect student interest, so you will have to think carefully about what you want to reveal about your personal life. You can expect to be quizzed on a variety of issues, and it is best to be prepared with responses. If you plan what you want to disclose about each topic before your students ask, then you will not be caught off guard. Here are a few areas of your personal life that you can expect your students to be curious about:

- Your social life
- Where you live
- Your living arrangements
- The kind of car you drive
- What you do in your free time
- Your pets
- Your family
- What you think of other teachers

Forestall questions by giving out some information in advance. Your students should see your human side. If you share innocuous information about yourself with your students, you will curb their curiosity, and they will be less tempted to pry. For example, at the beginning of the year, you should tell your students where you went to college and how hard you had to study. Or you can tell them about your family while asking about theirs. By offering information in advance, you can build on your common interests and prevent questions that are too personal at the same time.

Keep students too engaged to ask personal questions. Another technique that experienced teachers have found valuable for limiting the information they reveal about themselves is to structure class in such a way that there is little free time for personal questions.

If your students are busily engaged in learning all period long, they will not have time to speculate more than necessary about your personal life.

THE PROBLEM WITH BEING A POPULAR TEACHER

It is natural to want to be liked. It is a wonderful experience to be in a mall or a restaurant and hear a young voice joyfully calling your name or to look out over a classroom full of students who are hanging on to your every word. The problem with being a well-liked teacher is that it is sometimes such an exhilarating feeling that you are reluctant to give it up, even when you should.

> It took me a little while to just be me in front of the class. Early on, I was so concerned about classroom management that I was careful not to reveal too much about myself. However, it wasn't long before I realized that the kids crave a personal connection with their teachers and they love it when I am relaxed and am myself with them.
>
> *Melinda Conner, first-year teacher*

It is much more pleasant to hear your students cheer when you tell them there will be no homework than to hear their groans when you give a challenging assignment. Choices like this constitute a teacher's day. As a teacher, you should base your decisions not on what your students want at the moment but on what they need for the future. Students can be shortsighted; you should not be.

There are many legitimate reasons for your students to like you. Are your classes interesting? Do you treat everyone with respect? Are you inspiring? Unfortunately, there are many other reasons for your students to like you that are seductive traps; you must avoid these by thinking of your students' needs. If you ever overhear your students make any of the following statements about you, you are becoming popular for the wrong reasons:

- She's an easy grader.
- He's just like us.
- We're friends on Facebook.
- He never calls home, no matter what I do.
- She never makes us do real work in that class.
- We never have to take notes.
- She doesn't really care if we swear.
- He likes to joke around with us.

> Start by letting them know you care. Your actions and concern for their success speak volumes.
>
> *Dawn Carroll, 17 years' experience*

LETTING YOUR STUDENTS KNOW YOU CARE

You can plan the most fascinating lesson your students will ever have, but nothing will go well if your students believe you do not care about them. Show your interest in them by asking them about their activities or relating your lessons to their needs and interests. Research studies have proved what good teachers know from experience: students who believe their teachers like and respect them are far more likely to be successful than those students who don't perceive their teachers as caring or supportive.

From kindergarten to senior year, students of all ages need to feel that their teachers like them and approve of what they do. Fortunately, there are many ways to show that you care about your students:

- Agree with your students as often as you can.
- Set responsible limits for everyone in terms of behavior, and be fair when you enforce these limits.
- Use a kind voice when you speak with your students.
- Listen to all of your students. Encourage them to share ideas and opinions.
- If one of your students is in the newspaper for something positive, clip out the article and display it.
- Stress the things that you and your students have in common: goals, dreams, and beliefs.
- When a student speaks to you, stop and really listen.
- Maintain a birthday calendar for your students. Celebrate birthdays with birthday messages on the board.
- Attend school events. If your students play a sport or perform in a concert, go and watch them to show your appreciation for their hard work.
- Use good manners when you deal with your students, and insist that they do the same.
- When students confide in you, follow up. For example, if students told you that they were worried about a test in another class, take the time to ask about how they did.
- Make it very clear to your students that you want to help them achieve their dreams.
- Ask about a student's family. If you know someone is ill, show your concern.
- Show your sense of humor. Laugh when funny things happen in class—especially when they happen to you.
- Speak to every student each day. Leave no one out of class discussions.
- Write notes to your students. Use plenty of stickers, and write positive comments on their papers.
- Pay attention to your students' health. If students need to go to the clinic, send them. When students have to miss several days because of illness, call to see how they are doing, or send a get-well card. Be prompt in sending work to the student's home if appropriate.
- Use this sentence to convey your concern: "What can I do to help you?"

- Talk with students when you notice a change in their behavior. For example, if a normally serious student is neglecting his or her work, find out why.
- Take the time to tell your students what you like about them.
- Take photographs of your students, and display them.

PROMOTING TRUST

You and your students need to trust each other. Much of what happens at school is based on mutual trust. The following tips will help you and your students make trust a vital part of your relationship:

- Be a model of trustworthiness. Talk about such issues as plagiarism or accurate record keeping, and show how you avoid mistakes in these areas.
- Adopt a "we" attitude. Talk about trust as a mutual responsibility. If you make every student feel essential to the smooth functioning of the class, many of the problems that occur with distrust will vanish.
- Don't promise what you cannot deliver. If a student confides in you, do not promise not to tell anyone else as a condition of the confession. Some things must be shared with counselors and parents or guardians.
- Avoid situations that will destroy your students' fragile trust. Do not leave your personal belongings or answer keys where students might be tempted to take them. Situations such as these can undo months of patient trust building in a few seconds.
- Don't be a pushover. If students see that you believe every false excuse their classmates offer, they will not feel that they can trust you to make good decisions.
- Accept that some students will take a long time to trust you. Be patient and persistent.

> Don't be afraid to admit that you don't know an answer. Ask for students' help in finding the correct answer.
>
> *Edward Gardner, 36 years' experience*

TEACHING YOUR STUDENTS TO BELIEVE IN THEMSELVES

One of the greatest gifts that teachers can give their students is the gift of self-confidence. Students who are confident in their ability to succeed will also find it easy to feel positive about the class and about their relationship with you. When you instill self-belief in your students, you will see them transform into lifelong learners, regardless of their age or ability level. Every day, you can transmit your belief in the abilities of your students in a variety of ways:

- Post motivational signs to encourage students to give their best effort. Reward effort as well as achievement.

- Create an environment in which students can risk trying new things without fear of failure or ridicule.

- Tell your students about your confidence in their ability to succeed. Tell them over and over.

- Teach your students how to set and achieve measurable goals. Once they start achieving, students will want to continue.

- Remember that small successes lead to larger ones. Make it a point to arrange opportunities for students to be successful. Your students will soon be confident in their own ability to achieve.

- At the end of class, occasionally ask students to share what they have learned. Often, they are not aware of how much they have actually achieved.

- Teach your students how to handle the failures that everyone experiences from time to time. Help them understand that they can learn from their mistakes.

- Acknowledge and celebrate your students' successes as often as you can. After all, their successes are your successes.

BECOMING A CULTURALLY RESPONSIVE EDUCATOR

One of the most enduring strengths of the public school system in America is the variety of cultures that meet peacefully in thousands of classrooms each day. In classroom after classroom, students of all different races and cultural backgrounds study together. At a time when school systems are scrutinized and criticized from many sides, classroom diversity is one of our nation's greatest assets.

Although some people try to define culture in ethnic or racial terms, a broader definition is more accurate. Every person belongs to a variety of cultural groups delineated by such features as geography, age, economics, gender, religion, interests, or education level. If you ignore the cultural differences among your students, you will create strife and tension. Conversely, if you choose to accept and celebrate those differences, you will find them to be a rich resource for your class.

Teach your students to value their differences. When you do this, you are creating a truly global classroom. And by expanding students' appreciation of each other, you are showing them how to appreciate the rest of the world.

Here are some general guidelines you can use to incorporate the many cultures in your classroom into a successful and unified group:

- Be aware that your own attitudes are influenced by your own culture. If your students' cultures are different from yours, you should strive to be sensitive to the differences in attitudes that you may have.

- Expose your students to a wide variety of cultures throughout the term. This exposure will enable them to be more tolerant of each other's differences. Instructional materials should incorporate multicultural information and approaches whenever possible.

- Make discussing the cultures in your class an important part of what you and your students do together. You can manage a few minutes every now and then for an informal discussion without losing valuable instructional time.

- Because cultural differences can sometimes lead to misunderstandings, be alert to the potential for student conflict so that you can prevent or minimize it.

- Be very clear about your behavior expectations so that the classroom culture you create can serve to guide student actions and interactions in the classroom.

- Make it obvious that you appreciate and value your students' cultures. Provide frequent icebreakers so that you and your students can learn about each other. Other activities that allow students to learn about their classmates' cultures can include marking birthplaces on a large map; creating a word wall of common words, such as *thank you* or *please,* in other languages; and having students post photos or images from their culture on a bulletin board or class Web page.

- Accept that the concerns of a parent or guardian who is not part of your culture may be different from the concerns that you have. If you are sensitive to the potential differences when you speak with family members, you will find yourself asking questions that will help you determine what their goals for their child are before you attempt to impose your own beliefs.

- Stress to students the importance of an open-minded attitude about people whose beliefs or lifestyles are different from theirs. Make sure you model that acceptance yourself.

- Promote activities that will increase your students' self-esteem. Students who are self-confident are not as likely to taunt others to feel good about themselves.

- Because different cultures stress different ways of learning, you should design instruction that offers a variety of differentiated strategies that students can use to access the material. You should also offer as much appropriate scaffolding as possible.

- If students learn racism or intolerance at home, know that you will have a very difficult time stopping it in class. Your first step in combating intolerant attitudes should be to make your position of tolerance very clear to your students through what you say and what you do.

There are many excellent resources to help you become a culturally responsive educator, and these two books are particularly informative:

Developing positive relationships with students is the most important part of my classroom. If you have developed the relationships, then students will want to learn for you. The first day of school, I start my class with a story of the day. This idea is almost a mirroring of a family dinner situation in which each child gets to tell about his or her day. It creates a family within the classroom, and I am able to develop positive relationships with students.

Erin Sager, 8 years' experience

Delpit, L. *Other People's Children: Cultural Conflict in the Classroom*. New York, NY: New Press, 2006.

Ladson-Billings, G. *Crossing over to Canaan: The Journey of New Teachers in Diverse Classrooms*. San Francisco, CA: Jossey-Bass, 2001.

THE LIMITS OF YOUR RESPONSIBILITY TO YOUR STUDENTS

It is very easy to become involved in helping students when it is obvious that they need more than just classroom instruction to be successful. As teachers, we are in a caring profession that values service and encourages us to help the whole child. It's impossible to just stand by when our students struggle with hunger, homelessness, or any other serious issue that makes it difficult for them to learn. We should help. After all, our students depend on us to keep them safe from harm.

Although it is essential that we help our students, it is important that we do so in a professional manner so that success is more likely. First of all, think of yourself as the first line of defense in getting help for your students in need. Once you become aware of a student's need, you should act promptly.

Remember, too, that you are part of a team of caring professionals who are all trained to assist students. Never take it upon yourself to act alone to solve student problems. Instead, involve counselors, administrators, school resource officers, school nurses, social workers, and other appropriate personnel as quickly as you can.

Although you may have been trained as a classroom teacher, often your colleagues in specialized fields will have access to resources and support that you do not. Their assistance and support can be more extensive and better-suited to student needs than any help you can offer.

If you have students who are struggling with any of the issues in the following list, act quickly to contact other professionals to seek their help:

- Pregnancy
- Bullying
- Neighborhood threats
- Mental health issues
- Suicide threats or attempts
- Emotional, verbal, or sexual abuse
- Substance abuse issues
- Serious family problems
- Gang involvement
- Sexual orientation issues
- Attempts or threats to run away
- Chronic illness or injury

- A need for eyeglasses, a hearing aid, or other adaptive technology
- Hunger
- Homelessness

Help Students Learn to Relate Well to Each Other

Our students are social creatures just as we are. They long to be part of something bigger than themselves—to feel that vital connection with others that is so important to all of us. When students feel that they are valued members of a group, the results can be remarkable. Classroom harmony and academic success are certain to be achievable.

The need to feel a sense of belonging is intense for students of all grade levels. If you doubt the importance of a supportive class chemistry, ask yourself why any student would want to come to a class in which he or she feels like an outcast. If a student does not feel connected to the other students in your classroom, that child will find it impossible to see any benefit in attending your class. Not only is your role as a teacher important in helping students who are at risk for academic failure or dropping out but also the role of their classmates is vital.

Every class develops its own chemistry. Even very young children will perform characteristic interactions that shape the entire group. With this propensity in mind, the importance of guiding students to relate well to each other is one of the most important responsibilities we have.

WHAT A SUPPORTIVE CLASS CHEMISTRY LOOKS LIKE

Classes in which students have learned to relate well to each other can be found across grade levels, ability levels, and content areas. Visitors to this type of class often notice the obvious comfort of the students in the room. Although they may be fully engaged in either independent or collaborative learning, students in a class in which the chemistry is supportive are both keenly aware and accepting of each other.

Students in a supportive class routinely watch out for each other. They post reminders, hand out supplies when needed, invite classmates to join in when working in groups, and share jokes. They are empathetic and courteous. The result is a sense of inclusion that supersedes petty or unkind comments or reactions. They understand the importance of a shared purpose when doing assignments and work to help each other meet the demands of that purpose. These students view themselves as a family away from home. This type of class might seem too good to be true, but it is well worth the effort to plan how to promote activities and attitudes that can make it possible.

REMOVING BARRIERS TO PEER ACCEPTANCE

It is important for teachers to make it easy for their students to work well together—an undertaking that requires diplomacy as well as dedicated effort. Social inclusion is such a vital aspect of any student's life that the effort often results in beneficial dividends. Begin by identifying some of the barriers to social acceptance that could have a negative effect on your students.

What are some of the most common barriers to social acceptance in school? Many students could feel excluded because they do not know their classmates. It is a mistake to assume that students know each other well. Even students who have attended school together for several years may not know much about their classmates.

Another barrier is that your students may live in different neighborhoods. If you teach in a school where students may live at a distance or come from very diverse neighborhoods, it is likely that they have not had many opportunities to interact with each other outside of school.

In addition, students who have not been taught how to behave courteously or who have not learned socially acceptable ways to resolve conflict often struggle to form appropriate relationships with their peers.

Perhaps the greatest barrier that you will have to help your students overcome is the perception that they may not have much in common with a classmate whom they do not know well. With effort and persistence, you can assist students in learning to recognize their commonalities so that they can learn to accept and support each other. Use the tips in the list that follows to guide you as you work to help students remove the barriers to peer acceptance.

- Make sure that each student's strengths are well known to the rest of the class.
- If a student has an unpleasant history of failure or misbehavior, make it clear that it is time for a fresh start.
- Show your students the correct ways to interact with each other. They need plenty of models and monitoring until they have learned to cooperate productively.
- Let each student shine. Every student should believe that he or she is really your favorite.
- Be sensitive to the differences that divide your students and to the potential for conflict that those differences can cause.
- Make it a point to recognize students who work well with others. Whenever possible, praise the entire class for its cooperative attitude.
- Provide opportunities for students to get to know each other. These do not have to take up a great deal of time, but can be done in brief activities scattered throughout the year.
- Plan enough work for your students to do so that they are focused on school and don't have time to discover their classmates' negative character traits.
- Promote tolerance and acceptance with a display of posters and encouraging mottoes.
- Encourage students to share experiences and personal information about their family, culture, dreams, and goals while working together.

- Make it very easy for students to understand class routines and procedures and to follow directions well. Students who know what to do are less likely to make embarrassing mistakes for which they can be teased or excluded later.

- Be careful that you model appropriate behavior, thereby encouraging your students to do the same. Don't give in to the temptation of rolling your eyes or losing your patience when a student blunders in front of classmates. Your actions could set that student up for social exclusion later.

SHARED EXPERIENCES AND SHARED TASKS

Few things can establish a sense of community in a classroom as quickly as shared experiences and shared tasks. Students who learn to see themselves as a united group working and playing together quickly learn to be supportive of each other's efforts and tolerant of each other's idiosyncrasies.

Although any twenty-first-century classroom is a place where students share experiences and tasks, teachers who recognize and celebrate these common experiences and tasks can build a sense of pride, teamwork, and camaraderie among students. Here are several ways you can encourage your students to be part of a supportive classroom:

- Take frequent photos to encourage students to see how they have progressed and grown throughout the school year. Display photographs of students doing various classroom tasks, such as maintaining the classroom library or managing a classroom recycling center, as well as participating in field trips and other lively events.

- Keep a scrapbook of major events and experiences throughout the year. The scrapbook does not have to be elaborate to be effective. Even photos clipped into a three-ring binder will show your students that they are important to you and to each other. Students can even contribute to or maintain the scrapbook themselves as part of an ongoing class project or routine task.

- Use bulletin board space to show collages of the interests students have in common, their contributions to the class, and personal quotations or mottoes that are important to them.

- Set goals as a class and work together to reach them:
  - The entire class earns a certain grade
  - The class goes a certain number of days without tardies
  - The class earns a specified class average on a test
  - The class strives for a perfect homework completion rate

- Post rotating classroom chores that students have to complete for the benefit of classmates. Students of all ages can participate in tasks that make the class run more smoothly for everyone.

- Adopt a class mascot, secret sign, or catchphrase. Celebrate class in-jokes, traditions, or rituals.

- Observe milestones, such as the twentieth homework assignment or the tenth day with no tardies or the Hundredth Day. An excellent resource for Hundredth Day celebrations can be found at Enchanted Learning (www.enchantedlearning.com). Use "Hundredth Day" as a search term to access resources and lesson ideas to celebrate this occasion.

USING TECHNOLOGY TO PROMOTE A SUPPORTIVE CLASS

As even very young students become more tech savvy, it is easier than ever to use technology to promote a supportive class atmosphere. When using technology to promote a supportive class, take care that the activities you ask of your students are age appropriate and meet the guidelines for acceptable computer use established by your school district. Here are just a few of the many ways you can use technology to help your students relate well to each other:

- You can create a classroom blogging community at Kid Blog (http://kidblog.org). Kid Blog is a site created and maintained by K–12 teachers to establish safe classroom blogging communities for their students.
- Flickr (www.flickr.com) and Tag Galaxy (http://taggalaxy.de) are both enormous photo-sharing databases with millions of shared images. Although students, particularly younger ones, should be carefully supervised while visiting these sites due to the possibility of objectionable content in some photos, such sites can be used as sources for a variety of collaborative projects.
- Students can collaborate on group multimedia presentations using the tools in PowerPoint or Prezi (http://prezi.com).
- If it is possible for students to communicate with each other through discussion boards or wiki pages on your classroom Web page, encouraging them to do so will help build a sense of community in your classroom.
- Older students can create Facebook (www.facebook.com) or Tumblr (www.tumblr.com) pages through which they can communicate with each other about the topics in class.
- Students can use Twitter (http://twitter.com) to tweet messages and reminders to each other about class concerns.
- You can use your school e-mail account as well as your class Web page to broadcast notes, messages, and reminders to your students who have e-mail accounts of their own.

TEAM-BUILDING ACTIVITIES FOR THE ENTIRE YEAR

Many teachers use engaging team activities at the start of the school term to help students get to know each other, but team-building activities can help build a sense of community in your classroom all year long. Such activities serve to help students get to know each other, develop social skills, listen carefully to directions, cooperate with others, and feel more comfortable in class. Building teams in your classroom creates a sense of community and connectedness that makes learning easier and more fun for every student.

Teachers who want to include team-building activities in their classes will find it easy to access many different sources of ideas with just a quick Internet search. One very useful book that can provide plenty of ideas for team-building activities that are adaptable to the classroom is *Team Challenges: 170+ Group Activities to Build Cooperation, Communication, and Creativity* by Kris Bordessa. Published by Chicago Review Press in 2005, this book contains plenty of easily adaptable and interesting activities for students of all ages.

In the list that follows you will find a brief description of some easy team-building activities that require little or no advance preparation on your part but that can be effective ways for students to bond well with each other while having fun.

- **Lining-up games.** Teachers of younger students can use these games to line students up for a variety of routine activities. Those who teach older students can use these as quick energizers throughout the year. Ask students to line up according to a variety of categories, such as birthday, height, eye color, first letter of a pet's name, last name in alphabetical order, number of syllables in their name, shirt color, number of siblings, and favorite sports team.

- **Tic-tac-toe.** Arrange nine chairs into a tic-tac-toe grid of three across and three down. Divide students into two teams. Ask students to review questions. When students answer correctly, they may move to a spot on the grid. The first team to fill three chairs in a row wins.

- **Structure building.** Have students build towers or other structures using an assortment of unlikely construction materials, such as straws, paper clips, and sticky notes.

- **Survivor.** Create a disaster scenario and ask students to discuss how to survive the disaster or even to determine which survivors should be saved. Some scenarios that other teachers have found successful involve being shipwrecked on a deserted island, being in the path of an erupting volcano, or being lost on the moon.

- **Egg drop.** This old-fashioned favorite can easily be adapted to appeal to students of any age. Students will have to create packaging that will protect an egg dropped from a certain height. Other objects can be used instead of eggs, of course: pumpkins, tomatoes, and small plastic bags of water or flour are all good substitutes.

- **Balloon games.** Balloons lend themselves to a variety of cooperative games. In one of the easiest games, students develop strategies to keep one or more balloons aloft for a specified length of time with a predetermined restriction, such as no talking or no hands.

- **Ball toss.** Have students in either large or small groups toss a variety of balls while answering review questions, reciting their name, or stating interesting personal facts. You can add variety, having teams play against each other.

- **Recycling toss.** Assign students to teams that help clean the room at the end of class. Stage competitions whereby students ball up papers to be recycled and toss them into the recycle bin. Keep score and encourage teams to challenge each other as they keep the room tidy.

- **Spiderweb.** Have students sit or stand in a large circle. Hand a student a ball of yarn. Ask that student to state something that he or she believes other students will share a common interest in. Students who agree will raise their hand. The first student, while still holding on to the string, will toss the yarn to one of the classmates with a hand up. That student will continue with a different interest until all students are connected to each other. At the end of the activity, have students roll the yarn back into a ball for another day.

MAKING YOUR CLASSROOM A RISK-FREE ENVIRONMENT

Although at first there does not seem to be a strong connection between students' taking academic risks and social inclusion by their peers, the link is indeed a strong one. Students who are comfortable enough in their classroom to take a risk are students who are not afraid of being ridiculed by their peers. They have been taught that it is okay to make mistakes and that it is okay to laugh at themselves. To make it easy for students not to be intimidated, try the options that follow when someone makes a mistake or doesn't know the answer to a question or problem.

Here are a few general tips for creating a risk-free environment that you can do in advance of a question-and-answer session:

- Be open about the mistakes you make yourself. Model how to react appropriately when you make a mistake yourself.
- Encourage students to write out their answers before speaking.
- Make it clear that if students speak to you in advance, you will not call on them.
- Tell students that it is okay to say, "I am not sure, but _____."

Here are some tips for handling student responses when a student is struggling with an answer:

- Ask if he or she would like to "phone a friend" or get advice from a classmate.
- Ask if he or she would like to opt out or take a pass on the question.
- Tell the student to give his or her best guess.
- Offer to come back to the student later.
- Ask for clarification by saying, "Did I hear you say _____?"

- Say, "Almost. Can you add a bit more?"
- Ask another student to tell you what is correct about the answer, but then to add to it.

PEER TUTORING

Peer tutoring motivates students because it encourages academic success through pleasant social interaction. When students work together to help each other learn, both the person learning the material and the tutor can benefit.

There are two types of peer tutoring: formal sessions and informal sessions. Formal sessions are often planned to occur after school or during designated study times. Informal sessions can occur during free time in class, at the beginning or end of class, and as a quick review before a quiz or test. Make either type of peer tutoring an effective motivational tool for your class by implementing some of these pointers:

- Before you encourage students to work together, discuss with them what peer tutoring is and the behaviors you want from them while they are working together. You should encourage them to stay on task, keep their voices down, and be respectful of each other.
- Carefully monitor two or more students studying together to ensure that they stay on task. It is easy for students' conversation to stray to topics other than the one they're studying, so you must be careful to let them know that you are aware of what they are doing when they work together.
- Remember that peer tutoring will be most efficient when students have specific information to cover in a session. For example, instead of reviewing material for a unit test, students should focus on particular areas of weakness within that material.
- Limit the time that students work together to sessions of fifteen minutes or less during class and about thirty minutes after school. If you allow longer sessions, students will find it too easy to lose focus.
- Engage struggling students as tutors. Students who have to work hard to learn the material can grow more self-confident by teaching what they know to others.
- Be careful not to allow students in your class who are quick to understand the work to spend too much time tutoring their classmates. Although it is acceptable to ask your more able students to help their classmates on occasion, tutoring is not the best use of such a student's time if it is used too often. If you have several students who consistently complete assignments before the rest of the class, you should differentiate instruction to involve them in more challenging work or enrichment activities.
- Establish formal study groups. When students regularly work together in a study group, they quickly learn to rely on each other. For maximum study group

effectiveness, you should assign students to a study group that stays together for a specified period of time, such as a grading period or a semester. Some of the study group activities can include

- Taking notes for absent members
- Checking facts from the lesson
- Managing handouts or reminders about due dates
- Working on study guides or other shared assignments
- Reading aloud and doing guided assignments together
- Practicing and reviewing together
- Using flash cards to help each other learn.

> Make sure you enter this profession because you want it to be your life's work. Don't enter it as a stopgap measure ("I'm waiting to go to graduate school" or "I don't really know what I want to do with my life yet"). Children deserve more than just a layover in your life.
>
> *Luann Scott, 37 years' experience*

Collaborative work is one of the most enjoyable activities you can assign to your students. Because of its popularity and because it allows students to share ideas in a structured and focused manner, collaborative work is a classroom strategy that is well worth the effort it requires. To learn more about how to manage collaborative groups in your class successfully, study the bonus material about this subject included on the DVD that accompanies this book.

TEACHING COURTESY AND CONFLICT RESOLUTION

Although we want our students to be consistently pleasant to each other, the reality is that we have a classroom full of young individuals who may not always know the best way to act or the right thing to say. As teachers, we need to make sure that the social groups in our classes function well.

To accomplish this, we need to teach our students that we expect them to be courteous all of the time, and we need to show them how to resolve conflicts successfully. The reward for our diligence in teaching social skills and helping students resolve conflicts is a positive, supportive classroom environment in which students relate well to each other. Everyone wins when this happens. To help you decide which social skills are most important for your classroom, use Teacher Worksheet 5.3 later in this section.

Teaching Courtesy

Teaching courtesy is a task you will have to assume if you want to have a smoothly running classroom. Not only do you need to teach your students the social skills they require to function well in your class but also you will have to enforce those skills by insisting that they treat each other and you with courtesy.

Your students observe you far more you than you can imagine. They want and need your guidance, not just in academics but in social skills, too. When you take the time to teach and model life skills, such as courtesy, you are teaching your students how to be successful in your classroom and in life.

It is easier to make this effort if you keep in mind that the rewards are great. Your bond with your students will be strong enough to reduce the discipline problems in your classroom. Here are a few suggestions for teaching courtesy in your class:

- **Make sure that everyone understands which behaviors are courteous and which are not.** Not all of your students mean to be rude when they shout insults at each other, interrupt, or put their head down on their desk when you are talking. Social rules, particularly those in schools, vary widely. Some teachers tolerate behavior that other teachers find offensive. This confuses children of all ages. Be direct, specific, and clear about what you expect. Do this early in the term so that you can prevent mistakes.

- **Reward good behavior.** Offer little rewards and lavish words of praise when a class has been courteous. This is especially important at the start of a term when students are still not sure of their boundaries. When you see a student or a group of students being courteous, take notice. Point it out so that everyone else can see what you mean when you talk about being polite.

- **Exploit the power of peer pressure.** You can steer students in the right direction by making sure that everyone in the class is courteous. When this happens, discourteous students will see that there is no peer support for bad behavior. Soon, they will police themselves.

- **Encourage students to accept each other's differences.** Many of the negative behaviors in a class can be eliminated by encouraging students to be tolerant of each other. You can do this by modeling acceptance and respect for each of your students, particularly the ones who struggle with social skills.

- **Model courteous behavior.** Rules are useless if you do not model the behavior you want from your students. If you are rude to your students, you can be sure that they will be rude to you, and possibly to each other. Each day, you have hundreds of opportunities to show your students how to be polite. Take advantage of each one. Being able to show that you are a courteous person is a powerful tool.

Resolving Peer Conflicts

There are many different ways to help students learn to resolve their differences and be supportive of each other. Whenever you can, promote the values that can make it easier for students to avoid conflicts: respect for each other's views, tolerance of each other's differences, and willingness to work together for the mutual good of their classmates. Try using some of the suggestions in the list that follows to help students resolve conflicts before strife can rob your classroom of any chance of achievement.

- Help students understand the concept of creating a win-win situation instead of just emerging victorious over an opponent.
- Help students understand the issues that may have caused the conflict. How did each one contribute to the conflict?
- Do what you can to help students learn to listen attentively to each other. Everyone in a dispute should listen carefully to each other and work to understand the viewpoints of everyone else involved.
- If a conflict seems to be more complex than you feel comfortable handling, involve other staff members in the mediation process.
- Be careful not to take sides while you are helping students work out their differences.

A useful online site for more information about conflict resolution in the classroom is Peace Education Foundation (www.peaceeducation.org). This organization offers various resources to help students learn to resolve their conflicts in a positive and productive manner.

I was surprised at how much fun you can actually have in class. The enthusiasm and playfulness of the students are truly infectious!

Alanna Dougherty, first-year teacher

Another helpful online resource to learn more about classroom conflict resolution is Teaching Tolerance (www.tolerance.org), maintained by the Southern Poverty Law Center. At this site, you will find links to more resources, classroom activities, and free teaching kits on a variety of topics.

TEACHER WORKSHEET 5.3

Checklist of Social Skills All Students Should Master

Use this checklist to target the social skills that you may need to emphasize with students.

All students should

1. _____ Use "please," "excuse me," and "thank you" when speaking with each other and their teacher

2. _____ Use an appropriate volume when talking. This includes at the start and end of class

3. _____ Not interrupt others unnecessarily

4. _____ Make an effort to control angry outbursts or other unpleasant comments

5. _____ Ask permission before taking something that belongs to someone else

6. _____ Refrain from using inappropriate language, such as profanity or insults

7. _____ Drop used tissues in the trash

8. _____ Stay upright in their seat unless they are ill

9. _____ Not clutter the aisles with their personal belongings

10. _____ Slip quietly into class when tardy or when returning from being excused so as not to disturb others

11. _____ Raise their hand as a signal for attention, and then wait to be called on

12. _____ Show that they are attentive by looking at a speaker

13. _____ Clean up their work area

14. _____ Respect others' values, outlook, and life experiences

15. _____ Address each other and their teacher by using appropriate names

PROTECTING YOUR STUDENTS FROM BULLIES

Schools are not always safe places for teachers. Each year, thousands of teachers report that they have been insulted and threatened by their students. School can be an even tougher place for students. Every year, thousands of students report that a classmate has physically attacked them. Others report that they have been too afraid to attend school on at least one occasion. These statistics reveal only what is reported to authorities; far more harassment occurs than is ever reported.

One of the worst aspects of the problem of harassment is that teachers have been slow to react to complaints from victims in the past. Some teachers seem to feel that victims of harassment bring it on themselves or are overreacting. Many teachers, despite recent incidents of school violence, are still inclined to overlook harassment. The situation is exacerbated by the fact that many teachers are not sure about when they should intervene.

The first step you can take to stop this serious threat is to understand exactly what harassment is. It can take three forms: physical abuse, verbal abuse, and cyber bullying. Cyber bullying is a growing threat as more and more students use social networking sites, cell phones, and other forms of electronic communication to connect with their classmates. When students are abused physically, teachers are usually quick to respond. However, verbal abuse in the form of rumors, racial slurs, name calling, and teasing is the most widespread form of harassment; unfortunately, it is far more likely to be tolerated by teachers. Cyber bullying is even more difficult to manage because it rarely takes place in a classroom, although its effects can be devastating. Finally, one particular type of bully, "mean girls," can present unique challenges for teachers of all ages. (More information on cyber bullying and "mean girls" follows later in this section.)

Your Responsibilities

- You are expected to take necessary steps to prevent harassment by teaching your students about it and by supervising them adequately.
- You need to be alert to signs that a student is being harassed by others. Act promptly.
- You must know your school's policy about harassment as well as your responsibilities.
- Because harassment is such a serious offense, you must involve administrators, parents or guardians, and other support personnel according to the guidelines specified by your district if one of your students is involved in harassment.

Mistakes to Avoid

- Never ignore the situation. If you observe an incident, no matter how mild it may appear to you, take action.
- Don't make things worse for the victim by causing him or her unnecessary public humiliation. Be sensitive to the embarrassment such a student feels at being a target and having to ask for help.

- Never assume that victims bring it on themselves.
- Don't neglect to teach your students about harassment, the forms it can take, the consequences of perpetrating it, how to report it, and why they must report incidents to adults.

What to Do Before an Incident Occurs

- Make teaching social skills part of your classroom procedures, no matter how old your students are. Some of your students simply do not know which behaviors are appropriate and which are not.
- Make sure your school's policy on bullying is clear and up to date. Every staff member should have a copy of the policy. Students should also be aware of the school's policy and the consequences involved.
- Be alert for the early signs of bullying. Often teachers only see the tip of the iceberg because bullies prefer to target victims in unsupervised areas. If, for example, you notice that several students have targeted one of their classmates or that a student is having trouble making adjustments to your class at the beginning of the term, be alert that more may be going on that you don't see.
- Strive to build a sense of teamwork among your students so that they learn to value everyone's contributions to the class.
- Promote acceptance by praising students when they are helpful to each other. It is particularly effective when you can label an entire class as helpful, initiating a positive self-fulfilling prophecy.
- Boost the self-esteem of all students, particularly those who may be tempted to harass others because of their own poor sense of self-worth and those who may be targets of harassment.
- Make sure that students have the basic skills they need to deal with peer conflicts.
- Be aware of how students treat each other. Listen carefully to what they have to say both to and about each other.

What to Do After an Incident Occurs

- Put the school's procedures into action by speaking with an administrator. It is important to prevent more abuse by acting quickly.
- Meet with the students whom you suspect of having harassed a peer and ask them to tell you about the incident. Then ask for the details in writing. It is important that you not speak with the victim first so that there will be few reprisals for tattling.
- Meet with the victim to discuss the incident. Have this student write a report of the incident, too.

- Support the victim. Often, just talking with an adult will help the child relieve some of the anxiety that he or she is feeling.

- Talk with the parents or guardians of the students involved to let them know what has been reported. They should understand not only what happened but also that there is a school policy about harassment and that the incident has been reported to an administrator. Elicit their support in working with you to prevent further abuse.

- Work with both students together to reconcile their differences. The abuser should apologize to the victim. At the end of their conference, both students should have a better understanding of their behavior.

Cyber Bullying

Cyber bullying is a relatively new harassment phenomenon that continues to spread as more and more students gain access to social networking sites, cell phones, and other forms of electronic communication. Cyber bullying is just what its name implies—harassment through electronic means.

Cyber bullying is often more insidious than other types because victims are never free of the threat as long as they carry a cell phone, check e-mail, or belong to one or more social networking sites. Cyber bullies, too, are often more aggressive because they are not face-to-face with their victims.

Although it is not our responsibility to police how our students use their personal electronic media to communicate with each other when they are not in class, teachers do have a privileged position in the lives of their students. Here are some tips on how to handle a cyber bullying incident should you have to:

- If a student confides to you that he or she is the victim of a cyber bully, the first step that you should take is to talk with the student to learn the details of the harassment.

- You should involve other professionals who can help your student at once. Contact your school's technology support personnel and the administrator whose responsibility it is to cope with your school's policy for fair use of the Internet to enlist their assistance.

- At this point, the other personnel should assume the primary role in helping your student with the issue. You should, however, continue to offer your support and encouragement to help the victim.

To learn more about what you can do to prevent and deal with digital harassment, there are several national organizations that can offer you and your students advice and support. One of the foremost of these organizations is Wired Kids. This group maintains an informative and helpful site at www.cyberbullying.org. Another group is the Cyber

Bullying Research Center. Their site at www.cyberbullying.us offers constructive prevention and response tips for teens in general, cyber bullies, victims, parents and guardians, and educators.

"Mean Girls"

A particular type of bullying that can have a negative impact on any classroom is the phenomenon of harassment by "mean girls"—pretty and popular girls of any age who engage in power struggles with other girls. Although the 2004 movie *Mean Girls* explored a make-believe stereotype of this type of bully, the misery caused by "mean girls" in countless classrooms is very real. Relentless teasing and ostracism of a female student by either one girl or a clique with the aim of spreading pain, intimidation, and humiliation can undermine any teacher's efforts to create a positive classroom environment. Teachers often have a challenging time dealing with "mean girls" for several reasons:

- Often the "mean girl" can be so popular that she plays a powerful role in the lives of her classmates.
- The intimidation tactics of the "mean girl" can be so cleverly disguised that it not easy for a teacher to notice and halt them.
- Sometimes, sadly enough, a "mean girl" is supported by doting parents or guardians who ignore or even silently approve of their daughter's cruel behavior.

Teachers who have learned to cope with "mean girls" readily admit that this type of bullying is challenging to manage. Your first step should be to recognize that this type of bullying is possible in any classroom. Next, if you do notice the subtle signs of intimidation, act as swiftly and decisively as you would in the case of any other type of bullying. Take care to make your position clear to the bullies and to offer support to the victim. Finally, involve counselors and other support personnel at your school who are accustomed to dealing with bullies of either gender and can help you keep your classroom a safe place for all students.

HOW TO MANAGE NAME CALLING

Forget the "sticks and stones" rhyme of your childhood. The hateful names that students can call each other do indeed cause a great deal of hurt. From the obscene to the silly, the names that students across all grade levels, cultures, and social groups choose to use as weapons to degrade each other can be staggeringly effective. Anguish, humiliation, and anger result when students tease each other with name calling.

As educators, we cannot allow name calling to be a part of our school environment. Fortunately, there are some positive actions that any teacher can take to manage name calling successfully. Use these suggestions to help your students learn to relate to each other in a positive way instead of resorting to calling each other names:

- Model adult behavior at all times. Students can be quick to pick up on a teacher's problem with pronouncing a classmate's name or frustration at a student's misbehavior.

- Be alert. Even pleasant and cooperative students can call each other hateful names. Often the offense happens when the teacher's back is turned; when students are moving from one place to another; or in a less supervised place, such as the cafeteria, playground, or hallway.

- Although racist name calling is clearly not tolerable, remember that some students may not be aware that all hurtful names are still painful to the victims.

- Be aware of the students in your class who may be at risk for name calling. Students whose appearance and behavior differ from those of their classmates are particularly vulnerable.

- Act quickly and decisively as soon as you hear name calling. Stop the misbehavior at once. Be matter of fact and calm, but make it obvious that name calling will not happen in your class.

- Don't accept excuses. Some students will try to convince you that they meant no harm. Continue to be firm in your efforts to stop the name calling.

- As unobtrusively as possible, offer appropriate support to students who are the victims of name calling. Please note, however, that the appropriateness of the support you should offer can vary according to the student and the offense. If you are not sure of the types of support you should provide, consult a school counselor, a colleague, or your mentor for advice.

- Create a bulletin board display of a trash can and the words that you do not want to hear from your students. Even words that are commonly accepted (by other students), such as *loser* or *dummy*, get placed in the trash can display. You can manage offensive words by labeling them by their group instead of specifically: *swear words* or *homophobic words* instead of actual examples.

HOW YOU CAN HELP STUDENTS COPE WITH NEGATIVE PEER PRESSURE

Experienced teachers are aware of the powerful role that peer pressure plays in the classroom. Students of all ages want to fit in, to get along with their classmates, and to feel accepted. When this need promotes good behavior, the positive energy it generates is welcome in any classroom.

The need for acceptance can be so strong, however, that sometimes it can cause inappropriate behavior in even the best-managed classrooms. Although there are many social causes of negative peer pressure, teachers can successfully control a few of them. Try some of these strategies to help your students cope with the negative effects of peer pressure:

- Provide students with an occasional opportunity to reflect on their learning and behavior. This will allow them to clarify their thinking.

- Don't allow students to bully or intimidate each other. Be vigilant, and stop these behaviors as soon as you can.

- Increase your students' self-esteem and confidence by focusing on their successes.

- Give your class a positive identity so that students do not create a negative one for themselves. (See Section Four for more information about how to give a class a positive group identity.)

- Help your students set both long-term and short-term goals for themselves.

- Work to build a positive relationship with each student. A caring teacher can be a force stronger than peer pressure in a child's life.

Best Practices Checklist

1. Reach out to your students. A strong teacher-student bond is necessary for the smooth running of your classroom and for the success of your students.

2. Learn to view your role as one of a "guide on the side" rather than a "sage on the stage." Encourage students to be responsible and self-directed learners.

3. Make sure your relationships with your students are appropriate. Remember the simple test: would a member of the school board regard what you say or do as appropriate and in the best interests of your students?

4. Work to ensure that your class is as risk-free an environment as possible for your students. Consistently employ a variety of approaches to make students comfortable and willing to share and support each other.

5. Use reflective practices to examine how well you meet your students' expectations of what a teacher should be.

6. Never forget that you are a role model. This applies not just in your classroom but also in the eyes of your community.

7. Before students work in collaborative groups, take care to teach appropriate behavior, including signaling for assistance and self-regulating their noise level, for example.

8. Spend time each day as necessary to teach appropriate social skills, including courtesy. Be careful to model courteous behavior yourself.

9. Pay attention to the various types of potential bullies in your classroom. Be decisive in your actions once you determine that a student has been bullied.

10. Don't ignore the problems caused by negative peer pressure in your classroom. Use a variety of techniques to help students overcome its destructive effects.

Time to Reflect
Develop Positive Classroom Relationships

Use the information in this section to guide your thinking as you reflect on these questions. They are designed to encourage you to think more deeply about the issues in the text or to discuss those issues with colleagues.

1. Assess your own strengths and weaknesses in terms of classroom immediacy. What are you already doing to be a teacher who is friendly and approachable? What aspects of how you present yourself would you like to improve?

2. What kind of a role model are you currently? What kind of role model do you want to become? What can you improve? Who can help you with this?

3. How can teachers show that they care about students while maintaining a respectful emotional distance? Why is this distance necessary for both students and teachers?

4. What have you observed another teacher doing to forge a positive connection with students? Brainstorm a list of actions you can take to make sure that your connection with your students is strong and positive.

5. Discuss what you did to help your students be successful this week. How do you know they were successful? How did your students react to your actions?

SECTION SIX

Control Class Time

As a teacher, you can't control many of the more challenging aspects of your profession, but there is one very important factor over which you do have control: class time. You have door-to-door control over the ways your students use the all-too-few hours they spend with you in your classroom. Teachers control whether class time is wasted or productive.

You can choose either to engage students in meaningful and engaging learning activities or to condemn them to boredom and missed opportunities. Although some time will be wasted in unavoidable disruptions and interruptions, you can and should strive to minimize this loss. You can allow students to have nothing productive to do for much of the time they spend with you, or you can arrange to have students engaged in a variety of learning tasks while developing a positive, productive attitude about their academic responsibilities.

You Control the Time Your Students Have with You

You may be tempted to believe that your day is so consumed by interruptions and distractions that these circumstances regulate what happens in your class, but this is not true. Although there are certainly many things you can't change about your school situation, you do have control over how your students spend their time while they are with you.

Sometimes it will seem that such interruptions as intercom announcements, commotions in the halls, or unruly students disrupt your class much too often. Just as other teachers do, you will have to find ways to cope successfully with these obvious disturbances as well as with many more subtle disruptions of your class routines.

If you do not control the use of time in your classroom, what are the consequences? If you waste only two minutes of your students' day—a few seconds at the opening of class, a distraction or two, a lost handout, maybe even a minute of free time at the end of class—over the course of a typical school year, those two minutes a day will add up to more than six hours of lost instruction. That's an entire school day.

The results of misused instructional time can be grim. Teachers who do not use class time wisely experience far more discipline problems than teachers who make use of every minute. Students who waste class time are less able to succeed academically. Discipline problems and academic failures not only make a teacher's workday unpleasant but can eventually lead to burnout as well.

What can you do to avoid the hazards of wasted class time? Start by making a commitment to yourself and to your students that you will teach them during every minute that they are with you. Resolve to make good use of the time that your students are in your class.

How Teachers Waste Time

One way to use class time to the best advantage is to be aware of how easy it is to waste it. Some of the ways that teachers misuse class time include the following:

- Teaching lessons that are not relevant or interesting to students
- Not having clear procedures for student computer use
- Not using the first few minutes of class effectively
- Allowing students to goof off for the last few minutes of class
- Not intervening quickly enough to keep problems manageable
- Confusing digressions from their topic with teachable moments
- Neglecting to set up equipment in advance
- Not establishing routines for daily classroom procedures
- Not double-checking links in Web sites your students will need to use
- Calling roll instead of checking attendance with a seating chart
- Not enforcing a reasonable policy for leaving the classroom
- Not providing assistance for students without materials
- Allowing students to decide when class is over
- Not determining students' prior knowledge of new material
- Assigning an inappropriate amount of work
- Giving confusing directions
- Making poor transitions between activities
- Giving homework that is only busywork

How Well Do You Use Class Time?

To determine how well you use class time at this point in your teaching career, use the self-assessment that follows. The actions listed in the first column are positive ones that all teachers should cultivate.

	I Always Do This	I Sometimes Do This	I Don't Do This
I expect students to begin working on established class routines as soon as they enter the classroom.			
My students can pick up handouts and other materials as they enter class.			
My students and I follow a predictable routine for the end of class.			
I delegate as many chores as appropriate given the age and ability levels of my students.			
I always make a few extra copies of handouts so that students who have lost theirs can begin right away.			
I provide small pencil sharpeners at various places around the room.			
When I show videos, I show only the most relevant clips.			
When groups need to pick up materials, only one student picks them up for the entire group.			
When students need to pick up various types of materials, I avoid long lines and congestion by scattering the materials in various stations around the room.			
I make a point of testing equipment before students arrive to make sure that it is in working order.			
I give directions verbally one time while students follow along with a written or posted copy.			
I have extra pencils and paper available for students who lack supplies.			

(continued on next page)

(continued from previous page)

	I Always Do This	I Sometimes Do This	I Don't Do This
When I plan lessons, I focus on the activities that students will be doing and the time constraints of each one.			
I always have a backup plan in case a lesson does not work well or there is a disruption.			
I design lessons to meet state and district objectives.			
After an interruption, I focus on instruction to minimize time loss.			
I offer "wiggle breaks" at regular intervals so that students find it easy to remain on task.			
My students and I stop periodically during a lesson to review and recap.			
I routinely use a timer to help students focus.			
I encourage students to watch the clock and set time limits for their own work.			
I realize that all students can experience difficulty transitioning from one topic to another and adjust my plans accordingly.			
I hold students accountable for how well they use the time that they are in class.			
I use formative assessments to determine my students' readiness for a particular unit of study.			
I teach my students how to keep their notes and other materials in order so that they can find them quickly.			

When you believe you have filled a class period, go back and plan a few extra activities—or identify an activity that can be stretched to fill time—just in case you have extra time. I live in fear of finishing my lesson plan with time to spare on the clock and always make sure I have more than enough to do to keep the students engaged until the bell rings.

Melinda Conner, first-year teacher

Principles of Effective Classroom Time Management

Learning to use class time wisely is a skill that will take time, patience, and practice to acquire; however, the rewards are well worth the effort. You and your students will benefit every day from classes that run smoothly. You will eventually gather many tips from your colleagues and learn even more from your own classroom experiences; until then, you can start with these general principles for using class time wisely:

- **Reduce distractions.** The old image of restless students staring dreamily out of the window has much truth in it. Students of all ages are always able to entertain themselves by paying attention to distractions rather than focusing on the teacher. Look around your classroom for things that might distract your students. Some obvious sources of distractions might be windows, desks too close together, doorways, pencil sharpeners, trash cans, screen savers, too many posters or banners, graffiti, or—the most enticing one of all—other students.

- **Raise student awareness.** Your students need to learn that time is important in your class. This doesn't mean that you should rush them through their tasks, but you should discuss the importance of using class time wisely, making sure that your students understand that you expect them to work productively while they are in class.

- **Establish routines.** If you have routines for daily activities in your class, your students will save minutes each day and hours each week instead of wasting time because they don't know what to do.

- **Monitor constantly.** Monitoring your students is of primary importance for the smooth running of your class for a variety of reasons, not just for efficient time use. Walking around the classroom instead of sitting at your desk will allow you to help students while their problems are still manageable.

- **Be very organized.** If your students have to wait while you find your textbook or a handout, that is a poor use of their time. Make it a point to be so organized that you will be able to keep yourself and your students on task.

● **Have a backup plan.** If a lesson isn't going well, if a guest speaker cancels, or if the equipment you need to use isn't working, you will need an alternative way to teach the material you planned to cover. Have a backup plan in place so that you can quickly shift gears if your first plan doesn't work out. (See Section Ten for more information about backup plans.)

● **Take a door-to-door approach.** Engage students in learning from the time they enter your classroom until the time they leave. Many teachers make the mistake of thinking that students need a few minutes of free time at the start of class and at the end of class to relax. Although students do need time at both ends of class to make effective transitions, they do not need free time to do this. Instead, give them interesting activities that relate to the day's lesson.

● **Use small blocks of time.** Just as you can accomplish many of your own tasks with brief bits of concentrated effort, so can your students. If you only have five minutes until dismissal, refuse to allow students to do nothing just because it will take too long to get them working on a new assignment. Instead, use this time and other snippets of time in class to review or to teach a new fact.

● **Teach to an objective.** If you teach a subject that you enjoy personally, it is tempting to spend more time on certain topics than the curriculum dictates. Stick to your plan so that your students won't be shortchanged on other topics. In addition, keep the purpose of the work that you are asking of your students clearly in mind and communicate that purpose to them. If you are unclear about why your work together is important, your students will also be unclear, and you will have trouble keeping them on task.

● **Assign enough work.** If students finish a task, there should be another waiting for them. For example, students who sit around after a test waiting for others to finish before going on to the next activity are obviously wasting time. Always make sure that your students know what they are supposed to do after they finish their current assignment.

> Having downtime in class is just asking for behavior problems. If they are busy with interesting work, they'll be more inclined to stay on task.
>
> *Megan Kelly, first-year teacher*

Raise Your Students' Awareness of Class Time

You are not the only person in your class who is concerned about how your students spend their time. Your students are, too. They want to spend their days successfully doing the work that you ask them to do—and to have fun while doing it.

When you have to deal with a series of petty forms of misbehavior, it is easy to forget that your students want to do well in school and that they want to spend their time doing interesting and useful work. You can take this natural interest and use it to help your students learn to become efficient at their classroom tasks. Obviously, you cannot manage this feat by yourself; it makes sense to enlist the support of the people you are trying to help.

A good way to make your students aware of how they spend their time is to discuss it with them. When students see that you are not just nagging them or rushing them through their work, they will be more willing to work well with you. Discuss the benefits they enjoy when they use class time well.

Teach your students key word signals, such as "Focus" or "Concentrate," so that they know exactly what to do when they hear you say these words. Make concentration an expected behavior in your classroom so that students will be aware when they are not as attentive as they should be. Offer to teach your students study skills and show them how to achieve good grades without having to spend hours on their work.

Display constant reminders of the importance of using time well. Use some of the study tips from Section Eleven to create banners and posters that address the issue. You can also use your own tips, ask students to share their tips, or find quotations about time management that can serve to raise your students' awareness of the importance of using class time wisely.

How to Handle Interruptions

Many teachers feel frustrated when their carefully planned lesson is interrupted by a fire drill, a class visitor, or even too many students who need to sharpen their pencil. Interruptions destroy instructional time not just because they distract you but also because they tend to distract every student in the class. The best defense you have against losing instructional time to interruptions is delivering an interesting lesson. Students who are fully engaged in meaningful and interesting work would rather stay on task than pay attention to yet another classmate sharpening a pencil. You can minimize the negative effects of interruptions by meeting three goals:

Goal One: Prevent as many interruptions as you can. Some teachers find that putting a sign such as "Learning in Progress—Please Do Not Disturb" on the door serves as a gentle reminder to those visitors whose business may not be urgent. Others work with colleagues whose classrooms are nearby so that one teacher does not schedule a noisy class activity on the same day that another has planned a test or other quiet activity. Still others have talked with their principal about poorly timed intercom announcements. Work with your colleagues in a similar fashion to solve problems when you can.

Goal Two: Minimize the disruption caused by an interruption. Although you can prevent many interruptions during your school day, some are unavoidable. For example, you cannot prevent the interruption caused by a message from the office requesting a student for an early dismissal. In such situations, your goal must be to keep the other students on task. If you remind yourself that your goal is to minimize the disturbance, you are likely to create a solution to the problem.

Goal Three: Prepare for predictable interruptions. Having a plan in place for unavoidable, predictable interruptions will give you confidence, and your students will behave better because you will know what to do in almost any situation. When you make plans for predictable interruptions, keep the solutions simple so that your students will be able to respond appropriately when interruptions occur. Here is a list of some of the predictable interruptions that teachers have to handle successfully. Use it to plan how you will manage each one.

- A student has no paper, and no pencil or pen.
- Students ask to leave the class to use the restroom, see the nurse, or go to their locker.
- Students need to listen to intercom announcements.
- A visitor asks to speak with you.
- A computer doesn't work properly.
- Students leave class early or arrive late.
- The class needs to rearrange desks for group work.
- Students need to sharpen pencils, staple papers, or dispose of trash.
- A student from another class asks to speak with one of your students.
- There is a commotion in the hallway or another classroom.

Pacing Instruction

Pacing instruction is the art of making sure that you assign just the right amount of meaningful work to keep students engaged in learning activities all class long. Developing the skills needed to be effective at pacing instruction correctly requires that you know your students and your subject matter, and that you also pay close attention to the speed at which students are expected to accomplish their work. Pacing instruction well is not a skill that is easy to master because the dramatic variations in students' readiness levels, preferred learning styles, processing speeds, and work habits make it difficult to design assignments that all students will finish at the same time.

Although pacing instruction for maximum learning is a skill that usually requires a great deal of experience to master, the guidelines that follow can make it easier for you to design instruction that will keep students engaged in learning for the entire class period.

- Provide plenty of assistance early on as assignments progress so that those students who need help completing assignments do not fall behind other students.
- Use a mixture of whole-group, small-group, and individual instruction to manage the pace of assignments.
- Consider providing high-interest enrichment and remedial activities for students to work on when they complete their basic assignments. Offering attractive optional assignments will engage students constructively.

- Post a list of activities for students who finish their work early. Suggested activities might include starting homework early, working at a learning center, playing online games for review, reading a library book, working with another student on an extra project, or organizing notebooks.

- Provide directions in the form of checklists for students to follow as they complete their work so that they know how to plan for themselves how to accomplish their assignments.

- Always have the next assignment ready for those students who complete their assignments early. Allowing students who finish other work early to begin their homework in class is a reasonable use of their time if they know how to complete the work.

> My goal is to get my students' brains working as soon as the bell rings. When I plan, my goal is to create a learning environment that touches on as many of the five senses as possible. My classes involve listening, speaking, and, most important, DOING.
>
> *Kathleen Stankiewicz, 10 years' experience*

The First Ten Minutes of Class

Teachers often overlook the potential power of the opening minutes of class. They watch as students drift into class, visit with their friends, and leisurely rummage around to find last night's homework. After finding their materials, students are frequently content to just sit and wait to be told what to do. Often, if they are quiet enough and if there are many pressing demands on a teacher's time at that moment, more than ten minutes can vanish before class starts. It's no wonder that students are tardy to class; they have little reason to be on time.

You can use the first ten minutes to get your class off to a great start, or you can choose to waste this time. The first minutes set the tone for the rest of the class. If you are prepared for class and have taught your students an opening routine, they can use this brief time to make mental and emotional transitions from the last class or subject and prepare to focus on learning new material.

You should establish a comfortable and predictable routine for the opening of class. Here is a simple opening routine that many teachers follow and that you can adapt to meet the needs of your class:

Step One: Greet each student as he or she enters the class. You can hand out any papers you need to distribute at this time. You can also answer questions, collect attendance notes, and check the emotional states of your students. Your students will appreciate that you care enough to stand at the door to greet them.

Step Two: Have students go immediately to their respective seats. You will avoid many problems if you strictly enforce this part of the routine. Students who wander around the room while you are busy at the door can cause problems that will last throughout class. Furthermore, students will often carry problems from earlier in the day to your room. By insisting that your students take a seat right away, you will help focus their energy on your class and on learning.

Step Three: Have students check the board for a predictable organizing exercise. The organizing exercise gives them time to settle down, organize their materials, and shift mental gears to what is going to happen in class. Your message on the board might include directions such as these:

Today's Tasks

1. Open your textbook to page 23.
2. Please get out a pen and paper.
3. Copy tonight's homework assignment into your planner.
4. Place last night's homework on your desk.
5. Read the objectives for today's classwork.

Step Four: Have students complete an introductory or warm-up activity. The activity should arouse curiosity and relate the day's new learning to previous knowledge. It should be interesting yet simple enough for students to complete independently. The activity will thus increase their confidence, so that they are even more interested in the day's lesson.

Use your creativity to design activities that your students will enjoy as they look forward to the day's lesson. For example, ask students to do one of the following activities or modify one to suit your students' needs. Students can

- Complete a storyboard of a process or series of events. A good source for this is Education World (www.educationworld.com). On the home page, use "storyboard" as a search term to be directed to storyboard templates.
- Work with classmates to combine puzzle pieces containing information about the material being studied.
- Complete a word-sorting activity. There are thousands of online sites containing various levels of vocabulary words to sort. Just use "word sorts" as a search term in your browser.
- Survey classmates to gather reactions to a quotation related to the unit of study.
- Read and teach a set of directions to classmates.
- Complete a graphic organizer. A site with many easy-to-use organizers is maintained by Education Oasis. (www.educationoasis.com/curriculum/graphic_organizers.htm).
- Participate in energizers, such as a ball toss game or racing the clock.
- Display their homework for classmates to evaluate with colored dots. (See Section Eleven for more ideas on how to use colored dots.)
- Work with classmates to skim the day's reading and make group predictions.

- Relate a photo or series of photos to their current lesson.

- Listen to lively music associated with the lesson. A good site to explore the various types of music you can use for this purpose is Free Play Music (http://freeplaymusic.com).

- Create electronic flash cards of key facts.

- Work with a partner to solve a problem related to the lesson.

- Respond to an intriguing, open-ended question.

- Make a one-minute presentation on a topic that interests the entire class.

- Work with classmates to share ideas about their homework or previous learning.

- Use "screen beans" to illustrate a concept or event. These computer stick figures can be found by using the search term "screen beans" at Microsoft's site for its Office products. (http://office.microsoft.com).

- Select two or three objects from a box containing many items and then predict how they will relate to the lesson.

- Open class with a review game of their own devising.

- Play a timed PowerPoint game. An excellent source for a variety of free games is a site maintained by Jefferson County Schools in Dandridge, Tennessee (http://jc-schools.net/ppt-teachers.html).

- Write a rhyme to help recall information.

- List what they already know about the day's lesson.

- Skim the day's reading materials and predict what they will learn.

- Create or study flash cards with a partner.

- Solve a brainteaser. Brain Bashers (www.brainbashers.com) is an excellent site to search for brainteasers. Managed by British mathematician Kevin Stone, it features thousands of games, riddles, puzzles, and illusions.

- List three reasons to study the day's topic.

- Read a news article and summarize the information in it. To find articles in eighty languages from all over the world, try searching the leader in online news: World News (http://wn.com).

- With another student, combine information from their notes.

- Watch a video clip and write about it. You can find thousands of short audio or video versions of historical events as well as clips from movies and television broadcasts at American Rhetoric (www.americanrhetoric.com).

- Brainstorm ideas with a partner about an assignment.

- Label or draw a map. A helpful Internet source for free maps of all types and interactive activities to go along with them is Maps.com (www.maps.com).

As you can see, there are countless ways to open class with a predictable routine that your students will enjoy. Use Teacher Worksheet 6.2 as a template to make interesting and beneficial plans for the start of each class.

TEACHER WORKSHEET 6.2

Plans for Starting Class Effectively

With just a bit of careful planning you can make the opening minutes of your class a productive time that sets a positive tone. Use this worksheet to ensure that the first few minutes of class are ones that you and your students will find useful.

Lesson topic: _____ Date: _____

Handouts to be distributed:

_____

_____

_____

_____

Routine procedures posted:

_____

_____

_____

_____

Day's agenda for students:

_____

_____

_____

_____

Activity to open class:

Purpose: _____

_____

_____

Materials needed: _____

_____

_____

Time needed: _____

Activity procedure:

_____

_____

_____

_____

_____

_____

From *The First-Year Teacher's Survival Guide, 3ʳᵈ Edition*, by Julia G. Thompson. Copyright © 2013 by John Wiley & Sons, Inc. Reproduced by permission.

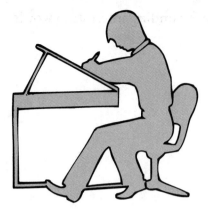

The best way to control class time is to get a timer that has a magnet. You can put the timer on your whiteboard or chalkboard. When students are doing practice activities, I set the timer to keep students responsible for working within the limit I have set. If you do not set time limits, students will spend most of their time off task and only work hard at the very end.

Erin Sager, 8 years' experience

Productive Transitions

Because your students are accustomed to the fast-paced action of modern life, they may lose interest in a lesson that seems to last too long. Experienced teachers create a positive learning environment by designing lessons around several brief activities. Although having several activities is sensible, it requires transitions that encourage students to be productive between activities.

Transitions are difficult to manage well because they require students to do three things in a very brief amount of time: mentally close out one task, prepare for the next one, and refocus their mental energy on a new topic. Fortunately, a wise first-year teacher can do several things to help students handle transitions effectively:

Design activities that flow naturally from one to the next, requiring a minimum of large-group instruction from you. Sequencing instruction in this way encourages students to manage their own learning.

Try using a kitchen timer to set a time limit for a change in activities. When students know that they have only a minute or two to switch from one activity to another, they are more likely to move quickly. You can also use an electronic timer and an interactive whiteboard. A good source for a kitchen timer is TimeMe (www.timeme.com).

Make transitions productive by providing your students with activities that will convert useless waiting time into learning opportunities. Using small blocks of time to engage your students in active thinking and learning can be enjoyable for both you and your students.

Such small activities, called *sponges* because they soak up class time that could be lost, can add interest and new information to a lesson. These activities are brief, but their impact on productivity in your classroom can be significant. You can use these activities as they are, or you can adapt, adjust, or add information to them to create others that will keep your students involved in productive learning throughout class. Ask students to

- Justify the rules for _____.
- Apply the information in the lesson to a real-life situation.
- Defend a position.

- Write the definition of an unusual word. A useful site for finding interesting words is Word Dynamo (http://dynamo.dictionary.com).
- Match words and meanings.
- Unscramble vocabulary words.
- Create a to-do list for a project or other activity.
- Explain the correct procedure for _____.
- Complete a word sort.
- Modify a procedure so that it is more efficient.
- Modify a tool so that it is more efficient.
- Explain what they learned in the lesson.
- Read a brief newspaper article and respond to it.
- Create a time line of _____.
- Explain what to do in an emergency involving _____.
- Create a brief outline of _____.
- Fill in the blanks in a brief outline.
- Brainstorm as many _____ as they can.
- Read a brief Internet article and respond to it.
- Put a series of events in chronological order.
- Read an online shopping catalogue to find _____.
- Practice the process of elimination on the answers to some sample standardized test questions.
- Paraphrase information.
- Respond to a political cartoon. You can choose from among hundreds of cartoons at Political Cartoons hosted by Slate Magazine (www.politicalcartoons.com).
- Respond to a humorous cartoon. A good source of cartoons appropriate for students is Today's Cartoon by Randy Glasbergen (www.glasbergen.com).
- Respond to a picture. You can search the millions of images at Google Images online.
- Respond to an advertisement.
- Review information with a partner.
- List important facts from the last few days of class.
- Explain why the day's lesson is useful.
- Recall facts from the last lesson.
- Predict the outcome of a story.
- Predict an outcome that can be inferred from information in the chapter under study.
- Explain why it is important to use time wisely.

- Use two of the key terms from the lesson in a sentence.
- Answer trivia questions related to the lesson.
- Find places on a map.
- Draw a map.
- Color a map.
- Write a key term on a scrap of paper and pass that scrap to a classmate, who has to explain it.
- Circle or highlight keywords in their notes or reading.
- Play a game of hangman to review vocabulary words. An excellent site for online hangman games is maintained by Oxford Dictionaries (http://oxforddictionaries .com/words/hangman).
- Make quick flash cards to review vocabulary.
- Proofread a paragraph containing many grammatical errors.
- Proofread a paragraph containing many factual errors.
- Read the opening paragraphs from an assigned reading and tell a partner what they learned from the reading.
- Brainstorm a list of keywords from the lesson.
- Offer solutions to a variety of problems.
- Create a mnemonic.
- Brainstorm a list of ten important concepts from the lesson.
- Brainstorm a list of ideas for a creative project based on the lesson.
- Explain the day's objectives.
- Explain a study skill.
- Brainstorm the causes of a current event.
- Brainstorm the effects of a current event.
- Summarize the lesson orally with a partner.
- Describe an object in the room in twenty-five words.
- Draw a concept from the lesson.
- Use stick figures to draw idioms.
- Make up a true-or-false quiz on the lesson.
- Take a true-or-false quiz on the lesson.
- Time a classmate as he or she reviews the main points of the lesson.
- Scan the text to find _____.
- Complete a logic puzzle or brainteaser.
- Copy and define the word of the day.
- Read a newspaper article and respond to it.

- Go to a learning center and _____.
- Complete analogies. You can find many free online analogy practice sites. A very good one is Analogix—a part of the online game site BrainCurls (www .braincurls.com).
- Put words in alphabetical order.
- Explain what they learned in another class that they can use now.
- Explain what they learned in this class that they can use in another class.
- Classify groups of words.
- State the reasons for _____.
- Create a brief word search puzzle for a classmate to solve tomorrow.
- Create test questions (with answers).
- Create relationships among the vocabulary terms in the lesson.
- Practice math problems.
- Drill a friend in math facts.
- Complete a math word problem.
- Make up a math word problem.
- Make up math problems for review.
- Quiz themselves on the words on a word wall.
- Brainstorm a list of the similarities between themselves and the people mentioned in the lesson.
- Define some of the words on standardized tests that trouble students: *imply, infer,* and so on.
- Follow directions to create a simple origami figure.
- Brainstorm a list of people who epitomize such words as *politician, healer, explorer,* and so on.
- Follow specific directions to star, underline, or circle certain words in a passage.
- Create a cause-and-effect web about an event in the lesson.
- Make a Venn diagram illustrating a concept or a relationship in the lesson.
- Write about the meaning of a quotation.
- Write a question about the lesson they will study tomorrow.
- Find as many synonyms as they can for a word.
- Clean out their book bag.
- Clean out or organize their binder.
- Finish famous proverbs, such as "The early bird gets the _____."
- Decide how and when they will complete their homework assignment.
- Find three dissimilar objects and describe what they have in common.
- Explain a favorite line from a song.

How to Handle Requests to Leave the Classroom

"Can I go to the restroom?" "Can I go to my locker?" "Can I take this lunch money to my brother?" Sometimes it may seem as if you are the only person who does not want to leave the room.

Learning how to manage student requests to leave class will save you lots of time and trouble. The time you spend in planning how to cope successfully with these requests will be rewarded when students develop the self-discipline to manage such requests themselves.

In handling student requests to leave class, you first need to determine whether students are being truthful about why they need to leave class. If your hall pass has places for the signatures of other professionals, such as the nurse or the media specialist, check the signature when students return to ensure that they went where they told you they needed to go.

Where do your students want to go when they leave your class? Here is a list of some of the places to which students at all levels of schooling ask to go when they leave class, along with suggestions for how to effectively handle each type of request:

- **The media center.** You can allow students to go to the media center, because they will have adult supervision there. If you are sending more than one or two students, you should check with the librarian first. Make sure that your students have a specific task there and that they know when you expect them to return.

- **The clinic.** You can also send students to the school nurse's office without worry, because there is adult supervision there. If a student asks to go to the clinic too often, check with the nurse to see whether the requests are genuine. If a student is gone too long, make sure that you check to see whether there is a problem. Also, if a student is obviously ill, consider sending another student along to assist the ill child.

- **Another classroom.** Sometimes a student will ask to go to another teacher's class; for example, cheerleaders may want to make posters for the big game, or drama students may want to rehearse. These requests should not come from students. Speak to the other teacher before you send students to another class. You should also refuse to be pressured into letting students leave if you do not believe that they can make up the work they will miss in your class.

- **Their locker.** If you have a bank of shared supplies for students to use, and if you allow students to turn in any assignments they have left in their locker immediately after class without a penalty, you will eliminate some requests. You can determine the validity of other requests on a case-by-case basis. At times, you can allow students to go to their locker, but you must also avoid giving the impression that students can use such requests whenever they feel like taking a little break from class.

- **The parking lot or their car.** Never send a student out of the building without checking with an administrator first. If a student has something that needs to be turned in during class, offer to accept it after school with no penalty rather than send a student to the parking lot.

- **The guidance office or student services.** Before you send a student to speak with a counselor, make sure that a counselor will be able to see the student. Students have been known to wait patiently for a counselor for hours rather than attend class.

- **The office.** If a student asks to see an administrator, make sure that the administrator is available and willing to see the student before you honor the request.

- **To see another student.** Sometimes, in the middle of your class, students will remember that they have the lunch money for their sibling or a note excusing a younger family member's tardiness. Do not allow students to leave your class to attend to this nonemergency business. Instead, allow students to take care of it between classes or during a break.

- **Water fountain.** Unless a student is coughing or obviously in need of a drink of water, say no. Students use this request as a way to stretch their legs and break up a monotonous class. Make sure that you design your class so that you break up the monotony caused by sitting too long and that you encourage students to stretch their legs at appropriate intervals. Even older students periodically need a wiggle break.

- **The restroom.** You should never refuse a student's request to use the restroom. If you do and the student is ill, you may make the situation worse. Instead of refusing outright, you can say, "Have you finished your work? Can you please wait a few minutes?" If the student insists, then honor the request.

GUIDELINES FOR HANDLING STUDENT REQUESTS TO LEAVE THE CLASSROOM

Making good decisions about whether or not to allow a student to leave the classroom is not always easy, no matter how much teaching experience you have. Consider the following guidelines as you begin to formulate your policy on leaving class:

- Do not allow more than one or two students to leave at one time.

- Do not refuse to allow students to go to the restroom or to the clinic. Use your best judgment about other requests.

- If a student seems to be making too many requests to leave the classroom, speak privately with him or her about the problem. If this does not work, call a parent or guardian. If there is a problem, the parent or guardian can apprise you of it. If there is not a problem, enlist that person's help in keeping the student focused and in class. Often, just knowing that you take the problem seriously enough to call their home will convince students to make fewer requests.

- Prevent too many requests to leave the room by presenting fast-paced and interesting lessons that keep your students so engaged that they will not want to miss anything exciting.

- When you send students out of the room, make sure whenever possible that an adult will supervise them. You are responsible for your students until that responsibility is assumed by another adult.

- Never allow students to leave the building without contacting an administrator first. Older students may wish to retrieve items that they have left in their car, but school parking lots can provide opportunities for violence and other misbehavior.

- Consider using laminated passes for each student. At the beginning of the year, you can photograph students and then use the photographs to make individual hall passes. Individual hall passes are particularly useful because they allow hall duty supervisors to quickly identify students who are not in class.

- When it is necessary, refuse requests in a polite but firm manner. Instead of brusquely refusing, try one of these phrases:
  - Can you wait a few minutes?
  - Have you finished your work?
  - Let me check to see whether _____ is in the _____ office.
  - Can you do that right after class?

Sample 6.1
Hall Pass

Student name: _____ Date: _____

Time out: _____ Time returned: _____

_____ Restroom

_____ Guidance office

_____ Locker

_____ Clinic

_____ Media center

_____ Water fountain

_____ Principal's office

_____ Classroom

_____ Other: _____

Teacher signature: _____

HOW TO ESTABLISH A FAIR POLICY FOR STUDENTS TO LEAVE THE ROOM

You will need to establish and enforce a fair policy about leaving the classroom. Ask your mentor or a colleague whether there is a school policy or how other teachers handle this matter. If there is no formal school policy, consider these issues when creating your own policy:

- How often is it acceptable for a student to leave your class during a grading period?
- Where will you allow students to go without first consulting another adult?
- How can students ask permission so that the interruption is minimal?
- How will you maintain records of which students have left your class?
- Where will students sign out?
- When students return to class, where will they put their hall pass for you to keep?
- How will you enforce your policy? What consequences will your students face if they do not comply?

KEEPING TRACK OF STUDENTS WHO LEAVE THE CLASSROOM

Because you will need to keep track of students who are out of your class, you should have a sign-out sheet as well as hall passes. A sign-out sheet can take many forms. You can post a sheet for students to fill out as they leave, have them sign out on a computer, or maintain a class logbook. If you are fortunate enough to teach in a school that is very small or peaceful, a generic hall pass may be acceptable. If you don't use a generic hall pass, your school probably has a hall pass form for you to use. You will need to keep plenty of these forms on hand.

Having a sign-out sheet, such as the one in Teacher Worksheet 6.3, will make it easier for you to keep accurate records of when your students leave your class and where they go.

TEACHER WORKSHEET 6.3

Student Sign-Out Sheet

Name	Date	Destination	Time Out	Time Returned

> Keep students engaged. If students are allowed free time, they will often abuse it and get out of hand. If you have even a few minutes at the end of class, allow the kids to pack up and spend those few minutes reviewing vocabulary, spelling, or content orally.
>
> *Charlene Herrala, 31 years' experience*

The Last Ten Minutes of Class

You have two goals for the end of class: to have students who are reluctant to leave and to have students retain the information you have just taught them. The last ten minutes of class are the ideal time to accomplish both goals.

The routine you create for the end of class should be predictable, but also one that students can look forward to. Here is a simple two-step plan for the end of class that you can follow to make sure that the last few minutes of your class are as productive as all the rest.

Step One: Do an eight-minute closing exercise. Use this brief period to help students retain information by reviewing what you have just taught and by looking ahead to what students will be learning next. Here are some activities that you can adopt or adapt to end your class on a positive note:

- Have students individually list several things that they have just learned. Have them share this list with a classmate or with the entire group.
- Ask students to predict what they will learn next.
- Ask students to predict the meaning of the key terms for the next part of the unit.
- Have students write a quick explanation of the most interesting aspect of the day's lesson.
- Hold a quick review, vocabulary practice, or spelling bee.
- Ask students to explain the directions for their homework. Be sure to ask them to estimate how long it should take them to complete the assignment successfully.
- Unveil a final thought for the day that you have hidden under a sheet of paper that was taped to the board earlier in the day.
- Give your students a brief text passage to read and ask them to comment on it.
- Show a relevant cartoon or illustration on the overhead projector.
- Assign an exit slip activity.

Step Two: Implement the two-minute dismissal. After the closing exercise, you should allow two minutes for your students to prepare to be dismissed at your signal. During this time, they should have a routine to follow that includes the following activities:

- Disposing of trash
- Stowing away books and materials
- Checking to make sure they don't leave anything behind

During the last two minutes of class, you should move to the door so that you can speak to students as they leave. This will prevent any last-minute misbehavior and show your students that they have a teacher who cares about them. You should not allow students to congregate at the door or jump up and bolt when the bell rings. Insist that you will dismiss class and that they should wait for your signal. You should not detain students after the bell has rung.

Plans for Ending Class Effectively

Lesson topic:_____ Date: _____

First Eight Minutes

Review activity:

_____

_____

_____

_____

Homework discussion and clarification:

_____

_____

_____

_____

Prediction activity:

_____

_____

_____

_____

Reflection on day's learning activity:

_____

_____

_____

_____

Last Two Minutes

Students clean their work area and gather their belongings to prepare to exit. Students exit on a dismissal signal from you.

From *The First-Year Teacher's Survival Guide, 3rd Edition*, by Julia G. Thompson. Copyright © 2013 by John Wiley & Sons, Inc. Reproduced by permission.

> Do not let the end of your class block disintegrate into a "do your homework" half hour. In doing so, you will have forfeited a significant amount of your instructional time.
>
> *Luann Scott, 37 years' experience*

How to Use Any Time Left at the End of Class

Sometimes, despite your best efforts, there may be an awkward three to five minutes left at the end of class. This can happen naturally when students unexpectedly finish up the end-of-class exercises early. Although many teachers may be tempted to allow students to just sit and wait for the bell to signal the end of class, you should consider how you and your students can benefit from these tiny gifts of free time. With just a bit of preparation and planning, you can use even these short moments to connect with your students. In addition to using any of the sponge activities mentioned earlier in this section, here are some ideas for you to consider:

- Show a short story from an inspirational segment on TeacherTube (http://teachertube.com) or YouTube. (www.youtube.com).
- Keep a list of riddles or jokes to read so that your students can leave class smiling. A good source for this is Riddles.com (www.riddles.com).
- Conduct a quick informal survey. Ask students their opinions about school events, sports, songs, or just about anything that they are interested in outside of school.
- Ask students each to state something new that they have learned during the class or the week.
- Ask students to share their favorites—favorite colors, foods, music, sports teams, _____.
- Ask students to share their pet peeves.
- Ask students their opinion about a class problem.
- Read a biographical paragraph or story to inspire your students.
- Ask students to tell you something that surprised or confused them on the first day of school or when they were younger.

Best Practices Checklist

1. Make a point of using your students' class time wisely. You have control over how well your students use the time allotted for your class.

2. Create routines and procedures for daily class activities so that students can become self-disciplined at managing their use of time.

3. Make plans so that you can minimize the time lost to various predictable interruptions, such fire drills or intercom announcements.

4. Pace instruction so that students always have meaningful work to do. No student should wait idly for others to finish working.

5. Stand at your door at the beginning of each class to greet students and help them settle down to work right away.

6. Use a variety of activities during transition times to engage student interest and enhance student learning.

7. Plan ahead so that the beginning and end of class are productive periods for your students.

8. Make plans to manage student requests to leave the classroom.

9. Be sure to keep track of students once they have left your class.

10. If you have any free time at the end of class, use it productively instead of just letting students sit.

Time to Reflect
Control Class Time

Use the information in this section to guide your thinking as you reflect on these questions. They are designed to encourage you to think more deeply about the issues in the text or to discuss those issues with colleagues.

1. Discuss the ways that teachers unintentionally waste their students' time. What can you do to avoid misuse of instructional time?

2. What does the expression *door-to-door* mean when applied to class time management? How do your colleagues use their door-to-door time? What have you observed other teachers doing that made class time more productive?

3. What is your policy concerning students' leaving the room? What is your school's policy? If you had to adjust your school's policy, what would you change?

4. Which of the warm-up activities in this section would work well with your students? Brainstorm other activities you can use to relate new learning to your students' previous learning.

5. The beginning and end of class are times you can use to your students' advantage. What routines do you have planned to open and close class on a positive and productive note?

SECTION SEVEN

Manage Your Classroom

The most noticeable characteristic of a well-managed classroom is almost tangible: the students know what to do. They are confident, comfortable, and, most of all, focused on learning. Students in a classroom in which their teacher has made prudent management decisions on their behalf are aware and accepting of the high expectations that their teacher has for the daily operation of the class.

The practical affairs of the well-managed classroom are accomplished with almost effortless ease, such that the real business of the class, the mastery of skills and the acquisition of knowledge in the mandated curriculum, are the focus instead of crowd control or the antics of disruptive students.

A Well-Managed Classroom

A well-managed classroom does not happen by accident. Instead, it is the result of a series of deliberate choices made by a teacher who cares for students, is consistent, is fair minded in the way he or she deals with all students, and has the imagination to predict student behavior.

In a well-managed classroom, students operate within a reassuring framework. A well-managed classroom is one in which their teacher has put a systematic arrangement of complementary policies, procedures, and rules into place so that students can manage their daily tasks with ease and comfort. To learn more about the practical aspects of a well-managed classroom, try some of these resources:

- **National Education Association (www.nea.org).** Use "classroom management" as a search term to access helpful articles about how to manage a classroom successfully.
- **TeacherVision (www.teachervision.fen.com).** Use "classroom management" as a search term to find dozens of articles and other useful resources.

- Teaching Channel (www.teachingchannel.org). Again, use "classroom management" as a search term to find dozens of videos to help you make sound management decisions.

How to Focus Your Class on Good Behavior

When students behave cooperatively and stay focused on their work, the classroom just hums with a flow of positive energy. Lessons are learned, students are self-disciplined, and your own workday is a successful one. To get your students on the right track and then keep them there, combine a variety of strategies with a consistent emphasis on good behavior. In the list that follows, you will find strategies that can help your students focus on good behavior.

- Make it easy for students to know what is expected of them by having clearly expressed class policies, rules, and procedures. Students who know what to do are far less likely to misbehave than students who are not sure of expectations or boundaries.

- Increase student willingness by enlisting cooperation from your students rather than demanding it. For example, try asking, "Could you please help put the scissors away?" instead of sternly telling students to quit playing around with the scissors.

- Periodically stop and ask questions designed to make students think about what they are doing correctly. For example, "What is everyone doing well right now?" "What made this assignment successful?" and "Why do you think class went so well today?" are questions that will focus attention on the positive things that happened in class and encourage students to continue their good behavior.

- Be liberal in your use of the positive labels you have created for your class. (See Section Four for a list of positive labels.)

- Don't leave time for misbehavior. Often students misbehave because they have nothing better to do. Keep your students too busy to be anything but focused on good behavior.

- Praise good behavior more than you fuss about poor behavior.

- Be pleasantly matter of fact about your expectation of good behavior. Act surprised at behavior that is less than excellent to make sure that students know what the norm should be. Expect good behavior and it is likely that you will receive it.

- Make a graphic display of the positive behaviors in your class. Even something as simple as hash marks on the board for every right answer in a review can help students know what to do.

- Consider offering small tangible rewards for the first few students who do something correctly—the first three in their seat and working when the bell rings, for example.

- Have students create a class motto that is affirmative and success oriented. Harness the power inherent in the chanting of even a simple motto, such as "We are smart.

We are hardworking. We are successful." To find other affirmations that can help your students focus on good behavior, try the site TeachersNetwork (www. teachersnetwork.org), using "affirmations" as a search term.

The Importance of Clear Expectations

Although it may seem obvious that we should make our expectations for good behavior known to our students, it is often easy to overlook this task in the press of the other responsibilities we have to manage. Making our expectations for classroom behavior clear to our students is a vital component of a successfully managed classroom, however.

The same techniques that make it easy for our students to understand our expectations for academic success can be applied to their classroom behavior. Students need to have a clear idea of what success should look like so they know how to attain it for themselves. Some easy-to-implement suggestions for making your behavior expectations clear to your students can include these:

- Try modeling the good behavior that you want from your students. Have students practice it after you have modeled it for them. You can also try modeling the behaviors that you do not want to see from your students so they know what not to do.

- Make visual displays of reminders about how you want students to behave. Photographs, posters, and bulletin board displays are all effective ways to manage this.

- Show a brief video of students performing an expected behavior correctly so that others may see how to do it for themselves.

- Create a pithy scrapbook of illustrated good behaviors for students to flip through or even add to from time to time.

- Create charts of "What to Do and What Not to Do" behaviors so students can see that they can choose to do well instead of making a mistake.

- Leave time for students to seek clarification about expected behaviors. Ask students to restate your behavior expectations in their own words so you can be sure that everyone knows them.

> I set very high standards for my students, and I don't hesitate to let them know if they are not reaching the goals I have set for them. I feel like students need to know that you are anticipating that they will succeed, even if they don't expect it of themselves.
>
> *Melinda Conner, first-year teacher*

Procedures, Policies, Rules: When to Apply Each One

Using a combination of sensible policies, procedures, and rules to run the daily business of your classroom will create a safety net that allows students to function well because they will know what to do and how to do it properly.

Although all three elements of a classroom management system should work together, each differs from the others in significant ways. Classroom policies differ from procedures in that policies cover a wide range of expectations, whereas procedures are more action oriented. Policies differ from rules in that rules govern very broad aspects of student behavior, whereas policies cover specific topics.

For example, you may have a policy that states that students who have forgotten their materials for the day may borrow from the shared materials bank. A procedure that could apply to that same situation is that students are expected to borrow supplies at the start of class and return any unused ones at the end of class. A rule that could apply to this situation would be "Be prepared for class each day."

Policies You Will Need to Develop

Before you can develop a set of policies for your own classroom, you should first consult the policies of your school district, the policies of your school in general, and those policies that the other members of a grade-level or content area team to which you may belong already have in place. By paying attention to these broader policies, you will find it easier to develop policies that can serve as guidelines for your students to follow.

For example, your grade-level committee may have a policy that allows students who do not show mastery on an assessment to retake it. Your classroom policy could be that students can retake assessments during daily study periods. Because policies will differ from classroom to classroom, it is important that you make it easy for your students to know what your policies are. Some of the areas for which you may need to design policies include these:

- Students who need extra help
- Classroom cell phone use
- Food in the classroom
- Missing work
- Cheating
- Class discussions
- Tardiness
- Late or missing homework
- Appropriate homework help
- Conflicts with classmates
- Technology use
- Grading
- Forgotten materials
- Interactive technology responses

You may want to use Worksheet 7.1 to plan for various policies you will need to develop for your classroom.

TEACHER WORKSHEET 7.1

Planning for Classroom Policies

Use this worksheet to record your research and brainstorms as well as your final policies on some of areas in which a developed policy is most commonly needed. As you complete this worksheet, consider the policies of your district or school as well as those of your grade or subject area committees or teams when planning for your own classroom policies.

Students Who Need Extra Help

District or school policy:

_____

Committee input:

_____

Classroom policy:

_____

_____

Classroom Cell Phone Use

District or school policy:

_____

Committee input:

_____

Classroom policy:

_____

_____

Food in the Classroom

District or school policy:

_____

Committee input:

_____

Classroom policy:

_____

_____

(continued on next page)

(continued from previous page)

Missing Work

District or school policy:

_____

Committee input:

_____

Classroom policy:

_____

_____

Cheating

District or school policy:

_____

Committee input:

_____

Classroom policy:

_____

_____

Class Discussions

District or school policy:

_____

Committee input:

_____

Classroom policy:

_____

_____

Tardiness

District or school policy:

_____

Committee input:

_____

Classroom policy:

_____

_____

Late or Missing Homework

District or school policy:

_____

Committee input:

_____

Classroom policy:

_____

_____

Appropriate Homework Help

District or school policy:

_____

Committee input:

_____

Classroom policy:

_____

_____

Conflicts with Classmates

District or school policy:

_____

Committee input:

_____

Classroom policy:

_____

_____

(continued on next page)

(continued from previous page)

Technology Use

District or school policy:

_____

Committee input:

_____

Classroom policy:

_____

_____

Grading

District or school policy:

_____

Committee input:

_____

Classroom policy:

_____

_____

Forgotten Materials

District or school policy:

_____

Committee input:

_____

Classroom policy:

_____

_____

Interactive Technology Responses

District or school policy:

_____

Committee input:

_____

Classroom policy:

_____

_____

Establish Procedures

All students share some characteristics in common; one of the most significant is the need for structured time. From energetic kindergartners to sophisticated seniors, students need routines or recurring procedures in their school day to keep them on track.

The particulars of these procedures will vary from teacher to teacher and from grade level to grade level, but adhering to specific business procedures for the classroom will give teachers and students the best chance to achieve successful and harmonious learning.

Before school begins, you should decide how to handle the classroom procedures you want your students to follow. If you have these in place before the first day of class, you will be rewarded with a positive classroom environment and successful students. Use Teacher Worksheet 7.2 to help you begin to formulate your class procedures.

From *The First-Year Teacher's Survival Guide, 3rd Edition*, by Julia G. Thompson. Copyright © 2013 by John Wiley & Sons, Inc. Reproduced by permission.

TEACHER WORKSHEET 7.2

Where to Find Help with Establishing Procedures

Following are some of the basic, essential classroom areas many teachers have to manage that require carefully planned procedures. To determine the best course of action to take for each item, will you need to talk with a mentor? Consult members of one of the school communities you belong to? Brainstorm your own ideas? In the blank beside each item, indicate where you can find information about each one.

Beginning class: _____

Ending class: _____

Being tardy to class: _____

Making up work when absent: _____

Handing in work: _____

Using cell phones: _____

Keeping the work area clean: _____

Formatting written work: _____

Using the classroom library: _____

Finishing work early: _____

Pledging allegiance to the flag: _____

Listening to intercom announcements: _____

Being a classroom helper: _____

Lining up: _____

Going to the clinic: _____

Using a computer: _____

Asking questions: _____

Handling emergencies: _____

Managing restroom breaks: _____

Having materials needed for class: _____

Making up missing or late work: _____

Sharpening pencils: _____

Assigning homework: _____

Turning in money: _____

Taking attendance: _____

Taking lunch counts: _____

Coming to attention: _____

Taking tests: _____

Sharing supplies: _____

Conducting fire and other drills: _____

Other procedures: _____

_____

_____

_____

Suggestions for Establishing Three Necessary Procedures

Although procedures will vary from classroom to classroom, there are some common situations that most teachers have to manage successfully. Three of these situations—sharing supplies, passing out papers, and giving directions at the start of class—are ones that you need to manage with carefully planned procedures so that your class can run smoothly from start to finish.

PROCEDURE ONE: SETTING UP A SHARED SUPPLIES BANK

Off-task behavior and discipline issues are just two of the things that can go wrong when students come to class unprepared. Keeping extra supplies will help you avoid many problems.

Try to have extra textbooks and other everyday classroom items, such as pencils and paper, on hand to lend to students if they forget theirs. You could consider assigning a responsible student to be in charge of issuing and collecting borrowed items. When you lend an item to a student, make sure that the student writes his or her name on the board or in another safe place so that you have a record of where the borrowed item is. If missing pens or pencils are a particular problem, set up a shared bank of supplies that students can borrow from. Here's how:

- **Step One:** Select one or two students to be in charge of the supplies bank.
- **Step Two:** Ask every student to donate a new pen or pencil.
- **Step Three:** Mark each pen and pencil with a number.
- **Step Four:** When a student needs to borrow a pen or pencil, have the students who are in charge of the bank record the number of the item and the name of the student who borrowed it.
- **Step Five:** Have the students who distribute the supplies also be the ones who remind the borrowers to return them at the end of class.

PROCEDURE TWO: PASSING OUT PAPERS AT THE START OF A LESSON

Even though it seems as though passing out papers would be a simple task, not having a plan for doing this efficiently can waste valuable class time. Creating procedures for passing out papers that will work for you and your students can not only save time but also reduce off-task behaviors that result when students are not sure of what to do.

Distributing Handouts

- **Scenario One:** At the start of class, either give students each a handout as you greet them when they enter the room or have the handouts for the day in a convenient area so that students can just pick them up on the way to their seat.

- **Scenario Two:** For younger students, place papers in individual folders. You can either have them each pick up their folder or place it on their desk before class.

Lost Papers

What to do if students have lost their papers? Keep a folder or bin of extra handouts so that students who have misplaced their handouts can simply pick up extras without further disruption.

Teamwork

When students are in groups, they can designate one team member to pick up papers for everyone in the group, thus reducing congestion and off-task traffic.

PROCEDURE THREE: GIVING DIRECTIONS AT THE START OF CLASS

Giving directions at the start of class is one of the most important parts of any school day. When students have directions that they can follow with ease, they can settle down to work quickly and remain on task. To make sure that this happens, take care to create a procedure for giving your students directions and then teach that procedure to your students.

- At the start of class, have written directions on the board in the same place each day so that your students know what is expected of them. Use numbered step-by-step directions to keep students on task. Word the information as simply as possible.
- For repeated tasks, such as copying homework into assignment books or placing homework on desks, follow the same sequence each day so that it becomes a routine for students.
- Check for understanding when you go over directions with your students. Often, in spite of our best efforts, what we think we are saying isn't what our students understand at all.
- Ask for clarification of the directions after students have had an opportunity to read and follow the posted ones and then listened to you as you went over them.
- Provide your students with a numbered checklist if the directions are complicated so that they can cross off each task as they complete it.

Teach and Enforce School Rules

You will prevent many discipline problems and create a positive classroom environment if you take the time to teach and enforce the rules that govern all students in your school. Consistent enforcement is especially important because some of the conflicts you will have with your students will arise from teachers' having inconsistently enforced rules in the past. Use the following guidelines to create a positive classroom environment:

- **Know the rules thoroughly.** To teach and enforce school rules successfully, you must be thoroughly familiar with them. Ask colleagues about rules that you are not sure how to enforce.
- **Follow the rules yourself.** Students are quick to point out hypocrisy. For example, a particularly sensitive area for many students is the dress code. You will find it very difficult to enforce the rules for student dress if you violate them yourself.
- **Take the time to teach school rules to your students.** One mistake that many teachers make is assuming that someone else will teach school rules to students. Even though the administrators at your school may have reviewed the rules with students, you should discuss them again during the first few weeks of school to make sure that everyone knows what to do. You will have to repeat the rules from time to time to ensure that students maintain a clear understanding.
- **Enforce school rules consistently.** If you have a serious reservation about a particular rule, you should speak with an administrator about it. No matter what you personally think about a school rule, however, you should enforce it. Students are quick to take advantage when teachers are not consistent in enforcement.

> I give students second chances. I think it is important to give students a chance to correct their mistakes and make a situation better.
>
> *Joshua Culver, first-year teacher*

Creating Classroom Rules

Class rules provide guidelines for acceptable behavior and protect your right to teach and your students' right to learn. Rules also send the message that good behavior is important and that you expect students to work productively. Although your students may earnestly try to convince you that rules are not necessary, they really do not want total freedom. Students of all ages benefit from the guidance that classroom rules provide in establishing a tone of mutual respect, trust, and cooperation. When creating rules for your classroom, you should follow three guidelines to ensure their success. Class rules should be

- Stated in positive terms
- General enough to cover a broad range of student activity
- Easy for students to remember

The rules you create for your classroom should be appropriate to the age and ability levels of your students. When you create a set of rules, you establish a common language for discussing your expectation of good behavior. Here is a step-by-step approach creating workable classroom rules:

Step One: Determine what areas your rules need to cover. Begin by asking yourself these questions:

- What are some behaviors that make it possible for students to succeed?
- What are some behaviors that make it difficult for students to succeed?
- What limits can I set to guarantee that all students can exercise their right to learn?

Step Two: Draft a rough set of rules. After you have determined the areas your rules should cover, write a rough draft. At this point, you may want to show your rules to a colleague to make sure they are in line with school rules and appropriate to the age and ability levels of your students.

Step Three: Word classroom rules positively. Take your rough draft and change the wording as needed to state all of your rules in positive terms, conveying a tone of mutual respect and consideration.

> My biggest challenge this year was learning to discipline my students. I wanted them all to like me, even the troublemakers. I would make a lot of threats and not follow through. If you say you are going to do something, do it. I have had to learn that even if you give students detentions or some other unpleasant consequences, they'll still like you at the end of the day.
>
> *Megan Kelly, first-year teacher*

Step Four: State rules in such a way that they are easy to remember. Can you combine any of your rules to cover a general range of student behavior? For example, you could combine "Bring your textbook every day" and "You will need paper and pens in this class" to read, "Bring the materials you will need for class." Your students will also find it easier to recall your class rules if you only have a few.

Many experienced teachers recommend having about five rules for middle school and secondary students. Reduce the number of rules for younger students. If you are not sure whether your classroom rules will work, here are some that experienced teachers have used successfully. Adapt them to meet the needs of your students.

- Use class time wisely.
- Do your work well.
- Treat other people with respect.
- Follow school rules.
- Bring your materials to class every day.

If you would like more information about creating class rules that will work well for your students, try visiting Education World (www.educationworld.com). On the home page, use "classroom rules" as a search term to yield dozens of articles and strategies for creating useful class rules for students at all grade levels.

Checklist to Determine If Your Rules Will Be Successful

Use this checklist to determine if the rules you have created for your class will be effective. Place a check mark before each statement that applies to your classroom rules. The more check marks you have, the more likely it is that your classroom rules will be successful.

To be effective, classroom rules must

1. _____ Be easy to remember
2. _____ Create an orderly classroom
3. _____ Fit within a school district's policies for student behavior
4. _____ Be stated so that students understand them
5. _____ Be enforceable
6. _____ Be as fair to as many students as possible
7. _____ Satisfy the parents and guardians of your students

Teaching Classroom Rules

In the rush to cover the academic material that your students need to learn, it is easy to overlook the importance of actually teaching the classroom rules you have created. A set of well-expressed rules is useless if your students do not know what they are.

You can help your students understand the importance of following rules by spending time teaching them how to behave correctly. Teaching appropriate behavior is not something you can complete in one class period; rather, it is a process that will last the entire year. It is better to spend a few minutes each day or week with minilessons on various aspects of your rules than to spend an hour early in the term and then ignore them afterward.

Students who know how to behave correctly will not lose time in bad behavior. Incorporate the strategies that follow, and the time you spend teaching the rules will save you precious instructional time later.

- Post a letter about your classroom rules on your class Web page or send a copy home with your students, thus enlisting the support of parents and guardians.

- Post a copy of your class rules in a prominent spot to serve as a quick reminder for everyone in the class.

- Although teaching classroom rules is a process that will last all term, focus on teaching them during the first three weeks of the term to let your students know that you are serious about creating a positive classroom climate. Revisiting the rules periodically will reinforce this early teaching.

- When you are ready to talk about rules with your students, don't try to bluff your way through a brief presentation. Instead, present your rules in a dynamic lesson. Try some of these activities to make the lesson interesting:
  - Have students create a Venn diagram comparing the rules that they have at school with the rules that adults have at work.
  - Place students in groups. Have some groups brainstorm reasons why everyone should follow various rules. Ask other groups to list what could happen if no one followed a rule.
  - Have students write the class rules in their notebook. Ask them to see whether they can improve the wording of a rule or whether they can create examples to explain each one.
  - Have students debate the positive and negative effects on the entire group when students follow or don't follow rules.
  - Ask students to explain the rules to you in their own words.
  - Divide students into groups and assign each group a rule to present in a skit.

- To determine whether you should reteach your rules, ask yourself the questions that follow for each one. If the answer to either one is "no," then you should allow time to reteach that classroom rule.

- Do all students understand the rule?
- Do students understand the rationale for this rule as well as its importance?

Enforcing Classroom Rules

Classroom rules empower teachers who want their students to understand that they are serious about good behavior. By consistently enforcing classroom rules, you can prevent many serious discipline problems. When a student breaks a rule and you care enough to spend the time enforcing that rule, you send a powerful message not just to the rule breaker but also to every student in the class, thereby preventing many other infractions.

When a student breaks a class rule, calmly and quietly enforce the rule. Don't threaten, nag, or lose your temper. Instead, try this five-step procedure:

- **Step One**: Ask, "What rule have you broken?"
- **Step Two**: Help the student understand that the rule applies to this occasion.
- **Step Three**: Ask the student to explain the reasons for the rule.
- **Step Four**: Ask the student to tell you the consequences of breaking the rule.
- **Step Five**: Carry out the consequences you have for students who break that rule.

One fact in which you can take comfort is that frequently students will break a rule not from a desire to misbehave but from a momentary lapse in good judgment. By calmly enforcing your rules, you acknowledge that lapse and remind students not to repeat the offense. Here are a few more tips to help you successfully enforce your class rules:

- The first time students break a rule, talk privately with them to make sure they understand the rule and the consequences of breaking it.
- Before you rush to judgment, determine why your students broke the rule. Do they need more attention from you? Did they run out of meaningful work to do? Do you need to explain the rule again?
- Reward good behavior as often as you can. Rewarding students for behaving well will encourage them to continue.
- Accept that enforcing rules is part of your job as a teacher. Be patient. Your students are going to misbehave from time to time.
- Don't be a pushover. Although it may be tempting to make an exception to a rule, think carefully before you do so. You should balance the needs of all of your students with the needs of the student who broke the rule.
- If you find you are having trouble enforcing a particular rule, consider asking yourself these questions to see how to get back on track:
  - Do all students understand this rule?

- Do students understand and accept the need for this rule? Can they see how it is necessary for the smooth running of the class?
- Has your enforcement of this rule been consistent, or have you sent a confusing message by allowing too many exceptions?

Enlisting Student Support for Class Rules

Many ways of encouraging students to follow class rules will be more effective than just imposing your teacher power over students. Spending time at the start of a term enlisting your students' support for class rules will result in a more productive classroom environment all year long. Follow these strategies to solicit your students' support:

- Involve students early. The more involved your students are with class rules early in the year, the more likely those rules are to be successful. This success will be generated by the sense of ownership your students will gain through their involvement.
- Have several informal discussions about rules; discuss, for example, why rules are useful, how to observe them, or the benefits they bring to every student.
- Have students role-play scenarios illustrating various aspects of the rules.
- Occasionally quiz your students orally about the rules in rapid-fire bursts of questions at the start or end of class.

Positive or Negative Consequences?

Although it is inevitable that some consequences of broken rules will be negative, astute teachers know that a more effective approach to encouraging students to embrace the rules of their classroom is to promote the positive consequences that arise when everyone works together to follow reasonable rules. From higher grades and tangible rewards to solid feelings of accomplishment, positive consequences are a powerful way to motivate students to behave well.

The key to classroom management is to be firm, but fair. If a situation does arise in the classroom, try not to let your emotions come out. If you react to your students in a calm manner, the situation may defuse itself more quickly than if you show your students your emotional side.

Erin Sager, 8 years' experience

To help students understand that all actions have consequences and that they choose the kinds of consequences that they will experience, make the connection between behavior and consequences clear to your students. If students are older, a brief class discussion or a few gentle reminders may be sufficient to make the connection clear, whereas younger students may need extra help, patience, and such incentives as stickers or other tangible rewards.

Best Practices Checklist

1. Develop a framework of carefully planned policies, procedures, and rules to make the day-to-day business of your classroom run smoothly.

2. Use your classroom management systems to focus your students on good behavior more often than on their misbehavior to create a positive classroom environment.

3. Model the productive behaviors that you expect from your students as part of daily classroom routines so that they know what to do and how to do it well.

4. Align your classroom policies with the policies of your school and school district for peak effectiveness.

5. Establish simple-to-follow procedures for a variety of recurring classroom tasks and take the time to teach those procedures to your students.

6. Set a good example for your students by following school rules yourself and insisting that they do the same.

7. When you create class rules, be sure that they are appropriate for your students and that they are stated in a positive way.

8. Spend enough time at the start of the year and then periodically thereafter teaching the class rules to your students. The time you spend will be earned back in productivity.

9. Enforce classroom rules as consistently as possible to prevent or minimize serious discipline issues.

10. Make it as clear as possible to your students that their choices result in positive or negative consequences. Make the positive consequences rather than the negative ones the focus of your teaching.

Time to Reflect
Manage Your Classroom

Use the information in this section to guide your thinking as you reflect on these questions. They are designed to encourage you to think more deeply about the issues in the text or to discuss those issues with colleagues.

1. What types of policies do you anticipate needing for your class that are not on the list given earlier in this section? How can you plan for them?

2. What other types of procedures besides the ones highlighted in this section would be beneficial to your students? How can you plan for them?

3. What can you do to enforce your classroom rules in such a way that the disruption caused by the rule breakers is minimized? How can you help those students refrain from repeating their errors?

4. What classroom management systems do you currently have in place that are effective? What makes them effective? What can you add to your other classroom management systems to increase their effectiveness?

5. What classroom management techniques have you observed in other classrooms that you would like to try in your own class? How easily could they be adapted to meet the needs of your students?

SECTION EIGHT

Motivate Students to Succeed

For most professions, motivation is simple and straightforward: it is the act of stimulating something to happen. In an educational setting, however, motivation has a much more complex meaning. For teachers, motivation is the *sum* of everything that we do to inspire our students to want to do their work, to cooperate with classmates and teachers, and to strive to do their best. Highly effective teachers know that it is important to use as many techniques, strategies, and activities as they can to engage their students as often as possible. As teachers, we know that without the vital component of motivation built into every lesson, nothing else matters. If our students do not do the work we have planned for them, our plans are useless.

Motivating students is a complex task because there are many reasons why students may not be motivated to perform well in school. Some students may lack the skills or background knowledge they need to approach their work with confidence. Others may not see the relevance of a school assignment if their home lives are chaotic and if no one outside of school encourages them to succeed academically. Still others may have failed repeatedly in the past because they live in a culture with values that are vastly different from the ones we attempt to instill in them.

No matter the causes of the lack of motivation in your students, taking the time to inspire your students to succeed academically and behaviorally is one of the most worthwhile endeavors you can undertake. Teachers who make the effort to inspire their students are those memorable educators who change lives.

The Self-Fulfilling Prophecy

You have enormous power over the lives of your students. In fact, you can make the students in your classroom into successful scholars, or you can make those same students into academic failures. Your beliefs about your students form a self-fulfilling prophecy.

The self-fulfilling prophecy begins with the expectations you have about your students. These expectations are your unconscious as well as your conscious attitudes about your students' ability to succeed. You communicate those expectations to your students in many subtle ways—for example, through your body language, by the assignments you make, in the language you use, and through how much time you spend with individual students.

Because humans tend to behave as they are treated, your students will react to the way in which you communicate your expectations to them. If students believe that you do not think them capable of hard work, they will not deliver it. Students are often more capable than their teachers believe them to be. If you motivate your students to do their best, they will strive to live up to your expectations. If you think highly of your students, they will tend to behave better for you than they do for teachers who obviously do not enjoy being with them.

If you believe that the students in your class are capable of good behavior and academic success, then your students are highly likely to behave well and strive for success. When you begin to think about how you will motivate your students to succeed, don't disregard the remarkable power of the self-fulfilling prophecy. After all, somewhere along the way, a teacher had faith in you and empowered you through that faith.

> I have found that the best way to motivate a student both academically and behaviorally is to use positive reinforcement. Students love being told when they did something right and having something to feel good about. Notice when they are being good and mention it.
>
> *Alanna Dougherty, first-year teacher*

Be Positive If You Want Positive Results

Unfortunately, the three most common classroom motivational strategies are punishment, threats of punishment, and grades. These three can be compelling motivators, but they can also generate unpleasant and even harmful teaching practices. Although punishment can work in the short run, it does not encourage students to self-manage their behavior. Threats of punishment are even less effective and more prone to misuse by teachers who rely on them too often. Grades, despite being the least objectionable of these three strategies, are also problematic because they are external to the work. Students who are easily motivated by grades tend to be more interested in earning a high score than they are in mastering the material.

Deciding to use a positive reinforcement approach to motivating students is a sound choice that will create students who are self-motivated in time. Even though it may seem that you should take a stand and firmly punish students for misbehaving, you will have more success in getting students to behave by encouraging and praising their good behavior instead. If you want students to act a certain way, you should reinforce that action. When you choose to adopt a positive attitude instead of a negative one, you will spend your time inspiring your students, not nitpicking over their faults.

One of the reasons why a positive reinforcement approach to motivation works well is that many students are so accustomed to negativity at school that it no longer motivates them to improve. Positive reinforcement, in contrast, creates a supportive atmosphere that allows students to see the connection between their efforts and the results.

> Sometimes they will play you. They will lie to get more time; they will push your boundaries and then some. But in between the games that they play, they will let you know if what you are doing is connecting with them. It will take some time to filter through the whining, but this idea is essential to building the trust that creates a positive learning environment.
>
> *Matt Kissling, 20 years' experience*

Lay a Solid Foundation

Successful motivation does not happen by accident. To reach the students in your class, it's necessary to lay a solid foundation for success to occur. The first step, of course, is for you to have a very clear idea of what that success will entail. What skills do you want your students to have acquired by the end of the term? How will their knowledge base have been enlarged? What modifications to improve their behavior or study habits will be constructive and effective? Once you have determined what success will look like for your students, you will be able to make plans to help them achieve it.

The next step is to learn as much as you can about the various ways to motivate your students by observing the activities or strategies to which they respond positively. As you try different ways to motivate them to succeed, gather data on what you observe. Once you know what tends to motivate your students, you can take a prescriptive approach to designing activities that will boost their interest and engagement.

And finally, experienced teachers have found that it is efficient and productive to use an organization system such as a three-ring binder, a file folder, a series of index cards, or e-files to record data they've observed and to organize ideas and materials used to motivate students. When you make the effort to do this, you will find that you will be able to quickly access helpful ideas for motivating students when you need to kindle interest in a lesson.

> The difficult part about motivating students is that each child responds differently to different motivators. I believe the best way to motivate students is to have many different ways to motivate them.
>
> *Christina L. Myren, 4 years' experience*

Motivate Your Students with a Variety of Methods

As a new teacher, you will quickly discover the obvious: there is no silver bullet that will allow you to motivate all of your students all of the time. In fact, it can be very frustrating to observe an activity that appealed to your class one day fall flat on another. Effective classroom teachers have found that it is important to employ a variety of motivational techniques in hopes of appealing to a wide range of students. In the list that follows you will find some general tips to keep in mind as you work to motivate your students by using a variety of methods.

- Make sure that all of your students have the prerequisite skills and knowledge needed to achieve mastery of the material.

- Deliver instruction that encourages students to be active rather than passive learners.

- Provide as many opportunities as you can for students to make choices about the work they are required to do. When students can make sensible choices about their assignments, they are highly likely to engage themselves more fully in their work.

- Include strategies that will help students understand the value of the work they have to do in each lesson. Every student should have a clear understanding of why his or her hard work is necessary.

- Be enthusiastic about the subject your students are studying. Students may not always be interested in every topic you teach, but they will never be interested in a topic that you do not teach with enthusiasm.

- Provide timely and positive feedback that is not just praise but also encouragement so that students know what they have done well and the steps they need to take to improve their work.

- Be flexible and creative when planning instruction to engage as many students as possible. Rote learning is rarely successful or fully engaging; dynamic lessons involving higher-order thinking skills and problem solving are far more likely to engage students.

- Appeal to your students' diverse learning styles as often as you can. This practice will make it easier for them to unlock the information in the lesson and make them more likely to persist in learning.

- Call on every student every day. Students who know they will not be held accountable for answering a homework question or responding in a class discussion are not going to try as hard as students who know you are going to call on them.

- Ask students to evaluate themselves. If students know in advance that they will have an opportunity to assess how well they did in accomplishing their goals, they will work harder to meet those goals. Evaluating assignments as a group or with a partner has a similar effect of encouraging students to have a serious attitude toward their work.

- Involve students in collaborative assignments. Collaboration encourages responsibility, and the division of labor and mutual encouragement make students' work easier to manage.

- Keep in mind that you are a role model for your students. They will observe how you manage your own workload as well as how you help them with theirs, and will react in accordance with what they notice.

- Provide authentic audiences for student work. If your students know that their work will be placed on display, published, read aloud, or shared in other ways, they will take it more seriously than they would if you were the only person who would see it.

- Help students understand the connection between effort and success. Students should be aware that it is their effort that brings about positive outcomes.

- Offer work that is challenging, but not too demanding. Ideally, the difficulty level of the work you ask students to accomplish should be just above their comfort level, requiring them to expend a reasonable amount of effort to complete it.

- Ask open-ended questions. Posing open-ended questions gives students the opportunity to employ higher-level thinking skills and to take creative approaches to problems, and it reduces the risk of failure. Many students who hesitate to answer objective questions will welcome the challenge of open-ended questions.

- Offer in-depth assignments. It is better to cover less material well than to try to cover everything in the textbook as fast as you can. Although you do need to meet your objectives, you do not have to assign every problem or question at the end of a chapter. Spend enough time to enable your students to do independent, challenging assignments that stretch their imagination.

- Provide novelty and variety in the types of assignments you ask students to complete.

- Design instruction so that the work progresses from easy assignments at the beginning of a unit to more difficult ones at the end. The small successes that compound with each phase of an assignment will build confidence and encourage students to keep trying.

- Encourage a sense of belonging in your classroom by establishing a positive and inclusive atmosphere in which all students share classroom tasks as well as learning experiences.

- Make an assignment dependent on the successful completion of an earlier one. Help students recognize that to understand the next topic they will have to know the current material.

- Involve parents and guardians in class activities. Keep them advised of due dates and other information that will help them encourage students to stay on task.

- Combat students' piecemeal approach to their education by using a course outline or a syllabus. Too often, students are not aware of the big picture and don't understand how one assignment will lead to the next.

- Include opportunities for discussion in your class. Encourage students to debate topics of interest and to share their mastery of a lesson. In a math class, for example, you can have teams of students solve a problem and then explain to the class how they derived their answer.

- Encourage your students to be open minded and tolerant so that they will not be afraid to take intellectual risks. Students often are not motivated to attempt their work because they are afraid of failure.

- Strive to establish a productive classroom environment that uses a mixture of collaborative and competitive activities to keep students focused on their work.

- Make sure that students can see that the work is personally relevant to their present and future needs. This can be managed through such simple techniques as incorporating their interests into practice work or using real-life issues or community concerns as contexts for learning.

- Arouse students' curiosity. If you do things like asking provocative questions, showing an odd painting, or even holding up a large box and asking students to tell you what's inside, you'll get their attention and make them want to learn more.

- Provide opportunities for students to assess their own progress. Students who can see that they are developing skills or increasing their knowledge are likely to continue to work hard.

- Ask students to write a response before giving them the opportunity to engage in a discussion. This will automatically involve all students in thinking about a response instead of just listening to their classmates.

- Do your utmost to become a teacher who projects an aura of caring and concern about students and their success. Research indicates that students who like their teachers and believe that these teachers care about their students' success tend to be much more highly motivated than students who perceive their teachers as skilled but uncaring.

> If you can post your grades online, keep them up to date. I try to have current grades on Fridays so families can use them to reward their child or schedule time for grade improvement during the weekend.
>
> *Stephanie Stock Mahoney, 35 years' experience*

Extrinsic Motivation

Researchers classify the various ways that we attempt to motivate students as extrinsic motivation or intrinsic motivation. Extrinsic motivation is a type of positive reinforcement that offers external or tangible rewards to students as behavioral motivators. There are two categories of external rewards: activities that students find enjoyable and desirable items that students receive.

Although many different types of rewards can be considered extrinsic rewards, the most common example of an extrinsic reward is a good grade. Assigning a grade for a student's success or failure on an assignment is an action that is not inherent to the assignment and does not come from within the student. Because of these factors as well as others, such as the subjective nature of many grading practices, grades are not always the best motivator of student success.

Extrinsic motivation, unlike intrinsic motivation, is a controversial practice because its effects do not appear to be as long-lasting as those of intrinsic motivation. Students tend to be too focused on the reward being offered rather than on the successful mastery of the material. Other problems with extrinsic motivation include some teachers' tendency to overuse it and the high monetary expense for teachers who attempt to be fair and offer many students tangible rewards.

Despite all of these negatives, however, extrinsic motivation can play a valuable role in motivating students to succeed. Its greatest advantage is that it makes an immediate connection between the reward being offered and the work students are expected to complete.

If you choose to use various types of extrinsic rewards in your class, keep in mind that they work best when students know about them in advance of the work and can anticipate earning them. You should also take care to combine any such reward with praise so that students clearly understand that they have earned the reward through their own actions. Finally, take care that you offer extrinsic rewards only occasionally so that they are novel enough to be coveted by students.

TANGIBLE REWARDS STUDENTS ENJOY

You do not have to spend a fortune on rewards for your students. The most effective rewards are activities that students enjoy. Instead of going shopping for stickers or other prizes, offer students some of these free rewards:

- Extra time on the computer
- Time to play an educational computer game
- Being team captain
- Time to work on a puzzle or other enjoyable activity
- Bookmarks made by other students
- A walk for the entire class
- A bulletin board featuring their work
- Having their name displayed on a wall of fame
- Having their work displayed
- Watching a film
- Using the library during free time
- Time to do homework for another class
- Being on a class honor roll
- Having a decorated desk

- Being the "Student of the Week"
- Participation in a paper airplane contest
- Extra time to complete an assignment
- Sitting in a special desk or chair
- Borrowing a book from the classroom library
- Time for independent reading
- Encouraging notes on their work
- A free pass to a school sporting event
- A positive note from you to take home
- Having you call a parent or guardian with a positive message
- Having their photograph in a class newsletter or on a class Web page

WHY YOU SHOULD NOT USE FOOD AS A REWARD

For many years, educators used candy, snacks, and other sweet treats to encourage students to do their work and behave well. These edible rewards were fun not only for students but for their teachers, too. Recently, however, educators have begun to realize that using food as a reward is not a sound practice. Here's why you should not offer sweet treats to your students:

- Childhood obesity is a national epidemic. As caring adult role models, teachers have a responsibility to help students stay healthy.
- Using food as a reward contradicts the information about fitness that students learn in health or nutrition classes.
- When teachers offer candy and other snacks to students, they make life more difficult for students who do not want to overeat.
- You may have students with serious medical conditions, such as diabetes or food allergies.
- When you reward students with food, you establish a connection between food and behavior that can lead to problems later in life.
- Parents often object to food as a reward because it may undermine the values about nutrition that they are trying to teach their children.

Make Sure Intrinsic Motivation Is a Classroom Constant

Intrinsic motivation is an incentive to work that is satisfying in itself. Although extrinsic motivation can be effective in boosting students' self-confidence and their desire to do well, intrinsic motivation is the most effective way to promote a fundamental change in student effort and achievement. The potential for intrinsic motivation is always present, even when there is no tangible reward; therefore, its effects last longer than those of extrinsic rewards.

There are countless ways to harness the power of intrinsic motivation in every assignment. For example, many students really enjoy being able to use recently acquired knowledge in new ways or to engage in a community event related to the work at hand. It does not take long to determine that students are far more engaged in activities that encourage them to discover, inquire, or play, rather than just listen passively to a teacher droning on and on.

Thoughtful teachers find ways to increase the intrinsic motivation in assignments by considering how they can make assignments appealing to their students. To make your assignments appealing to your students, include one or more of these techniques in each lesson:

Offer assignments that provide novelty and an unexpected departure from routine activities:

- Writing on anything other than lined paper
- Making a demonstration
- Watching short videos
- Listening to music that matches the day's assignment
- Listening to guest speakers
- Completing only the odd or even problems in an assignment
- Creating their own quizzes, worksheets, games, or puzzles
- Communicating only through notes instead of conversation
- Making three-dimensional graphic organizers
- Unscrambling jumbled facts or events

Offer assignments that students find enjoyable:

- Taking mini–field trips within the school
- Participating in small-group discussions
- Sharing personal reactions to their work
- Sketching
- Peer tutoring
- Role playing
- Playing games
- Setting something to music
- Competing against another class

Offer assignments that arouse student curiosity:

- Answering riddles
- Discussing paradoxes
- Solving mysteries
- Exploring mazes
- Determining what unlike things could have in common
- Solving brainteasers
- Answering open-ended questions
- Drawing inferences from interesting case studies
- Exploring an unusual artifact
- Examining a photograph for incongruities

Offer assignments that students find interesting:

- Using manipulatives
- Finding hidden facts or clues
- Being the first to _____
- Earning a silly reward or bragging rights
- Getting up and moving around the class
- Racing the clock
- Racing another team in the class
- Making a movie or audio recording
- Performing in a class skit
- Participating in a scavenger hunt

Offer assignments that encourage students to be creative:

- Making a Prezi or PowerPoint presentation
- Tweeting an opinion or fact about the lesson
- Posting in a class wiki
- Making a stick figure sketch
- Brainstorming
- Reacting to a startling statement
- Working with simulation problems
- Creating an assignment for a class Tumblr page
- Defending or refuting a point in a class debate
- Participating in a class discussion without using words from a list of forbidden terms related to the assignment

Make Success Attainable

It only makes sense. If students do not believe that they can be successful, why should they even try? One of the most important actions that we can take as teachers is to make sure that our students know they can succeed at the tasks we ask them to complete. Sometimes the roadblocks to accomplishments are ones that are easy to manage, whereas others may require a bit more time and effort on our part.

No matter what the obstacle is, though, teachers who want the best for their students will make school success something that is achievable for all learners. Here are some actions that you can take to help students feel that success in your class is within their reach:

- Teach students to pay attention when you are giving directions. Good listening skills and the ability to understand and follow directions will enable students to proceed with confidence because they will have a clear idea of what to do and how to do it correctly.

- Offer plenty of models, samples, and examples of finished products so that students know how their own work should look. If you also offer examples of incorrectly done work, your students will be aware of the mistakes they need to avoid.

- Offer detailed rubrics when you make assignments so that students are aware of the criteria for success.

- When you make assignments, be sure to discuss the best study skills and time management tips that will allow students to make good choices when they begin working. Teachers who take the time to help students figure out the most efficient ways to do their work make it easy for students to do well.

- Even if students are not officially working together on a project, provide opportunities for them to consult each other or periodically check each other's work. Allowing them to do this often clears up mistakes before they become permanent ones.

- Make sure students know how to seek help from you while they are in class or even after class. Making yourself available at appropriate times to help students can really make a difference for those students who may be struggling with an assignment.

- Break down larger projects into smaller increments with specific mini-due dates so that students are not overwhelmed.

- When you are working with student formative assessments, take the time to offer specific encouragement instead of just praise or error catching.

- Check to be certain that all of your students have the resources they need to do their work. If a project calls for online research, for example, students will need access to a computer and printer. Even something as insignificant as the lack of a pencil can make it difficult for students to do their work well.

- Be prepared to allow students who need extra time to complete an assignment to have that time. Be flexible and work together with them to determine an acceptable deadline. Sometimes just a bit of extra time is all that students need to really do a good job on an assignment.

- Use the electronic resources available to you to share information and notes about class on a class blog or Web site. Be careful to keep your postings about such important information as homework, classwork, grades, and other requirements updated regularly.

- Appeal to your students' learning style preferences whenever you can so that they can access the material as easily as possible.

- Offer assignments that allow students to present their work in different modalities so that they will be motivated to work well. In addition, vary the types of finished products you require whenever you can. Giving students a choice in the type of final product they need to produce will encourage them to work to completion.

- Show students how to take good notes for your class and how to maintain an organized notebook. Keeping up with notes and papers is an important skill that can make it easier for students to succeed. Experienced teachers know all too well the frustration of watching students search through overstuffed book bags for missing papers.

- Design assignments such that the work begins with items that are easy to manage in terms of difficulty level and then progresses in complexity. This promotes student confidence and willingness to persist in completing the assignment.

- Provide appropriate enrichment and remediation opportunities as often as you can. Offer students a chance to both improve skills and develop knowledge.

- Make frequent checks of student progress so that students are aware of what they need to do to succeed.

- Encourage students to reflect on and assess their own work. Students who engage in metacognition in regard to their assignments and work habits tend to be more successful than those who do not.

Teach Your Students to Follow Directions

One of the most important steps you can take to make it easy for your students to be successful is to make sure that they know what to do and how to do it properly. By teaching your students to follow directions well, you encourage them to be self-motivated.

Teachers often expect their students to follow complicated directions with ease, even though many students just cannot do this. Why? Part of the problem lies in our students' impatience with reading long sets of directions (more than three steps) or listening to what they perceive to be a long explanation (more than three seconds).

Following directions well is an important skill that is neither hard nor time consuming to learn. Teach your students this skill early in the school year and your efforts will be rewarded daily. Here are some tips to get you started:

- **Make following directions well a part of the culture of your classroom.** Talk about it every day. Work on it until your students see that following directions is not just something their teacher thinks is important but rather a necessary life skill.

- **Expect and command attention.** When you are ready to go over written or oral directions, expect your students to stop what they are doing and pay attention to you from the beginning of your explanation to the end.

- **Seek clarification.** Ask students to rephrase directions until you are sure everyone knows what to do.

- **Give students practice in step-by-step sequences.** One way to raise your students' awareness of the importance of following directions in a certain order is to give them a paragraph consisting of a jumble of directions and ask them to sort it into manageable steps in the correct sequence.

- **Play a silly game.** To help your students practice following oral directions, try a modified game of Simon Says. Ask your students to do such silly things as placing both hands over their ears, standing by their desk, nodding three times, or holding up one thumb and three fingers.

- **Ask students to focus when you read test directions.** When you are giving a test, teach students to read the directions on the test as you are giving them aloud. They should not be trying to complete the first page as you explain the directions on the last page.

- **Be alert to impatient students.** Don't be fooled by students who inform you that they know what to do. These impatient students just want to get started; they do not always have a clear understanding of the assignment.

To learn more about how to teach students to follow directions, begin with Education World's Web site (www.educationworld.com), where you can find excellent lesson plans and activities for teaching the skill of following both written and verbal directions. Browse the lesson plan archive to find the activities that meet your needs.

HOW TO GIVE WRITTEN DIRECTIONS THAT ALL STUDENTS CAN FOLLOW

Many teachers are puzzled when students cannot follow brief directions for written assignments. One of the problems, of course, is that students do not always see the importance of following school directions. Sensible teachers take care to build relevance into every assignment. Here are some ideas on how to help your students succeed in following written directions:

- Divide large tasks into manageable smaller ones.

- Express directions in the form of logical steps that students should accomplish to complete the assignment. List and number the steps in the order you want your students to complete them.

- Pay attention to the verbs you use. Be as clear and as specific as possible. For example, "Look over page 17" is not a clear direction. "Read to the bottom of the first column of page 17" is more specific.

- Keep each statement brief. For example, try "Write your answers on your test paper" instead of "Be sure to put all the notebook paper on your desk away because I want you to just write on the test."

- Provide concrete examples to help your students understand what to do. It is better to give too many examples than too few.

- If giving directions for a long assignment, use a checklist for students to mark as they go.

- If the various parts of an assignment are worth different amounts of points, be sure to indicate the point values.

- Take the time to go over directions orally with students. This is especially important on tests that have several sections, each with different directions.

- If you want to call attention to an item, try a bold font, underlining, capital letters, or other eye-catching strategies.

- Check for understanding by asking students to restate or ask for clarification on the directions and by monitoring students' work after they begin the assignment.

HOW TO GIVE VERBAL DIRECTIONS THAT ALL STUDENTS CAN FOLLOW

Giving clear verbal directions is a key element in delivering effective instruction. Imagine students' frustration at hearing a teacher say something like this: "Turn to page 167 in your books and begin reading all of Section Eighteen. Then answer questions 1 to 9 and 11 to 17 at the end. You have forty-five minutes to complete this." While this teacher is giving directions, two students slip in tardy, three rummage in their book bag, two more realize their book is in their locker, and no one really knows what to do.

How can you avoid the mistakes that this teacher made? It will not be hard if you remember these guidelines:

- Don't rely only on your voice to convey your message.
- Don't present your students with a maze of steps to follow.
- Don't begin to give directions until you have everyone's attention.

Here are some strategies to guarantee that every student in your class understands your oral instructions:

Before Class

- Write the instructions where students can read them as you review them orally: on the board, on slips of paper for each student, on a transparency sheet, on a computer display, or on a large piece of bulletin board paper.

- Word each step simply and positively. For example, "Turn to page 117" is a well-expressed direction because it is brief and specific. "Turn to page 117 and begin about halfway down the page on the left-hand side; you don't need to read the top of the page or to do the questions at the bottom" is not as easy to follow because it contains a flurry of directives.

During Your Presentation

- Call for your students' attention by using the same signal every time. Something as simple as "May I have your attention, please?" is enough to let your students know to listen to you.
- Stand in the same spot every time you give oral directions. Wait until all students have stopped what they are doing and can look at you. Take as long as you need to ensure that students are focused on you and are no longer opening books, rummaging in book bags, or trying to borrow pens.
- Speak clearly and loudly. Use a serious tone.
- Check for understanding by asking a student to restate the directions. If necessary, ask students to seek clarification and explain until everyone is clear about what to do.
- Consider having students each clear their desk so they can listen or take notes as you speak.

After You Have Given Instructions

- Stay on your feet and monitor students to see that they are starting the work correctly. Circulate to answer questions or provide encouragement.
- If you see that several students are having trouble with one of the steps, do not hesitate to stop the class and clarify the step for everyone.

Purposeful Learning

Everything that your students do should have a clear purpose. As teachers, we have the educational experiences to understand the rationale for studying the more esoteric parts of our respective curricula, but our students do not. Even worse, unless students know the purpose of their learning, they are not going to care enough to want to do a good job on it. In fact, the idea that students want to learn just for learning's sake is not a sensible one considering the many attractive and enjoyable distractions that surround them each day.

If you find your students questioning why they have to complete an assignment, you have failed in one of your most important tasks: making students aware of the benefits of the instruction they are receiving. Students often do not automatically understand the connection between sitting for hours at an uncomfortable desk and the successful lives they envision for themselves when they are adults. You must help them make these connections. Preempt your students' doubting questions by teaching them why they need to know what you are teaching them. Here's how:

- Put the benefits of the lesson on the board so that students will know them right away. Tell students how their lives will be better when they know the material you intend to teach. Focus on why students need to know the information right now as well as why they will need it in the future.

- Begin a unit by connecting it to previous learning, so that students can see a progression of knowledge and skills in their schooling.

- Be very specific. Say, "At the end of class today you will be able to _____" or "You need to know this because _____."

- Take time every now and then to ask students to tell you why they need to know the information you are presenting. Make a list of their ideas and post it in a conspicuous spot.

- Draw connections between what your students are doing now in your class and what they will be doing later in the term in your class.

The answers that follow are ones you should not give when students ask, "Why do we have to learn this?"

- You need it for your test next week.
- Your teachers next year will expect you to know it.
- You will need it for college.
- Because I told you so.

Given the importance of making sure that all students know the purpose of every assignment, it is the task of each classroom teacher to make sure that students know why they are required to do their work and the benefits that will accrue from doing it. As you plan a lesson, consider the suggestions in the worksheet that follows to make sure that your students benefit fully.

TEACHER WORKSHEET 8.1
Assignment Checklist

Place a check mark in the blank before each statement that applies to the assignment under consideration. The more check marks you can award an assignment, the more likely it is that your students will have a clear understanding of the purpose of their hard work.

Purpose of this assignment: _____

1. _____ The assignment is designed to help students master at least one of the state or district objectives for students involved in this course of study.

2. _____ I have made students aware of the purpose of the assignment.

3. _____ Students know that they will need the information in this assignment as a stepping stone to future learning.

4. _____ Students know the short-term benefits of completing this assignment.

5. _____ Students know the long-term benefits of completing this assignment.

6. _____ Students are able to state the practical applications of the material they are studying.

7. _____ Students know how to express the information they are learning in their own words so that it is personally meaningful.

8. _____ Students know how they can use this material to solve authentic problems.

9. _____ Students are able to state how they can use this material in other classes.

10. _____ Students are aware of how this assignment will help them meet their own goals (as expressed on Student Worksheet 8.1).

Take a Goal-Oriented Approach to Learning

Students need many positive messages from the adults in their lives if they are to succeed in school. One of the most powerful messages we can send our students is that they can achieve their dreams. We send this message to students when we give them a solid reason to study: to achieve a dream by setting worthwhile goals and working consistently toward them.

When students work toward a goal, they work with a focused purpose and direction. Because they can begin to see the relationship between the actions they take now and their future, students with goals achieve more than do students who just come to school because they are legally required to. Setting goals also motivates students because it allows them to see their progress as they advance toward an accomplishment. Another benefit of teaching students to set goals is that students who work to achieve goals learn how to be successful. They learn to take responsibility for their own actions instead of waiting for others to intervene in their lives.

Most experts agree that it is a sensible practice to use SMART goals. These are goals that are specific, measurable, attainable, relevant, and timely. SMART goals are not vague wishes for the future, but rather are carefully conceived and planned statements of intent. When students set SMART goals, they make sure that their goals are stated as specifically as possible, are able to be measured, are attainable, are relevant to their larger life goals, and are structured so that there is a time when the goal will be accomplished.

Once students have set their goals, set aside a regular time to work with them to examine their progress and make suggestions for success. It does not have to take more than a few minutes on a fairly regular basis for students to update their goals and measure their progress. Once students see that achievement is possible, continue to help them develop strategies to meet their goals through class discussions and individual conferences when appropriate.

Although encouraging students to set life goals should be a vital part of any teaching practice, adopting a goal-oriented approach to smaller tasks is also extremely productive. This can be done very simply. Just ask students to jot down the grade they are aiming for and one or two things they know they must do to achieve it at the top of an assignment. Doing this will not take more than a minute or two, but this brief metacognitive activity will get students to focus their attention on what they need to do to succeed instead of just blindly working through an assignment.

To help your students set worthwhile goals and work to achieve them, offer Student Worksheet 8.1 to help them think about their goals and what they need to do to make that future success a reality.

STUDENT WORKSHEET 8.1

Setting and Achieving SMART Goals

Use this worksheet to set goals that are specific, measurable, attainable, relevant, and timely (SMART).

Goal One

Specific: What am I trying to achieve?

_____

_____

Measurable: How will I know when I have been successful?

_____

_____

Attainable: What do I need to do to succeed?
Steps I need to take to achieve my goal:

_____

_____

One problem I will have to solve to achieve my goal:

_____

_____

Relevant: How does my goal match other plans I have for my life?

_____

_____

Timely: By what date will my goal be accomplished?

_____

_____

Goal Two

Specific: What am I trying to achieve?

_____

_____

Measurable: How will I know when I have been successful?

_____

_____

(continued on next page)

(continued from previous page)

Attainable: What do I need to do to succeed?

Steps I need to take to achieve my goal:

_____

_____

One problem I will have to solve to achieve my goal:

_____

_____

Relevant: How does my goal match other plans I have for my life?

_____

_____

Timely: By what date will my goal be accomplished?

_____

Make Success Visible

One of the most productive ways to motivate students is to make their success visible. A classroom environment in which student engagement is valued and student success is celebrated in a wide variety of ways is a positive one in which students thrive. There are many different ways to make your students' success visible. Here are just a few of the methods of visually encouraging student success that you can adapt for your classroom:

- Using stickers on student papers
- Rubber-stamping student work with positive messages
- Writing positive notes to students on their papers
- Sending home positive notes or e-mails to parents or guardians
- Using buzzwords, such as "WooHoo!" in unison as class "shout-outs"
- Using a class hand signal, such as a group thumbs up, in unison to acknowledge success
- Displaying photographs of students with their good work as well as the work itself
- Holding brief recognition ceremonies periodically
- Setting aside a special section on a bulletin board as a display area for student work
- Awarding certificates for such qualities as persistence and dedication
- Creating large bulletin board graphs to chart the success of an entire class
- Having students who do well on an assignment put their name on a paper cutout in the shape of a star, and then displaying their stars

> I try to motivate students by designing engaging lessons and learning activities, which is probably the standard answer for most teachers. However, the part of motivation that is oftentimes the most important is that I work to have a rapport with every student. I ask about how students are feeling in general about the school year, and I try to get to know each individual student's interests.
>
> *Kristin Reagan, first-year teacher*

Teach Students to Track Their Own Mastery of Material

Because the real purpose of including motivational techniques in a lesson is to move students toward self-efficacy, it is important to encourage them to assume responsibility for their success as often as possible. One way to accomplish this is to teach students to track their own mastery of the material they are studying. Even with today's transparent classrooms in which students and their parents or guardians have easy access to their grades, it is necessary to help students understand not only the impact of those grades but also how they relate to mastery of the content they are studying.

One of the most obvious ways to do this is to spend a few minutes each week asking students to evaluate their goals and the progress they have made in accomplishing them. This can be done as a brief whole-class discussion at the end of the week or in individual conferences if time permits.

Another technique that many experienced teachers have found effective is to offer a checklist of skills or areas of knowledge that students must master at the start of a unit, and then have students work systematically though the checklist.

Yet another useful way for students to track their own progress is to have them reflect on this topic in an exit slip, free-form writing response, or journal entry. They could use this exercise to determine how well they are doing, to establish what they still need to work on, and to make future plans to complete their work.

A final way you can enable students to track their own progress is to offer them Student Worksheet 8.2, in which students record their assignments and how well they did on each one.

Progress Tracking Chart

As you receive graded assignments, record the grades for each one on this chart so that you can keep track of your progress on each assignment.

Assignment	Date	A	B	C	D	F	Incomplete

> If you constantly point out what a student is doing wrong, eventually he or she will stop caring what you think altogether. Show students that you care about them and they will naturally want to please you.
>
> *Alanna Dougherty, first-year teacher*

How to Survive the Homework Debate

If you find yourself struggling to motivate your students to do their homework consistently and well, you are not alone. The tension created between students and teachers, teachers and parents, and parents and students over homework has grown in recent years into a contentious national debate. For decades, the issue of homework and its impact on home life has been a concern for families and schools. Although the pendulum of the debate seems to swing with the social climate, homework has remained a staple of education despite the problems associated with it.

Teachers at all levels of experience are judged by their homework assignments. If you assign too much, you are too strict. If you assign too little, you are too lenient. The parents and guardians of your students may also represent two extremes: those who take an active role in homework and those who resent the demands of homework assignments. One thing is clear: teachers cannot please everyone.

There are many steps you can take to make sure that the homework you assign serves its intended instructional purposes and does not cause conflict between classroom and home. In the paragraphs that follow, you will learn about the strategies that can make homework a positive learning experience for you and your students alike.

CREATING A HOMEWORK PARTNERSHIP

You can overcome many homework hassles by creating a strong partnership with students and their families. The best way is to communicate your expectations in regard to homework in a letter or e-mail home and to be as consistent as possible in adhering to your homework policy.

Many school districts now make it easy to have a transparent classroom by providing homework hotlines, voice mail, e-mail accounts, and class Web pages that students and parents can use to access homework information at home. Take advantage of every possible method of communicating with your students and their families about their homework assignments. This is an especially important step if you want to promote the importance of learning as something that continues outside of school. If it is easy for parents and guardians to figure out what you expect in terms of homework assignments, then it will be easier for them to offer support.

Sample 8.1
Homework Letter to Parents or Guardians

Following is an example of a letter to parents and guardians outlining a homework policy that you can use to build a homework partnership with students' families.

Dear Parents or Guardians of _____,

Homework is a powerful tool for learning and a necessary part of any student's successful mastery of skills and knowledge. You can expect that your child will have homework on Monday through Thursday nights. These assignments will usually take no longer than thirty minutes to complete. On weekends, I will make no formal assignments, but students can use this time to read, do research, and work on projects.

Homework due dates will be given on the day the work is assigned. I expect students to turn work in on time. If there is a problem, please let me know so that I can help your child. The first time an assignment is not completed, I will speak with your child to see if I can help. After that, I will contact you when assignments are not completed on time.

I will make sure that my students write their assignments down each day. I will also record the assignments on my voice mail, which you can reach at _____, and on our class Web page at _____.

You can help your child do well on homework assignments by setting aside a study time each night, encouraging good work habits, and contacting me if there is a problem we can solve together.

Please discuss these points with your child. Please sign below and return the bottom portion of this letter to school with your child. Keep the part above the dotted line for your reference.

Sincerely,

. . ..

I have read this homework policy and discussed it with my child.

Parent or guardian signature(s): _____

Student signature: _____

If you teach young students, consider a homework folder. Many teachers have found that this is a convenient way to contact parents and guardians. These teachers laminate a folder for every child to take home each night with returned papers and the day's homework assignment tucked safely inside.

If you teach older students, send home frequent progress reports and return other graded work promptly so that everyone involved can see what is required and how to meet those requirements. Don't hesitate to call home to ask for assistance when a student seems to be struggling with homework completion.

HOW MUCH HOMEWORK IS APPROPRIATE?

Part of the resistance that fuels the debate over homework concerns the amount of work that students are asked to complete. Parents and guardians complain of assignments that take their children hours and hours of tedious work to complete or that require expensive resources. Because it is not always easy to gauge how long it will take students to complete an assignment, especially before you become familiar with your students and the speed at which they work, you should expect to have to make adjustments as the year progresses, as you get to know your students, and as they develop the skills that will make it easier for them to do their work.

As a general rule, younger students should be assigned much less homework than older students. Many teachers have found that assigning frequent brief homework assignments to younger students not only reinforces classroom learning but also helps students develop good work habits.

Older students can be expected to handle longer assignments with more comfort and success. Their homework assignments should also involve more independent preparation and practice than the work expected of younger students who may need assistance in completing their assignments.

Although the expected amount of homework time will necessarily vary from class to class, it is generally an acceptable practice to assign about ten minutes of homework per night per grade level. At this rate, young elementary students will have only brief assignments, sixth graders should have no more than an hour, and high school students should have no more than two hours a night.

If a student has more than one teacher who will be assigning homework, those teachers should take care to not overload a student if he or she already has a heavy assignment workload in another class. You should talk with those other teachers to make sure that the overall homework load is reasonable.

DEVELOPING A HOMEWORK POLICY

Experienced teachers know that making appropriate homework assignments that students will want to complete does not just happen; it requires the same degree of planning and preparation as the assignments that you expect students to complete in class. Remember, you will avoid many of the problems associated with homework if you involve parents and guardians early in the year, communicate with them frequently, alert them promptly if a problem arises, and are organized about homework. One way to begin is by developing a homework policy for your class.

Start by finding out whether there is a formal homework policy for your school district or your school. If there is no formal policy, then you should find out how the other teachers in your school handle homework. When all of the teachers in a school have the same expectations for homework assignments, the likelihood of complaints will be reduced.

All homework assignments should be purposefully designed to help students reach mastery of a specific learning objective. Usually homework assignments can be grouped into three basic kinds: assignments that can prepare students for the next day's instruction, such as preparing advance organizers; practice work to review previously taught facts or terms, such as making flash cards; or assignments or independent reading that can extend or enrich the content of a lesson, such as doing WebQuests (see Section Nine).

In general, your homework policy should provide work that is reasonable in length and in the resources required, designed to reinforce or extend classroom learning, and interesting enough to engage student attention. Homework assignments should never be given at the last minute or assigned as punishment work. Use Teacher Worksheet 8.2 to reflect on and plan for the homework policies you would like to use in your own teaching practice.

From *The First-Year Teacher's Survival Guide, 3rd Edition,* by Julia G. Thompson. Copyright © 2013 by John Wiley & Sons, Inc. Reproduced by permission.

TEACHER WORKSHEET 8.2

Plan Successful Homework Assignments

As you begin to think about the types of homework assignments you want your students to complete, use the questions that follow to guide your planning.

1. What is the purpose of homework in your class?

   _____

   _____

2. How much weight will you assign to homework grades?

   _____

   _____

3. How long should each homework assignment take?

   _____

   _____

4. When will you assign homework? When will your students not have homework?

   _____

   _____

5. How will students know what their assignments are?

   _____

   _____

6. What types of homework will you assign?

   _____

   _____

7. How will you communicate with parents and guardians when problems arise?

   _____

   _____

8. How will you grade homework?

   _____

   _____

9. What will you do when students turn in late homework?

   _____

   _____

10. What will you do when students do not do their homework?

   _____

   _____

MOTIVATE STUDENTS TO SUCCEED 249

SPECIFIC STRATEGIES TO MANAGE HOMEWORK ASSIGNMENTS SUCCESSFULLY

Homework assignments need not be a headache for you or your students and their families. Instead, homework assignments can function as you intend them to: as a logical and helpful extension of the classroom material that you teach. Here are several general homework strategies you can use to help your students find success:

- **Allow your students as many choices as you can.** For example, you can let students choose to answer the even or the odd problems in their textbook or one of several essay questions. Ask students to research a topic of their own choosing using a database, or to review using games from among a selection of online review game sites.

- **Consider designating some nights as homework-free nights.** This is a good way to dispel some of the complaints about too much homework. If you leave weekends free of new homework assignments, your students can use that time to read for pleasure or to catch up on long-term projects and other work.

- **Show plenty of examples, samples, and models.** To work with assurance, students need to have a clear idea of what the final product should be.

- **Make the work as interesting as possible.** Use real-life examples, television shows, popular songs, actual student names, sports, or other eye-catching details to engage students.

- **Allow students to consult each other when they all have the same assignment.** You should expect that your students will help each other on homework assignments, even ones that you may want them to do independently. Build in collaboration when you can to help your students avoid the temptation to cheat.

In addition to these general strategies, there are several different things to consider when you design and give assignments. Giving effective homework assignments can be broken into three components: before, while presenting, and after the assignment. Use the following suggestions to make homework a successful experience for you and your students:

Before the Assignment

- Teach the academic work skills that your students need to complete their work with little or no anxiety.
- Allow students to design their own homework assignments when appropriate. If they did not finish an assignment in class, they should have the option of completing it for homework, for example. If students are working in a group, they should have time together to plan the work they need to complete outside of class.
- Have a well-published schedule for homework so that students can anticipate assignments.

- Allow as many options as you can for assignments so that students can do work that is interesting and that encourages them to want to learn more.

While Presenting the Assignment

- Spend enough time going over the assignment and checking for understanding that students know you are serious about it.

- Give plenty of models, samples, and examples, letting students know what their final product should be.

- Don't wait until the last few minutes of class to assign homework. If you want students to take an assignment seriously, it should not be a last-minute item. A sound practice is to go over it at the start of class and at the end of class. Be sure to ask for clarification to make sure all students know what is expected of them.

- Write the homework assignment in the same spot on the board each day. Write it on the board even if you also give your students a syllabus, post it online, and record it on your voice mail.

- Ask students to estimate how long it will take them to do the assignment so that they can set aside the time to do it. With time, students will become adept at planning their work.

After the Assignment

- Send an e-mail, note, or phone call home when a student does not complete an assignment. This will often correct the problem of missing work. If nothing else, it alerts parents or guardians to be more vigilant about checking on their child's homework.

- Offer help to students who may need extra assistance in doing their work. A bit of extra time with you after school will often clear up problems and give students a confidence boost.

- Be reasonable if a student brings in a note from home requesting an extension. Sometimes unforeseen events can cause even the most conscientious child not to complete homework on time.

- Check homework at the start of class on the day it is due. If you do not take homework assignments seriously enough to collect or check them on the day they are due, then your students won't either.

- Because grading homework can be overwhelming, follow these tips to make giving prompt feedback a manageable task:

  - Collect and grade only some of the assignments.

  - Go over the work together as a class. Give a grade for completion.

  - Go over the work with your class, and then give a quiz on it.

- Check the work every day. Have students slip their assignments into a weekly portfolio and then select their best work for you to assess.
- Have students work in small groups to discuss their answers.

WHAT TO DO WHEN STUDENTS DON'T DO THEIR HOMEWORK

When students don't do their homework, it becomes more than just an assignment; it becomes a headache for parents and guardians, students, and teachers. It can be particularly frustrating if the problem is chronic; has a detrimental effect on the student's mastery of important material; or occurs after you have made sure that the assignment is reasonable, purposeful and clearly explained. You should make sure that it is posted for students on the board and on a class Web page (if you maintain one), and recorded in their assignment book.

One of the first things you should do is talk to individual students to find out what the problem is. There are many reasonable explanations for why students might not have done their homework: chronic family dysfunction, a lack of resources, insufficient skills to do the work, and even disorganization, just to name a few. After you know why the problem is happening, you can act to help students overcome the issues that prevent them from doing their assignments.

You should also make sure that you have an explicit homework policy in place so that the positive and negative consequences are clearly spelled out for your students. Once a student has not completed a homework assignment and you have talked with him or her about the problem, you may want to enact your policy if it would be appropriate for that circumstance.

You can also encourage students who have not done their homework to do it and turn it in later. If your school has a policy about accepting late work, you should follow that policy. The most important thing is that students should do the assignment and learn the material it covers.

Finally, if a student appears to have steady problems with getting homework turned in on time, then you should contact the student's parents or guardians to make sure that they are aware of the situation and to ask for their support. One tool that may help you with this conversation is Student Worksheet 8.3. On this form, students have to explain why they did not do their work. Going over the form with your students or their parents or guardians will make it easier for you to identify any behaviors that may be causing the problem.

Missing Homework Explanation Form

Please complete this form and then return it to your teacher.

Student name: _____ Date: _____

Assignment not completed: _____

_____

_____

I do not have my homework today because

_____

_____

_____

_____

_____

_____

_____

_____

Student signature: _____

This information may be shared with a parent or guardian.

ONLINE HOMEWORK HELP

Another way to help students develop good homework work habits is to encourage them to find online assistance. Although some homework help sites are limited to a specific content area or grade level, many are not. You can help students and their families by checking out a few sites and then recommending the ones you feel would work best for your students.

A great place to begin your search for online homework help is to check out the resources offered on your state's department of education Web site. In addition, many states offer extensive free homework help through local public library Web sites. There are also many other online sites that you may want to recommend to your students. YouTube (www.youtube.com) and TeacherTube (http://www.teachertube.com) are both excellent places to search for videos that may appeal to and help your students as they work independently at home. Still others include these helpful sites:

- **B. J.'s Homework Helper (www.bjpinchbeck.com).** The moderator of B. J.'s Homework Helper is B. J. Pinchbeck, who offers more than seven hundred links to sites that students can access for homework help.

- **Multnomah County Oregon Public Library (https://multcolib.org/home work-center).** The librarians at this extensive site have collected helpful Web site links, databases, and many other resources.

- **Homework Spot (www.homeworkspot.com).** This site offers many helpful resources for a variety of subjects, and is designed primarily for K–8 grade levels.

- **National Geographic (www.nationalgeographic.com/education).** National Geographic offers a student-friendly site with such topic categories as animals, history, culture, and science.

- **Khan Academy (www.khanacademy.org).** With the goal of offering a free education to anyone in the world, this inspiring site offers over three thousand videos created by volunteer coaches on a variety of subjects.

WHAT TYPES OF HOMEWORK HELP ARE ACCEPTABLE

One of the most frustrating problems concerning homework is that once students leave the classroom, you have no control over who helps them with their work and how much help they receive. Although you want your students to have the assistance they need to do their work well, some types of help are just not appropriate or helpful in the long run. Inappropriate help tends to fall into two categories: too much help offered by other students and too much help offered by parents or guardians.

When other students are involved, the situation is somewhat easier to manage. Begin by making sure that you have thought out the interactions you would like your students to have with each other when it comes to homework. Be explicit in explaining your expectations to them when you give the assignment. Make these expectations as clear as possible so that students will know when they are cheating on homework assignments.

The second category, too much help offered by parents or guardians, is not as easily managed. Instead of accusing parents or guardians of offering their child too much help, a more effective approach may be to be as encouraging as possible about the types of help that you would appreciate from them. In general, parents and guardians should help their child by setting aside a time and place for homework, being aware of the homework that their child is required to complete, encouraging solid work habits, and communicating with you when there are concerns. As a rule of thumb, if parents and guardians find themselves teaching content at home instead of just supporting good work habits by encouraging successful homework completion, then there may be a problem with the homework assignments.

If you notice that a student appears to be getting what seems to be inappropriate help from home, contact the adults responsible. Never put the student in the awkward position of having to defend parents or guardians.

HELPING STUDENTS MAKE UP MISSING WORK

When a student asks you, "Did we do anything when I was out?" resist the nearly overwhelming urge to respond sarcastically. Your student is only asking for a chance to make up work. Because only very few students have perfect attendance, helping students make up missing work is a responsibility you will have to undertake almost every day.

Assisting students in making up missing work will not be difficult if you establish a policy, make sure that your students understand it, and enforce the policy consistently. Here are some guidelines that will help you:

Establish a Policy

- Learn your school's policy on making up missing work, and align your policy with it. If there is no formal policy at your school, ask if there is one for your department or grade level.

- When coming up with a workable policy for making up work, include the revised due date of the assignment, how much and what kind of help a student may receive from others, when you are available to help students make up work, the point at which you will contact parents or guardians, and the penalty for late work.

- If you use a syllabus, encourage absent students to follow it as closely as they can so that they will find it easy to catch up when they return.

Make Sure That Students Understand What to Do

- At the beginning of the term and at subsequent intervals, discuss the issue of making up missing work in class.

- Divide your students into study teams early in the term. Within each team, students can help each other make up missed assignments by calling or texting absent members, sharing notes, collecting handouts, and reviewing the difficult parts of the assignment. Even very young children can help each other by being part of a study team.

- Consider having students rotate the task of recording class events and assignments on a large calendar, on your class Web page, or even in a binder each day. When students return from an absence, they can check the class record or logbook to see what they missed and what work they need to do. You will find a sample of a class log page that you can adapt for your own classroom use in Student Worksheet 8.4.

- Keep all papers to be handed back and new handouts in a designated area of the room so that students can pick up missing papers when they return.

- Set aside time each week to meet with students and help them make up work. Post your hours, and be sure to inform parents and guardians about them.

- If a parent asks you to send work home to an absent student, be prompt and very specific. Give details that will enable the child to complete the work at home. Include a note offering extra help. Such a gesture not only is professional and courteous but also will show your students that you care about their welfare.

Enforce Your Policy Consistently

- Avoid allowing students to make up missing work during class time. Although this practice is certainly convenient, it allows students to miss yet more work. It is better to have students make up their work before or after school rather than miss more class.

- Make time to speak about missing work with each student who has been absent. Make sure that the child knows what is due and when it is due.

- If a due date is approaching and a student has made no effort to make up the missing work despite reminders from you, call the student's parent or guardian. This sends a clear message that you are serious about students' making up their work.

- Be flexible. Inevitably, some situations will require you to alter your policy, using your best judgment. For example, if a student is absent because of a serious illness, you should respond with compassion. You will need to adjust the makeup work and the amount of support you offer a student in such a situation.

Class Log Page

Day of the week and date: _____

Student reporter: _____

Here's what happened today in period _____:

Homework assignments and due dates:

_____

_____

_____

_____

Handouts:

_____

_____

_____

_____

Class activities:

_____

_____

_____

_____

Work turned in:

_____

_____

_____

_____

Advice:

_____

_____

_____

_____

From *The First-Year Teacher's Survival Guide, 3rd Edition*, by Julia G. Thompson. Copyright © 2013 by John Wiley & Sons, Inc. Reproduced by permission.

If you would like to learn more about how you can motivate your students by instilling in them the habits and attitudes for success that they need, consult the bonus material concerning these strategies on the DVD that accompanies this book. You can learn ways to help your students see the connection between their effort and achievement, how to incorporate work habit instruction into every lesson, as well as several other methods to help students learn to be successful.

Best Practices Checklist

1. The inclusion of motivational activities or strategies should be a routine part of every lesson planning session.

2. Make success attainable by using a wide range of instructional strategies to meet the needs of every learner.

3. Incorporate a blend of extrinsic and intrinsic motivation into your motivational strategies, with an emphasis on intrinsic motivation.

4. Make sure that you communicate your high expectations and faith in students' ability to succeed if you want them to believe that they are capable learners.

5. Communicate the purpose of every assignment so that your students will have a reason to complete their work.

6. Learn as much as you can about what motivates your students so that you can take a prescriptive approach to designing effective strategies to engage their interest.

7. Take the time to help students understand the connection between their own efforts and success.

8. Let your students see you as an enthusiastic teacher who cares about their success.

9. Take a goal-oriented approach to every assignment and activity, no matter how small it may be.

10. Plan homework assignments as carefully as you plan classwork or other assignments. Create a homework policy that can encourage students to become self-disciplined learners.

Time to Reflect
Motivate Students to Succeed

Use the information in this section to guide your thinking as you reflect on these questions. They are designed to encourage you to think more deeply about the issues in the text or to discuss those issues with colleagues.

1. How high are your expectations for your students? How do you convey your belief that they are capable learners?

2. What can you do to include intrinsic motivation in every lesson?

3. Brainstorm a list of tangible rewards that would appeal to your students. How can you find other rewards to motivate your students?

4. How can you make every lesson relevant to the needs, concerns, and interests of your students? How can you determine what those needs, concerns, and interests are? How can your colleagues help you with this?

5. Students of all ages benefit from teachers who make it easy to be successful while still challenging their students. How can you motivate your students in this way? What problems should you take care to avoid?

SECTION NINE

Choose Appropriate Instructional Strategies and Resources

One of the biggest advantages that first-year teachers have as they begin their career is the abundance of new instructional strategies and resources available for classroom use. In fact, there are so many new strategies, so many new approaches, and so many options for classroom equipment and other resources that it is sometimes difficult to make fully informed choices. In this section, you will learn about just a few of the educational choices you have before you.

Take Advantage of the Advances in Educational Research

Constructivism? Blended learning? Neuroscience? As you were studying to be a teacher, you were probably aware of some of the ongoing developments in educational research that are rapidly transforming how we think about our role as teachers and how we design and deliver instruction. Educators at countless colleges and universities and in thousands of classrooms are involved in constant research in an attempt to learn more about how humans learn, the best way to reach and teach every student, and the qualities that make instruction effective for all students.

As an educator, you have access to a great deal of this research with just a small bit of effort. Through your state's department of education, you should be able to find links, books, and other resources that can keep you informed about the latest information in regard to educational theory and practice. Professional development opportunities on the local level will also help you keep abreast of the latest research in education. In addition, you can educate yourself by doing independent research online. Three informative sites to help you begin to learn about and take advantage of the advances in recent educational research are listed here:

- **University of Michigan's Center for Research on Learning and Teaching** (www.crlt.umich.edu/tstrategies/tslt). At this site, you will be able to access many different resources on educational research, various educational theories, and valuable articles on practical applications for instruction.

- **Learning-Theories** (www.learning-theories.com). Here you will find overviews of the major learning theories that are in use in twenty-first-century classrooms.

- **Innovative Learning** (www.innovativelearning.com). At this site, Richard Culatta and other innovative educators offer a great deal of information about educational theories, best practices, and how to integrate technology into instruction.

Why Small, Strategic Steps Are the Keys to Success

As you are probably already aware, it is better to begin any small household project with careful planning, gathering the best possible resources, and making sure you know what to do before you begin. If these steps are important for an ordinary household project, just imagine how vital it is to plan ahead when trying to implement various instructional strategies in your classroom. Instead of taking on too much and failing to help your students, be cautious. Take your time. Educate yourself. Prepare. Be deliberate in your approach.

If you learn of a strategy that seems interesting and that you predict would work well with your students, implement it strategically and in small steps. First, learn all that you can about it. Talk it over with your mentor or with others in your school communities. Next, be thoroughly prepared and have a backup plan in case your untried plan does not work well. Gather data as you implement the strategy so that you can be as accurate as possible when assessing its effectiveness. Finally, take time to reflect. What went well? What do you need to tweak? How can you make sure that this strategy is as effective as possible next time?

Overview of Just a Few of the Instructional Options Teachers Have

In the compilation of instructional options that follows, you will find some of the most popular and adaptable strategies or activities that may work well for your students. Of course there are many more strategies, but these have been selected for their popularity and the ease with which they can be adapted to most classrooms.

Because this compilation provides only a brief overview of each instructional strategy, you will probably have questions about individual strategies and how they would work in your class. It is relatively easy to search for information about instructional strategies online; however, here are two very helpful books that offer sound practical advice on implementing various instructional strategies in your classroom:

Marzano, R. J., and others. *Classroom Instruction That Works: Research-Based Strategies for Increasing Student Achievement*, 2nd ed. Alexandria, VA: ASCD, 2012.

Tate, M. *Worksheets Don't Grow Dendrites: Twenty Instructional Strategies That Engage the Brain.* Thousand Oaks, CA: Corwin Press, 2010.

REFLECTIVE DISCUSSIONS

- **Definition**: In reflective discussions, students make connections between what they have read or learned and their personal experiences or past learning.

- **Most appropriate uses**: Such discussion is best used when talking about literature; interpreting text passages; and thinking though processes, such as problem solving. It is most helpful when incorporated into collaborative activities.

- **In-classroom practice**: The teacher begins by asking an open-ended question designed to encourage students to reflect on an aspect of the unit under study. Students are asked to reiterate or explain ideas and to connect them to previous learning or experiences. The teacher encourages students to apply the essential concepts in different ways.

- **Advantages**: Reflective discussions create high student engagement, encourage higher-order thinking skills, and foster collaboration. They can enlarge and extend learning.

- **Disadvantages**: It is difficult to assess student understanding of the material under discussion.

ACTIVE LEARNING

- **Definition**: Active learning occurs when students assume the responsibility for their own learning through engagement in various learning activities rather than being passive receptors of knowledge disseminated by an expert.

- **Most appropriate uses**: All students benefit from active learning strategies.

- **In-classroom practice**: The possibilities for active learning assignments are endless. Some of the most common include online or face-to-face discussions, collaborative projects, written exercises, problem-based instruction, peer tutoring, experiments, and games.

- **Advantages**: Students benefit by doing instead of passively listening and through active engagement.

- **Disadvantages**: There is an increased need for careful planning in regard to the use of resources and materials as well as explicit directions and expectations for student behavior.

INTERACTIVE LEARNING

- **Definition**: Interactive learning uses various social networking platforms as an integral part of classroom activities.

- **Most appropriate uses**: This type of learning is best employed in real-world problem solving, collaboration with peers within the school community and beyond, in videoconferences, and in playing educational games.

- **In-classroom practice**: Students can create and share blogs and microblogs, meet with others via Skype, contribute to online discussion boards, post videos on YouTube, and share podcasts.

- **Advantages**: Students are no longer limited by their geographic location, but can connect with others via digital tools.

- **Disadvantages**: Students will need access to the technology tools that make interactive learning possible.

PROBLEM-BASED LEARNING

- **Definition**: Problem-based learning is a method whereby students learn material by collaboratively solving realistic problems.

- **Most appropriate uses**: Middle school and older students will benefit most by being able to solve problems in a variety of different contexts, such as current science issues, open-ended social problems, or similar authentic problems.

- **In-classroom practice**: Presented with a broad problem, students will first analyze and define it, then identify methods of solving it while gathering data and information about the problem, before implementing strategies to solve it.

- **Advantages**: The authentic and collaborative nature of problem-based learning brings about high levels of intrinsic motivation.

- **Disadvantages**: Done correctly, problem-based learning is a complex activity. Students who have had some limited exposure to the process in their earlier school years tend to do better than students who are expected to jump right in without careful preparation.

INQUIRY METHODS

- **Definition**: Inquiry methods of instruction all involve students drawing on background knowledge, using higher-level thinking skills to create meaning, conducting authentic research, and evaluating their results.

- **Most appropriate uses**: Inquiry methods are most often used in science and science-related classes, but they can also be used in other disciplines, such as social studies.

- **In-classroom practice:** Students are either given a general problem or asked to generate one of their own. Next they gather information and generate a solution or explanation. They will then prove the soundness of their thinking with an evaluation of their solution or explanation.
- **Advantages:** Inquiry methods are closely aligned with real-life problem-solving processes, high student engagement, and critical thinking and collaboration.
- **Disadvantages:** Inquiry methods are not always applicable to all classes, and they are not appropriate for all grade levels.

HANDS-ON INSTRUCTION

- **Definition:** Hands-on instruction is a type of active learning that involves students manipulating objects, conducting experiments and evaluating their results, or participating in active collaboration in the classroom.
- **Most appropriate uses:** All students can benefit from hands-on instruction.
- **In-classroom practice:** Students play games in teams, work with partners to review flash cards, conduct experiments or surveys, use individual whiteboards, or participate in similar activities involving movement.
- **Advantages:** Learning becomes real when students can actually see it happen as they engage in hands-on activities.
- **Disadvantages:** Some activities can create a focus on having fun rather than on acquiring knowledge or developing skills.

DIRECT INSTRUCTION

- **Definition:** Direct instruction is a common, traditional method of delivering instruction through oral presentations, lectures, or demonstrations.
- **Most appropriate uses:** All students can benefit from direct instruction if it is delivered in an effective and engaging manner appropriate to the age and ability levels of students.
- **In-classroom practice:** Students learn by listening to an instructor who is giving an explicit explanation of the material under study. Older students often are expected to take notes.
- **Advantages:** Direct instruction is a quick way to deliver a great deal of information.
- **Disadvantages:** Not all students are successful at processing information delivered in an auditory mode. Because they are not actively part of the lesson, students find it hard to be engaged.

COOPERATIVE LEARNING

- **Definition**: Cooperative learning is an instructional approach that encourages students to work together in groups. It emphasizes the importance of cooperation rather than competition in solving academic problems and completing assignments.

- **Most appropriate uses**: Students at any age and studying any topic can benefit from cooperative learning activities if the activities are carefully planned and if students are made aware of their responsibilities and roles in working toward the group's success.

- **In-classroom practice**: Small groups or student pairs organized for a specific purpose work well. For example, members of a group are commonly asked to divide a task, with each one completing his or her part of the whole. In other instances, group members might divide reading passages and then share the information with other members of the group.

- **Advantages**: There is high engagement when students share a task and an increased sense of teamwork or community as students work cooperatively rather than competitively.

- **Disadvantages**: Students who are not willing or cooperative group members can negatively affect the learning experience for the entire group.

BLENDED LEARNING

- **Definition**: Blended learning is an approach to instruction that combines classroom interactions with computer or other digital activities.

- **Most appropriate uses**: All students can benefit from blended learning.

- **In-classroom practice**: Students working individually, in groups or pairs, as well as in various combinations of these options use a digital device, such as a computer, cell phone, or iPad, to complete assignments.

- **Advantages**: There is high engagement, a wealth of available information and activities, and real-world applications that allow student access to material regardless of geographic location. Blended learning also prepares students for the future

- **Disadvantages**: Not all classrooms have adequate access to technology, and not all teachers are equally skilled at making use of available resources.

CURRICULUM COMPACTING

- **Definition**: Curriculum compacting is an educational approach designed to assist students who have already mastered at least part of the material under study. It is a type of differentiated instruction geared for higher-achieving students.

- **Most appropriate uses:** This approach is used after a teacher has collected data indicating that a student already knows the concepts being studied or has mastered the required skills. Students in any content area or at any grade level can benefit from curriculum compacting.

- **In-classroom practice:** After determining that a student has achieved mastery, the teacher offers alternative high-interest enrichment or accelerated materials, usually in the context of learning centers, choice boards, or other guided activities.

- **Advantages:** This approach is respectful of the needs of individual learners, provides intrinsic motivation, and allows students to engage in creative or higher-level thinking activities.

- **Disadvantages:** Difficulties can arise in determining the most appropriate alternative activities or establishing how to assess those activities fairly.

CONTRACT LEARNING

- **Definition:** Contract learning is an instructional technique that involves an individualized written learning contract between student and teacher indicating the specific terms of an agreement about how a student will master the content of a unit of study.

- **Most appropriate uses:** Although all students can benefit from a learning contract, it is most effectively used for either remediation or enrichment purposes, when the expectations for alternative assignments need to be mutually determined.

- **In-classroom practice:** Teachers can offer learning contracts to students who need remediation in a specific area or students who have mastered the material and need an opportunity for enrichment.

- **Advantages:** Because learning contracts are specific to individual students, they tend to generate engagement and enthusiasm. Learning contracts also allow for differentiation based on student needs. Students often find contracts intrinsically motivating because they have worked with their teacher to determine the terms of their individual contract.

- **Disadvantages:** Some students need more close supervision of their contract work than others. Teachers who enter into learning contracts with students need to be explicit in how students will be held accountable for their learning.

WEBQUESTS

- **Definition:** WebQuests are engaging activities that ask students to solve problems or conduct investigations using the resources found at various sites online.

Students will be asked to create a final product using the information gathered during the WebQuest.

- **Most appropriate uses**: Many WebQuests are used to arouse student interest at the beginning of a unit of study or as a culminating exercise. WebQuests are adaptable to any content area and for all grade levels.

- **In-classroom practice**: Students are given an open-ended problem to solve or investigate using online resources. The teacher offers practical advice and resources and sets the parameters of the assignment. Students investigate the problem and then create a product in response to their investigation. Product possibilities are wide ranging, but can include written responses, creative projects, or oral reports.

- **Advantages**: WebQuests encourage students to gain online experience and competence, promote critical thinking skills, and foster student independence and responsibility.

- **Disadvantages**: Teachers need to be very careful in planning WebQuests so that students know how to do their work well and how to evaluate online sites for reliability.

SOCRATIC SEMINARS

- **Definition**: A Socratic seminar is an instructional strategy that requires students to participate in an open discussion of a designated text, video, piece of art, or similar object in a formal, well-prepared manner. In this case, the teacher acts as a facilitator and evaluator.

- **Most appropriate uses**: Although Socratic seminars may prove to be useful with much scaffolding when used with younger students, middle and high school students will benefit most.

- **In-classroom practice**: Students prepare by either creating or reviewing questions related to the assignment. Thoughtful preparation is a key element if the seminar is to succeed. During the seminar, students sit in a circle so that they can listen carefully and respond appropriately. The teacher's role is to guide students as they explore the topic under discussion.

- **Advantages**: Through discussion and careful listening, students learn to be thoughtful in their responses to the topic as well as in their communication with each other.

- **Disadvantages**: Students need to be taught how to prepare for Socratic seminars; not every student can handle the intense but controlled discussion format.

FLIPPED LEARNING

- **Definition**: Flipped learning (sometimes called flip teaching) is a strategy whereby a teacher assigns online work to be completed outside of class. Frequently, the online work consists of videos created by the teacher. Students do the online work and then come to class with questions or prepared for guided practice from their instructor.

- **Most appropriate uses**: Older students who are willing to assume, and capable of assuming, responsibility for their own learning are an appropriate target audience for this strategy.

- **In-classroom practice**: Students watch a video at home and then come to class prepared to practice the skills taught in the video. This is particularly good for introductions to math topics, but the strategy can be used in almost any content area.

- **Advantages**: There is a potential for more personal interaction between teacher and student, as the introductory work is already accomplished when students come to class. Students assume responsibility for their own learning.

- **Disadvantages**: A lack of technology resources, or students who are not responsible enough to master even basic material on their own, can make this approach problematic.

RECIPROCAL TEACHING

- **Definition**: Reciprocal teaching is an instructional strategy that involves students taking turns teaching the material or coaching each other. In short, students assume the traditional teacher role.

- **Most appropriate uses**: All students can benefit from reciprocal teaching.

- **In-classroom practice**: Reciprocal teaching is most frequently used as part of collaborative activities in which students read a text, and then take turns leading discussions and questioning sessions about that text until all members of the group have mastered the material.

- **Advantages**: There is high engagement, with an increased sense of responsibility to classmates as well as for personal learning. Reciprocal teaching also requires students to engage in metacognitive reflection. Another advantage is that no additional resources are required.

- **Disadvantages**: Some students may not be mature or self-disciplined enough to assume responsibility for helping classmates master the material.

Classroom Technology Resources to Aid Your Instructional Practices

Although it can be very tempting to want to incorporate as many technology resources as possible into every lesson, remembering to use small, strategic steps while deciding how to incorporate the latest interactive Web page or personal device into next week's lesson plans is a sound idea.

No matter how comfortable you may be with a device or a certain type of software, integrating technology resources into your instructional practices takes careful thought and planning to ensure success. One of the most significant issues that you will have to manage is the inequity that exists in technology use. It is simply neither fair nor reasonable to expect that all students will have the same access to technology resources. As you begin planning how to integrate these resources into your classroom, you will have to determine the best ways to overcome this limitation.

It is best to begin by mastering a base of several resources that you know your students will find useful and then add other technology resources as you have time. To help you get started with this, six of the most common technology resources are listed here, along with tips for how to integrate them successfully in your lesson plans.

> At first I was nervous about saying to my students, "Okay, take out your phones and . . ." but I found that if I set boundaries and encouraged positive use of technology, I got buy-in from my students. I allow my students to use their phone to take a picture of the homework board. If students ask me a question I can't answer, instead of panicking, I tell them to take out their phone and find the answer from a reliable source. Even if you are not ready to immerse your classroom in technology, meet your students halfway.
>
> *Kathleen Stankiewicz, 10 years' experience*

CELL PHONES

Once the bane of many a teacher's existence because of their propensity to distract students or because they make cyber cheating possible, cell phones are now regarded as valuable classroom tools. Here is a list of just some of the easiest ways in which cell phones can be used to facilitate instruction.

Students can use their cell phone to

- Photograph their notes and share them with classmates
- Record homework assignments by using the phone's note features and use the alarm feature to set reminders
- Text questions to each other in advance of a class discussion
- Remind each other of an upcoming project or assignment
- Check a social networking account that they have set up for the purpose of studying together with classmates
- Stage a scene from a book, photograph it, and share the photo
- Photograph important information on the board that they do not have time to copy, to be downloaded later for use at home
- Record (with permission) a lecture or oral presentation
- Record themselves or classmates studying notes aloud and then play the notes back
- Access school e-mail or a class Web page while away from home

- Text absent classmates about missing work
- Create brief summaries of important passages or other material and share them
- Create a photoblog using the phone's camera
- Access maps and related information of different types
- Read e-books or listen to audiobooks
- Watch videos recorded by their teacher in a flipped classroom
- Make videos about the lesson and share them
- Time themselves and classmates during class activities
- Use various apps to access such tools as dictionaries or search engines
- Check or solve problems using the phone's calculator function

INTERACTIVE WHITEBOARDS

There are hundreds of different Web sites with information, ideas, and lesson plans for using interactive whiteboards. These engaging lesson ideas and activities appeal to all students—from our youngest students to the oldest. In the list that follows you will find just a few of the ways you can use an interactive whiteboard in your classroom.

Teachers can use interactive whiteboards to

- Share student multimedia presentations, PowerPoints, or Prezis
- Have students play review games on interactive Web sites
- Find and mark errors in written work as well as examples of excellent writing
- Create and share diagrams or other graphic organizers
- Edit assignments and share the results with students
- Have students write exit slips to share
- Provide opportunities for students to take virtual field trips together
- Teach students how to analyze a passage, photograph, film clip, or work of art
- Show students how to compare and contrast different passages or texts
- Have students solve problems while working with classmates
- Share photos of students as they work on projects
- Display interactive maps
- Share exemplary work done by students
- Work out solutions to puzzles with students

- Show review videos in a flipped classroom
- Teach students how their work will be assessed using a rubric
- Work with students to create class poems, stories, or quotations of the day
- Use interesting words from the day's lesson appropriately so that they become part of students' vocabulary
- Show students how to create and use spreadsheets and tables of various types
- Highlight key features of a text
- Show a brief inspiring video
- Have students correct errors in sentences or problems
- Show a student-made project
- Conduct discussions through a blog, wiki, or discussion board thread
- Show students how to research databases and archived information

> We are sharing ideas in class and finding what works best for sending work, taking notes, and using the iPad as an agenda. We have had to learn ways to help students who don't have Internet access at home. We are all figuring this out together.
>
> *Jane Lankford, 31 years' experience*

- Have students create graphs and other nonlinguistic representations
- Ask students to create various types of time lines or flowcharts
- Share a daily current event, news article, cartoon, riddle, or unusual fact
- Have students write and share sentences using the word of the day, roots and affixes, or target vocabulary words

iPADS

As innovative now as laptops were just a few short years ago, iPads can be invaluable in the classroom. Although they do function in different ways than laptops and other computers, iPads can serve as helpful and versatile resources in any classroom. If you have even one iPad in your classroom, you can have your students

- Connect with others via global learning project sites; service project sites; and social networks, such as Tumblr or Twitter
- Complete e-projects and share them
- Evaluate the reliability and credibility of Web sites
- Create interactive time lines
- Create and post book trailers
- Brainstorm collaboratively
- Create and post videos of various types
- Create and share e-books

- Photograph their work and share it with their parents or guardians
- Read and edit each other's work
- Share videos from YouTube, the Teaching Channel, or TeacherTube
- Access the photos at Tag Galaxy
- Donate rice through Freerice (http://freerice.com) by playing learning games
- Collaborate with other students via Skype
- Use Google Docs to interact with each other's work
- Make and share electronic flash cards
- Listen to podcasts on various topics
- Create a photoblog or photocollage
- Take electronic notes on readings or on face-to-face presentations

BLOGS

Blogs are among the most versatile technology resources that teachers and students can use and enjoy. Blogs make online sharing an easy and manageable task for even very young students. If you would like to use blogs in your classroom, you can ask your students to

- Maintain a class blog with daily news and updates for absent classmates
- Maintain electronic journals about projects from start to finish and share them online
- Embed videos or artwork that they have made into their postings
- Share ideas about how to study or prepare for assessments
- Compare their work with the work of other students
- Access links and online resources that you have embedded into the class blog
- Review and edit classmates' work
- Complete and share graphic organizers
- Share notes about what they have read or learned
- Respond to writing prompts of various types
- Write entrance or exit slips
- Write responses as they read for pleasure or for a class assignment
- Offer solutions to local problems
- Write reviews of products or books
- Post ideas on a common topic
- Share predictions about what they are reading or upcoming class events
- Practice random acts of kindness and share what they have done with classmates

- Collect and analyze data for a future report posting
- Survey classmates on a topic of interest and share the results
- Create tutorials and post them for classmates
- Share autobiographies or opinions
- Complete daily practice work and share what they have done
- Connect their classroom with another classroom in a faraway location

PODCASTS

Podcasting is simply a way of making digital audio or video files available on the Internet so that others can access them. It is also an intrinsically engaging activity for classroom use because it requires students to apply what they have learned in a new and authentic way. Its rapidly growing popularity is based not only on its usefulness as an instructional tool but also on the ease with which podcasts can be incorporated into lessons.

The process is simple. First, prepare your podcast content and then record it. Next, upload your podcast to a server and publish it. Another good reason to try podcasting is that the equipment you will need to begin podcasting in your classroom can usually be found in any school: a computer with Internet access and a microphone (preferably a USB one) that can record your voice. In addition to the actual equipment you will require, you will need suitable software to broadcast your students' work. Fortunately, there are excellent free software programs available for educators. You'll find a list of sites where you can download these programs later in this section.

Podcasting is a versatile learning activity that can be used with students of all ages. There are limitless possibilities for classroom use. Here are just a few of the many uses suitable for students of all ages for you to consider experimenting with in your classroom:

- Discussion of current events or other topics
- Multimedia presentations of a field trip experience
- Advice on projects or homework assignments
- Demonstrations or explanations
- Tutorials, especially peer tutoring
- Alternative assignments
- Remediation or enrichment work
- Class newsletters or daily logs
- Study guides
- Data gathered for student assignments
- Teacher lectures
- Activities to improve listening comprehension

- Debates
- Riddles, puzzles, and brainteasers to promote critical thinking

Podcasting is an emerging classroom activity, but there are many useful resources to help you get started. Here are a few of the more user-friendly sites that are geared toward classroom teachers:

- **Podomatic (www.podomatic.com).** This popular site offers tutorials as well as many podcasts you and your students could access for inspiration.
- **Kid-cast.com (www.kid-cast.com).** This site, with its emphasis on online safety, makes it easy for students to create and share their podcasts.
- **Podcasting Tools (www.podcasting-tools.com).** This site hosts a great deal of information, such as tips and directories, for any potential podcaster.
- **Audacity (http://audacity.sourceforge.net).** Audacity is a site that offers highly-regarded free software for editing and recording sounds.
- **Edudemic (http://edudemic.com).** At Edudemic, use "podcasts" as a search term to access helpful articles about podcasting.

Useful Web Sites for Educators

Although the Internet changes rapidly as more and more educators find ways to take advantage of the wealth of information to be found online, some sites remain consistently valuable for teachers. In this list, you will find twenty classroom-tested sites that can enrich your classroom.

- **Edublogs (http://edublogs.org).** This site offers a user-friendly way to create and share blogs.
- **Skype (www.skype.com).** Skype is a service that can make it easy for students in your classroom to communicate with students in other classrooms.
- **Wikispaces (www.wikispaces.com).** Wikispaces offers educators a free space to gather materials and other resources suitable for a wiki.
- **Edudemic (http://edudemic.com).** At this resource-rich site, you can follow the latest trends in educational technology.
- **Knowmia (www.knowmia.com).** At Knowmia, teachers can create and share videos. The site also contains thousands of high school–level videos for visitors to view.
- **Animoto (http://animoto.com).** Animoto is a site that makes it possible for teachers to create and share videos.
- **Timetoast (www.timetoast.com).** Students can use this site to create and share time lines in just a few minutes.

- **Instructify (http://instructify.com).** This site, maintained by a group at the University of North Carolina at Chapel Hill College of Education, offers many useful and practical tools and tips for integrating technology in classrooms.

- **Tumblr (www.tumblr.com).** An easy-to-use, free blogging platform, Tumblr can make it easy for you and your students to create and share blogs.

- **Poll Everywhere (www.polleverywhere.com).** Poll Everywhere offers a free service for educators that will allow students to create, take, and share polls of various types.

- **Live Binders (www.livebinders.com).** The Live Binders site allows users to maintain an online three-ring binder or portfolio. Teachers can store materials in a binder as well as share binders.

- **Smart Tech (www.scholastic.com/smarttech/teachers.htm).** At Scholastic's Smart Tech page, teachers can find dozens of ideas and resources concerning how to use interactive whiteboards.

- **Twitter (https://twitter.com).** Twitter is a very popular microblogging site at which students can share their ideas in 140-character increments. You can also join other educators in one of the many professional learning networks (PLNs) available on Twitter.

- **Mastery Connect (www.masteryconnect.com).** At Mastery Connect, educators can manage information and data relating to the Common Core standards (see Section Ten).

- **Pinterest (http://pinterest.com).** Pinterest is a popular and user-friendly online pinboard where you and your students can collect, organize, and share images.

- **SlideShare (www.slideshare.net).** At SlideShare, teachers can access and download PowerPoint presentations as well as create and share their own.

- **TED (www.ted.com).** At this site, you and your students can access videos delivered by great thinkers and experts covering a wide range of topics

- **4Teachers (www.4teachers.org).** This extensive site offers many different tools and helpful resources to make integrating technology easy.

- **Free Technology for Teachers (www.freetech4teachers.com).** Richard Byrne, the creator of this site, offers a wealth of helpful information and links to free educational sites.

- **Tag Galaxy (http://taggalaxy.de).** Tag Galaxy is a free photo-sharing site that students and teachers can access to find photos for projects and lessons.

"There's an App for That!"

It is likely that the fastest-growing advance in technology for the average consumer—the apps for our mobile devices—will remain popular and useful for some time. As an educator, you will find that there are apps for just about every aspect of your professional life:

- Tracking grades and data
- Accessing documents when you are not at school
- Reading books with students
- Helping students build vocabulary
- Providing study guides for students
- Having students view a fact or word of the day
- Accessing reference materials of all types
- Finding games for your students to play
- Organizing your classroom
- Ordering supplies
- Editing papers
- Creating lesson plans and sharing them
- Finding video clips to engage students
- Accessing blogs, microblogs, and podcasts
- Searching the Web
- Collaborating with colleagues
- Sharing documents with your professional learning community or PLN members
- Coming up with lesson plan ideas

To learn more about the apps that can increase your knowledge and improve your teaching skills and productivity, one of the best places to begin is with the pages devoted to apps for educators at Kathy Schrock's Guide to Everything site (www.schrockguide.net/bloomin-apps.html), where visitors can access information about hundreds of carefully selected educator-recommended apps categorized by device as well as by how they can be used in the classroom.

Best Practices Checklist

1. Be sure to make informed choices about which instructional strategies and resources to use. Gather data, seek advice, share ideas, and do your best to make sound instructional decisions.

2. Begin your search for more information about the advances in educational research at your state's department of education Web site. As time permits, explore other resources so that you can remain up to date in your knowledge and skills.

3. When you learn of a strategy that seems interesting and that you predict would be successful for your students, be sure to implement it after careful deliberation and planning.

4. Use learning strategies that encourage students to assume responsibility for their own mastery of the material. Experiment with the strategies that appear to work best with your students.

5. Take advantage of every possible technology resource as you begin to implement instructional strategies in your classroom.

6. Do not overlook the importance of making sure that a strategy is well planned and carefully prepared before implementation. A hasty implementation will waste precious instructional time and create negative reactions among your students.

7. Keep in mind that although a strategy may be enjoyable and novel, for it to be effective it must enable students to learn the material they are studying.

8. With every implementation of a new strategy or resource, take time to reflect on its effectiveness and on what you need to improve before you use it again.

9. Pay careful attention to the differences among your students when it comes to their access to technology resources. Unless your students use devices provided by the school, there may be significant gaps in what they are able to do at home.

10. If you are not sure if a strategy or technology resource is appropriate for your students, take the time to talk it over with a colleague or administrator to gather ideas and troubleshoot problems before implementation so that the experience can be positive for everyone.

> Surviving your first year of teaching is like making it through army boot camp; most teachers have tremendous sympathy for first-year teachers and will willingly provide aid, but they are oh so happy that they won't ever have to go through their first year again.
>
> *Melinda Conner, first-year teacher*

Time to Reflect
Choose Appropriate Instructional Strategies and Resources

Use the information in this section to guide your thinking as you reflect on these questions. They are designed to encourage you to think more deeply about the issues in the text or to discuss those issues with colleagues.

1. How would you rate your current level of knowledge about educational research? How does your knowledge affect the choices you make about the instructional strategies you use in your classroom?

2. What successful learning strategies have you observed other teachers in your school using that you would like to adapt for your students? Who can help you with this? What problems can you anticipate, and how will you solve them?

3. What are the advantages of taking small, strategic steps in implementing instructional strategies in your classroom?

4. Of the various strategies in this section, which ones appeal to you? How will you implement them? What additional help will you need to be able to do this successfully?

5. As you look over the brief lists of suggested technology resources in this section, which resource can you begin using right away? Where can you learn more about this resource? What can you do to ensure that implementation is successful?

SECTION TEN

Design Effective Instruction

Lesson planning is one of the most important tasks you have as a first-year teacher, as a second-year teacher, as a third-year teacher . . . and it will be just as important when you are a seasoned veteran with years of experience. Planning effective lessons is the foundation for success in your classroom and, ultimately, success in your career. There can be no substitute for this process. Successful teachers know that they must carefully plan every lesson.

The Benefits of Careful Planning

When you make the decision to plan lessons carefully, you and your students will benefit in many different ways. Here are just some of the benefits you will receive when you make this sound decision:

- You will be more likely to prepare interesting lessons that engage your students' critical thinking skills, leverage their preferred learning styles, and appeal to their interests rather than relying on lackluster routines.

- You will gain confidence from having a clear plan for each lesson. This added confidence will translate into a more successful delivery of material for your students and increased professional credibility for you.

- You will be able to pay attention to the details that will make your lessons successful, such as including technology and real-world assignments.

- You will be able to create a logical progression of learning instead of just presenting bits and pieces of information without a clear purpose.

- Most important, you will be better able to teach the curriculum that your state and district require of you. With well-planned lessons, you can cover the standards that your students need to master.

Backward Design: Think Big, but Start Small

The iconic term *backward design* was coined by Grant Wiggins and Jay McTighe in their groundbreaking 1998 book, *Understanding by Design*. Backward design is a productive approach to instructional planning based on the idea that teachers should begin the process by determining the desired end results of instruction. With the final outcomes in mind, teachers can then efficiently design and deliver appropriate instruction tailored to help students achieve those predetermined results. To learn more about the innovative ideas in the backward design approach, consult the following resource: Wiggins, G., and McTighe, J. *Understanding by Design*, Expanded 2nd ed. Upper Saddle River, NJ: Pearson, 2005.

Although thousands of teachers follow the principles of backward design when planning lessons, countless others make the mistake of planning small increments of instruction instead of building a framework of carefully sequenced skills and knowledge. When you begin designing lessons to help your students master the information and skills that your school district's curriculum requires, begin with the big picture. What do your students really need to know to establish a base of knowledge on which the next unit will build? What do your students need to know to be successful in the upcoming years of their education? What skills will they need to compete successfully in the workplace or in college?

Once you have determined the big picture of the purpose of the material, you will find that it becomes easier to design lessons that will encourage your students to succeed. At this point, think small. What daily lesson plans will enable your students to reach those end results? With the big picture firmly in your mind, it will be easier to lead your students forward with carefully constructed lessons that combine to form a satisfying sequence of instruction.

Cover the Curriculum or Teach Your Students?

It can be frustrating and discouraging to assess your students' readiness and background knowledge, only to learn that many of them are underprepared and unable to manage even the most basic work that you ask of them. The frustration and discouragement intensify once you realize that you cannot just ignore the mandated curriculum but rather are expected to help every student master the material successfully enough to perform well on high-stakes tests.

Although there will never be an easy way to solve the problem of students who are not prepared for grade-level work, teachers do not have to choose between teaching their students and covering the curriculum. Learn to see students with learning deficiencies as students who can succeed and who do need to learn the material rather than as problem students. Make a plan to differentiate instruction, scaffold lessons, offer extra help, and involve other concerned adults in a sustained effort to help every student succeed. If you teach the curriculum with sensitivity to your students' needs, you will not have to make this unfair choice.

> Don't think that you can wing it. Prepare for class! You will quickly lose credibility with students if you are caught floundering in class.
>
> *Debbie McManaway, 19 years' experience*

How Prepared Should You Be?

One of the easiest mistakes for first-year teachers to make is to not prepare adequately. This is understandable because of the overwhelming newness of each day and the volume of unfamiliar material that you must master, but it is not a sound practice. Put simply, if you are not thoroughly prepared for class, your students will struggle to be successful. Although the amount of necessary preparation varies from teacher to teacher, here are some guidelines on how prepared you should be, at a minimum:

At the start of a school year

- You must be thoroughly familiar with your state's standards.
- You must know the material you will be expected to teach each term.
- You must have a course overview in place as soon as possible.

At the start of a grading period

- You must have plans for each unit you intend to teach.
- You should have enough daily plans for at least two weeks. Try to have at least two weeks of daily plans prepared at all times.

Common Planning Problems

Although it is true that all teachers may have occasional problems planning effective lessons, some problems seem to be especially prevalent during the first few years of teaching. The biggest disadvantage you have in creating lesson plans as a novice teacher is that you do not have a storehouse of tried-and-true materials. Every lesson plan you write in your first year is an experiment. No matter how much effort you put into your plans, a lesson can fail simply because it has unforeseen drawbacks. You can reduce the likelihood of an unsuccessful lesson by paying attention to some of the incorrect ideas you might have about writing your plans. Here are a few of the problems concerning lesson plans that many first-year teachers encounter:

- Neglecting to follow state and district standards and guidelines
- Rushing to cover material instead of teaching students
- Failing to connect current learning to previous learning
- Spending a disproportionate amount of time on one unit
- Failing to include activities to engage critical thinking skills
- Not allowing for differences in learning styles
- Failing to assess students' prior knowledge before starting new instruction
- Testing students on material they have not adequately mastered
- Failing to provide enough formative assessments before a summative evaluation
- Mistaking a list of activities for a lesson plan
- Failing to write a course overview, unit plans, and daily plans

How to Find the Time to Plan

One of the excuses teachers give for not writing detailed lesson plans is that the process takes too much time. Whether you choose to create your plans at home or at school, you can master this task. Follow these suggestions to save time as you write lesson plans:

- As soon as you have familiarized yourself with your state's standards, begin reading the textbook and other materials you will need to cover. If you do this at the start of the term, you will have an understanding of the scope of the material you need to teach.
- Go online to research sites for lesson plans on the topics that you teach. You will find a list of online sites offering free lesson planning resources later in this section.
- Talk to other teachers in your school who have lesson plans, materials, resources, and good ideas to share.
- Create a course overview before you begin unit plans or daily plans. With this in place, you will have a quick reference for all other plans, and you will be able to pace and sequence instruction correctly.
- Make lesson planning a priority. Planning lessons should be just as important as photocopying handouts, grading papers, or any of the other tasks that can take up so much of a teacher's day.
- Set aside an uninterrupted block of time to plan. If you plan at the same time each week, it will be easier for you to stick to a routine and to make any necessary adjustments to your plans.
- Be organized. Have your textbook and other necessary materials ready before you begin.
- Use Teacher Worksheets 10.1, 10.2, and 10.3, given later in this section, to streamline the planning process.

Your State's Standards

Each state's department of education has created and published the standards that indicate the material students must master by the end of each course or grade level. As you begin the process of designing a course of study for your students, the foundation of your lesson plans should be your state's standards. You should plan all lessons with mastery of the state standards as your final objective. To learn more about the standards that apply to you and your students, try these tips on potential resources:

- Access your state's department of education Web site.
- Access your local school district's Web site.
- Investigate the ancillary materials that accompany the textbooks you will teach. Many textbook companies provide excellent support geared to the requirements of individual states.

The Common Core State Standards Initiative

The Common Core State Standards Initiative (CCSSI) is a far-reaching reform movement in education coordinated by the National Governor's Association for Best Practices and the Council of Chief State School Officers in an effort to provide students with a first-rate, twenty-first-century education regardless of their geographic location.

Concerned at how poorly our students have performed in recent years in comparison with other students from around the globe, and at the growing dissatisfaction with the low skill levels of students in college and the workplace, the teachers, educational experts, and administrators who are the designers of the Common Core standards have attempted to remedy both of these issues with a carefully researched and planned initiative slated for full implementation in 2014.

The scope of the Common Core standards will reach far. Teachers across the United States will share common objectives and a clearer understanding of what students will need to be successful once they leave their classroom. Transient students will be able to adjust to new schools because the expected outcomes for their learning will not change from school to school. Because students will have the same assessments no matter where they live, educators can make more precise comparisons across state and local school districts. Most promising is the hope that the CCSSI will enable students to compete successfully in the global workplace of the future because of the increased emphasis on the skills that they will need for the rest of their lives and not just until the next standardized test.

Classroom teachers will be profoundly affected by the implementation of the Common Core standards. K–12 math teachers; K–12 English and language arts teachers; and 6–12 social studies, history, science, and elective teachers will all have a major role in helping students master the literacy skills needed for their respective content areas as implementation goes into effect. More than ever before, teachers will be called on to work together to help students develop the critical thinking and literacy skills that will enable them to build on the knowledge that they already possess to synthesize new learning.

HOW THE COMMON CORE STANDARDS AFFECT YOU

The Common Core standards are results oriented. Accurate data collection and disaggregation will be crucial components in instructional planning. The various computer-based benchmark tests as well as the summative assessment at the end of the year will not be limited to multiple-choice questions but will incorporate a variety of item types, including constructive responses that call for students to explain and defend their work. Teachers will be expected to use formative and summative assessments to accurately gauge their students' progress and areas of deficiency.

One very important shift brought about by the Common Core standards is the emphasis on a shared responsibility for literacy across content areas. No longer will the development of good reading skills be limited to the work of language arts or reading teachers; every teacher will share the task of helping students become adept at reading and understanding a variety of complex informational texts. This will include an increased emphasis on historic, scientific, and technical sources as well as literary nonfiction. All teachers will be involved in helping students develop word-decoding skills, reading skills, critical thinking skills, and academic vocabulary.

Although the Common Core standards themselves are quite specific, educators will have a great deal of flexibility in designing appropriate instruction. There is not a prescribed curriculum that teachers are required to follow. Successful teachers will find that a creative approach and careful planning will help their students meet the expectations of the CCSSI. Educators will examine their curriculum guidelines to determine what currently works best and then find and implement the best ways to revise the areas that need improvement.

Under the terms of the CCSSI, students will have wide exposure to digital media across content areas. The increased emphasis on employing digital resources in instruction will require teachers to be cognizant of the current best practices in using electronic media and how such media can be used to greatest advantage in their classroom.

The Common Core standards are rigorous. Students will be expected to think critically, to make accurate inferences and judgments about the material they are studying, and to then express those inferences and judgments in a logical manner. Teachers will be expected to help their students rise to meet these higher expectations through instruction that is carefully designed and delivered.

HOW TO LEARN MORE ABOUT THE COMMON CORE STATE STANDARDS INITIATIVE

Although your school district will be able to provide you with the local-level information that you need to succeed, here are several other excellent resources that offer useful information on the CCSSI:

- **Common Core State Standards Initiative (www.corestandards.org).** At this informative site, teachers can educate themselves about the scope and history of the CCSSI, and can access a wide array of Webinars and PowerPoints about the Common Core standards and their implications for educators.

- **Partnership for Assessment of Readiness for College and Careers (www .parcconline.org).** At this site maintained by one of the two consortia involved in the development of the Common Core standards, teachers can learn about the standards themselves as well as about diagnostic assessments, instructional materials, and tools to help make implementation successful.

- **Smarter Balanced Assessment Consortium (www.smarterbalanced.org).** At the Web site of the Smarter Balanced Assessment Consortium, the second major consortium involved with the development of the Common Core standards, teachers can find valuable teaching resources, information on best practices, and practical strategies for successful implementation of the Common Core standards.

Assess Your Students' Prior Knowledge

Your students' prior knowledge is a gift that they bring to class each day. Before you can make final decisions about what you are going to teach, you first need to collect data about what your students already know.

Determining your students' prior knowledge is crucial because it dictates the approach you will take with a unit of study. For example, on the one hand, if most of your students understand a concept, then you may wish to review it only briefly as a springboard to studying the next concept. On the other hand, if most of your students are unfamiliar with information you assumed they would already know, your approach will need to be more comprehensive. Because prescriptive teaching practices are integral to successful instruction, determining background or prior knowledge is essential in diagnosing students' strengths and weaknesses.

To assess your students' previous learning, there are many techniques you can use. Try adapting some of these ideas to find out what your students already know about a topic:

- Ask students to write out a quick list of three facts they already know or think they know about a topic. After they have passed their responses to you, read some of them aloud without revealing the author and ask the entire class to judge their veracity.

- Ask students to write a brief description of what they have already been taught about the topic you are about to study. You could even ask them to tell you when and how they learned the information.

- Create a brief sampling of some of the questions you plan to include on a quiz or test later in the unit. Ask students to predict the correct answers.

- Divide your students into small groups and ask them to share everything they know about the topic under study. Set a time limit. After the time limit is up, have a representative from each group share the group's knowledge with the rest of the class.

- List the main points of the unit you are about to teach, and ask students to write what they already know about each one. Share their answers with the entire group.

- List the key terms that students will study. Have students write what they believe each term means based on what they already know about the topic. They should share their answers with the entire group.

- Ask students to work in pairs, and hand each pair a sheet of poster paper. Have each pair brainstorm, listing everything they know about the topic. Share the lists with the class, or display them.

- Offer a puzzling scenario, and ask students to solve it using what they already know about the topic. Have students keep their responses so they can verify their knowledge as they progress in their study.

- Show students a photograph, cartoon, diagram, quotation, or brief article related to the topic you are about to study. Ask them to share their reactions.

- Ask your students to create a Know/Want to Know/Learned chart. The first two sections of the chart will give you a good summary of their previous learning.

How to Begin Planning Instruction

Successful lesson planning proceeds in an orderly sequence. After you have thoroughly familiarized yourself with the curriculum that you are expected to teach and gathered the diagnostic data that you need to assess your students' readiness, here's how to begin:

- **Step One**: Create a course overview. This will give you an idea of the scope of the information your students need to master during the entire term.

- **Step Two**: Create unit plans. Divide the material you must teach into smaller units of information, and then plan how to teach each one.

- **Step Three**: Create daily plans. This final step in the lesson planning process is the most detailed. At this level, you have the most flexibility in determining the activities your students will complete.

CAPTURE THE BIG PICTURE WITH A COURSE OVERVIEW

Before you can write successful daily plans, you must have a clear idea of what your students will have to learn by the end of the school term. You must plan for the entire year before you can plan for each day. Here is how to create a course overview that will serve as a useful guide all term long:

- **Start with your state's standards.** You should begin by thoroughly reviewing the standards for the entire course so that you know what your students are expected to learn by the end of the year.

- **Use your district's resources.** Review your local curriculum guidelines; they will be aligned with your state's standards.

- **Determine the units you need to teach, and prioritize their importance.** Make a list of the units you will have to cover to meet state and district objectives. Prioritize your list into three tiers of importance:

  - Units you absolutely must cover

  - Material you would like to cover if you have time

  - Units you plan to offer to students as enrichment or remedial work

Use Teacher Worksheet 10.1 as a template for creating your course overview.

Format for a Course Overview

Use this worksheet to create a brief overview of the material that you are expected to cover before the school year ends.

Essential Units	Time-Permitting Units	Enrichment Units	Remedial Units

From *The First-Year Teacher's Survival Guide, 3rd Edition*, by Julia G. Thompson. Copyright © 2013 by John Wiley & Sons, Inc. Reproduced by permission.

CREATE UNIT PLANS

Unit plans are the intermediate step between a course overview and daily plans. When you create unit plans, you divide the material into smaller blocks and determine roughly how you will teach it. In the list that follows you will find some of the features that will guide you as you plan each unit. You can also use Teacher Worksheet 10.2 to guide your planning process and as a template for your written unit plans.

- **Determine your students' prior knowledge.** A crucial step in preparing unit plans is to first determine what your students already know about the topic. This will dictate the activities you will include because it will provide you with information about how you should approach the various topics in the unit.

- **Determine essential knowledge.** Using state and district guidelines as well as your textbook and other materials, identify the essential knowledge that students must gain to master the material in the unit.

- **Determine the length of the unit.** To create plans for a unit of study, you must first decide how long the unit will take, from the first objective to the final assessment. The length of time you plan to spend on a unit will be an important factor in determining the activities you need to plan.

- **Brainstorm and research appropriate activities.** Take time to brainstorm and conduct research to generate activities that will interest your students as you cover the material in the unit. You will need a variety of activities that will interest students, appeal to students with different learning styles, and provide opportunities for students to engage in critical thinking.

- **Select appropriate activities.** List the activities that you believe would be most useful to your students in the sequence in which you want to present them.

- **Select materials and resources.** With a timeline and prior knowledge firmly established, you can search for the materials you need. Although there are many places in which to find interesting materials, it is best to start nearby. Begin with your textbook and the supplementary materials that accompany it. Then, turn your attention to the resources in your building. Are there movies or other options for you to use? Do your colleagues have materials to share? Finally, turn to other sources, such as the Internet.

- **Create assessments.** It may seem strange to create the assessments for a unit of study before you write your daily plans, but if you do this, your daily plans will align with the information you plan to assess.

> Do not lecture for the entire block. You'll bore yourself.
>
> *Kay Stephenson, 33 years' experience*

Format for a Unit Plan

Use this worksheet to guide your planning as you create unit plans.

Unit title: _____

Dates: _____

Objectives: _____

_____

_____

_____

Materials and resources needed: _____

_____

_____

_____

Essential knowledge for mastery: _____

_____

_____

_____

Activities: _____

_____

_____

_____

Assessments and dates: _____

_____

_____

_____

Formative assessments: _____

_____

_____

_____

Summative assessments: _____

_____

_____

_____

_____

From *The First-Year Teacher's Survival Guide, 3rd Edition*, by Julia G. Thompson. Copyright © 2013 by John Wiley & Sons, Inc. Reproduced by permission.

CREATE DAILY PLANS THAT WORK FOR YOU AND YOUR STUDENTS

Productive lessons do not just happen. A course overview and unit plans are the basis for your curriculum planning, but your daily plans are what will make instruction come to life for your students.

Your daily plans should follow a standard format that makes it easy for you to consult them during class. Your school district may have a format that you will be expected to use. If not, then you should create a format that you can use with ease. Many teachers design their own planning templates and photocopy them, so that they just have to pencil in information for each section. If you use a computer-generated template, you may need to print out a copy for quick reference during class.

With your format decision under control, keep these pointers in mind to make sure that the lessons you plan are not only effective but also easy to manage:

- **Although you should vary your lessons, routines will keep students on track.** Establish some routines so that students can predict what their days will be like. For example, your routines could include a quiz every Thursday, a review game every Monday, or no homework on Tuesday nights.

- **You should not expect to cover every element on a lesson plan template every day.** Different activities take different amounts of time, and it is impossible to fit them all in.

- **No matter what you have planned to do each day, you must include two vital lesson elements.** First, you must have an engaging opening that will encourage your students to recall what they did in your class during the last meeting and to look ahead to the current lesson. Second, you must also include a satisfying closure to your lesson. This will help your students recall what they learned and reinforce their knowledge of the day's material.

- **Your lesson plans should be written for your own use.** Even though administrators or other evaluators will probably want to see your plans from time to time, you should plan for your own benefit. Learning to write useful plans will take time. If you are in doubt about how much to write, begin by writing detailed plans to give yourself a needed boost of confidence.

What to Include in Your Plans

The following list will help you as you begin to write your daily lesson plans. There may be other items that you will find useful to include in one class, but the listed items will constitute a good beginning. You will also find that you do not have to cover all of the items in this list in one class period. Instead, choose the items from this list that will be most effective in helping your students learn on the particular day for which you are creating plans.

- **Standards.** Refer to your district's or state's guidelines to make sure that the instruction you design is aligned with the standards in the curriculum you are required to cover.

- **Specific objectives.** Objectives indicate what the result of a lesson will be, not which activities students will complete. The objectives for a lesson should be stated in specific terms and must follow state and district guidelines. For example, an objective for students in a geography course could be, "Learners will be able to identify forty-five of the fifty state capitals."

- **Materials and equipment.** You should determine what resources you need to teach an innovative and interesting lesson.

- **Assessment of prior knowledge.** You must assess your students' prior knowledge before you begin teaching a lesson to determine exactly what you need to review or introduce.

- **Opening activity.** Creating anticipation among your students should be an integral part of the opening activity in your class each day. An engaging opening allows students to shift gears mentally from what they were doing before class began and leads them into the lesson they are about to begin. (For more information on opening and closing strategies, see Section Six.)

- **Direct instruction or teacher input.** Your input is necessary for a successful lesson. Carefully plan what you are going to do or say to make your points during the day's instruction.

- **Student activities.** Use a wide range of independent and guided practice activities that will appeal to students with a variety of learning styles. Be careful to include critical thinking activities.

- **Alternative activities.** Allow for differences among students in regard to ability, readiness, and speed of mastery by preparing alternative activities that provide enrichment or remediation. You can also add extension activities for students who finish before their classmates.

- **Closure.** Close each class with an activity designed to reinforce learning. Allowing students to drift from one class to another without formal closure fails to make use of students' tendency to recall the beginning and end of a lesson with clarity.

- **Homework.** Homework assignments should arise naturally from the lesson. Because they are part of what you teach, you should record specific assignments in your plans.

- **Assessments.** You should include a variety of assessments in each unit of study. Be sure to include formative and summative assessments to make it easy to evaluate your students' progress.

- **Student reflection.** If your students are old enough for this to be appropriate, include time for them to reflect on what they have learned during class, connections with other topics, and what they still need to do.

● **Teacher reflection.** Leave space in your daily plans to record your successes, failures, or any other information that will allow you to teach this lesson more successfully in the future.

Use Teacher Worksheet 10.3 as a template for creating your daily lesson plans, customizing it as necessary to fit your needs.

Easy-to-Use Format for Daily Lesson Plans

You can use this format to create daily lesson plans that will be easy to follow by filling in the sections you need to cover each day. Although you would not expect to cover all of the items in this worksheet every day, you can see at a glance what you have covered and what you may still want to include in your instruction.

Lesson topic: _____ Date: _____

Standards: _____

_____

_____

Specific objectives: _____

_____

_____

Materials and equipment: _____

_____

_____

Assessment of prior knowledge: _____

_____

_____

Opening activity: _____

_____

_____

Direct instruction or teacher input: _____

_____

_____

Student activities: _____

_____

_____

Alternative activities: _____

_____

_____

Closure: _____

_____

_____

Homework: _____

_____

_____

Assessments: _____

_____

_____

Student reflection: _____

_____

_____

Teacher reflection: _____

_____

_____

Successful Learning for Nontraditional Schedules

A widespread trend in recent years is nontraditional scheduling. There are countless versions of nontraditional schedules. For example, some classes may meet every day for an extended period for half the school year; some classes may meet every other day for the entire year; still others may meet for varying lengths of time a few days a week for only one grading period. Many districts are also trying year-round school schedules or modified summer schedules.

Although nontraditional schedules have many benefits, they also have drawbacks. In particular, it can be difficult to cover all the material the curriculum requires in the allotted time. If students need enrichment or remediation, it can be even more challenging.

Student absenteeism while students are on a nontraditional schedule is another serious matter. When students miss a class, they may be missing the equivalent of at least two classes, depending on the type of nontraditional schedule they have.

It is also easy for teachers to waste class time while on a nontraditional schedule because many nontraditional schedules allow for longer class periods. Wasting the end of class by allowing students unstructured time is a poor use of a student's time when classes are on a traditional schedule, but it becomes a serious misuse of students' time when a nontraditional schedule is in effect because of the compressed time constraints of most nontraditional schedules.

Despite these problems, many school districts have moved to nontraditional schedules to take advantage of the many benefits such schedules offer:

- With longer class periods, students can finish lengthy assignments, such as experiments or projects, before the end of class.
- With less hall traffic, there are fewer opportunities for discipline problems.

As already indicated, nontraditional schedules have disadvantages and advantages, just as traditional school schedules do; in both cases, you must learn to use the time you have with your students as fully as possible. Here are some strategies that may assist you as you work to master the challenges of a nontraditional schedule:

- Divide the class period you have with students into smaller blocks as you plan. Vary the activities in each of these smaller blocks to keep students alert and interested in working.
- Expect your students to work independently for at least part of the period. Very few teachers are able to lecture for a sustained length of time and keep the interest of a room full of restless students who are used to a fast-paced world.
- Plan the entire term carefully. You have a limited amount of time to cover the material your students need to know. You must keep your students on track if you are to succeed.
- Plan each day carefully. Always have backup plans to avoid running out of things for students to do.

- Make connections for your students. Spend time at the start of class reviewing the previous day's learning and the last few minutes of each class reinforcing the material that students have just learned.
- Take advantage of innovative activities that require extended periods of time, such as simulations, debates, seminars, or online learning games.

How to Adjust a Lesson

It is not uncommon for students to feel frustrated or to have trouble staying on task. When such behavior seems to last more than a few minutes, you must be prepared to adjust your lesson plan to meet your students' needs. Although the methods of adjusting your plan will vary from class to class, you can quickly correct most situations. The following tips will help you turn a frustrating lesson into a successful one as quickly as possible:

- Resist the temptation to give in to your own frustration by reprimanding your students. Think about why they are off task, and solve that problem instead.
- Remember that often just switching to another learning modality will engage students enough that they will work harder to overcome any small frustrations.

Change activities every thirty to forty-five minutes, depending on the ability levels of students. Honors kids can work longer; slower kids may need to take a break every twenty minutes. If your activities need to be long, give the kids a thirty-second or one-minute break so they can stand and stretch.

Charlene Herrala, 31 years' experience

- Either reduce the amount of drill and practice you have assigned or make it more palatable by allowing students to tackle it in pairs or small groups.
- Call a stop to the lesson and assess the situation. Determine what your students already know to avoid needlessly repeating information or leaving them behind by moving to a subject they are not ready to process.

Always Have a Backup Plan

Few situations in a classroom are more dismaying than realizing that your students have nothing constructive to do. In a situation like this, you must have a backup plan ready. When you write your daily plans, you should jot down ideas that would be useful as backup plans. To help you write backup plans, here are two possible ideas that you can adopt for your students:

First, you can brainstorm a list of interesting activities that are related to the general topic under study and will last anywhere from ten to thirty minutes. When you need to use a backup plan, you can quickly scan your list to select an appropriate activity.

Still other teachers keep an eye out for good backup plans all year long. They maintain collections of reading passages, games, and other learning activities. You can begin by compiling a few simple puzzles or other high-interest activities that will provide your students with opportunities to use their time constructively.

In the following list, you will find backup plan options that will help you keep students engaged in learning all period long. Although most of these activities require at least a modicum of planning or preparation in advance, once the activity is set up, the effort and time you spend on this activity will be rewarding.

> Be flexible. Overplan and have a backup. Always remember: you can't demand respect; you have to earn it. Be firm and consistent.
>
> *Dawn Carroll, 17 years' experience*

- Play an active game, such as Hot Potato, Twenty Questions, or any of the other games in Sections Eleven and Twelve).

- Group students into pairs to share the workload. Have some students do the even problems and others the odd problems, for example. Or have partners take turns tutoring each other.

- If a game is becoming too competitive or rowdy, group students into smaller teams and allow them to consult with each other. They can write their responses as a group instead of shouting the answers.

- Adapt any of the transition activities in Section Six that would help your students stay on task.

- If students have access to a computer, have them make multimedia PowerPoints or Prezis using the material in the lesson.

- Have students write a lesson reflection or prediction in fifty words and then share it with the class.

- Divide the material under study into several parts and have groups of students make presentations that teach the material to their classmates.

- Do a round-robin, whereby students pass around a sheet of paper sharing their ideas about the material in the lesson.

- Pass out learning cubes and have students work together to answer questions or engage in critical thinking activities. (See Section Eleven for information on learning cubes.)

- Have students illustrate the lesson's main concepts in a nonlinguistic manner by drawing or using clip art.

- Have students reorganize the material into their own words by using graphic organizers.

- Ask students to record answers or comments using a Webcam or the audio recording features on a computer.

- Have students use Blabberize (http://blabberize.com) to record themselves reciting the key facts as silly images "move" their mouths.

- Have students cover the required material by taking notes as part of a team effort.

- Have students each draw a shape that relates to the lesson on an oversize sheet of paper. After they have done this, have students record their notes inside the shape. They can trade their papers around the room to make sure that they have complete information.

- If a group is not working, move the students to independent work. If independent work is not going well, try collaboration.

- Offer students a choice board of six different activities that will help them master the material.

- Provide a checklist of the essential tasks that students must complete before they can move on to alternative activities.

- Have students either complete a puzzle or create their own puzzle using the puzzle creation feature at Discovery Education (http://puzzlemaker.discoveryeducation.com).

- Have students list key facts from the lesson and compare their list with those of other students.

- If students are having trouble understanding the material, ask them to decide on several key points and then explain those points to classmates.

- Hold a class discussion in which students have to offer evidence from a text to support the statements they make.

- Have students create silly three-dimensional models of the key concepts in a lesson using common objects in the classroom.

Free Online Resources for Lesson Plans

Although there are dozens of online sites devoted to lesson plans, the sites in the list that follows offer a comprehensive assortment of free lesson plans and lesson planning resources for K–12 educators. These sites are not limited in the topics that they cover, allowing teachers to access lesson plans that span a wide variety of content areas. At some sites, teachers may need to register to be able to fully use all of the site's resources, but at the time of publication, all of these sites are free resources for educators.

- **A to Z Teacher Stuff (www.atozteacherstuff.com).** A to Z Teacher Stuff is a teacher-created site designed to help teachers find lesson plans, thematic units, teacher tips, discussion forums, printable worksheets, as well as many more online resources.

- **Discovery Education (www.discoveryeducation.com).** Discovery Education offers an enormous wealth of resources for teachers—digital media, hundreds of easily adaptable lesson plans, worksheets, clip art, and much more.

- **Explore (http://explore.org).** Sponsored by the Annenberg Foundation, Explore's library consists of hundreds of brief, original films and more than thirty thousand photographs from around the world on a wide range of topics, such as animal rights, health, poverty, the environment, education, and spirituality.

- **Federal Resources for Educational Excellence (http://free.ed.gov).** At this site, teachers can access more than 1,500 federally supported teaching and learning resources submitted by dozens of federal agencies. Although they are not actual lesson plans in themselves, these resources can be invaluable tools in designing instruction.

- **ForLessonPlans (www.forlessonplans.com).** ForLessonPlans is an online directory of free lesson plans for K–12 teachers. Created by teachers, this site offers lesson plans that cover many different subjects as well as links to other resources.

- **Lesson Plans Page (http://lessonplanspage.com).** At this site, maintained by HotChalk, teachers can access over 3,500 lesson plans. The extensive selection of lesson plans at this helpful site was first developed by students and faculty at the University of Missouri in 1996 and later expanded to include contributions from Web site users.

- **Independent Television Service (www.itvs.org).** The Independent Television Service presents award-winning documentaries and dramas as well as innovative new media projects on the Web. Teachers can find interactive games and lesson plans that accompany the media presentations.

- **Lesson Planet (www.lessonplanet.com).** Founded in 1999, Lesson Planet enables teachers to search more than four hundred thousand teacher-reviewed lesson plans, worksheets, and other resources in an online professional community. A free trial is available.

- **LessonPlans.com (www.lessonplans.com).** Maintained by the Educators Network, LessonPlans.com offers thousands of teacher-created lessons plans in an easy-to-search format organized by topic as well as by grade level.

- **National Education Association (www.nea.org).** This site offers thousands of lesson plans in an easily searchable format. Teachers can also find a variety of lesson planning resources as well as practical tips for classroom use.

- **Share My Lesson (www.sharemylesson.com).** Share My Lesson is maintained by the American Federation of Teachers and TES Connect. Developed by teachers for teachers, this free platform provides over 250,000 teaching resources and hosts an online collaborative community. Share My Lesson also has a significant resource bank for the Common Core standards.

- **Teachers Network (http://teachersnetwork.org).** Teachers Network, a New York City–based nonprofit organization for educators, offers thousands of lesson plans and lesson planning resources covering a wide assortment of topics in a variety of formats for teachers at all grade levels.

- **Teaching Channel (www.teachingchannel.org).** Funded by the Bill and Melinda Gates Foundation and the William and Flora Hewlett Foundation, Teaching Channel is a video showcase of innovative and effective teaching practices. Teachers can watch brief videos of effective teaching ideas that they may want to implement in their own classroom.

- **Thinkfinity (www.thinkfinity.org).** Thinkfinity is the Verizon Foundation's online professional learning community, providing free access to over fifty thousand educators. This site houses thousands of digital resources aligned to state standards and the Common Core standards, as well as blogs and discussion groups.

Best Practices Checklist

1. Begin the process of lesson planning with consideration of the outcomes for student learning. Ask yourself what you want your students to know or be able to do after the unit of study is over and proceed to build instruction based on those outcomes.

2. Don't give in to frustration when students are not ready to cover the mandated curriculum. Instead, work to improve your students' skills and knowledge as soon as you can so that you can cover the curriculum.

3. Make a point of writing detailed daily lesson plans so you can be confident that you can manage your class and the lesson at the same time. Plan every lesson carefully.

4. Your state's standards and guidelines must form the foundation of the curriculum plans that you develop.

5. Use a variety of assessment techniques to gauge your students' background knowledge so that you have enough data to create meaningful and appropriate lessons.

6. Spend enough time planning. Manage your time such that you have structured time set aside for this purpose. Never attempt to teach improvised, off-the-cuff lessons.

7. Begin lesson planning with a course overview, followed by unit plans and daily plans.

8. Adopt a methodical and efficient approach to planning so that you can be sure to meet your students' needs and cover the curriculum you are expected to cover.

9. If your students are struggling with a lesson, adjust it as quickly as you can. Take care to have an array of backup plan options available so that you can use class time wisely.

10. Take advantage of the many online resources to ensure that the lessons you teach are engaging, appropriate, and successful.

Time to Reflect
Design Effective Instruction

Use the information in this section to guide your thinking as you reflect on these questions. They are designed to encourage you to think more deeply about the issues in the text or to discuss those issues with colleagues.

1. How can you improve the way you plan lessons? What can you do to make planning effective lessons easier? How can you make sure that you find time for this crucial activity? What suggestions do your colleagues have to help you?

2. How can you tell when your lessons are engaging and appropriate for your students? What specific activities can you include to make sure your lessons are interesting and challenging?

3. What steps can you take to ensure that you cover the material in your state's standards that your students need to know? What suggestions do your colleagues have to assist you with this?

4. One of the biggest headaches for any teacher is teaching a lesson that is not working well. What plans can you make now to prepare for when this might happen to you?

5. What online resources have you already found helpful in planning instruction? Which of the resources given earlier in this section can you use to meet the needs of your students?

SECTION ELEVEN

Deliver Engaging Instruction

Even the best-prepared teachers can have unsuccessful students. A teacher may have the most detailed lesson plans in an entire school, but if he or she does not deliver instruction effectively, students just will not be able to learn. When a lesson is delivered skillfully, however, a cycle of success gains momentum. Confident teachers inspire their students. Successful students, in turn, create confident teachers. This cycle is one of the most satisfying reasons to teach.

What is effective delivery, and how does it give a teacher control? Many teachers believe that effective delivery of instruction means speaking well in front of students. Although a teacher does need outstanding speaking skills, those are only one part of delivering instruction well. Other components of a good lesson can include class discussions, appealing seatwork, and innovative activities, just to name a few. Best of all is the result of putting all of these elements together; when teachers know that students have learned the material in a lesson, they can feel that they are having a positive impact on their students.

Guidelines for Improving Your Classroom Charisma

If you look back on your own student days, you can easily recall the teachers who made learning fun; you wanted to be in their classes. What makes certain teachers exceptional? Charisma—the elusive quality that makes ordinary people into leaders—is the key. Fortunately for many of us, classroom charisma can be learned. You should begin to cultivate your charismatic appeal on the very first day you step to the front of a class, and you will still be working on it on the very last day you teach.

Here are some general guidelines to help you become a charismatic teacher. Begin by selecting the steps you know you can manage with ease, and then move on to the ones that will require a more determined effort.

- **Your class should be about your students and their work.** Make them the focus of your attention. Some inexperienced teachers make the mistake of talking about their own lives too often while ignoring students, who are quietly tuning out.

- **Smile at your students.** No one likes a grouch. A teacher with a pleasant demeanor has half of the charisma battle won. What if you don't feel like smiling? Do it anyway. You owe it to your students. Remember that your difficult students are the very ones who most need your smiling support.

- **Stand at the door to greet your students as they come into the classroom.** You should greet your students to convey the message that you are glad to see them.

- **Overlook what you can.** Although it is certainly okay to be strict with your students, there is a fine distinction between a strict teacher and a too-strict teacher. If you spend your day quibbling over minor problems with your students, you will not have enough time to attend to larger issues.

- **Early in the term, establish the procedures and routines your students should follow, and then stick to them as much as reasonably possible.** Students who know what they are supposed to do and how they are supposed to do it are much more comfortable than those who are uncertain about what you expect.

- **Laugh at yourself.** Although you should not be the focus of the class—your students and their work should be—you should let your students know that you have enough confidence not to take yourself too seriously.

- **Make sure to eliminate distracting personal habits that might annoy students.** Some of the most obvious behavior factors that interfere with classroom charisma are a monotone voice, poor eye contact, sloppy speech patterns, and distracting gestures.

- **Use multiple modes of learning to make sure that your lessons are as dynamic and exciting as possible.** Include visual aids, technology, music, and other active learning strategies to involve every student in every lesson every day.

- **Talk less than your students do.** Ask questions that will encourage students to share their ideas with you.

> I think about teaching as a building art form. You make a little progress each day. Some days you need to rebuild.
>
> *Carole Platt, 35 years' experience*

Pitfalls That Plague Too Many Teachers

Many factors can interfere with a teacher's delivery of instruction. Teachers who are stressed, too tired to plan appealing lessons, or not quite in tune with the needs and interests of their students are likely to lack a smooth flow of instruction. Happily, you can avoid most of these pitfalls with just a bit of awareness, common sense, and planning. Here is a list of considerations that will help you avoid mistakes when you deliver instruction:

- **Whose voice is heard?**

  Don't talk more than your students do.

  Do design activities that encourage your students to speak to each other and to you.

- **Who does the work?**

  Don't create lessons that allow your students to be passive.

  Do skip the worksheets that require only recollection by rote, and ask students to solve puzzles, highlight notes, debate points, or engage in other open-ended thinking activities.

- **Are you letting teaching opportunities go by?**

  Don't let the national push for accountability intimidate you into neglecting to use those serendipitous moments that sometimes arise in every classroom.

  Do turn any occasion into a learning event in your classroom. Seize every opportunity, and capitalize on current events and student interests whenever you can.

- **How much material can you teach in one class?**

  Don't allow yourself to drift when it comes to finding the correct pace for the delivery of instruction. This takes practice, organization, and planning.

  Do make sure to plan alternate lessons in case the pace you initially set for a lesson needs adjustment.

- **How much time do you really need to teach the material?**

  Don't allow your students to sit around with nothing important to do while they wait for class to begin or end or for their classmates to finish an assignment.

  Do follow this practical advice from veteran teachers: plan more work than you think your students will be able to accomplish.

- **How will your students know what to do?**

  Don't confuse your students by giving hurried or unclear directions.

  Do be sure to deliver a combination of written and oral directions and to check for students' understanding of directions.

Improve Your Oral Presentations

One of the most important things to remember about speaking to a potentially bored group of students is that you need to practice what you are going to say and how you are going to say it. Rehearse, and then rehearse some more. In a few years, you may be comfortable enough to teach without rehearsals, but for now, consider rehearsing to be an important part of your lesson preparation.

In addition to practicing, there are several other techniques you can use to improve the way you speak in front of a class. Try the following ideas to make your oral presentations as interesting as possible.

VIDEOTAPE YOURSELF

One of the most effective ways to evaluate your delivery of instruction is to videotape yourself several times during the term. If you tape yourself several times, you will see how you have improved and which weaknesses still exist. Of course, it is not enough to just videotape and then watch. To assess your presentation, consider these questions:

- What annoying verbal and nonverbal tics do I have?
- Is my voice loud enough for all students to hear?
- Do I include all of my students by calling on them?
- Do I project enthusiasm, authority, and confidence?
- Do I command my students' attention when I speak?
- What messages am I conveying through my body language?

MASTER THE ART OF THE PAUSE

Practice the art of the pause by training yourself to refrain from enthusiastically "walking over" student responses. When a student speaks, mentally count to three before speaking or allowing others to jump in. Similarly, when students are slow to respond to a question, do not rush to save them from an awkward silence. Pause long enough to allow your students to think.

LEARN TO MAINTAIN EYE CONTACT

Another important skill you must refine is maintaining eye contact. As you speak with your students, refrain from looking at the wall or even the floor. Focus your attention on every student by making it a point to keep your eyes focused on two or three students for a few seconds and then moving on to another group.

It can be especially difficult to maintain eye contact while writing on the board. The trick to this is to not face the board at all, but rather to almost face the class by turning to the side while writing and continuing to talk. Students will feel you have spoken directly to each of them if you maintain direct eye contact throughout class.

SET THE STAGE

Before you begin an oral presentation, set the stage for a successful presentation by previewing the topic in such a way that students will want to know more about what you have to say. If you begin a lecture or presentation in a traditional, dull way, many of your students will quickly tune out. However, if you incorporate one or more of these preview techniques, your students will be motivated to pay attention:

- Post a motto, slogan, or other catchy phrase related to the lesson in a conspicuous spot, and ask students to comment on it.
- Display and talk about an unusual object related to the lesson.
- Make a provocative statement and ask students to respond to it.
- Read part of a passage to the class. Be sure to stop reading at an exciting part of the text. Finish the passage in your lecture.
- Tell students what new skill or knowledge they will have after the presentation is over. Show them how the lecture will benefit them.
- Pass out a handout with missing parts. Your students can fill in the missing information as they listen.
- Give students part of a scenario before the presentation. Stop and discuss it. Finish the scenario during the presentation.
- Have students enact a brief scene related to the topic under study.
- Do a demonstration, and then ask students to explain what they observed.
- Play a game related to the topic of your lesson.
- Take a poll of your students on some aspect of the topic.
- Pose a problem for students to decipher. Use the presentation to solve the problem.

PAY ATTENTION TO YOUR AUDIENCE

Establish an atmosphere of mutual respect. This is a day-to-day process that involves thoughtful work with every student in your class. Begin by being careful that your body language and tone of voice convey your respect for your students.

Good speakers pay attention to nonverbal cues from their audience. You need to add some pizzazz to your delivery if you notice that your students are doing any of the following:

- Watching the clock
- Looking confused
- Flipping through their notebook
- Staring off into space
- Talking to someone sitting nearby
- Refusing to look at you
- Putting their head down on their desk to sleep
- Doing homework for another class

- Asking to go to their locker, the restroom, the nurse, or the phone
- Tying and retying their shoes
- Sighing loudly and rolling their eyes

COMMAND ATTENTION

Few things can be as frustrating for a teacher as being ignored, and yet it happens in classroom after classroom, day after day. Although it is certainly understandable that we occasionally lose our students' attention, allowing students to zone out briefly or, even worse, ignore us as we give directions or relay important information is not an acceptable teaching practice.

Instead of trying to talk when your students are not ready to listen, wait until you have everyone's attention. Arrange a signal with students so that they know that they are supposed to stop what they are doing and listen. If you teach older students, a simple signal, such as "May I have your attention please?" spoken while you are at the front of the class obviously waiting for their attention is often effective. For younger students, a variety of signals may be more useful. Some of the most popular and effective signals include these:

- Stand in front of the class and begin a series of actions that you want students to copy: touching your nose, tugging on an earlobe, putting your hands on your hips, and so on. Once they are copying your actions, you will have their attention.
- Teach your students to hold up a hand and stop talking when they see you holding up yours.
- Count backward from ten.
- Say, "One, two, three, freeze!"
- Have a class catchphrase, such as the popular "Hocus, pocus, everybody focus" or "One, two, three, eyes on me."
- Display a timer or a clock on an interactive whiteboard and count down until students are paying attention.
- Sing a line or two of a song and expect students to finish it.
- Designate students to be the official "shushers" for the day or the week and put them to work.
- Play a song that they like so that they know they must be ready to pay attention at the end of it.
- Establish a rhythmic clapping pattern that students will follow once you start.
- Have a bell on your desk so that students can stop working and focus as soon as they hear it.

Another effective way to command your students' attention is to make sure your students know that you will not endlessly repeat yourself. Before you begin to speak in front of your class, warn them that they need to listen attentively because you want them to learn information the first time they hear it.

Finally, be aware of your audience. Students do not have long attention spans. They become restless after just a few minutes. Break up activities and allow wiggle breaks periodically to allow them to stay on track. Don't get so caught up in your lesson that you forget that even the best-planned lesson is useless if no one is listening.

USE YOUR VOICE EFFECTIVELY

One of the most important tools in your teacher's toolbox is your voice. Your voice is really one of the things that people notice first about you as a teacher. Your students certainly learn to respond to it quickly. If you are not sure of what to do, quick-witted students can be quick to pick up the hesitation in your voice and move off task. Conversely, a confident, credible voice can convey information in such a no-nonsense fashion that it can convince a roomful of rowdy students that you mean business.

When you take a deliberate approach to using your voice effectively to help you manage your classroom, there are several things to consider. First, consider how you can best use different volumes. One of the most important tips that veteran teachers can share with you is that shouting to be heard is never effective. If you want a class to listen to you, catch their attention and dramatically and slowly lower the volume of your voice. If you really want to make students pay attention, a dramatic stage whisper works wonders.

Another way to make sure to use your voice effectively is to match your tone to your purpose. Teachers who do not use a serious tone when the situation warrants it can confuse students who quickly pick up on the discrepancy between the tone of voice their teacher is using and the seriousness of the moment.

You may recall teachers in your past who had unfortunate verbal mannerisms—repeating "you know"; or clearing their throat; or using annoying filler words, such as "like." If you suspect that you may have a potentially distracting verbal mannerism, one of the best ways to be certain is to record yourself and listen critically. You can also ask for honest feedback from colleagues or even from your students.

A final way to modulate your voice to make it more effective as a teaching tool is to vary the speed at which you speak. Teachers who talk very quickly or in a slow monotone in front of the class are not tuned in to their audience. Remember that when you are in class, you should not be in the same conversational mode that you would use with your friends. Instead, use your voice to make it easy for your students to understand you.

USE BODY LANGUAGE TO MOTIVATE YOUR LISTENERS

Your students can tell right away when they have your full attention. They can also tell when you like them, when you find a lesson interesting, and when you are reaching the limits of your patience. The nonverbal language you use in your classroom can be a powerful way to capture your students' attention and motivate them to work.

First, you must learn to use it effectively. You have to make sure that the body language signals you send match the verbal ones. For example, if you try not to laugh when you are attempting to scold a student who has misbehaved in a way you find funny, no one will take you seriously. If you frown unconsciously while praising your class, you will confuse your students. To avoid sending such mixed signals, review this list of confusing or negative body language cues:

- Pointing at your students
- Standing with your hands on your hips
- Putting your hands too close to a student's face
- Speaking too loudly or in a monotone
- Jabbing a finger at a student's chest to make a point
- Tapping your fingers to show impatience
- Leaning away from students
- Snapping your fingers at students
- Laughing while delivering a serious message
- Rolling your eyes as if in disgust
- Ignoring a student who is upset
- Slamming doors or books

You can also use nonverbal language to send a positive message to your students. The following signals convey such a message:

> Put your students in the best position for them to be successful. Don't let the students dictate the classroom; they can have input, but you are in charge, and they need to know that.
>
> *Joshua Culver, first-year teacher*

- Leaning forward to indicate that you are interested
- Making eye contact
- Nodding your head
- Lightly touching a student on the arm
- Smiling
- Giving a thumbs up

How to Make a Point Students Will Remember

Although there are endless creative techniques to help your students remember the main points of your presentation, you will have to plan and prepare to make each technique successful. Successful teachers often experiment with a variety of approaches to help their students find success.

The following techniques are some you can use to help your students stay alert and interested in a lesson. Do not be afraid to modify or combine these ideas to get your points across to every student.

- **Help your students make a personal connection to the lesson.** They should be able to identify with the material under study. One easy way to do this is to include the names, interests, hobbies, experiences, or cultures of your students when creating worksheets or questions.

- **Present a slide show.** Using yours as a model, have your students prepare and present a slide show of their own.

- **Invite guest speakers to talk to your students as part of a unit of study.** Hearing a community leader talk about the importance of local government, for example, will reinforce any point you are trying to make about this topic.

- **Use plenty of models or examples and a variety of media when you demonstrate how to do something.** Try these: newspapers, advertisements, T-shirt slogans, cartoons, movies, art, computers, television shows, magazines, videos, or music.

- **Hide items related to the lesson in a large box.** Ask students to guess what the items could be. As they open the box, have students explain or predict the significance of each item.

- **Play music that fits the lesson of the day.** As you play parts of songs, ask students to tell how each relates to the lesson.

- **Hand out blindfolds and have your students put them on.** Give them objects related to the information you want them to recall and have them identify them without peeking.

- **Display a statement that you want your students to recall.** Guarantee that they will do so by immediately playing a video clip that supports it.

- **Surprise students with a bit of theater.** This not only will make your lesson enjoyable but also will make it one your students will recall for a long time. Try some of these ideas to develop your dramatic flair:
  - Say something outrageously startling and interesting.
  - Stage a reenactment.
  - Videotape your students as they work.
  - Wear a costume, or have your students wear costumes.

How to Help Students Stay on Track During a Lecture

Few classroom proceedings are as discouraging as preparing a fascinating lecture for a roomful of students who don't listen. Sometimes teachers assume that their students are paying attention, only to find out later that the entire class missed the fine points of a presentation. Through planning and preparation, you can avoid this disappointment. Here are some suggestions on how to help your students stay on track during a lecture:

- Tell students a specific number of facts they will learn during the course of the presentation. As you cover each one, mark it off, resulting in a countdown of the facts.

- Tell students that you only have a certain amount of time to lecture. Set a timer to make students aware of the passage of time as you speak.

- Give students an outline of the lecture.

- Stop periodically to review notes by calling on students to share a fact. Keep at it until all the points have been mentioned.

- Announce that there will be an open-note quiz after the lecture is over.

- Stop and ask students to share their notes with a partner so they can fill in any missing information.

- Hand each student two sets of ten cards. On each card from one set, have the first part of a fact from the presentation. On each card from the other set, have the second part of the fact. As the lecture progresses, students can match the cards from the two sets based on the information they are learning.

- Ask students to complete a graphic organizer as they listen.

- Stop and ask for a quick recap.

- Have students mark off items on a checklist.

- Give students a word bank of keywords, dates, or other items to use in their notes.

- If the lecture involves events in a particular order, give students a handout with the events in scrambled order, and ask them to rearrange the events in the correct order.

- Put ten words from the lecture on a handout. Ask students to mark them off as you speak. Tell them that you will discuss nine of the words, and that they are responsible for telling you which one was not in the lecture.

Conduct Class Discussions That Engage Every Student

If you have fond memories of classes in which everyone seemed to be involved in discussing a topic of burning importance, you probably want to help your students have that experience, too. Remember how you left the room exhilarated, still debating your points, and in full possession of strong opinions that you did not hold when class began?

Class discussions are an excellent way to deliver instruction that students will remember long after the class is over. Best of all, class discussions create active learners who are perfecting their thinking skills while expanding their knowledge of a topic.

What role should you take in a class discussion? First, envision yourself as the facilitator of the discussion. Your job is to plan the discussion, keep things running smoothly, and wrap up at the end. Think about your role in making this a successful and stimulating method of delivering instruction in three easy components: what to do to prepare for the discussion, what to do during the discussion, and what to do after the discussion is over.

BEFORE THE DISCUSSION

- **Post procedures in a prominent place in the classroom.** You should consider how you want your students to relate to each other and to you. Here are some guidelines you could establish:
  - Wait until the moderator recognizes you before you speak.
  - Do not speak after you have reached your limit of speaking opportunities.
  - Treat other people's opinions with tolerance and respect.
  - Listen more than you speak.
- **Determine the purpose of the discussion.** What outcomes do you want? Do you want students to analyze an issue? Combine information in a new way? Brainstorm new ideas? You should convey the purpose of the discussion to focus the conversation.
- **Create the questions your students will discuss.** Successful questions for class discussions require higher-order thinking skills. For the first discussion session, prepare ten thought-provoking questions. Use the reactions of your students to gauge how many to prepare for future sessions. When appropriate, give students advance copies of questions so that they can prepare.
- **Move the chairs.** Set up chairs so students can see each other's faces. Taking time to arrange the seating as you wish the first time will help you establish how you want it done in the future.

DURING THE DISCUSSION

- **Enforce procedures.** As the discussion gets under way, remind students of the importance of the conduct procedures for class discussions. Be steadfast in enforcing them. It may be difficult for your students to adjust to them at first, but with persistence, you will succeed in having productive class discussions.
- **Introduce the topics of discussion.** You can display questions using an overhead projector, write them on the board, or ask students to review their advance copy of the questions.
- **Teach your students the importance of supporting their opinions.** When someone makes a point, keep probing until enough support has been presented. Students need to realize that it is not enough to express their opinion; they must also be able to defend and support it.

- **Encourage deeper thinking.** Elicit thoughtful responses by trying these techniques: invite a student to comment on someone else's response, ask for elaboration, ask another student to refute what has been said, or ask for a restatement.

- **Allow everyone to participate.** Keep outgoing students who want to express themselves at the expense of everyone else in check. One easy way to do this is to give all students the same number of slips of paper. Each time someone speaks, he or she has to give up one of the slips. When a student is out of slips, he or she is out of opportunities to speak.

- **Recognize speakers.** To determine who gets to speak, have an unbreakable object, such as a book or stuffed toy, for students to hand to each other as they take turns speaking.

- **Encourage risk taking.** Make it easy and nonthreatening for all students to risk answering. Encourage and validate answers when you can.

- **Step back.** Refrain from dominating the discussion. A class discussion works best when all students are prepared and when all students join in.

AFTER THE DISCUSSION

Have students reflect. Ask students to reflect on the discussion by asking for

- Written or oral feedback on what went well
- Suggestions for improvement
- A retelling of the important points
- A written summary

The Power of Play: Using Toys to Capture Attention

Rubber ducks in math class? Spinning tops in history class? Not only do toys capture the attention of children of all ages but also the intrinsic contrast between a toy and an academic setting is enormously appealing to almost every audience. Successful teachers who want their students to enjoy a lesson know that few things are as useful as toys in capturing their students' attention.

Toys of all types can be effective manipulatives that spark students' curiosity and encourage them to use their imagination as well as their critical thinking skills. Harnessing the power of play in your classroom encourages students of all ages to be engaged with the lesson and invested in collaborating with their classmates.

Depending on your imagination, the lesson, and the ages of your students, toys can be used in many different ways before, during, and after a presentation. Try some of these activities to help your students relate the toy to the information in your instruction. Ask students to

- Describe the toy
- Tell how the toy works
- Explain how it relates to the lesson
- Research the history of the toy
- Give other uses for it
- Brainstorm a list of reasons why it is appealing
- Create other names for it
- Share memories about similar toys
- Take it apart
- Find out where the raw materials for it are from
- Estimate information, such as its weight, length, or height
- Use it to illustrate a point

> Make learning fun! Engaging students in fun activities allows them to learn without stress. It's kind of like a sneak attack. They are having so much fun in class that they don't realize they are mastering a difficult chunk of information until the close of the lesson.
>
> *Debbie McManaway, 19 years' experience*

Games Your Students Will Enjoy

Your students love to play games. You can capitalize on this natural interest by playing games often in your classroom. Games are positive learning experiences for the same reasons that activities incorporating toys are: they provide opportunities for interaction, offer immediate feedback, make the work relevant, allow plenty of practice, and motivate students to collaborate on higher-order learning tasks. Consider arranging team games to help students review, teach each other information, or simply work together in a structured fashion.

Before your students engage in a classroom game, you must establish ground rules so that the activity will be a successful one for everyone. Here are some suggestions for managing games in your classroom:

- Consider the geography of your room before you begin. Move furniture, put breakable items in a safe place, and plan how you will put the room back in order at the end of the game.
- Teach good sportsmanship in advance of game day. Be very clear with your students about what behaviors you expect from them and what behaviors are not acceptable.
- Make sure there is a sound educational purpose for each game, and that you are not simply using it as a pleasant way to pass time.
- Pay attention to safety. If you see that students are so excited that the competition is becoming too intense, stop play at once.

- Select the team members yourself so that no one will be left out. Allow students to make decisions about scoring procedures and rules of sportsmanship. Keep a container of numbers or other markers on hand for students to draw from to determine who goes first or makes other decisions.

- Although you don't really need prizes for class games, consider offering ribbons, stickers, trinkets, or bookmarks.

- Add realistic touches, such as music or other props. These will make it easier for your students to get into the spirit of the game.

- Have students assume the roles of scorekeeper, timekeeper, and master of ceremonies so that you can monitor activities.

- Prepare to move your class to a location where they won't disturb other students if the game gets noisy.

- After a game is over, ask your students to tell you what they learned.

In addition, you can always adapt games you enjoyed as a child. To give you some ideas as you begin your adaptations, here are some suggestions:

- **Flyswatter Badminton.** Use masking tape to mark off a small badminton court. Blow up a balloon and hand each student a flyswatter to use as a racket. Divide students into teams and arrange them on either side of an imaginary net (indicated by a taped line on the floor). As you ask questions, students earn points for moving the balloon across the net and for answering questions correctly.

- **PowerPoint games.** The assortment of PowerPoint games available to teachers is almost limitless. You can either create the games yourself or use some of the many templates available for downloading.

- **Talk Show.** Have your students stage a talk show to interview characters from fiction or history or in any other discipline. Choose an outgoing and reliable student to be the host, and let that student interview other students, who pose as guests.

- **Storytellers.** Have students sit in a circle. To play, one student begins a story, stops after a few sentences, and then points to another student, who continues the story. You can adapt this activity to teach vocabulary, the order of events, facts, or other information.

- **Quiz Bowl.** Set up a tournament of quick questions and answers involving as many of your students as possible. To add interest, vary the level of difficulty, rules of play, way of scoring, and incentives.

- **Board games.** Design your own board games to fit your topic. You can make small boards and photocopy them for students to use in a small group, or you can make a large board for the entire class to use. The tasks you assign your students in a board game can range from simply answering questions to solving problems.

- **Name That Person (or Battle, or City, or . . .).** This game is similar to Twenty Questions in that students try to guess answers with as few clues as possible. You should make up the clues in advance. On game day, you'll call the clues out one at a time until someone can name the target person, battle, city, or other item.

- **Ball Toss.** Line up your students in two teams facing each other. As soon as a student correctly answers a question you ask, that student tosses a soft foam ball to a student on the other team. That student has to answer the next question.

- **Chain Making.** This is an educational version of the old alphabet game that small children play. One player begins thinking of an object related to the unit of study and beginning with the letter *A*. The next student has to repeat that clue and add an object beginning with the letter *B*. The game continues until students are stumped or until they reach the end of the alphabet.

- **Simulations.** Although most simulation games are often sophisticated computer ones, you and your students can enjoy low-tech simulations that are simple to construct. Plan the scenario you want your students to enact, then involve them in it by reading them a written description or by role-playing. A very popular version of this game is to have your students imagine that they are shipwrecked on a deserted island and have to plan ways to survive. Simulation games can be used to help your students think creatively, learn to work cooperatively, or examine their values—or to satisfy just about any purpose you have in mind when you create the game for them.

- **One, Two, and You're Outta Here.** Stand at the door at the end of class with a set of flash cards or questions that require quick answers. For a student to leave class, he or she has to answer two questions correctly.

- **Tic-tac-toe.** Students advance play on a tic-tac-toe board by giving correct answers to questions. Creating a board is easy. Make a grid of three blocks across and down for a total of nine blocks. Photocopy the grid so that students can play in small groups.

- **Bingo.** Many teachers use this game to review vocabulary words. Photocopy a game board with sixteen or twenty-five blocks. Give students a list of words to place in the blanks. They can use bits of paper to cover the words when you call out definitions.

- **Hangman.** In the traditional version, students guess letters in a word or phrase to keep the figure "alive." In other versions, students can give correct answers to short-answer questions or define vocabulary terms. If you do not want to have your students draw a hanging man on the board, consider using a spider hanging from a web instead. Instead of drawing the head and limbs of a human, your students could add legs to the spider.

- **Student-created board games.** Many students can be very skilled and creative in designing their own board games. Often they will create games based on such old favorites as Candy Land or Battleship, but using the material they have learned in class.

- **Sporting events.** Divide your students into teams, and use the chalkboard to play games of football, soccer, or whatever sport currently interests them. Students advance by correctly answering questions or completing assigned tasks.

Another useful repository of classroom games is the Internet. With just a few clicks, you can find many puzzle and game sites that can engage students in meaningful learning activities. Many teachers, for example, have found that using the search term "free Power-Point games" will yield dozens of free templates to download. At some sites, teachers even share their own games with others who are teaching the same material.

The sites listed here are ones that contain a wide variety of puzzles and games that would be appropriate for students of all ages.

- **Boardgames.com (www.boardgames.com).** This commercial site offers a large variety of electronic and traditional board games at reasonable prices.
- **Dave's ESL Cafe (www.eslcafe.com).** Dave Sperling's site lists dozens of classroom games, along with rules and suggestions. Click on the "Stuff for Teachers" tab and then the "Games" tab to access the large list. This site has many other resources for teachers, too.
- **Discovery Education (http://school.discovery.com/brainboosters).** This page on the Discovery School site offers dozens of brain twister puzzles, activities, and games for students of all ages and ability levels.
- **Out of the Box Games (www.otb-games.com).** This is also a commercial site with a large assortment of games for sale. You can find classic board games, dice games, and word games, as well as newer types of games.

Use Graphic Organizers to Engage Students

Can you imagine how hard it would be to make up a seating chart without the chart? You would have to write sentence after sentence explaining who would sit where. Instead of writing it out, you save time by using a graphic organizer.

Not only do graphic organizers help students decode, process, and understand material but also they do so in a way that helps students retain information. Further, graphic organizers can help students solve problems and comprehend material quickly. When students create graphic organizers, they can see the relationships among the important elements in the assignment. Moreover, students of all age and ability levels can use them successfully for a variety of purposes:

- To take notes on lectures and reading
- To describe people, places, events, ideas, or objects

- To compare and contrast
- To determine the validity of assumptions
- To classify and categorize information
- To determine relevant details
- To see how parts make up a whole
- To solve problems
- To predict outcomes
- To plan reading and writing activities
- To understand cause and effect
- To support arguments
- To organize concepts into key components
- To analyze vocabulary words
- To organize textual material

You will find that there are several common patterns for graphic organizers. Here is a very brief list of some of these patterns, short descriptions of what they can be used for, and the names of some of the graphic organizers that could be associated with each one:

Pattern One: Concept maps. These allow students to understand the attributes of a concept. Some examples include

- Herringbone maps
- Venn diagrams
- Spider maps
- Network trees
- Outlines
- Novel or story matrices
- Hierarchy maps

Pattern Two: Description maps. These allow students to comprehend the facts that describe a person, place, thing, idea, or event. Some examples include

- Characterization maps
- Family trees
- Clustering
- Webbing
- Episode maps

Pattern Three: Time sequence maps. These allow students to put items in chronological order. Some examples include

- Time lines
- Continuum maps
- Storyboards
- Story maps
- Chain-of-events maps
- Cycle diagrams

Pattern Four: Cause-and-effect maps. These allow students to see the relationships that result when one event causes another. Some examples include

- Flowcharts
- Stepladder charts
- Problem-and-solution charts

It is easy to find and use comprehensive Web resources for help with graphic organizers. To access graphic organizers that are already designed for you and your students, try these sites:

- **Houghton Mifflin (www.eduplace.com/graphicorganizer/index.html).** Here you will find more than three dozen useful graphic organizers to download.
- **Education Oasis (www.educationoasis.com).** At Education Oasis, you will find more than fifty printable graphic organizers.

A special type of graphic organizer is the three-dimensional graphic organizer. To make this type of graphic organizer, students cut, fold, and glue paper in various configurations to create hands-on manipulatives. The best resource for this type of very popular and effective graphic organizer is an educational entrepreneur, Dinah Zike. You can learn more about how to use three-dimensional graphic organizers in your classroom at her informative and helpful Web site, Dinah-Might Adventures (www.dinah.com).

> Be ENTHUSIASTIC about your subject! If you enjoy yourself at your job, your students will embrace what you're showing them.
>
> *Kay Stephenson, 33 years' experience*

Two Simple Techniques: Learning Cubes and Colored Dot Labels

Two popular and inexpensive ways to deliver instruction sure to engage your students involve learning cubes and colored dot labels. Appropriate for students of all ages and versatile enough to be adapted to any content area, both of these simple ideas can enliven lessons.

LEARNING CUBES

Learning cubes can easily be made with just card stock, a marker, and scissors. Either find a cube-shaped box (several brands of tissues have suitable boxes) or make one from the card stock. On each side of a cube, write a direction or question. Students then roll the cube to determine which question to answer or which direction to follow. Although they can be used by individual students, learning cubes are most effective when pairs or teams of students work with them. To show you how versatile learning cubes can be, here are lists of just some of the directions or questions you can adapt for your classroom:

Idea Set One

1. What is _____?
2. Where is _____?
3. How did _____ happen?
4. Who caused _____?
5. Why did _____ happen?
6. What happened to _____?

Idea Set Two

1. Add _____ and _____.
2. Multiply _____ by _____.
3. Divide _____ into _____.
4. Subtract _____ from _____.
5. Solve _____.
6. Find the square root of _____.

Idea Set Three

1. List _____.
2. Explain _____.
3. Describe _____.
4. Justify _____.
5. Recall _____.
6. Prove _____.

Idea Set Four

1. Summarize _____.

2. Interpret _____.

3. Extend _____.

4. Demonstrate _____.

5. Rephrase _____.

6. Illustrate _____.

Idea Set Five

1. Classify _____.

2. Compare _____.

3. Support _____.

4. State in your own words _____.

5. Contrast _____.

6. Infer the meaning of _____.

Idea Set Six

1. What is the main idea?

2. What are the supporting ideas?

3. What essential concepts are you trying to prove?

4. Which facts provide valid proof?

5. What can you conclude?

6. What is meant by _____?

Idea Set Seven

1. How can you organize _____ to show _____?

2. How can you prove your understanding of _____?

3. What would be the result of _____?

4. What facts would you choose to prove _____?

5. What questions should you ask to _____?

6. What examples can you use to _____?

Idea Set Eight

1. Make use of _____ to _____.

2. Create a model _____.

3. Solve this puzzle: _____.

4. Make a plan to _____.

5. Construct a new _____.

6. Use _____ to _____.

Idea Set Nine

1. Use _____ to simplify _____.

2. Why do you believe _____ is true?

3. What is the chief cause of _____?

4. What conclusions can you draw from _____?

5. What is the evidence to support _____?

6. What is the relationship between _____ and _____?

Idea Set Ten

1. Justify the _____ of _____.

2. Categorize the reasons for _____.

3. Survey classmates about _____.

4. Create a test for _____.

5. Inspect _____, and make inferences about _____.

6. Determine the motives for _____.

Idea Set Eleven

1. What can you deduce from _____?

2. What caused _____?

3. What are the effects of _____?

4. What is the value of _____?

5. What are the criteria for _____?

6. How can you prioritize the steps for _____?

Idea Set Twelve

1. Why did _____ do _____?

2. What can you recommend for _____?

3. What determines the success of _____?

4. What explanations can there be for _____?

5. Which data are most valid to prove _____?

6. How would you disprove _____?

Idea Set Thirteen

1. Evaluate _____.

2. Classify _____.

3. Prove _____.

4. Interpret _____.

5. Support _____.

6. Assess _____.

Idea Set Fourteen

1. Design _____.

2. Elaborate on _____.

3. Predict _____.

4. Theorize about _____.

5. Improve _____.

6. Discuss _____.

Idea Set Fifteen

1. Analyze _____.

2. Compare and contrast _____ and _____.

3. Discuss _____.

4. Describe _____.

5. Summarize _____.

6. Justify _____.

Idea Set Sixteen

1. What should have happened to _____?

2. What would happen if _____?

3. What should not have happened to _____?

4. How can you minimize _____?

5. How can you maximize _____?

6. What is the best way to _____?

Idea Set Seventeen

1. What did you learn today?

2. What do you still need to learn?

3. What surprised you today?

4. What was easiest to learn today?

5. What was hardest to learn today?

6. What was covered today that you already knew?

Idea Set Eighteen

1. What can you design to _____?

2. What can you predict about _____?

3. What facts can you compile about _____?

4. What can you improve about _____?

5. How can you estimate the final outcome of _____?

6. What can you construct that will _____?

Idea Set Nineteen

1. Give an example of a person who _____.

2. Give an example of a place that _____.

3. Give an example of a thing that _____.

4. Give an example of an idea that _____.

5. Give an example of an event that _____.

6. Give an example of a group that _____.

Idea Set Twenty

1. What can you add to what you learned today?

2. How can you use what you learned today?

3. What is important about what you learned today?

4. What is not important about what you learned today?

5. What did you already know about the lesson before today?

6. What can you teach to someone else from the lesson today?

COLORED DOT LABELS

Colored dot labels are an inexpensive staple in most office supply stores. Found in a variety of bright colors and sizes, colored dots can be used in a number of engaging ways in a classroom because of their appeal to various learning styles and multiple intelligences and their easy adaptability. To put it simply, students just enjoy sticking the dots on things. Fortunately, it's easy to take advantage of this inherent appeal. Consider asking students to use colored dots to manipulate items, ideas, concepts, or steps in the following ways:

- To classify ideas
- To identify key concepts
- To group items
- To rearrange ideas
- To categorize concepts
- To place events in chronological order
- To distinguish traits
- To label characteristics
- To match elements
- To reorganize items in a process
- To differentiate items according to various criteria
- To determine cause and effect
- To agree or disagree with statements
- To prioritize items in order of importance
- To recommend as good, better, and best
- To choose items to be combined
- To rank items in order of significance
- To combine multiple ideas
- To evaluate using established criteria

> Even with all of the mandated testing and standards, keep creativity alive! Work hard to find a way to do it all!
>
> *Stephanie Stock Mahoney,*
> *35 years' experience*

Providing Models, Examples, and Samples

In the rush of planning, it's very easy to overlook this important part of making sure that your instruction is delivered successfully because you are quite naturally focused on the final products that your students will be turning in. However, providing models, examples, and samples of the kinds of work that you expect from your students is key to ensuring that they know what to do and how to do it well. As a new teacher, you may not have very many exemplars on hand to show your students. To overcome this, create one or two yourself and ask other teachers at your school for help. As soon as good student exemplars are turned in, display them for others to see. These three ways of obtaining good models, examples, and samples are well worth the effort because these items will build your students' confidence and knowledge.

To make sure that you will have plenty of excellent models, examples, and samples for future use and still have sufficient storage space in your classroom, photograph your exemplars and store them in an electronic file for later use. Imagine how convenient it will be next year to show a quick slide show of some of this year's work when you present new instruction!

How to Make Seatwork Appealing

Dull worksheets have no place in today's classroom. Although students do need to complete work at their desk, that work does not have to be tedious. Instead, you can make seatwork engaging and interesting as well as productive.

To give seatwork pizzazz, think of what would delight your students as they sit down to work. Do your students like bright colors? Political cartoons? Clever graphics? Options? You should take advantage of your students' preferences to make their work agreeable. Consider these suggestions to make seatwork a pleasant learning experience in your class:

- Personalize handouts with student names, local places, or interests of your students. Be sensitive about how you use personal facts to avoid inadvertently embarrassing a student.

- Provide access to a key so that students can check their progress on drill work.

- Provide scrambled facts, words, terms, or other items for students to unscramble.

- If the seatwork has several sections, create a small bar graph for students to fill in as they finish each section. This allows them to see their progress.

- Assign matching exercises, which students of all ages enjoy.

- Offer optional work. When students finish an assignment, they may opt for another activity.

- Allow students to use colored paper, crayons, and colored pencils or pens when appropriate.

- Have students solve puzzles, which hold built-in appeal for learners. Even a brief puzzle or riddle at the bottom of a page will be interesting to your students.

- Allow students to work with a partner or to have access to a study buddy when a question arises.

- Offer choices within the seatwork itself. For example, offer two sections, and allow students to choose which one they would like to tackle.

- Ask students to create potential test questions with answers.

- Reward students for working well or for completing seatwork on time.

- Allow students to be creative. Even such simple activities as making up their own problems or drawing to illustrate a point will please many students.

Don't be the students' pal. They've got plenty of those.

Kay Stephenson, 33 years' experience

- Ask students to give their opinions or to respond to questions in a personal way.
- Make all handouts as attractive as possible. Use a readable font, organize each handout clearly, and add clip art when appropriate.

Best Practices Checklist

1. Plan to work steadily all year to cultivate your communication skills in the interest of becoming a charismatic classroom leader who inspires students and engages them in learning.

2. Take care to plan and prepare for oral presentations. Good delivery of dynamic and interesting instruction does not happen by accident.

3. When working to improve your oral presentation skills, remember to pay attention to all aspects of your delivery: voice, demeanor, and body language.

4. Be proactive! Make sure to plan ways to encourage your students to stay on track and on task during presentations. They will not be focused unless you help them.

5. Take advantage of the power of play in all of its different guises when designing lessons that will appeal to your students' sense of fun.

6. Incorporate online sites offering games, brainteasers, puzzles, and other interesting and challenging activities into instruction whenever you can.

7. Use graphic organizers of various types often to help students access previous learning, master current material, and think though complicated problems.

8. Use hands-on manipulatives, such as learning cubes and colored dot labels, to enliven many different lessons.

9. Remember that if students are to succeed, they need to understand what you expect of them. Provide examples, samples, and models.

10. Make even such mundane class activities as seatwork appealing with creativity and careful planning.

Time to Reflect
Deliver Engaging Instruction

Use the information in this section to guide your thinking as you reflect on these questions. They are designed to encourage you to think more deeply about the issues in the text or to discuss those issues with colleagues.

1. What can you do to avoid having your students tune out? How can you use your strengths as a speaker to improve your delivery of instruction?

2. If your students were to compare you to a celebrity, who would it be? What can you learn from this? How can you improve your classroom charisma?

3. When delivering instruction, what student behaviors should teachers overlook? What can a speaker do to hold students' attention and prevent misbehavior? How can your colleagues help you with this?

4. What kinds of games do your students like to play? How can you incorporate their interests into learning activities? Where can you learn about more games or enjoyable activities that would work well in your classroom?

5. What can you do to make sure class discussions are valuable and enjoyable learning experiences for your students? What do you need to teach your students about their role in class discussions? What do you need to do to prepare for a successful class discussion? What suggestions do your colleagues have in regard to conducting class discussions?

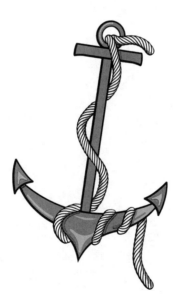

SECTION TWELVE

Meet the Needs of All of Your Students

There is no such thing as a homogeneous classroom. Although some classes may be grouped by age, ability level, standardized test scores, or some other special quality, even in those classrooms, which seem to be filled with students who are more similar than different, just a quick glance around the room reveals that there are many very real differences among the students. Whether our students are active or calm, energetic or quiet, focused or off task . . . our classrooms are complex communities composed of students whose differences and how well we accommodate those differences can determine the success or failure of the entire class.

In the past, educators erred by attempting to teach their students using one lesson plan and expecting that the material in the lesson would make sense to every student. Now, research and practical classroom experience have shown us that we cannot afford to ignore the educational needs of even one student in our classroom. Instead, we need to view our students as individuals and not just as faces in the classroom crowd.

In this section, you will first learn some of the basics of differentiating or modifying instruction so that all of your students can be successful. You will then learn some strategies to help some of the special populations of students you may have in your classroom.

Differentiated Instruction to Support All Learners

One of the most exciting shifts in educational practice in the twenty-first-century classroom is the movement from one-size-fits-all instruction to differentiated instruction. In almost any classroom, it is not unusual for advanced learners to work alongside other students whose background experiences, readiness levels, or preferred learning styles can vary greatly from one learner to the next. Other differences in today's classrooms include such factors as physical disabilities, diverse cultures, and varying levels of home support.

Educators today respond to these variations by differentiating instruction, a process by which teachers enhance learning by matching student characteristics to instruction and assessment. Although the activities and strategies are limitless, each one is designed to meet the needs of individual students, unlike the traditional approach in a one-size-fits-all classroom.

Differentiated instruction is an effective strategy because it meets students at their various readiness levels and then offers instruction geared to meet their needs. It also works well as a part of a classroom discipline plan because the focus on allowing students to work on appealing assignments that encourage self-efficacy and academic success engages students so fully that they have something better to do than misbehave. There are several important ideas to keep in mind when differentiating instruction:

- The focus of a differentiated classroom is on the needs of individual students as they learn the mandated content and skills rather than just on the material to be covered.

- Many different approaches to the delivery of instruction are necessary to reach all students.

- The main components of classroom instruction—content, process, and product—can all be adjusted to promote student growth and achievement.

- Instruction revolves around a proactive stance toward dealing with learning differences among students. Formative assessments are a key element in helping teachers design and adjust instructional activities.

At its most basic level, differentiating instruction is being fair to all students. It means creating many paths so that students of different abilities, interests, or learning needs experience appropriate ways to learn. Everyone has a chance to succeed when teachers differentiate.

One of the most respected authorities in this field of education is Carol Ann Tomlinson (http://caroltomlinson.com). To learn more about differentiated instruction, consult these resources:

Dodge, J. *Differentiation in Action*. New York, NY: Scholastic, 2005.

Kaplan, J., Rogers, V., and Webster, R. *Differentiated Instruction Made Easy: Hundreds of Multi-Level Activities for All Learners*. San Francisco, CA: Jossey-Bass, 2011.

Tomlinson, C. A. *How to Differentiate Instruction in Mixed Ability Classrooms*, 2nd ed. Alexandria, VA: Association for Supervision and Curriculum Development, 2004.

WHAT DIFFERENTIATED INSTRUCTION IS AND IS NOT

Although differentiated instruction is used in thousands of classrooms, some teachers may still have some misconceptions about it. They may be confused about what it is and how it can be used to help their students succeed. Here you can see what differentiated instruction is as well as what it is not:

> In the 1960s a student was placed in my general mechanics class because he could not read. I asked him what he liked to do. He said he liked to mess with motors. He had taken his diesel tractor motor out and put it in an old pickup truck. This is what he drove to school. In the spring, the motor went back in the tractor for spring plowing. Other teachers had told me this boy was dumb.
>
> *Edward Gardner, 36 years' experience*

What Differentiated Instruction Is	What Differentiated Instruction Is Not
A carefully planned and proactive approach to teaching	A disorganized and passive approach to teaching
Adjusted frequently based on regular assessments	Inflexible instructional strategies designed to appeal to almost every student
Varied approaches to help students master material	The same material and learning activities for all students
A blend of activities and different types of instruction	Individualized lesson plans for each student
Prescriptive and student centered	Another way to provide homogeneous instruction
Flexible, responsive to student needs, and respectful of student abilities	Used primarily for remediation alone
Variations of content, process, and product for all students	Easier work for some students and more difficult work for others

"HOW CAN I POSSIBLY MEET EVERYONE'S NEEDS?"

One of the overwhelming concerns that many teachers have when they first meet their students is how to accommodate the needs of every learner. After all, it is daunting to try to teach a roomful of students who come from different cultures, have different learning styles and widely varying maturity levels, have different levels of academic readiness, and even have very different interests. Once teachers become aware of the range of differences among their students, they can be tempted to just design a lesson with only one instructional strategy and hope that it will somehow magically be effective for all learners. Although that approach may appeal to a busy teacher, it will definitely not appeal to students.

It can be confusing at first to work out different ways to differentiate instruction, especially because most students have several learning style preferences, but really it is not difficult to meet the needs of the learners in your classroom. The trick to success is simple: *rotate every student through a variety of task types. You will strengthen weak areas and allow students to enjoy their preferences.* Not all students are visual learners, for example, but many students are, and they will benefit from being able to use their learning style preferences. At the same time, the auditory and tactile learners in your class will be able to strengthen an area of weakness as they work through tasks that would normally appeal mainly to visual learners. Rotating students through a variety of tasks makes accommodating the needs of every learner a reasonable and achievable endeavor.

To help you make informed decisions about how to rotate your students through a variety of activities, use Teacher Worksheet 12.1 as a planning guide.

TEACHER WORKSHEET 12.1

Individualized Instruction Worksheet

To ensure that your plans to offer a differentiated lesson are on the right track, you can use this worksheet to design instruction that will meet the needs of all of your learners.

Lesson topic: _____ Date: _____

Concepts and essential questions:

_____

_____

_____

_____

_____

Outcomes, objectives, and goals:

_____

_____

_____

_____

_____

Learning style preferences (circle the preference[s] that the lesson is designed to appeal to): Visual   Auditory   Kinesthetic

Prelearning activities:

_____

_____

_____

_____

_____

Lesson activities:

_____

_____

_____

_____

_____

Postlearning activities:

_____

_____

_____

_____

_____

BASIC GUIDELINES FOR DIFFERENTIATION

Although there are many useful resources both in books and on the Internet to help you begin to implement differentiated instruction in your classroom, there are some common-sense, basic guidelines that will make the process easier and more successful for you and for your students. In the list that follows you will discover some of these basic guidelines for use in making the transition from traditional to differentiated instruction.

- **Remember that what's fair for one may not be fair for all.** If you can offer alternative approaches to learning, try to do so. All students in your class are individuals with different needs.

- **Work to find ways to make differentiation feasible.** Differentiated instruction should be highly individualized, but still manageable. Pay attention to your students' various preferred learning styles, readiness levels, and abilities. Don't forget to include your students' interests if you want highly motivated students.

- **Use as much data as you can gather to adopt a prescriptive approach to instruction.** Formative assessments are a key factor in making sure you and your students know how they are supposed to proceed. Think of such assessments as a way to help you teach rather than as a way to find out what your students didn't learn.

- **Emphasize quality of thought rather than the size of the workload.** If a student has obviously mastered how to solve a particular type of problem, for example, don't continue to assign more of the same problems. Instead, offer alternative problems or allow the student to move ahead. Expecting every student to do the same work is often not productive.

- **Focus on student growth instead of grades.** One way to do this is to have students self-assess their skill or knowledge level several times within a unit of study. Teach students to reflect and then evaluate themselves if you want them to become self-disciplined learners.

- **Rotate your lessons through the three basic learning styles to meet everyone's needs.** Everyone needs variety. Offer opportunities for various collaborative activities whenever possible.

- **Plan for quiet work days.** Not every class has to be a lively and fun experience. You do not have to be "on" every day, and neither do your students. Allow time for students to work steadily on assignments that are engaging, but not necessarily thrilling.

- **Offer active learning experiences.** When learning is active, everyone wins. Don't forget to include hands-on options. Take advantage of every technology resource that you can.

- **Be flexible.** Always have a few backup plans ready. You will need them.

- **Have explicit directions for all activities.** Provide specific procedures for those students who may need to ask for clarification. The more comfortable students are with the procedures they are to follow when doing their work, the easier it will be for them to be successful.

- **Always, always begin with your district's standards.** No activity, no matter how exciting it may be, is useful if it does not serve to move your students' knowledge and skills forward toward mastering a specific learning objective.

- **Provide a balance between teacher-assigned work and student-selected work.** Allow students as much choice as is appropriate and reasonable to manage.

- **Begin with tiny steps and proceed at a pace that is comfortable for you.** It is better to be cautious than to have an out-of-control classroom.

TEACHER WORKSHEET 12.2

A Planning Tool for Differentiation

You can use this worksheet as a way to think through or begin to plan an activity that is differentiated to meet the learning needs of your students. As you work through the questions, you should be able to determine how you can effectively differentiate the activity.

1. What need do you hope to serve by including the activity in your instruction?

   _____

   _____

2. Which learning styles will your activity appeal to?

   _____

   _____

3. What materials will you need?

   _____

   _____

4. What preparation is necessary for you to include this activity in your instruction?

   _____

   _____

5. What routines or procedures do you need to establish or reinforce?

   _____

   _____

6. What problems can you anticipate? How can you prevent or solve them?

   _____

   _____

7. Which formative assessments will you use to gather data before and during the activity?

   _____

   _____

8. What will the products of the activity be? At what stages will these products be assessed?

   _____

   _____

9. How will you know if differentiated implementation is successful?

   _____

   _____

From *The First-Year Teacher's Survival Guide*, 3rd Edition, by Julia G. Thompson. Copyright © 2013 by John Wiley & Sons, Inc. Reproduced by permission.

FOUR KEY STRATEGIES OF DIFFERENTIATION

Successful differentiated instruction involves the use of four key strategies to modify instruction. These four strategies form the bedrock of the choices that informed teachers make when they design and deliver differentiated instruction activities for their students.

Key Strategy One: Design Respectful Tasks

Respectful tasks are ones that recognize and honor individual students' learning differences. When designing respectful tasks, teachers pay attention to the readiness level of each student, expect all students to grow and learn, and offer all students opportunities to explore according to their own readiness level. Teachers who design respectful tasks do so with the intention that all tasks should be equally interesting, important, and engaging. Teachers will make sure not just that each task is appropriate and fair but also that they have taken a proactive approach in determining how best to accommodate student needs. When you set about creating respectful tasks for your students to undertake, ask yourself these questions for each task:

- Will the task be appropriate for students' various readiness levels?
- Does the task take into account student interests so that it is intrinsically appealing?
- Will the task allow students to use their learning style preferences?
- Does the task allow all students to be successful?
- Will the task be one that is practical and easy to manage?

Key Strategy Two: Use Flexible Grouping

Flexible groups are purposeful collaborative groups that allow students to be appropriately challenged and help you avoid labeling a student's readiness or skill level as unchanging. During the course of a school year, your students should work as members of many different groups depending on the task and content. It is important to permit movement between groups because interests and skills change as students move from one topic to another.

Flexible grouping also has other advantages in a differentiated classroom: it allows for a variety of ways to match students to necessary tasks; makes it easier for you to observe and assess students; and, most important, allows you to assign appropriate instructional activities to meet each student's learning needs.

What types of flexible groups are possible in a differentiated classroom?

- Readiness level groups
- Homogeneous ability groups
- Heterogeneous ability groups

- Interest groups
- Learning style groups
- Impromptu study or discussion groups
- Just about any type of group that you think would benefit your students

Key Strategy Three: Create Tiered Instruction

Tiered instruction is made possible when teachers evaluate their students and then use the data they collect to provide a different tier of instruction for each student. The most common types of tiers offer instruction to students on these three levels: students who do not know the concept or who do not have the skill, students who have some understanding of the concept or skill, and students who have mastered and understand the concept or skill.

Tiered instruction is an extremely flexible strategy. Every aspect of a lesson can be categorized into one of the three tiers. Teachers can differentiate process, content, and product into the three tiers, for example. Other opportunities to create tiered instruction can include in-class assignments, homework, learning stations, and even assessments. In the example of one set of possible tiers that follows, you can see just how adaptable this strategy can be:

For Struggling Students

- The teacher introduces vocabulary words.
- Students read with learning buddies.
- Students use guided questions to aid comprehension.
- Students use a word bank.

For Students Who May Just Need Practice

- Students read a text independently.
- Students take notes on the text independently.

For Advanced Students

- Students determine the parts of the topic they would like to explore further.
- Students do independent research about the topic using multiple sources.

If you would like to begin using tiered instruction in your classroom, the process is not complicated. Follow these steps for successful implementation of this key strategy:

- **Step One**: Identify the standards or concepts and skills you want students to learn.
- **Step Two**: Collect data to determine if students have the background necessary to be successful with the lesson.

- **Step Three**: Assess students' readiness, interests, and learning profiles.
- **Step Four**: Create an activity that is focused on the standard or concept and skills of the lesson.
- **Step Five**: Adjust the activity to provide tiers of difficulty that will lead all students to be successful.

Key Strategy Four: Provide Anchor Activities

Anchor activities are ongoing activities that students may do at any time when they have completed their primary assignments or when their teacher is busy with other students. These activities can be part of the daily routines of the class, or part of an ongoing assignment or a long-term project. Teachers who use anchor activities often find that such activities are most successful when the expectations for academic work and behavior are explicit, and when students know that their work is meaningful and will be assessed. Examples of anchor activities include these:

- Independent reading
- Writing projects
- Flash card review
- Online games or review
- Word games of various types
- Puzzles
- Student blogs
- Reflection journals
- Games that reinforce content or skill acquisition
- Binder or learning portfolio upkeep
- Vocabulary work
- Problems of the day
- Learning centers
- Multimedia presentations
- Art projects
- Portfolio maintenance

MANAGEMENT TIPS FOR THE DIFFERENTIATED CLASSROOM

It's reasonable to wonder just how you are going to manage a classroom in which students are engaged in different activities. For example, what is the rest of the class going to be doing when you are helping a small group of students? Although the management challenges of a differentiated classroom can be difficult at first, once your students are accustomed to the routines and expectations for their class, they will find it easy to remain on task because the work itself will drive instruction. Here are some of the management tips that can make creating a differentiated classroom a workable solution to how you will accommodate the needs of all of your students:

- Encourage classroom ownership and a sense of shared responsibility for the success of the entire class. Ask students to self-evaluate, make informed decisions for the good of the group, articulate their learning goals, and help each other be successful.
- Always begin and end class with a common activity that all can enjoy and learn from.
- Appoint student experts who can help their peers.
- Have clear, written directions for all activities so that students know what to do. Many teachers find that checklists and daily agendas are effective in making assignments and expectations clear.
- Establish clear timelines for assignments so that students know that they are expected to produce work within a set period of time. This will help everyone stay focused.
- Post a list of procedures for those students who finish early. Provide plenty of high-interest, independent work for these students.
- Use signals to control noise—even good noise can get too loud sometimes.
- Establish class routines for turning in work, passing out materials, moving to groups, and so on.
- Keep the pace brisk, businesslike, and purposeful.

STRATEGIES AND ACTIVITIES FOR DIFFERENTIATED CLASSROOMS

- **Choice boards.** With a choice board, students are given a menu of possible tasks to accomplish. This is a structured way to allow for student choice.
- **Alphabet boxes.** Students are given a grid of squares with a letter of the alphabet in each square. They then brainstorm and recall words, ideas, and concepts related to a unit. For example, in an alphabet box for a unit on global warming, a student would write "Polar bears endangered" in the *P* box, "Ozone" in the *O* box, and so on for every letter.
- **Dialectical journals.** Students write two-column notes about information they read or hear. In one column, they are given or select a topic to write about, and in the other, they write a response to the topic.
- **Write-pair-shares.** In a write-pair-share, students write a response to a question. They then share their response with a partner first and with the entire group afterward.

- **Audio materials.** For students who are auditory learners, audio materials offer another approach to learning. Students listen to recorded materials as they read or instead of reading. Audio materials can be used to study, review, or introduce information, and in many other ways.

- **Vocabulary charades.** Students work in triads to act out vocabulary words and definitions. This also works well for reviewing key terms and facts in a unit of study.

- **Artifact boxes.** Items from a unit of study are displayed in a box for students to use to analyze and predict information. An artifact box may be used for enrichment, teaching, or remediation.

- **Case studies.** Students investigate real-life situations through reports, articles, and other observations. They complete their investigations in cooperative groups.

- **Chalk talks.** Five students go to the board and stand so that they cannot see each other's writing. The teacher calls out a topic and has everyone in the class write about it for one minute. Students discuss the work of the five chalk writers and compare it to the work of their classmates.

- **Exit slips.** Before leaving class, students write responses to questions about what they learned in class that day. They can also record information about what they still need to learn and what remaining questions or concerns they have.

- **Clickers.** Students use handheld devices to answer questions electronically.

- **Agendas.** Students are offered individualized personal checklists of work to complete within a set period of time—usually a week or so. Although students may have some assignments in common, agendas allow for differentiation by offering work that is less or more challenging while appealing to diverse learning style preferences.

- **Chunking.** Assignments are broken into smaller, more manageable parts, with structured directions offered for each part.

- **Hot Potato.** Similar to the Tingo Tango game later in this list, each student has a note card with a question about the lesson on it. Learners trade their cards as quickly as possible for thirty seconds. When time is called, each student will have to answer the question on his or her card either in writing or orally.

- **Task cards.** Because of the various activities possible in one differentiated class, students read explicit directions for an activity instead of hearing a quick flurry of verbal directions at the start of class. They can then refer to the directions as class progresses.

- **Interactive bookmarks.** Students use premade bookmarks specific to a unit of material to record notes, answer questions, define words, and make observations as they read.

- **Minilessons.** Students are given brief lessons designed to target specific areas for remediation or enrichment.

- **Jigsaws.** Students in a group divide the material to be studied into various sections. Each group member becomes an expert on his or her section and teaches it to the others.

- **One-sentence summaries.** Students write a quick summary of a passage, procedure, or other new learning.

- **Learning circles.** Students gather to discuss a piece of literature or a reading passage in depth. The concept can be applied to reading of all sorts and to working out common problems in math or science courses.

- **Manipulatives.** Hands-on activities can be used to help students in all disciplines learn. From science labs to word sorts, manipulatives benefit the tactile learner in that he or she is able to associate movement and the material to be learned.

- **Open-ended problems.** Students solve open-ended problems periodically throughout a unit of study. For example, during a unit about the American Revolution, students might be asked to view portraits of the leaders of the day and make predictions about their social status based on clues in the paintings.

- **Save the Last Word.** As students read, they write down words, phrases, or sentences that catch their attention. Once they have completed the reading, students share their choices in small groups. The other members of the group react to what was shared. The student who wrote the material then has the last word about why the choices were significant.

- **Sticky note note taking.** Students write brief notes on sticky notes as they work or read.

- **Note checks.** Students review and highlight each other's notes.

- **Roundtables.** Students discuss their work by sitting in a circle and taking turns. This works best if they have had time to write questions, concerns, or responses to a question first.

- **Online collaboration.** Students work together to create and post blogs or to collaborate with other students in activities involving podcasts, virtual projects, tweets, or wikis.

- **Paper discussions.** Small groups of students are seated in circles. Each group is handed a sheet of paper, and one student in each group writes a response to a question or idea pertaining to a topic. That student then passes the sheet to the next student, who adds to the response and passes it to the next student, and so on as quickly as possible in a specified time limit.

- **Student observations.** Students watch video clips or live demonstrations and record and share their observations.

- **Shaping-Up Review.** Students write the four main points of the day's lesson on the corners of a square, one thing they loved inside a heart, three questions they have on the three points of a triangle, and one thing they can apply in another way inside a circle.

- **Tingo Tango.** Students stand in a circle rapidly passing a soft ball around the circle as the teacher repeatedly says, "Tingo." At random intervals, the teacher say "Tango" instead of "Tingo." The student holding the ball at that point has to answer a question or call out a fact.

- **Two-minute questions.** The teacher poses a question and gives students two minutes to write responses before sharing with group members, the entire class, or a study buddy.

- **Word splashes.** Students generate a list of words associated with a particular unit of study before beginning the unit to increase background knowledge. Students can also be given a list of words to be alert for as they begin studying.

RESPONSE TO INTERVENTION

In the broadest sense, Response to Intervention (RTI) is a form of differentiated instruction in that it offers modifications to content, process, and product to help students master curriculum material. Although RTI is now a highly successful program in many schools, it differs from classroom differentiation in a significant way: RTI is a schoolwide intervention framework instead of differentiation delivered by an individual teacher.

Similar to other types of differentiated instruction, RTI offers a tiered approach to interventions. In the first tier, students are instructed by a general education teacher using solid, classroom-tested strategies, including differentiated instruction. Ongoing data collection through a variety of assessments is used to help determine the needs of all students in the class.

Students who, according to the collected data, are not mastering the content or acquiring the necessary skills required by the curriculum are moved to the second tier of instruction. Students in the second tier continue to remain in their general education classroom and receive the same instruction as their classmates. In addition, however, students in the second tier also receive more intensive instruction targeted to help them overcome their learning difficulties. Such instruction is usually delivered in small-group format, in learning centers, and even by an additional staff member. After a specified time limit, if students in the second tier have mastered the material, they then move back to the first tier of instruction. If they are still experiencing difficulties, they move to the third tier.

Students in the third tier receive instruction that is more intensive and individualized than that offered in the first two tiers. Often this instruction is provided on an individual basis by a specialist or a special education teacher, although the general education teacher can still be involved. Instruction is specifically targeted to assist individual students. Ongoing assessments at this level continue to play an important role, as students may be referred to a screening committee that will consider them for eligibility for special education services.

Although there may be experts at your school who are already involved in an RTI program and who can assist you in learning more about it, there are also two very good sites where you can access much more information:

- National Center on Response to Intervention (www .rti4success.org). At this carefully researched and maintained site, nationally recognized experts offer resources and advice to help schools implement RTI programs successfully.

- Intervention Central (www.interventioncentral .org). Here you can find expert advice and many helpful resources on how to implement RTI assistance for students with behavior problems as well as academic problems.

Students Who May Need Special Care

> I really believe that kids want to do well in school. No one spends seven hours a day motivated for failure. Teachers have to meet kids where they are educationally. Curriculum can be taught and mastered without having to water it down. Give the students a chance to succeed, and keep raising the bar.
>
> *Charlene Herrala, 31 years' experience*

Although every student deserves the best from you, there are some students who may require more attention and care from you than others. In the remainder of this section, you will learn about how to help some of these special populations. From students with attention disorders and 504 Plans to students with special needs, these students require the very best in skills, knowledge, and understanding from their teachers.

STUDENTS WITH ATTENTION DISORDERS

Students with attention deficit disorder (ADD) or attention deficit/hyperactivity disorder (ADHD) usually require intervention from supportive adults to be academically successful.

If you are not a special education teacher, a special education teacher will probably talk to you at the beginning of the term about your students with attention disorders. That teacher will suggest appropriate accommodations and will review each student's Individualized Education Program or 504 Plan with you.

To learn more about how you can help students with attention disorders, search the Internet, beginning with the Web site of the Attention Deficit Disorder Association (www.add.org). This site offers many practical tips, links to other sites, articles on a variety of issues pertaining to attention disorders, and information on legal issues of concern in regard to students with attention disorders.

Here are some general guidelines to assist you in teaching students with ADD or ADHD:

- Enlist support from other professionals and from the parents and guardians of students with ADD or ADHD. These people will be an excellent source of support and advice as you work together to assist students.

- Teach school success skills. Students with ADD or ADHD have not always mastered effective school-related skills, such as taking notes or following directions. Take time to show them how to accomplish some of the tasks that other students find easy.

- Clearly define classroom procedures for students with ADD or ADHD to help them stay on task. They will benefit from seeing as well as hearing directions and other information.

- Monitor students with attention disorders unobtrusively by placing them near you. You should also seat them with their back to other students so they will be less easily distracted. Other distractions to consider are doors, windows, computer screens, pencil sharpeners, and high-traffic areas.

- Give students with attention disorders extra assistance during transition times; it is not always easy for them to adjust to a change.

- When you give directions, be sure to give them one step at a time. Because students with attention disorders tend to be easily overwhelmed by large tasks and need guidance in planning how to accomplish their work, you should help students understand that each task is a sequence of smaller steps.

- Photocopy parts of a text that students may find particularly difficult, then highlight key parts. Using this text as an example, show your students with ADD or ADHD how they can do the same thing themselves to help them focus on important information in the text.

- Offer alternative auditory modes of learning. Students with attention disorders usually do well when they can listen to an audiotape of a text as they read the selection; the soundtrack helps keep them focused on the text. Contact the publisher of your textbook, a special education teacher in your building, or your state's textbook adoption committee for copies of tapes.

- Encourage computer use. Using a computer is a skill that students with ADD or ADHD often find helpful because it enables them to work quickly and competently, thus making it easier for them to stay on task because much of the tedium they associate with written work has been removed.

- Review frequently so that students with attention disorders have the basic skills and facts mastered before you move on to the next topic.

STUDENTS WITH 504 PLANS

A 504 Plan is a legally binding document that protects students who have a documented physical, emotional, or mental disability that limits their ability to learn. Students with 504 Plans are those whose disabilities do not need to be addressed by a teacher specifically trained to teach special education students. Instead, students with 504 Plans have needs that can be addressed with modifications by a general education teacher.

Students with 504 Plans might have ADD or ADHD, chronic illness, anger management problems, or impaired vision or hearing; might be obese; or might be confined to a wheelchair. Although these students do not qualify for special education programs, their 504 Plans spell out special accommodations they must receive. The accommodations in a 504 Plan may include various types of assistance, such as extra time on assignments, an extra set of textbooks, classrooms that are wheelchair accessible, or preferential seating.

When the school term begins, you will receive copies of the 504 Plans of your students. You may also meet with the 504 Plan administrator for your school to discuss each plan and what your specific responsibilities are. Although each 504 Plan is unique because it is tailored to the needs of the child it protects, typical accommodations that you might see include

- Preferential seating
- Extended time on assignments
- Extra books or materials
- Reduced practice time
- Frequent contact with parents or guardians
- Early notification of parents or guardians when problems arise
- Written copies of notes presented orally
- Assistance with organization skills

Many times, students will mask their poor performance with poor behavior to save face. Students prefer misbehavior over a lack of ability as a reason for failure. Give the students work they can do.

Charlene Herrala, 31 years' experience

You must follow 504 Plans exactly. 504 Plans are different from other school documents in that if you fail to follow them, the parents or guardians of the child have the right to sue not just the school district but the classroom teacher as well. Even if you are personally uncomfortable with an accommodation, you must make that accommodation.

AT-RISK STUDENTS

At-risk students are those who are very likely to drop out instead of graduating. Like most students, their future success depends on their getting as much education as they can. Although there are many promising programs and a great deal of support available for students who are at risk in this way, too many students still drop out of school.

Students can be at risk for dropping out for many reasons. Here are just a few of the possible contributing factors:

- Family problems
- Poor academic skills

- Substance abuse
- Pregnancy
- Emotional problems
- Chronic peer conflicts
- Repeated failure in school
- Inadequate supervision by parents or guardians
- Undiagnosed learning problems
- Chronic illness

At-risk students depend on their teachers to help them stay in school. Although the strategies listed here will benefit all of your students, it is especially important for you to reach out to those who are at risk. Adapt the following ideas to meet the needs of your at-risk students:

- Be persistent in your efforts to motivate at-risk students. Do not hesitate to let them know you plan to keep them in school as long as you can.
- Spend time helping your students establish life goals so that they can see a larger purpose for staying in school. Without a purpose for learning, a student who wants to drop out may see school as an exercise in futility.
- Set small goals that will help students reach a larger one. If you can get them in the habit of achieving at least one small goal each day, they can build on this pattern of success.
- Involve students in cooperative learning activities. Feeling connected to their classmates empowers and supports students who may be considering quitting school.
- Invite guest speakers or older students to talk with younger ones about the importance of staying in school.
- Ask open-ended questions so that at-risk students can attempt giving answers without fear of failure.
- Be generous with praise and attention. Your kind words may often be the only ones your at-risk students will hear all day.
- Seek assistance from support personnel and family members. It takes many determined adults to change a student's mind once he or she has decided to drop out.
- Check on students when they are absent. Call their home. Show your concern.
- Create situations in which at-risk students can be successful. Perhaps they can tutor younger students, mediate peer conflicts, or help you with classroom chores. Focus on their strengths.
- Offer extra help and assistance to all of your students, but particularly to those at risk of dropping out.

- Tailor activities to students' preferred learning styles. When the work seems too difficult, at-risk students can often be successful if their teacher uses another modality to teach the material they need to know.

- Connect to at-risk students in a positive way. Make sure that they understand that they are important to you and to their classmates.

To learn more about at-risk students, begin with Education World (www. educationworld.com). You can access a wealth of information on how to help your students who are at risk of dropping out of school by using "at risk" as a search term on this site. You will also find links to other sites, articles, motivational tools, and strategies for teachers.

GAY AND LESBIAN STUDENTS

Headlines about bullied gay and lesbian students and the statistics that accompany them are as disturbing as they are sad. Gay and lesbian students are overwhelmingly more prone to commit suicide than their straight classmates. Gay and lesbian students of all ages also report a relentless barrage of harassment that begins as early as preschool and never stops. It is our responsibility as professionals to offer support and encouragement to all of our students, including those who struggle as much as gay and lesbian students are forced to.

As a caring educator, you can take many actions to support the students in your class who may be gay or lesbian. One good place to start is to educate yourself about gay and lesbian students and their very real struggles in regard to their education. A good resource for this is provided by Human Rights Watch (www.hrw.org), an organization that offers a wealth of information about the plight of gay and lesbian students as part of its mission to defend and protect human rights around the world. The organization's report *Hatred in the Hallways* outlines the difficulties that many gay and lesbian students face in school and offers suggestions concerning how educators can support this population in the classroom.

In addition to educating yourself, there are some commonsense actions you can take to assist the gay and lesbian students at your school:

- Be a role model of acceptance and support for all of your students, including gay and lesbian students.

- Be aware of your own attitudes or prejudices. For example, do you deny your students positive gay and lesbian role models in your instruction?

- If a gay or lesbian student confides in you, respect his or her privacy if possible. If it is not possible for you to do so—for example, if he or she has been sexually abused or bullied—inform the student before he or she confides in you further.

- Encourage and support diversity programs at your school and in the community. Diversity does not just mean culture, skin color, or ethnicity, but includes sexual orientation as well.

- Take action when you hear name calling, harassment, or other types of bullying. Many schools have a clearly defined antidiscrimination policy to address bullying. Enforce it.

- Be aware of harmful stereotypes and the common slurs that students can use against their gay and lesbian peers so that you can combat them effectively.

- Consider sponsoring events, such as the Day of Silence (www.dayofsilence.org), that make it easier for gay and lesbian students to have their voice heard and their rights protected.

- Educate yourself about supportive community organizations that can help gay and lesbian students. Be prepared to refer your students to these organizations.

STUDENTS WHO ARE NOT NATIVE SPEAKERS OF ENGLISH

In recent years, the number of students for whom English is not their native language has greatly increased in many U.S. schools. The cultural diversity these students bring enriches our classrooms even as it presents a perplexing problem for teachers who do not speak their students' native language. With sensitivity, courtesy, and insight, you can help your students who primarily speak a minority language. Here are some strategies that should make this process easier for you and these students:

- Keep in mind that students who speak little English not only have to learn the content that your other students must learn but also have to learn it in a foreign language.

- Make a point of learning to pronounce the names of these students correctly. Insist that your other students do so, too.

- Be aware of cultural differences and sensitive issues. For example, in many cultures it is rude to maintain eye contact.

- Give as many directions as you can in writing as well as orally.

- Label items in your classroom to help students learn simple words.

- Keep resources on your students' cultures on hand for other students to read. Library books and Internet sites are good sources of such material.

- Arrange for your students to interact. Students who can communicate with each other about their work tend to do better. It is also easier for students to learn English if other students engage them in conversation as much as possible.

- Use a variety of learning styles to help your students master content as well as a new language. Graphic organizers and other useful study devices will help students who are learning English as well as your other students.

- Encourage students to read aloud to you whenever it is appropriate. Be careful that your corrections of English learners are helpful and not overwhelming.

- Set realistic expectations for your students who speak little English. They are not going to be able to do as much work as your other students if the work involves intensive interaction with a text because it will take them longer just to figure out the language.

- Don't rush to answer questions or fill in words when students are struggling to think through their responses. You must be patient and supportive if you want your students to learn successfully.

- Find bilingual dictionaries in the languages that your students speak. Encourage them to use the relevant bilingual dictionary frequently. Model its use yourself.

- Use audiotapes and other technology appropriate to the age and ability levels of your students. Students benefit from both seeing and hearing the language.

- Keep your language simple. If at all possible, use words that students will be likely to know.

One of the best resources to help you with your students who are not native speakers is Dave's ESL Cafe (www.eslcafe.com). This excellent site offers a wealth of useful information, resources, links, and insights into teaching students who are not proficient in English.

STUDENTS WHO ARE UNDERACHIEVERS

Few students go through all of their school years without having moments when they could have done better. Occasional underachievement is to be expected, but this behavior becomes problematic when it is the overriding pattern in a student's school life.

Chronic underachievement is a problem for students of many ages and capabilities. Their parents or guardians are often quick to tell you that their child is either lazy or just doesn't try hard enough. The students often label themselves in these negative ways, too.

As you begin to work with underachieving students, you may find yourself calling their parents or guardians often, and you will find yourself frustrated when no punishment you can devise solves the problem. In fact, many underachievers accept punishment as their due.

Chronic underachievement is not just a bad habit. It is often an elaborate defense mechanism that students adopt to protect themselves from their anxiety about failing. Underachieving students often have successful, highly goal-oriented parents who are very involved in their lives. Parents of underachievers usually spend lots of energy trying to understand and help their children.

The problem compounds itself when underachievers are gifted students. These students often must live up to their parents' high expectations and their own exacting standards. They opt for certain failure instead of trying and possibly failing. The contrast between their potential and what they achieve is frustrating for everyone who works with them. Working with underachieving students can be made less frustrating with a combination of these strategies:

- Accept that these students' shortcomings are not the result of laziness, even though they may see themselves as lazy and worthless. Their anxiety often paralyzes them.

- Work with parents and guidance counselors to help underachievers, but be aware that overinvolvement can sometimes increase a student's anxiety.

- Strive to make assignments so appealing that all students will want to do their work. Underachievers need extra motivation. They seldom find the work intrinsically interesting.

- Don't expect your underachieving students to be more than briefly motivated by their own success. Too often, after a successful school experience, underachievers will stop putting forth any effort—a situation that frustrates their family and teacher.

- Work out a plan with these students and their parents or guardians to guarantee that work will be turned in to you on time. Underachievers often do not turn in work even when they have completed it.

- Use a checklist to show students how to accomplish their assignments. Underachievers need assistance in establishing their priorities so that they can work with purpose.

- Have extra supplies on hand for the times when an underachiever will forget to bring them to class.

- Teach study skills, time management, and organization strategies so that the work will not be burdensome for an underachieving student who is easily overwhelmed by school tasks.

- Be matter of fact about assignments. Expect students to do them, and offer extra help and encouragement where necessary. If you allow your anger to show, or if you reprimand underachieving students harshly for not completing the work, they will have difficulty finishing it.

- Be positive and supportive as you encourage effort and the attempts to work. One of the most effective strategies is to bolster self-esteem in your underachievers.

- Offer help soon after you give an assignment in class. For many underachievers, the hardest part of an assignment is getting started. They may make several beginnings before giving up.

- Be aware that underachievers seldom ask for help. Be proactive in offering assistance.

- Offer frequent and unobtrusive encouragement. Underachievers have a perfectionist approach to their studies that results in incomplete work—the opposite of what they wanted to accomplish.

- Don't allow students to give you such excuses as "I am just lazy" or "I never do well in math." Most underachievers passively accept criticism from the disappointed adults in their lives. They tend to use the negative labels to excuse themselves from not working.

- Form a close connection with underachieving students whenever you can. If they feel that you are counting on them, they have more incentive to work than if you indicate that you do not care whether or not they do their work.

- Boost students' self-esteem by encouraging them to tutor students who are less able. Underachievers often will help other students when they will not help themselves.

STUDENTS LIVING IN POVERTY

Millions of school-age students in America live in poverty. You don't have to teach in a blighted urban area or a depressed rural region to teach students who are from a poor family. The lives of poor students are often very different from those of their more affluent peers. They cannot look forward to an abundance of presents at Christmas or on their birthday. Back-to-school shopping is not an exciting time of new clothes and school supplies. Even small outlays of money are significant to students living in poverty; a locker fee, a soft drink for a class party, or a fee for a field trip may be out of their reach. In addition, because they do not wear the same fashionable clothes as their peers, poor students are often the targets of ridicule.

Economically disadvantaged students have a very difficult time succeeding in school. One of the most unfortunate results of their economic struggles is that students who live in poverty often drop out of school, choosing a low-paying job to pay for the small luxuries they have been denied instead of an education.

Despite the bleak outlook for many of these students, you can do a great deal to make school a meaningful haven for them. You can help your students who live in poverty by implementing some of these suggestions:

- When you suspect that your students are taunting their disadvantaged peers, act quickly to stop the harassment.

- If you want poor students to connect their book learning with real-life situations, spend time adding to their worldly experiences by involving them in such activities as field trips or internships. Students who live in poverty have not been exposed to such broadening experiences as family vacations, trips to museums, or even eating in restaurants.

- Listen to your disadvantaged students. They need a strong relationship with a trustworthy adult if they are to succeed.

- Work to boost the self-esteem of students who live in poverty by praising their school success instead of what they own.

- Provide access to computers, magazines, newspapers, and books so low-income students can see and work with print materials. School may be the only place where they are exposed to print media.

- Keep your expectations for poor students high. Poverty does not mean ignorance.

- Don't make comments about your students' clothes or belongings unless they are in violation of the dress code.

- Take time to explain the rationale for rules and procedures in your classroom. Students who live in poverty may not always know the correct behaviors for school situations. At home, they may function under a different set of social rules.

- Be careful about the school supplies you expect students to purchase. Keep your requirements as simple as you can for all students.

- Arrange a bank of shared supplies for your students to borrow when they are temporarily out of materials for class.

- Do not require costly activities. For example, if you ask students to pay for a field trip, some of them will not be able to go.

- If you notice that a student does not have lunch money, check to make sure that a free lunch is an option for that child.

- Be very sensitive to the potential for embarrassment in even small requests for or comments about money that you make. For example, if you jokingly remark, "There's no such thing as a free lunch," you could embarrass one of your low-income students.

- Make it clear that you value all of your students for their character and not for their possessions.

For more information on how to help your economically disadvantaged students, visit aha!Process (www.ahaprocess.com), an organization founded by Ruby Payne, a leading expert on the effects of generational poverty on students. Her book *A Framework for Understanding Poverty*, first published in 1996 by aha!Process, is significant because it explains how the silent culture clash between students and teachers in classrooms has a harmful effect on students.

STUDENTS WITH AUTISM SPECTRUM DISORDERS

One of the most encouraging results of neurological and educational research in recent years is that educators not only are more knowledgeable about the various types of disorders falling under the heading of autism spectrum disorders (ASD) that may affect their students but also now know more about how to help these students. ASD can be loosely defined as developmental disorders that can include autism, Asperger's syndrome, Rett syndrome, and others. Although individuals with ASD can have very different characteristics from one other, often these disorders can cause difficulties with social and communication skills, aversion to change and difficulty with transitions, atypical responses to sensory stimuli, and sometimes repetitive behaviors.

As a teacher, you are very likely to have students with ASD in your classes even if you do not work exclusively with students with special needs. To make learning attainable for students with ASD, the first step you must take is to educate yourself about the types of disorders that your students may have. Some of the best resources to help you with this include

- **National Institute of Child Health and Human Development (www.nichd .nih.gov).** At this division of the National Institutes of Health that deals with children's health, browse the "Health Information" tab to learn more about ASD and to access links to even more resources.

- **Autism Society (www.autism-society.org).** This large grassroots advocacy organization has many different chapters across the United States. At this site you can find specific resources as well as links to more help.

- **TeachersFirst (www.teachersfirst.com).** At this free site, teachers can use "ASD" or "autism" as a search term to locate a wealth of practical tips and suggestions for helping students with ASD.

Another very good resource is the second edition of the book *1001 Great Ideas for Teaching and Raising Children with Autism or Asperger's,* written by Ellen Botbohm and Veronica Zysk. This book, published in 2010 by Future Horizons, is focused on practical suggestions and strategies for teachers as well as parents and guardians of children with ASD.

In addition to learning as much as you can about ASD, it is also very important that you learn as much as possible about the individual students with ASD in your class. To do this, you should first reach out to the parents and guardians of your students, who can then inform you of the best ways to help their child. As with parents and guardians of all your students, a strong partnership between your classroom and your students' families is an excellent way to help your students. You should also take time to consult previous teachers your students may have had as well as any records your school holds. By educating yourself about ASD in general and about your students in particular, you will be in a better position to make success attainable for them. Other strategies that experienced teachers have found helpful follow in this list:

- Make your classroom as inclusive and as welcoming of students as possible. This may mean educating other students about ASD so that they know the most appropriate ways to interact with all of their classmates. Consider creating peer buddies to help students with ASD. Both the buddy and the student with ASD will benefit from such interactions.

- Be extra diligent about documentation and record keeping for your students with ASD. This will enable you to be able to work well with their parents or guardians as well as with other professionals who work with these students.

- Create a well-organized classroom where students with ASD, who can sometimes be overwhelmed by stimuli, can feel comfortable. Avoid clutter and overdecoration whenever you can. If possible, establish an area of the room where students who are feeling stressed can go for quiet time and recovery.

- Provide visual cues to help students stay on task and focused. Calendars, charts, and other informational cues are often helpful for students with ASD. Further, graphic organizers can help students master academic work.

- Plan daily routines that students can follow independently. This makes the school day more manageable for students with ASD, especially because transition times are often difficult periods for them.

- Plan how you are going to manage the behavior challenges that students with ASD can present. Ask yourself which behaviors you can ignore and which ones you must deal with. Promote and encourage positive behaviors.

GIFTED STUDENTS

Gifted students are usually fun as well as difficult to teach. When a lesson interests a gifted child, he or she will take the lesson far beyond the boundaries of the material. Gifted students are also a challenge to teach. They are impatient with topics they don't perceive as interesting, and they can be especially impatient with teachers and peers whom they perceive to be less than capable. To learn more about teaching gifted students, consult some of the many books and Web sites that other teachers have found valuable. Two helpful sites are listed here:

- **National Association for Gifted Children (www.nagc.org).** At this site, you will find excellent resources for educators: links to Web sites with advice for those who teach students with high potential, research articles, and helpful information about teaching gifted children.

- **TeachersFirst (www.teachersfirst.com).** On the home page, use "gifted students" as a search term to access reading lists; strategies for teachers; links to other Web sites, including interactive online sites; booklists for students; and information on how to modify instruction to appeal to multiple intelligences.

When you have gifted students in your class, you will need to modify the content of the material, the learning process, or both to accommodate their needs. Use or adapt the guidelines that follow for modifying the content and process of your instruction as well as teaching gifted students in a group of students with mixed abilities.

Modifying Learning Processes for Gifted Students

- When you assign a project to gifted students, give a reasonably loose structure, and then allow them to take the project as far as they need to.

- Allow students to have a strong voice in how they will accomplish their goals. Gifted students are often self-directed learners. Take this characteristic into consideration when you modify the process of learning.

- Set a rapid pace for instruction. Gifted students quickly grow bored with the slower pace of undifferentiated instruction.

- Focus on having students use higher-level thinking skills throughout a unit of study; gifted students quickly master the recall and comprehension levels.

- Use technology as often as you can. Your gifted students are likely to become proficient at accessing resources on the Internet with just a bit of guidance from you. Allow gifted students to work together. They benefit from being able to bounce ideas off each other.

Modifying Lesson Content to Challenge Gifted Students

- Focus on the broad concepts in a unit of study. Gifted students will quickly grasp the details of an assignment.

- Provide content that will not only challenge gifted students to learn but also appeal to their particular interests. For example, if one of your students is interested in a sport, capitalize on this in teaching mathematics, physics, history, or other subjects.

- When you work with gifted students, ask them to synthesize information from a variety of sources. For a gifted child, a textbook is only a jumping-off point from which to begin exploring a topic.

- Encourage student input in the selection of material. You may have a general unit of study, but allow students to study the details that most interest them. For example, you may teach a general unit on space first and then have each student work on a particular aspect of space, such as planets, asteroids, or comets.

- Don't ask gifted students to just solve problems; have them use real-life situations to formulate their own problems. For example, you could ask students to anticipate and solve the problems that they would experience if they were to create a new city or to solve a current problem in their own neighborhood.

- Focus on depth of content rather than quantity. For example, having students read three excellent books on a topic of study is better than asking them to read five books of lesser quality.

- Plan to move instruction out of the classroom whenever possible so that students can study material firsthand. Enrich lessons with trips to museums and other appropriate points of interest.

Teaching Gifted Students in a Group of Students with Mixed Abilities

- Although allowing gifted students to serve as peer tutors is acceptable, be careful not to overuse this technique. It reinforces what they already know, but it doesn't provide enrichment of their own skills in the subject they are tutoring past a certain point.

- When students are working in groups, place gifted students with other high-achieving students as well as with students who are less able.

- Provide a modified assignment as often as you can.

- Work closely with the parents and guardians of gifted students so that you can fulfill each child's needs and reduce gifted learners' frustration when lessons don't appeal to their abilities or learning styles. Parents or guardians often are excellent and knowledgeable advocates for their gifted children.

> The teacher may provide more scaffolding or prompts for students with special needs: a specific list of resources or Web sites; a visual (for example, a teacher-made storyboard); or examples of past student projects that could be used as a templates or guides. For gifted students, you may let them use their talents to do the assigned task through any method they feel would meet the objective.
>
> *Stephanie Stock Mahoney,*
> *35 years' experience*

STUDENTS WITH SPECIAL NEEDS

Special needs is a very broad term that encompasses a wide range of disabilities and conditions. Students with special needs will be the treasures of your first year as a teacher when you learn to work with them successfully.

In years past, most teachers did not see students with special needs in their classes. These students were segregated in special classrooms or centers, where they had little contact with the general school population. This practice ended with the passage of Public Law 94-142, which mandated that children be educated in the "least restrictive environment"—that is, that children with special needs be mainstreamed to the greatest possible extent. Because of this law, students who have special needs are now frequently part of ordinary school life.

The Internet provides a great deal of information about students with special needs. To learn more about this topic, try these Web sites:

- **LD OnLine (www.ldonline.org).** This site advertises itself as the world's largest Web site for students with learning disabilities and attention disorders. It offers advice on motivation, an excellent glossary of educational terms, many practical strategies, information about social skills for students with learning disabilities, and an online forum.

- **Council for Exceptional Children (www.cec.sped.org).** This site is the "voice and vision of special education." It offers current information on trends, online courses, information about national and local policies, guidelines for various types of exceptionalities, and an excellent overview of the field.

- **Learning Disabilities Association of America (LDA) (www.ldaamerica.org).** In existence since 1963, the LDA offers current strategies for handling such practical concerns as homework policies and test accommodations. The site is supportive of as well as informative for teachers who have students with specific learning disabilities.

You can expect to have many types of students with special needs in your classes, from students who need only a slight accommodation to help them learn to students with severe disabilities. How successfully you handle this challenge will depend on your attitude. Along with having a positive attitude, the following general strategies can guide you as you teach your students with special needs:

- Accept your students' limitations and help them overcome them. Although some teachers think students with disabilities that are not as obvious as others just need to try harder, trying very hard is not enough to create success for many of these students.

- Be proactive in dealing with students with special needs. Make sure you understand their specific disabilities and the required accommodations.

- Give your best when teaching students with special needs. They deserve your best effort. When you take this view, you will be in a good position to help them. Expect to work closely with the special education teachers assigned to help you modify your instruction to meet the needs of every learner in your class.

- Accept responsibility for your students' success. Don't anticipate extensive additional training on how to help your students with special needs. Continue to educate yourself about how to work well with these students by reading professional literature, researching relevant Web sites, attending workshops, and observing special education teachers as they teach.

- Be sensitive to the needs of each student, and anticipate them whenever you can. For example, be sure to seat students with special needs where they can see and hear you without distractions.

- Use the resources available to you. Study students' permanent records to understand the instructional strategies that have worked well in past school years. As soon as possible, contact the special education teachers who are working with your students with special needs so that you can learn the specific strategies that will help them learn successfully. Some of the other adults who can help you learn about your students are parents and guardians, the school nurse, counselors, and current or previous teachers.

- Talk with each student with special needs about his or her concerns. Make it easy for these students to communicate with you. Even young children can tell you when they learn best and what activities help them master the material.

Instructional Strategies for Students with Special Needs

Following are some helpful ideas for teaching students with special needs. Because students' needs vary, not all of the ideas will be appropriate for every one of these students.

- Limit the materials you ask students with special needs to manage at any given time. They should only have the materials necessary for the successful completion of a lesson on their desk.

- Limit the number of practice items. For example, instead of assigning fifteen drill sentences, ask students with special needs to complete ten.

- Consider each student's learning style preferences when you create assignments. When you can, modify the assignment to better fit his or her needs. If you can provide alternative materials, do so.

- Be sure to provide prompt feedback when a student with special needs completes an assignment.

- Limit the amount of written work that you assign to students with special needs.

- Offer a variety of activities. Change the pace several times in each class so that students will find it easy to stay on task.

- Structure your classroom routines so that students can predict what they will be expected to do. Go over the daily objectives at the start of the class, and offer students a checklist to keep them on task all day.

- Be generous with your praise when your students with special needs do something well.

- Give very clear directions. Ask students with special needs to restate what you want them to do. On written work, use bold type or other eye-catching design elements to distinguish the directions from the rest of the text.

- Offer collaborative learning opportunities often. Working with other students often reinforces learning, gives students with special needs a chance to interact in a positive way with classmates, and tends to build their confidence as learners.

- Help your students with special needs understand their progress. Set small, achievable goals, and celebrate together when students reach them.

Collaborating with Special Education Teachers

When students with special needs began to be included in all classrooms, special education teachers and general education teachers formed teams to help students who required special accommodations. The unique features of this type of collaboration are that frequently both teachers are present in the classroom at the same time and they take joint responsibility for the education of all students in their class.

These collaborative teams of teachers face an important challenge: sharing the duties of the class so that they have common goals for delivering instruction, assessing progress, and managing behavior. Successful collaboration is likely if team teachers see themselves as equal partners who are actively engaged in all parts of the teaching process. The general education teacher's responsibilities usually include the following:

- Creating activities to teach the content
- Finding and adapting resource material for all students
- Delivering effective instruction
- Meeting the curriculum requirements of all students

The special education teacher's responsibilities usually include these:

- Adapting material to meet the needs of students with special needs
- Adapting activities to match the learning styles of students with special needs
- Modifying assessments
- Meeting the curriculum requirements of students with special needs

What makes it possible for two teachers with different educational backgrounds to work together in a successful collaboration? The primary requirement for a positive working relationship is a commitment on the part of both teachers to working together for the common good of their students. Both teachers should also agree to

- Plan lessons together
- Follow the same classroom management procedures
- Discuss controversial class events in civil tones and in privacy
- Assume equal responsibility for what happens in class
- Present a united front to students
- Share resource materials
- Schedule time to work together on a regular basis

Best Practices Checklist

1. Differentiate instruction to meet the needs of all learners in your class. Instruction that is fair is instruction that is not the same for everyone.

2. Modify content, process, or product when you plan differentiated instruction, but do not lower your high expectations for all students.

3. Begin by learning as much as you can. Gather data to help you determine the learning needs and preferred learning styles of your students.

4. Rotate your students through a variety of tasks that appeal to all learning styles to meet the needs of all learners.

5. Start differentiation with small, carefully planned steps. It is sensible to begin differentiated instruction in your classroom with just a few easy-to-manage activities that are likely to be successful.

6. Use a variety of learning experiences, but let activities that engage and enliven your students predominate to ensure engagement.

7. Be persistent in your efforts to help students who may require special assistance from you to be successful.

8. Categorically refuse to allow any form of bullying of any student, regardless of the perceived cause.

9. When seeking to assist students, don't neglect to involve parents, guardians, and other staff members in a teamwork approach.

10. As you work with all of your students, take care to first accept their limitations and then help them overcome them.

Time to Reflect
Meet the Needs of All of Your Students

Use the information in this section to guide your thinking as you reflect on these questions. They are designed to encourage you to think more deeply about the issues in the text or to discuss those issues with colleagues.

1. How can you use what you already know about differentiating instruction to design instruction that will appeal to every student? What sorts of data will you need to gather? What instruments will you use to obtain this information?

2. What do you anticipate as your biggest challenge in dealing with the differences among your students? What can you do to meet this challenge? Where can you find assistance?

3. What do you already know about your students who may need special care and support? How do your supervisors expect you to help these students? How do the students themselves expect you to help them? Who at your school can help you learn the best ways to help these students?

4. What strengths do you have that will help you meet the diverse needs of your students? How can you use your strengths to help all the students in your class reach their full potential?

5. Who is struggling academically or behaviorally in your class? What should your attitude toward these students be? What schoolwide programs can help the struggling students in your class? What can you do to help them stay in school and be successful?

SECTION THIRTEEN

Assess Your Students' Progress

One of the most important shifts in the way we educate our students in the twenty-first century is the new emphasis on assessments of all types. No longer do teachers just present information, offer a quick quiz at about midpoint in the unit, and then give a long test on the material at the end of a unit. Instead, we use the findings of the researchers who study how students learn best and offer many smaller checkpoints along the way to assess not just what our students know but also what we can do to adjust our instruction to help them learn.

Data-Driven Instruction: Summative and Formative Assessments

Data-driven instruction is shaped by an analysis of the information collected through various assessments. Teachers who use the data-driven model of teaching first collect and then carefully analyze classroom data in an effort to set achievable learning goals for their students before differentiating instruction. Data-driven instruction depends on two broad categories of assessments: summative assessments and formative assessments.

Summative assessments are those that come at the end of a unit of study, at the end of a grading period, or at the end of a school year to measure how well we have aligned our instruction with the objectives in the curriculum and how well our students have mastered the material they were supposed to learn. Although most summative assessments are created and administered by the classroom teacher, standardized tests of all sorts are summative measurements of student progress. The data from summative assessments are often used by schools or even school districts to make broad curriculum decisions.

Formative assessments, in contrast, are created by classroom teachers as a way to collect data about student progress and lesson effectiveness. Formative assessments tend to be brief, and they can take a wide variety of forms depending on the age and ability levels of the students as well as the subject matter being taught. Frequent formative assessments and careful analysis of the data they yield will make it easy for you to focus your efforts on the instructional practices that will be most effective for your students. Formative assessments help teachers make informed, prescriptive decisions about the content and process of instruction.

During your first year, you will often hear the words *assessment* and *evaluation,* so it is helpful to know the difference between them, as they are not interchangeable. Assessment is the process of determining how well individual students have learned the material that you have taught. Evaluation occurs when you compare one student to another or an entire class to another class or even a student to a larger group.

As you prepare to assess your students throughout the year, it is important to adopt a balanced approach to the process. Formative assessments cannot yield all of the information about your students that you will require, and neither can summative assessments. You will need to give frequent and varied assessments if you and your students are to collaborate well in an effort to make sure that they achieve what they are supposed to during the school term or year that they spend with you. Finally, to be sure that your assessments serve your students well, avoid using assessment instruments that

- Are too long to complete in the allotted time
- Don't assess what you have taught
- Use a format that is hard to follow
- Don't list point values
- Ignore higher-level thinking skills
- Contain poorly worded directions
- Don't match your objectives
- Don't meet the needs of all learners
- Contain trick questions
- Don't match the test-taking skills of your students

As you read further in this section, you will find more information about formative and summative assessments and how you can use each type effectively to help your students master the material and skills mandated in your curriculum.

How to Use Formative Assessments

Formative assessments can be powerful tools for examining the way your students learn. Every formative assessment you give can provide valuable information to help you assess what your students know; what they don't know; and, most important, how you can adjust instruction to help every learner in your classroom succeed. If you take the time to analyze these data, you will learn a great deal. For example, if a number of students missed the same question on a quiz, take a closer look at the quiz and how you designed and delivered the instruction leading up to the quiz. As you reflect on the information that you have, you could ask yourself these questions:

- Did I adequately teach the material covered by the question?
- Did I word the question poorly?
- Did I provide enough practice or review?
- Do students need to change the way they prepare?
- How can I improve the way I teach this material?

In addition, you can ask your students questions about the formative assessments that you assign. Consider asking students to write explanations of why they missed the questions they did, how they prepared, and how the lessons leading to the assessment could have been more helpful. With this feedback from the formative assessments in your class, you can improve your students' learning and your teaching.

Assess often, but don't make the quick, formative assessments so long that it takes forever to grade. The benefit of formative assessments is that they give immediate feedback.

Christina L. Myren, 4 years' experience

Tracking Formative Assessment Data

You can use this worksheet to help you plan how you will administer and keep track of various types of formative assessments during a unit of study.

Unit of study: _____

Skills: _____

Formative Assessment Type	Date	Purpose or Objective	Feedback Type

TYPES OF FORMATIVE ASSESSMENTS

Just about any assignment or activity can serve as a formative assessment if it is used to collect data that will not only inform but also influence instruction. Because many formative assessments tend to be brief, they make it easier for a teacher to use them often without the loss of instructional time that can occur on days when students are taking longer tests or writing longer essays. To learn as much as you can about your students and then use what you learn to adjust instruction, try some of the suggestions for different types of formative assessments that follow.

Ask students to

- Answer brief questions, such as multiple choice or true-or-false
- Label or draw maps or diagrams
- Answer questions in complete sentences
- Put items in order of importance
- Place items in chronological order
- Complete self-evaluations
- Complete peer evaluations
- Teach material to someone else
- Restate material in their own words
- Complete various types of worksheets
- Complete or make graphic organizers
- Restate definitions
- Create definitions
- Play word games
- Complete puzzles
- Generate their own questions
- Identify main points
- Classify material into categories
- Combine various elements in a lesson
- Recognize characteristics
- Produce writing samples
- Recall facts
- Apply knowledge from one unit of study to another
- Conduct an experiment
- Summarize
- Make comparisons
- Draw contrasts
- Analyze information

HOW TO GATHER BASELINE DATA BEFORE BEGINNING A UNIT OF STUDY

Even though you may have access to information about your students' knowledge and skills from their previous school years, it is also important to learn what they do and do not know about the material in the new units of instruction that you teach. Collecting baseline data will allow you not only to design differentiated instruction activities and adjust the pace of learning as the unit proceeds but also to track student learning because you will have a clear starting point. There are many different ways to gather baseline data, but here are just a few that veteran teachers have found to be helpful and that you can adapt for your students:

- Give students a list of statements related to the unit and ask them to determine if they are true or false. Alternatively, you can ask students to agree or disagree with statements about the work.

- Ask students to predict the meaning of the vocabulary terms they will be studying.

- Have students write a two-minute paper in which they tell you what they know about the upcoming material.

- Verbally ask the entire class questions about the material and observe how many students can answer the questions correctly.

- Give students a Know/Want to Know/Learned chart and ask them to fill it out with what they know.

- Have students share ideas and brainstorm what they know about the topic together.

- Hold a class discussion in which you ask general questions about the material and observe your students' reactions and answers.

- Give students a list of items pertaining to the topic and ask them to rate or rank them.

USING REVIEW SESSIONS AS FORMATIVE ASSESSMENTS

If you want to improve the way you deliver instruction, you should treat review time as an integral aspect of instruction. Reviewing the day's instruction or the information covered in the homework is an excellent way not only to reinforce what students have learned but also to gather data before a summative assessment. Many teachers, especially of older students, tend to think of reviews as something students should do on their own as they prepare for a test. Although studying for a test is certainly a reasonable purpose of review sessions, it is not the only one—and students do not always have to do the reviewing independently.

Reviewing is not something you should force your students to do immediately before a test. It should be part of the daily fabric of the lessons in your class. Review can be used as a formative assessment tool because it will provide valuable insights into what your students do and don't know so that you can adjust instruction accordingly before a summative assessment.

If you think of lessons as layers of information that your students need to know instead of as large units, it will be easier for you to find ways to incorporate reviews into each day's work. When you assume responsibility for creating daily review opportunities and then taking care to collect and analyze the data that you gather from reviews, your students will be able to build their knowledge.

When is the best time to review class material with your students? Each day offers time for brief review sessions. Research studies identify the beginning and the end of a class as optimum times for increasing student recall.

If you use the small moments of time that are available each day instead of waiting until right before a test, you will not overwhelm your students with too much information. Here is a list of review activities that can enliven your class and reinforce what your students have recently learned:

- Use a few minutes to teach just one quick and interesting word, fact, or concept about the lesson your students have just learned. Relate it to the earlier lesson in such a way that students will leave your class with something new and interesting to think about.

- Have students predict five possible quiz questions. Ask each student to share one with the class and discuss the answer. To extend this activity, ask students to share how they made the prediction. This technique will not just review facts; it will enhance students' test preparation skills.

- Hold a rapid-fire drill session covering some of the facts you have taught recently. You could do this daily, keeping a running tally of the scores for your students or classes and transforming your review routine into a contest or tournament of knowledge.

- Because students of all ages love to play board games, design a giant one for the chalkboard or the wall. Divide your class into teams and allow them to roll dice to move their team's token along the board if they can answer drill questions correctly.

- Read a brief passage related to the day's topic to your students, and then ask for their reactions. An interesting twist on this idea is to read a passage that does not seem to be related to the topic and ask your students to explain how the two might be connected.

- Divide students into review teams of three or four. Hand each team a large sheet of paper and a marker. Allow three minutes for students to write as many review facts as they can. The real review occurs when students share their facts with the class.

- Use the last few minutes of class to review the underlying principles of the material in the day's lesson. Reviewing principles in this way on a regular basis will help students focus not just on detailed facts but also on the big concepts in their lessons.

- Have students each write three difficult questions and their answers, based on the lesson. Have them select one question to read aloud in an attempt to stump their classmates.

- Reveal a graphic organizer for students to fill out that will help them study the material in a new way. If you have been using an outline format, for example, a Venn diagram might be an effective way to reorganize and reinforce your students' learning.

- Have students go through their notes and list the important words. This will be much easier for students to do if you have them take notes in the two-column style—that is, if students leave a wide left margin so that there will be space for them to write key words or other comments about the material.

- Have students link ideas and facts in a knowledge chain. Begin by asking one student to state a fact from the lesson. Next, select another student to repeat the first student's fact and add another fact to it. The next student, in turn, repeats both facts and adds a third. The chain can go on until you run out of facts, students, or class time.

- Give students a crossword or word search puzzle in which just a few major words or concepts are hidden.

- Teach students to review their notes by underlining, circling, or highlighting the most important terms using colored pencils, highlighters, or pens.

- Review important information by making flash cards for your students. You can involve students even more thoroughly by having them create their own flash cards to share with the rest of the class.

A USEFUL FORMATIVE ASSESSMENT STRATEGY: EXIT SLIPS

Exit slips have been around for a long time because of their powerful appeal to students and teachers alike. As a method of assessing student learning, exit slips are effective for a variety of reasons. They are brief, focused on the day's learning, and easy for students to manage and for you to evaluate. Further, they can offer specific information about what students need to be successful. Another important aspect of exit slips is that they encourage students to be reflective about their own learning and to determine their own strengths and areas in need of improvement.

One easy way to have students complete exit slips is to ask them to complete a problem or set of problems or answer a set of questions directly related to the day's work. True-or-false statements, multiple-choice questions, or even brief short-answer questions can all work well as exit slips. The responses to these do not need to be graded, but rather quickly appraised to see where changes need to be made for the next day's lesson. Many teachers even differentiate this type of exit slip by offering tiered activities for students. (For more information on tiered instruction, see Section Twelve.)

One especially effective way to create exit slips that can yield useful data is to ask students to relate the information in the day's lesson to the essential question or the objectives for the unit under study.

Another helpful strategy for exit slips is to use 3-2-1 slips, whereby students are asked to write three things they learned, two things they found particularly interesting, and one thing they are still confused about.

Exit slips do not always have to involve writing. You can also ask students to sketch a fact, definition, or event from the lesson or to respond verbally to a question you ask as they leave the room. You can use a class roster to place a plus sign or a minus sign next to the names of students who know the material well enough to answer correctly or who still need help, respectively.

You can also ask your students to finish some of these sentence starters as a way for you to gather information as they leave the classroom:

- I was surprised when _____.
- I'm beginning to wonder _____.
- I think I will _____.
- I still need help with _____.
- I would have liked _____.
- Now I understand _____.
- In class tomorrow, I will _____.
- Today was valuable to me because _____.
- The easiest part of class today was _____.
- The hardest part of class today was _____.
- Because I need help with _____, I will _____.
- Today I changed the way I _____ because _____.
- Class would be more interesting if _____.
- I can be more successful in this class if I _____.

OFFER HELPFUL FEEDBACK

One of the most beneficial features inherent in formative assessments is the opportunity teachers have to provide students with helpful feedback about their work right away. Because we can offer assistance early in the learning cycle, students not only avoid making mistakes but also can proceed with confidence because they know they are on the right track.

There are several factors that can make feedback helpful for your students. First, try to keep your comments, whether written or verbal, as simple as possible. Be specific about what the student is doing correctly or needs to improve. Many teachers have found that their students tend to perform better if they comment on no more than three items at a time.

Instead of taking time to offer general praise about the student in general, stay focused on the issues that the student is experiencing with the work. Offering focused feedback about what the student is doing right and what needs to be improved is a much more effective method of helping a student learn than telling a student that he or she is a "Superstar" who is doing a "Great Job!"

Feedback also needs to be given as soon as possible so that students can know if their work is correct or not. Waiting for even a day or two to grade papers and return them can sometimes allow a student to continue making avoidable mistakes.

Finally, for feedback to be as useful as possible, it is necessary to keep track of it so that you and your students can see patterns of strengths and weaknesses in their learning as well as how they are progressing. You can use Teacher Worksheet 13.1 earlier in this section to help keep track of the formative assessments you give your students.

Use Podcasts to Respond to Student Work

One very easy and very engaging way to provide helpful feedback for your students is to podcast the comments that you would normally write on their papers. Instead of writing hurried comments in an illegible script that your students promptly ignore, you can simply place a number in the margin beside the part of the paper that you want to talk about and record your comment using a computer and one of the free software programs available for podcasting. Instead of seeing red ink, your students will hear your thoughtful responses or questions as they work their way from number to number throughout the paper. To ensure that your students are learning from listening to your comments, they should take notes on the comments that you make as they listen to you and then use those notes to correct their work. For more information about how to create and use podcasts in your classroom, see Section Nine.

Encourage Students to Learn from Their Errors

Even though formative assessments can be valuable classroom learning tools, one of the most difficult challenges involves helping students learn to use formative assessments as encouragement to stay on task and work hard. Sometimes, despite our best efforts, students become so discouraged that they quit trying to do their assignments well. Other negative reactions can include angry outbursts and other unpleasant class disruptions.

Teachers who are prepared for these potential reactions can help their students overcome their initial negativity and learn how to use the information they gain from formative assessments to improve their academic performance. In the list that follows, you will find a variety of ways to help students overcome their negative reactions and benefit from formative assessments.

- Be consistent in expecting students to correct their errors. Once it is part of their routine, students will be more likely to do it.
- To overcome the reluctance that many students have about completing work that won't be graded, consider grading only part of an assignment, giving a quiz on the

material instead of a grade, or allowing students to select their best work from a group of assignments.

- Have students correct their papers for a return of partial credit or for a chance to retest.

- Ask students to complete a brief self-reflection sheet about the assignment.

- Allow students to write an explanation of their thinking process on various questions. They can include an explanation of what they should have been thinking as well as what guided them to answer the way that they did.

- Have students explain to partners what they will do differently on the next assignment, how they prepared for this one, and what they learned from their work.

- Ask students to assess their readiness to move on to new material. If they are not ready, ask them what their next steps should be.

- Ask students to color-code their work, with one color representing material that they know well, another color representing material with which they are somewhat comfortable, and a third color representing material that they need help with.

- Remember that students are often willing to take more time and care assessing another student's paper than they would their own. Use this tendency to have students help each other determine their weaknesses and strengths.

Use Student Worksheet 13.1 as a way to encourage students to reflect on their work and take responsibility for their own learning.

Assignment Reflection

Fill out each part of this worksheet as you reflect on the assignment.

Student name: _____   Date: _____

Assignment: _____

_____

I did or did not achieve my goal of _____ on this assignment.

I am proud of the way I managed these parts of this assignment:

_____

_____

_____

I need to improve the way I

_____

_____

The work that I enjoyed most was

_____

_____

I can get help on the next assignment of this type from

_____

_____

The most important information that I learned was

_____

_____

The most important skill that I learned was

_____

_____

I will be able to use what I've learned from this assignment to

_____

_____

From *The First-Year Teacher's Survival Guide, 3rd Edition*, by Julia G. Thompson. Copyright © 2013 by John Wiley & Sons, Inc. Reproduced by permission.

The Two Most Common Written Assessments: Tests and Quizzes

Tests and quizzes are the chief written assessment tools that many teachers use to gauge their students' progress. Both tests and quizzes can be classified as either summative or formative assessments depending on the way teachers use the data they collect from them. Quizzes can be considered as formative assessments if they are brief and the data are intended to adjust instruction.

Although tests and quizzes both offer many advantages, using these instruments has a few disadvantages. Too often tests and quizzes focus on lower-level thinking skills and offer question formats that do not appeal to the learning styles of all students. However, you can successfully handle these problems and design effective assessments to measure your students' progress. The following strategies offer ways to design tests and quizzes that will be fair and valid.

- Remember that if a test or quiz is to be considered valid, it must accurately measure what it is designed to appraise. Aim for validity by making sure that the test or quiz covers the content you want to assess. One way to do this is to create the test or quiz when you plan each unit of study.

- Include a variety of question types on each test or quiz. Objective questions do not always give an accurate assessment of your students' thinking. A balanced combination of objective questions and essay questions will provide a better assessment of your students than either type will by itself.

- Write questions that require students to think beyond the remembering level of learning. You can still use an objective format if you model your questions on the format used on many standardized tests. These tests often offer a reading passage followed by questions that require students to apply their knowledge, judge the validity of a statement in the passage, or use another higher-level thinking skill.

- Prevent problems with cheating by presenting different versions of the same test or quiz to your students. Give different assessments within the same class, or give each class a different version. You should also plan to give future students different versions from this year's quizzes or tests .

- Share questions with your colleagues. If you and other teachers cover the same material, you can save time by using the best questions from each other's assessments.

- Make your tests and quizzes easy to follow by grouping similar question types together.

- Place the point value for each section beside the directions for that section so that your students can judge their own progress.

- Begin any test or quiz with simple questions that your students will find easy. This will help them get over their initial anxiety.

- Make sure to give clear directions that are easy to follow. When you change question types, you must give new directions, even if the procedure seems obvious to you.

- Number each page so that students can keep track of where they are in the assessment.

- Humanize your tests and quizzes with encouragement, hints, and advice. Suggest how long a section should take to complete, underline key words, or even wish students good luck.

- If you type your tests and quizzes, make sure to use a plain font that is large enough for students to read easily. If you write tests and quizzes by hand, make sure that your writing is extremely neat.

- Avoid vague questions that are difficult for students to comprehend easily.

- Don't make your assessments so long that your students will not be able to finish them. To judge the length of your test or quiz, take it yourself, and then allow two or three times that amount of time for your students to complete it.

- Save your questions electronically so that you will have ready access to them. Experienced teachers create banks of questions that they can use again in a different format or on future tests and quizzes.

Quizzes are similar to tests in that they require the same careful attention to fairness and validity. With a few exceptions, you should follow the same guidelines for designing quizzes that you use for tests. Here are some suggestions on how to make sure that the quizzes you design will accurately assess your students' progress:

- Design quizzes to last thirty minutes or less. Because they are less comprehensive than tests, quizzes should be much more brief.

- Use quizzes as formative assessments leading up to a longer assessment. If you give your students several quizzes before you give them a test, you will have a more accurate measurement of their test readiness than you would if you only offered one quiz.

- With fairness in mind, warn your students when you are planning to give a quiz. Students tend to regard pop quizzes as vengeful.

- Give students quizzes on paper instead of using a projector or a television or monitor, because some students may have difficulty reading a screen or monitor.

- Bear in mind that oral quizzes are very difficult for students who have trouble processing auditory information.

> I always knew that teachers worked hard, but I don't think that any new teacher can anticipate the sheer exhaustion associated with teaching. Every day is a new challenge and a new lesson to prepare. However, the rewards are too numerous to mention, and the job satisfaction is truly life altering.
>
> *Melinda Conner, first-year teacher*

- Grade and return quizzes promptly. One of the chief benefits of giving quizzes is that they offer immediate feedback to your students.

Create Useful Objective Questions

Objective questions have many advantages for teachers and students. Although it can take a very long time to construct objective questions that can fairly assess what your students know, they can be very easy to grade. Also, objective questions are not subject to the grader's subjectivity in the way that essay questions are. Use the tips that follow to create useful objective questions that allow you to assess your students' knowledge and understanding accurately.

TRUE-OR-FALSE STATEMENTS

- Remember that this type of question is less useful than others because students have a good chance of guessing the answer.
- Make sure that the answers don't follow a pattern.
- Avoid ambiguous statements.
- Take care to write statements that are similar in length. Often the true statements tend to be longer than the false ones.
- Avoid giving away the answers with such words or phrases as *not, none, at no time, never, all of the time,* or *always.*
- If you would like to increase the thinking skills required on a test with true-or-false statements, ask students to explain or rewrite the answers they find false.

MATCHING QUESTIONS

- Involve higher-level thinking skills by asking students to do more than just recall information. For example, instead of asking students to match a character with the title of a short story, ask them to match a character with a type of conflict the character may have experienced.
- Make sure that the answers don't follow a pattern.
- Be sure to work out the answers before you give a test so that you can find any words that may inadvertently be spelled with your answers.
- Allow students to cross out answer choices as they use them.
- Offer more answer choices than questions.

- Give several short lists of ten to fifteen items rather than a longer list that students will find difficult to follow.

- Arrange matching questions to fit on the same page so that students will not be confused by having to flip back and forth.

SHORT-ANSWER QUESTIONS

- Keep in mind that although it does not take long to create short-answer questions, it does take longer to grade them.

- Use short-answer questions to see how well your students write and how well they think.

- Provide opportunities for higher-level thinking by using short-answer questions; answers are not predetermined, so students have to think more to come up with their own responses.

- Design short-answer questions to yield responses that can be a word, a phrase, or even a paragraph in length.

- Avoid giving such clues as "a" or "an" to indicate the answer. Instead, use "a/an" to give your students a full range of choices for their answer. For example, your quiz might read, "A wheelwright is a/an _____."

- When you ask questions that require brief answers, make all the blanks the same length; otherwise, many students will interpret the length of the line as a clue to the answer.

MULTIPLE-CHOICE QUESTIONS

- Use multiple-choice questions to measure your students' mastery of both simple and complex concepts.

- Don't allow your answers to follow a pattern.

- Make each answer choice significantly different from the others to reduce confusion.

- Write the answer choices in such a way that they are similar grammatically.

- Avoid overusing one letter. You can do this by making up the answer pattern in advance and arranging the questions so that the answers conform to that pattern.

- Provide answer choices that are all roughly the same length to avoid giving away the answer.

- Make every answer choice a possibility by not including options that students can immediately eliminate as possible answers. For example, if your science test includes a question about who discovered DNA, don't give "George Washington" as one of the answer choices.

How to Grade Objective Questions Quickly

Among the chief advantages of using objective questions are the ease and speed of grading. Here are some tips to make grading objective questions even easier:

- Group similar items together. For example, place all true-or-false statements together and all short-answer questions together.

- Place questions with the same point values together so that you don't have to keep checking the value of each question.

- Keep the number of total points at 100 so that you will be able to quickly add up the missed points and subtract them from 100 to determine the percentage.

- If you ask students to write short answers, provide lines for their answers. They will find it easier to write on the lines, and you will not have to decipher answers that slant off the page.

- If the test or quiz is long, create a blank answer form on a separate sheet that students must use to record their answers.

- Teach students to use a plus sign for "true" and a minus sign for "false," allowing you to grade true-or-false questions very quickly. It is not always easy to distinguish students' answers when they use *T* and *F*.

- If a student leaves an answer blank, draw a straight line through where the answer would have been in addition to an *X* to prevent students from cheating by adding answers when you go over the graded papers together.

- Ask your students to use dark ink to take a test or quiz (when appropriate). Dark ink makes the answers easy for you to read.

- Grade all of the same pages at once instead of grading each test or quiz separately. For example, grade all of the first pages, then go back and grade all of the second pages.

Conduct Rules for Quizzes and Tests

When your students take quizzes and tests, they should not cheat, and they should not disturb others who may be struggling with an answer. You can prevent both of these forms of misbehavior from invalidating an assignment by teaching and enforcing rules for your students to follow while taking a quiz or test. These rules will make it easier for you to give quizzes and tests:

- Don't allow students a few minutes to study before a test or quiz. Ill-prepared students may take advantage of this opportunity to write cheat notes.

- Provide students with a cover sheet to allow them to keep their answers hidden from other students seated near them during the test or quiz. You and your students can create colorful ones with inspiring quotations and artwork. Laminate them and use them over and over.

- Limit the materials on students' desks to the minimum of necessary paper and one or two writing utensils. Students with extra paper can use it to hide cheat notes. If students want to pad their paper to make writing easier, allow them to fold their paper in half.

- Before giving an assignment, have students neatly stow their belongings under their desk and not beside it. All notes and loose papers should be inside a binder. If your students have cell phones, remind them to turn their phones off and put them out of sight.

- Require students to sit facing the front of the class with their knees and feet under the front of their desk. Allowing students to sit sideways during a quiz or test increases the chances that cheating will occur.

- If students need extra paper, pens, or pencils while they have a test or quiz paper, require them to ask permission before searching through their book bag.

- Monitor your students carefully until all papers are in. If students have a question, teach them to raise their hand and wait for you to come to them. Do not allow them to walk to you.

- Do not allow any talking until all students have turned in their paper. If you allow talking, other students could be disturbed and you will find it impossible to control cheating.

- Once students turn in their work, don't allow them to retrieve their paper to add answers.

- Set a reasonable but firm time limit. Students who take much longer than others to take a test or quiz have more opportunities to cheat and may cause the rest of the class to become restless while waiting for them to finish.

- If students have accommodations for testing, such as small-group testing or extended time, allow them to leave the room at the start of the testing period. Take care to make sure that they will be supervised adequately.

- Take time to check for cheat notes on your students' hands, desks, clothing, and shoes. Students who know you will check will be less likely to attempt cheating.

- Be sure to erase the board cleanly to remove any information that will be on the test or quiz.

- Make sure that you do not leave an answer key where students can see it.

What to Do If Many of Your Students Fail a Test or Quiz

Few things are as discouraging as having a number of students fail a test or quiz. When this happens, there are three possible causes: the test or quiz itself is flawed, students did not prepare adequately, or you did not sufficiently help students master the material before giving the assessment. Here are some suggestions on how to handle each problem:

- **The assessment is flawed.** Look at the assessment. Is the format easy for students to follow? Are the point values logical? Do the questions match the way you taught the material? You can correct this situation by designing another test or quiz and using the one that students failed as a pretest and study guide.

- **Students did not prepare for the test or quiz.** Determine the reasons why your students did not prepare. Ask them to describe how they studied and why they did not study more. Teach students how you want them to review. You can also correct this problem by designing a new test or quiz and using the one that students failed as a pretest and study guide.

- **You did not sufficiently help students master the material.** Sometimes teachers overestimate their students' readiness to take a test or quiz. When this happens to you, learn from your mistake and help students master the material better before the next assessment You can correct this problem by using the failed test or quiz as a review guide to help students determine what they don't know. Remedy the situation by providing additional instruction and then retesting.

Types of Authentic Assessments

Authentic assessments are alternative methods of determining the knowledge or skills your students have acquired that you can use in addition to traditional tests and quizzes to measure student achievement. Authentic assessments have become popular in the last few years as educators have come to realize that traditional summative assessments do not always meet the needs of all learners.

Students who do not read or write well struggle with tests and quizzes, even though they may know the material as well as students with stronger verbal skills. Recognizing the need for a variety of assessments, educators have developed a wide array of evaluation instruments to measure what their students know.

Begin slowly, choosing authentic assessments that are easy to manage. As you grow in confidence, and as you get to know your students' strengths and weaknesses, you can incorporate assessments that are more extensive. When you make up your next assessments, consider using some of the following types of assessments in addition to traditional measurements:

- Oral reports
- Research projects
- Creative projects
- Posters

- Work contracts
- Models
- Booklets
- Online assessments
- Class Web pages
- Self-evaluations
- Peer evaluations

How can you determine whether an authentic assessment will be successful with your students? Follow these suggestions:

- Make sure to align the assessment very closely with the material. For example, asking students to demonstrate a process is an appropriate assessment after you have taught them the steps of the process.
- Give scoring information to students when you make the initial assignment. No matter which method of assessment you use, your students need to know the criteria for success as they begin their work.

There are many different authentic assessments you can use throughout the school year. Here, however, is a brief list of some authentic assessments that you may find particularly easy to incorporate into your lessons.

OPEN-ENDED QUESTIONS

When answering open-ended questions, students can reveal what they know about a topic without the constraints of questions requiring fixed-answer responses. Skillfully worded open-ended questions can elicit a great deal more information about a topic than objective questions can. Asking open-ended questions based on real-world situations will yield meaningful responses that require students to use higher-level thinking skills. Here are some examples of open-ended questions:

- How did pioneer settlers in 1825 experience hardships similar to the ones you and your classmates experience?
- Predict the changes that the main character will have to go through before the end of the book, and tell whether each one is positive or negative.
- How do you think Thomas Jefferson would feel about the laws on illegal immigration today? Explain your answer.
- Describe several ways that you can learn about another country. If you were planning a trip, which one would you prefer to visit? Why?

VARIATIONS ON TRADITIONAL TESTS

There are many variations on traditional tests that can help you assess your students' knowledge. Use one or more of the following:

- **Group tests.** Students work as a group to answer questions.
- **Pairs tests.** Students work in pairs to answer questions.
- **Take-home tests.** Students work out the answers to the test at home.
- **Open-book or open-note tests.** Students can refer to their book or their notes when answering questions.

PERFORMANCE ASSESSMENTS

Instead of asking students to write answers, you can give them a task to perform to elicit the information you need to measure. Some examples of activities suitable for this type of assessment include these:

- Science experiments
- Oral reports
- Skits
- Demonstrations
- Book talks
- Projects

JOURNALS AND LEARNING LOGS

Journals and learning logs are particularly useful as authentic assessments because they allow students to reflect on their learning. Even though they are frequently grouped together under the heading of writing tasks, journals and learning logs are used for different purposes. When students write a journal entry, they react to the material under study in a personal, subjective way, expressing their opinions. When students write a learning log entry, they write a response that is factual, objective, and more impersonal than a journal entry.

In both types of writing, students write about what they learned and how they learn material. Both of these assessments are particularly easy to adapt to the needs of students of all ages and abilities.

INTERACTIVE RESPONSE SYSTEMS

One of the most exciting new alternatives to traditional assessments is interactive response systems, automated assessments that allow students to use a software program, computer, and handheld response pad to answer questions. When using an interactive response system, students usually read questions on a shared monitor or projector screen and record their answers by clicking buttons on individual response pads. Because the feedback is immediate, students learn quickly. The advantages of an interactive response system are immediate feedback and highly motivated students. Although such a system is too expensive for you to purchase by yourself, your school may already have such a system. If so, your students will enjoy the opportunity to assess their knowledge with a clicker. To learn more about how to use an interactive response system to assess your students, try searching these Web sites:

- **eInstruction Corporation (www.einstruction.com).** Over a million students have used eInstruction's user-friendly interactive response system, which was launched in 2000. To learn more about how to use the innovative Classroom Performance System, visit the eInstruction site and explore with a video tour.
- **Qwizdom (www.qwizdom.com).** This site offers a great deal of information about Qwizdom's various software products, which are designed to help teachers create lively presentations and interactive quizzes. Using Qwizdom's versatile site and online tutorials, you can easily access a great deal of useful material about interactive response systems.

RUBRICS

A rubric is a sophisticated assessment tool that more and more teachers are using to evaluate what their students understand. Like other good ideas, rubrics began simply and have grown in usefulness as more teachers have learned to adapt them for their purposes.

Both students and teachers can use rubrics. Students use them to complete assignments, whereas teachers use them to assess student performance. Although rubrics save teachers time in grading student work, the success of rubrics lies mainly in the clarity they provide about what is expected when students complete assignments.

The goals for an assignment are very clear when students receive a rubric before they begin. Because students know what to do, their work is usually of higher quality than it is with traditional assessments. An added benefit of rubrics is that they force students to critique and reflect on their own work. Rubrics often help students find and correct mistakes before their teacher has to subtract points for errors.

How can you use rubrics in your class? Although it takes practice and patience to learn how to develop a clearly expressed rubric, you can begin with these steps:

- **Step One:** Determine the criteria by which you will grade an assignment.
- **Step Two:** Decide on the levels of mastery you want in an assignment. Begin by determining the best and the worst levels, and then determine the levels in between.
- **Step Three:** Create your own rubric, using a chart format similar to the one in Sample 13.1. Using a chart makes it easier for students to see the relationships among the various assessment items.

- **Step Four**: Show students models of acceptable and unacceptable assignments. Demonstrate how you would evaluate each assignment using the rubric.
- **Step Five**: Encourage students to practice using the rubric with several model assignments before you move them to self-assessments.

Many Web sites are devoted to the various types of rubrics. To begin refining your knowledge and to access free models, try these outstanding sites:

- **4Teachers (www.4teachers.org).** At this helpful site, you will find RubiStar, a tool that allows you to create customized rubrics for all grade levels in English and in Spanish. You can save the rubrics you create online, and modify them whenever you need to.
- **Kathy Schrock's Guide to Everything (www.schrockguide.net).** This extensive site has dozens of articles about rubrics, along with examples and instructions for specific types. You can learn how to create useful rubrics and modify existing ones,

Sample 13.1
Simple Rubric

This very simple sample rubric is one that teachers and students could use with an assignment requiring learners to create a map of the United States.

Quality	Excellent	Above Average	Average	Needs Work
Neatness	Lettering is very neat. States are carefully colored.	Lettering is neat. States are colored.	States are colored. Lettering is sloppy.	States are not colored. Lettering is sloppy.
Accuracy	All capitals, states, cities, and features are correct.	Almost all elements are correct.	More than 75 percent of the elements are correct.	Less than 75 percent of the elements are correct.
Details	States, capitals, cities, and all major features are shown.	States, capitals, cities, and some major features are shown.	States, capitals, cities, and few major features are shown.	States, capitals, cities, and no other major features are shown.

how to use rubrics in your classroom, or even how to guide students in creating their own rubrics.

- **Educator's Network (www.rubrics4teachers.com).** This excellent site offers hundreds of free rubrics on a wide range of topics. It also offers information on how to create effective rubrics; many models of rubrics; and advice on how to use rubrics with a variety of students, grade levels, and subjects.

One of the most productive ways to use rubrics is to involve students in their creation. To do this, first present an assignment to your students. Show examples, models, or samples so that students know what the finished product should be. Next, have students work together in small groups to set their goals for the assignment and to establish criteria for assessment. After each group has made their decisions, they should share their ideas about the desired qualities of their work with the whole class. After a discussion, the whole class can suggest the elements that they believe should be included on a rubric. With this type of discussion in advance of the start of an assignment, students should have a clear idea of how to produce successful work.

> Minimize what you grade if possible. One approach: I have a daily warm-up problem that students work on when they come in. I circulate around the room while they are working on the problems and check homework. If it seems clear that one of the homework problems has caused trouble, I ask one of the students to do the problem on the board while I continue checking homework.
>
> *Bob Foley, 2+ years' experience*

Keeping Track of Grades

Although you hope it will not happen to you, many teachers have had to produce their grade book as evidence in court. Because a grade book is a legal document, you must maintain it meticulously throughout the year. Your school district will have strict policies about how you are to keep student grade records, and you should follow them precisely.

There are three ways you can record student grades: recording all grades electronically, recording all grades on paper, or using a combination of paper and electronic record keeping.

The combination approach is currently the most common way that teachers maintain grade records. Here's why:

- Electronic grade systems can fail.
- You can lose a paper grade book.
- A paper grade book is usually more portable than an electronic grade book.
- One method can serve as a backup for the other.

To manage both types of grade books—paper or electronic—successfully, you will have to be very organized. Following are some tips for success in managing grade books.

GENERAL INFORMATION ON GRADE MANAGEMENT

- You should perform a variety of assessments during a marking period to provide balance in the types of grades your students earn. For example, if you use classwork grades, quiz grades, project grades, portfolio grades, and test grades to determine a student's average, you will have a more accurate assessment of what the student knows than if you rely only on test and quiz grades.

- You should collect several grades each week so that you can have an accurate idea of each student's progress.

- You should determine how you will weight your grades before school begins. In general, you should have a greater percentage of objective measurements (as opposed to subjective ones).

- You must inform your students of how you will weight their grades. Many teachers post this information in a conspicuous place and also send it home in a letter to parents and guardians at the start of the term.

- When you plan your grades, you must also plan how you are going to handle missing work, makeup work, and assignments for students who are homebound.

- Students' grades are confidential; the Family Educational Rights and Privacy Act (first enacted in 1974) protects them. By law, you should never announce grades, post grades, tell a student's grade to a classmate, or allow students to look at your grade book.

PAPER GRADE BOOKS

- Never leave your grade book where a student can take it. Keep track of your grade book by keeping it in the same place each day. You should either lock it away securely at night or take it home with you.

- Use black ink in your grade book whenever you can. Be very neat.

- Record your students' names in alphabetical order. You should also include student identification numbers if you will be required to use them during the term.

- Record the dates when your class will meet at the top of each column if you will be maintaining attendance records in your grade book.

- At the bottom of each column, record the specific names of assignments. For example, write "Quiz on Chapter 1," "Fractions Test," or "Homework, page 17" rather than "quiz," "test," and "homework" so that you can quickly identify the assignment later in the term.

- When you record grades, place a line at the bottom of the box where a student's grade will be if the student is absent and needs to make up an assignment. Convert this line to a circle when the student makes up the work. This will be very useful when you need to transfer your paper grades to an electronic program or when you have to average grades by hand, because you can add in grades for made-up work quickly.

ELECTRONIC GRADE BOOKS

- Schedule a set amount of time each week to update your electronic grade book. Trying to record hundreds of grades the day before you are supposed to give report cards to students is almost impossible.

- Save your grades in several places. Be very careful to keep all copies secure, however.

- Be aware that students can read the screen when you record grades while they are present. Place your classroom computer in a spot where you can maintain confidentiality.

- Print grades for students often so that your students will be able to help you correct errors. To maintain your students' privacy, keep the printouts of their grades in a secure place, just as you would a paper grade book.

- If your school district requires you to keep electronic grades, use a password to protect them.

- If your school district does not require all teachers to use the same electronic grade book program, consider looking into the several good ones that you can purchase. Here are some Web sites offering grade books that other teachers have found easy to use:

  - **Learner Profile (www.learnerprofile.com).** The grade book on this site not only records grades but also tracks Adequate Yearly Progress information and allows users to access test objectives for Houghton Mifflin reading tests.

  - **Learn Boost (www.learnboost.com).** Here you can access a free electronic grade book along with a host of other organization tools.

In addition to keeping track of your students' grades throughout a grading period, you may also want to consider asking your students to track their own grades. When students monitor their grades, they will be more likely to become self-disciplined learners and much more inclined to improve their poor study habits than those students who are clueless about how well they are doing between progress reports. You can use or adapt Student Worksheet 13.2 as a tool to help your students self-monitor their own grades.

STUDENT WORKSHEET 13.2

Grade Tracking Form for Student Success

Use this worksheet to track the grades that you earn on each of your assignments so that you can see how well you are doing and what changes, if any, you need to make to improve your study habits.

Student name: _____ Date: _____

My grade goal for this class: _____

Two study strategies I am using are

_____

_____

Date	Assignment	Grade	Weight	Impact

How to Personalize a Grade Report

One of the best ways to send home meaningful grade reports is to personalize them. There are two types of information that you can place on a report: general information intended for all parents and guardians and information that is specific to each student.

Many types of general information can be included on a grade report. Parents and guardians will appreciate a notice of upcoming events, such as science fairs, project due dates, or parent conference days. You can also include your contact information, in case parents or guardians want to discuss the grade report with you.

In addition to the general information on a grade report, you should include information that is specific to the student. Here you can explain such matters as the due dates for any missing work or why the overall grade is what it is; if appropriate, you can write a brief note thanking parents or guardians for their support.

You should also be sure to make a positive comment about the child on each grade report. If you have trouble thinking of fresh ways to write comments about students, you can get ideas from other teachers who have had this problem and shared their solutions with others. For hundreds of comments that you can use on grade reports, try these terrific Web sites:

- **Teach Net (www.teachnet.com).** On this site's home page, use "report card comments" as a search term to bring up many useful results.
- **Teachers Network (www.teachersnetwork.org).** At this site, use "report card comments" as a search term to find great ideas for constructive comments to include in grade reports.

What You Should Do When Students Challenge Grades

It is only natural for students to challenge their grades throughout the term. If you do not handle their challenges well, the resulting problems may cause long-term resentment. Here are suggestions for dealing with student challenges in a way that benefits everyone involved:

- **Take a proactive attitude.** Anticipate that some of your students will challenge their grades, and prevent as many problems as you can by being proactive. Here's how:
  - Make sure that your assessments and the weight for each one are in keeping with your district's policies.
  - Publish the grading scale for your class so that students know just how much weight a particular assignment will have.
  - Be careful to have many assessments for your students and to vary the types of assignments you use so that your students will have many different opportunities to be successful.

- **Do not take the challenge personally.** Focus on the complaint and not on the fact that a student is questioning your judgment.

- **Listen to students.** Their complaints, even if they are not legitimate, are often the result of confusion. Take what students have to say seriously, and use their complaints to improve your teaching.

- **Expect challenges to daily or weekly assignments.** When you go over a graded assignment with students, tell them that you could have made mistakes. Ask them to let you know about mistakes you have made by putting a large question mark beside any item they would like you to look at again. They should also write a note to let you know why they are challenging the grade. Collect those papers and look at them again. By doing so, you are letting your students know that you will address their concerns. You will also benefit because you won't have a group of students shouting at you.

- **Expect challenges to progress reports or report cards.** You can preempt many of these challenges by letting students know their averages more often than when progress reports and report cards are distributed. If you use an electronic grading program, print copies of averages frequently. Another advantage of this practice is that students can help you correct errors you may have made in recording grades.

- **Be respectful of students who are mistaken.** When a student challenges a grade and is mistaken, take care to explain the error completely. Thank the student for checking with you, and encourage him or her to continue to be concerned about the work.

What to Do When You Suspect a Student of Cheating

When you suspect a student of cheating, be certain you have enough evidence before you speak to the student. Begin by speaking privately with the child. Do not be confrontational; instead, remain calm as you present your point of view.

If, after talking with the student, you are still sure that cheating has taken place, you must follow your school's guidelines for handling cheating incidents. The guidelines will probably direct you to contact the child's parents or guardians, inform an administrator, and withhold credit for the assignment.

If you suspect that several students are involved in a single incident of cheating, you still need to speak to students individually and handle the problem one student at a time. In such a case, it is important to involve an administrator early in the process because you will need support to deal with all of the students involved.

How to Manage Cyber Cheating

Even though many students who cheat in school still use old-fashioned methods, the incidence of cyber cheating has increased alarmingly in the last few years. Cyber cheating is on the rise across all grade levels as students are becoming more media literate. Other causes include the increased use of computers and the Internet in classrooms, larger numbers of students who bring their own phone or other device to school, increased pressures on students to achieve academic success, overscheduled students with little time to perform well on their assignments done at home, a proliferation of sites that offer essays for students to plagiarize, and a lack of training and awareness in regard to exactly what the parameters of cyber cheating are. Cyber cheating can take a variety of forms, just a few of which include

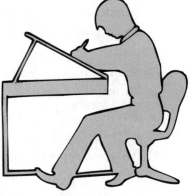

- Accessing information stored on a phone or other device during a test or quiz
- Photographing a test or quiz and sending the digital image to classmates
- Texting answers to classmates
- Purchasing essays from online plagiarism sites
- Plagiarizing parts of essays, reports, or projects

Although the problem of cyber cheating is widespread and growing rapidly with new developments in technology, there are several things that savvy teachers can do to manage the issue.

- Educate your students about what constitutes cyber cheating. Many students are so accustomed to cutting and pasting information and images into essays and reports or sharing information with classmates that they may not always understand what cyber cheating is.
- Make sure your students know that you are aware of the issue of cyber cheating and that you will be checking their work for evidence of this phenomenon.
- Ask students to show all of their work on projects and essays. They should submit notes and drafts as well as final copies.
- Hold conferences with students in which you discuss the methods they used to complete their work or ask them to summarize the main points of their essays or test answers.
- Browse some of the many online cheating advice sites maintained by less-than-ethical students. To access dozens of the most current sites, use a search term such as "how to cheat in school." When you browse these sites, you will learn some of the many ways that students cheat while in class as well as when they are cheating electronically.
- Pay attention to your intuition. If a student's work seems to be too good to be true, it may be work that is copied. Take the time to talk with the student about it.
- Don't recycle tests and essay topics year after year. Design assignments instead that are unique and that require students to do independent and creative thinking.

Extra Credit Dilemmas and Solutions

Extra credit is often a controversial topic for teachers. Some teachers are adamant about its usefulness, whereas others believe that offering extra credit encourages poor study habits. Either way, extra credit can be a trap for the unwary first-year teacher. When you are trying to establish a workable extra credit policy for your students, follow these guidelines:

- Make sure that your plan for extra credit is in line with your school's policy. If the policy is not in your faculty manual, check with several colleagues to learn what other teachers do.

- Before you give in to student pressure for extra credit, decide on your expectations. Don't give in on the spur of the moment just because students want extra points.

- Be aware of how easy it is to skew grades with extra credit points. If you assign work for extra credit without considering the impact it will have on grades, you may devalue the work you have assigned throughout the grading period.

- If you do offer extra credit, do so at the beginning of a marking period and assign a clear due date and point value for any extra credit assignment. If you don't do this, you will find yourself grading too many papers at the end of the term.

- Remember that extra credit assignments should have rubrics, just as other assignments do. Grade them on the quality of the work, not just on effort.

- Offer extra credit to every student in your class, not just to students who request it. If you don't offer it to everyone, you can legitimately be accused of favoritism.

- Don't offer extra credit for activities that require your students to spend money. For example, don't give students an extra credit assignment of going to see a local play. Some students will not be able to afford the admission fee, no matter how small it might be.

- If you offer bonus questions on a test, make sure they are not worth as much as the other questions. The purpose of such questions is to encourage a student to stretch his or her mind, not earn easy points to make up for what he or she did not know.

> Teach your students with confidence. Instill the confidence in them that they will be prepared. Don't let your anxiety about tests transfer to students.
>
> *Luann Scott, 37 years' experience*

Success with Standardized Tests

It is highly likely that your students will have to take at least one standardized test this year. School districts rely on standardized tests to assess not only the performance of individual students but also the performance of schools and how well teachers are achieving the goals of the school district. Because standardized tests have serious implications for everyone involved, the test administrators in your district will probably give teachers a great deal of information about the specific tests that students have to take. Standardized tests do not have to be a headache for you and your students if you take care to do three important things: prepare all year long, teach test-taking skills, and assume your professional responsibilities.

YEARLONG PREPARATION

There are several simple steps you can take, beginning at the start of the school year, to make sure that your students are prepared for a standardized test. Spending a bit of time periodically throughout each grading period is a much more sensible plan to help students succeed than just cramming right before the test. Here are some suggestions to follow all year long:

- Provide solid instruction that is aligned with your school district's and state's curriculum guidelines. If your focus is on carefully planning and delivering content instead of just covering the test, your students will have a greater chance of success.

- Talk about the test. Make students aware of the test, but don't threaten them with it. Too often teachers find it easy to warn students that they will have to take a standardized test seriously, but this can intimidate students who are less able.

- Offer a variety of testing formats and instructional activities all year long so that students can naturally develop skills as test takers.

- Use the materials offered by your state's department of education and your local school district as a planning guide. Often there will be course blueprints and ancillary materials that will help you cover the necessary content.

- Offer your students previous tests as practice as often as you can. When they are informed about what to expect, they can take the test with confidence.

- When students practice for the test, gather data, and use this information to offer differentiated remediation activities.

TEST-TAKING SKILLS

Prepare your students by making sure they are test wise. They should not feel intimidated by the format or process of a standardized test if you take the time to teach test-taking skills. The tips that follow can help you teach important test-taking skills.

- Teach students to take the time to listen as the test examiner reads the instructions, even if they believe that they are familiar with the directions. They should also reread the instructions for themselves as they work through the test.

- When your students practice taking the test, show them how to pace themselves. Make sure they know where to find a clock at the testing site.

- Practice reading test items together and analyzing what information the answers require. Many mistakes happen because students do not read the questions carefully.

- Be aware that students often become bogged down in a difficult reading passage and just skim the questions. Teach them to read the questions carefully first and then skim the passage, looking for the answers.

- When students have passages to read, teach them to underline the parts of the passage that are covered in the questions. They can also circle important words or write notes to themselves in the margins.

- Teach the process of elimination in regard to answer choices. Students should practice eliminating the answers that are obviously not correct until they arrive at a reasonable answer.

- Because marking a bubble sheet during a test can be stressful for many students, give your students lots of opportunities throughout the year to practice marking their answers on a bubble sheet.

- Encourage students to go back and check their work. If the test is a very long one, or if it is timed, teach students to check the questions they are unsure of first and then check the ones they are sure of as time permits.

YOUR PROFESSIONAL RESPONSIBILITIES IN REGARD TO TESTING

As a classroom teacher, you will have to manage weighty responsibilities when it comes to the administration of standardized tests. It is important that you take care to be as professional as possible when you administer them. It may be helpful to keep in mind that standardized tests are just that—standardized—so that the same testing conditions can be in place for every student. When tests are standardized, they are more likely to be fair assessments of what students know because the testing conditions are the same for every test taker.

In the list that follows, you will find some suggestions for making sure that you manage test administration in a professional and competent manner.

- Be aware that you will probably be asked to attend training sessions to prepare for test administration. Take the training seriously, and don't hesitate to ask questions.

- Allow yourself enough time in advance of the date of the test to carefully read the procedures and directions for testing. If you are not clear about what you are supposed to do, ask the staff member in charge of testing at your school.

- Familiarize yourself with the directions that you are supposed to read out loud to students during testing. Do not deviate from the script that you will be given.

- Make sure that you have a reliable way to time tests if they are supposed to be timed.

- Do your best to prevent violations of test security. Here are some specific suggestions for this:

  - Monitor students carefully during testing. Don't check e-mail or grade papers during the test, for example. Take care not to look at the tests as you administer them.

  - Don't give in to the temptation to quiz your students afterward about what was on the test.

  - Be sure to carefully count out the test materials as you distribute them, and make sure to account for all copies after the testing period is over.

  - Take care that all students turn cell phones or other electronic devices off and place them in a secure place during the testing period.

- Know that teachers are often asked to sign an acknowledgment that they have received information about the particular test that their students will be taking. When you sign such an acknowledgment, you are indicating that you understand the kind of help you will need to offer your students before and during the test. Gently refuse requests for help from anxious students during testing. If you are not sure how to do this in an appropriate manner, ask the testing coordinator at your school for advice. Refrain from offering hints or encouragement during a test, also.

- If students are supposed to receive testing accommodations, be scrupulous in providing those accommodations.

- If you encounter problems during testing, report them to the testing coordinator as soon as you can. Some of the problems that you may have to report could include a fire drill, loud noises, a ringing cell phone, a student bubbling in patterns instead of actually taking the test, or a disruptive student, just to name a few.

A final word about success with standardized tests: one of the biggest complaints about standardized tests is that they force teachers to teach to the test. Some opponents of standardized testing claim that the flaws inherent in standardized tests require teachers who want to have successful students to teach only the material that will be covered on the test. Although it is inevitable that there will be flaws in systems of standardized testing, teachers who want their students to be successful certainly do not teach to the test. In fact, teachers whose students are successful test takers make a point of covering the important concepts in the course curriculum instead of dwelling on what may or may not be tested. They may prepare their students by strengthening the test-taking skills specific to their subject or grade level, but teachers with integrity do not limit their students by teaching to the test.

> Teaching gave me the chance to share my love for my subject with new minds. I learned a good deal about my subject and life, even, from my students.
>
> *Carole Platt, 35 years' experience*

Best Practices Checklist

1. Let your instructional practices be informed by the careful collection and analysis of data throughout the school year.

2. Use formative assessments not just to determine your students' progress but also to adjust and differentiate instruction.

3. Begin each unit of study with assessments designed to gather baseline data so that you can create instruction to meet the needs of your students.

4. Take care to offer helpful, constructive feedback that will encourage students to learn from their mistakes.

5. Be aware of the various types of problems that can occur with any type of assessment and work to make sure that the assessments you offer your students are as fair as possible.

6. Use rubrics not only to assess student work but also to help define the qualities and expectations of the assignment.

7. Be scrupulous in managing your students' grades throughout each grading period. Remember that your grade book is a legal document.

8. Make a point of helping students keep track of their own grades so that they can see what they have to do to be successful.

9. Be aware of your school district's policies on student cheating and develop a classroom plan to manage cheating and cyber cheating.

10. Help your students achieve success with standardized tests by offering solid instruction all year long, teaching test-taking skills, and assuming your professional responsibilities as a test administrator.

Time to Reflect
Assess Your Students' Progress

Use the information in this section to guide your thinking as you reflect on these questions. They are designed to encourage you to think more deeply about the issues in the text or to discuss those issues with colleagues.

1. How important is the role of data in helping shape instruction in your classroom? What types of formative assessments work well for you and your students? How do you manage the data you gather? What can you do to improve how you manage formative assessments in your classroom?

2. Traditional tests and quizzes can be useful assessments. How can you maximize their effectiveness? How can your colleagues help you with this?

3. What kinds of authentic assessments would work well in your classroom? Discuss how you can incorporate these assessments into your lessons.

4. What plans have you made to manage your students' grades in an organized way? What does your school district expect of you? What tips can other professionals in your building share with you to help lighten your workload?

5. How have you prepared your students for any standardized tests they will take this year? What test-taking skills are important for them to know? How have you taught those skills? Where can you find more information on how to prepare students for standardized tests?

SECTION FOURTEEN

Level the Playing Field by Covering Basic Skills

There are sad inequities in our classrooms that we teachers cannot do anything about. We can't make a student from a dysfunctional family go home at night to a peaceful, supportive environment. We can't provide the safety and security that our students from neighborhoods threatened by constant criminal activity lack. We can't redistribute wealth so that all of our students can have the material comforts that some of them enjoy and others long for.

However, there are many inequities that we can resolve for our students. It is up to us, as caring education professionals, to assume responsibility for making sure that each of our students has opportunities to be successful and to learn. It is our responsibility to remove the obstacles that prevent our students from acquiring the knowledge and developing the skills inherent in our course curricula.

No matter how old our students are or how capable they are at learning, we need to make sure that they have the basic skills they need to be academically successful. In twenty-first-century classrooms, the basic skills that students need to succeed are very different from the skills that students in the past have required. In the past, students may have needed just the rudiments of reading, writing, and math to graduate from school, find a good job, and lead productive lives.

Today's students, in contrast, should be skilled at managing the information that barrages us all daily through various media outlets and at using different forms of media to communicate effectively; they should also be able to listen attentively, speak well in front of others, write clearly and coherently, recognize and use words with ease, think critically, and read well. These are the basic skills they require.

You cannot and should not expect that your students will have been taught these skills in the past. No matter what subject or grade level you teach, it is up to you to make sure that your students acquire the basic skills that are appropriate for their age and for your course. It is up to you to make sure that they have the skills they need to succeed.

Media Literacy Skills

Because our students, like us, are inundated with an overwhelming amount of information from a multitude of reliable and not-so-reliable sources, it is imperative that we teach them how to manage the information that comes to them and that they will themselves produce in our increasingly digital world. Experts agree that the basic definition of media literacy is the ability to access, analyze, evaluate, and create media in a variety of forms.

Media literacy is not just the ability to use various pieces of hardware or the newest software products, although both of these skills are covered in the broad sense of the term. Instead, working toward media literacy means that our students will develop the skills and knowledge they will need to become discriminating and informed global citizens. Our students not only will have access to the vast streams of media available to them through social media, phones, televisions, radio stations, the Internet, and other technology-dependent ways to communicate but also will be able to understand what they receive and send.

As a classroom teacher, you should make helping your students become media literate one of your priorities. You will not be able to do this in just a few lessons, even if you teach high-achieving older students. Instead, a more sensible approach is to integrate media literacy lessons into appropriate instructional activities. For example, if your students are required to bring articles on current events to share with the class, one of the skills that you should teach in advance of the assignment is finding articles that are from reliable sources. By frequently asking students to evaluate and analyze sources, information, and even images or advertisements and to discuss their findings, you will help your students develop their media literacy skills. Other ways to help your students become informed digital consumers and producers can include these activities:

- Expose your students to appropriate guided online activities as often as possible. For example, ask students to work together as a team to explore a site and then report back to other teams about the information they found as well as how it was presented and the information's reliability.

- Ask students to find examples of information targeted at specific audiences and then to provide evidence to support their findings.

- Encourage your students to make informed decisions on a variety of topics by having them research topics that are of personal interest to them and then share their ideas with their classmates.

- Ask students to create digital products, such as class Web pages, blogs, or multimedia presentations. Have them examine their own choices in terms of their products' suitability or purpose.

- Ask students to compare and contrast articles, cartoons, illustrations, or other digital materials on the same topic.

- Have students prepare a checklist of what makes a source reliable or unreliable.

- Ask students to develop a series of questions that they can use to discuss various media messages.

- Provide opportunities for students to share their ideas about current events or information that is related to a topic under study so that they can determine if their ideas arise from valid sources or not.

- Have students survey each other about their own media participation to determine if there are patterns in their shared experiences.

Here are some excellent resources on the topic of teaching media literacy skills:

- **National Association for Media Literacy Education (NAMLE) (http:// namle.net).** On the home page of this national organization devoted to media literacy education, you can learn about the core principles of media literacy as well as access NAMLE's many resources for teaching media literacy.

- **Media Smarts (http://mediasmarts.ca).** At this Canadian site, you will find a wealth of practical information, tip sheets, lesson ideas, and other resources for teaching students of all ages.

- **Project Look Sharp (www.ithaca .edu/looksharp).** Project Look Sharp is a media literacy initiative of the Division of Interdisciplinary and International Studies at Ithaca College. At this site, you will find a number of different practical strategies as well as links to many other classroom resources.

- **Center for Media Literacy (www .medialit.org).** Here you can learn about media literacy by reading numerous articles, incorporating the suggestions in the site's "Best Practices" section, and reviewing the many other resources this site offers.

> We ask our students to fail all the time. We push them. We set the bar high. We expect them to pick themselves up and learn from their mistakes. You will fail at many a lesson. Having a fallback plan is essential. This will come with time. And you will have more weapons in your arsenal as you continue to teach, but you will also take more risks if you think it might engage your students, and with those risks come failures. How you choose to respond to those failures will set the tone for your classroom.
>
> *Matt Kissling, 20 years' experience*

- **Media Literacy.com (www.medialiteracy.com).** At this site devoted to media literacy education, you will find many useful free resources of various types to engage and instruct your students.

In addition to the resources just listed, a very helpful and comprehensive book about teaching media literacy is *The Teacher's Guide to Media Literacy: Critical Thinking in a Multimedia World* by Cynthia L. Scheibe and Faith Rogow. Published in 2011 by Corwin Press, this book offers many practical suggestions for teaching media literacy to students of all ages.

Listening Skills

Good listening skills are crucial for academic success for students of all ages. Listening well is something anyone can learn to do over time and with practice. Fortunately, creative teachers can find many different ways to help their students improve their listening skills. For example, you could read aloud from a short news article each day and then quiz your students about what they heard. Or you could have students enact a real-life scenario, such as making a complaint, and then ask the student audience to recount what they heard.

The key is to offer many practice opportunities appropriate to the ages and interests of your students. You can also help your students become good listeners by teaching what it means to be an active listener who pays attention. Here are some tips to help you teach your students to be active listeners:

- Talk with your students about the importance of maintaining an open mind when someone is speaking. They should listen closely to their teachers and classmates and not quit listening when they disagree with what they hear.

- Teach students to listen for the key topics under discussion, an important skill for students who take an active role in their learning.

- Teach your students to generate questions as they listen to you, but to hold their questions until you call for them.

- Play a gentle classroom game in which you ask students to respond every time they hear you say a certain word. For example, they could tap their desk every time they hear you say "book." The competitive nature of this game will keep students alert.

- If students are not sure whether they have understood the main points of a presentation, ask whether they can summarize it. If they can summarize what they've heard, then they are competent in active listening.

- Find a simple drawing of a person, object, or scene and describe it to your students in vivid detail as they attempt to draw it from your description. You could even have pairs of students speak as well as draw to reinforce the idea of attentive listening.

- Stress the importance of looking at the person speaking. Often when students are not looking at their teacher, they can tune out.

Here are two excellent Web sites for teachers who want to help their students improve their listening skills:

- **Many Teaching Ideas (www.teachingideas.co.uk).** A British primary school teacher, Mark Werner, manages this site. Although many of the ideas are for teachers of younger children, the site has hundreds of useful games, activities, and teaching suggestions for all teachers.

- **Learning Through Listening (www.learningthroughlistening.org).** This site, maintained by the nonprofit organization Learning Ally, offers advice on helping students improve their listening skills.

Speaking Skills

In twenty-first-century classrooms, students are expected to actively participate both as listeners and as speakers. Many students, like many adults, have a fear of speaking formally in public. Even chatty students who are not afraid to shout across the room to friends may be overcome with stage fright when asked to make a presentation to the entire class. As a caring teacher, you can do a great deal to help your students learn to speak well in front of their classmates. Here are some suggestions on how to help your students become confident speakers:

- As early in the year as you can, give your students opportunities to speak to small groups. It is less intimidating for them to speak to a group of four or five classmates than it is to speak to the entire class.
- Painlessly habituate your students to public speaking by calling on every student every day. You should sometimes ask students to stand by their desk while speaking.
- Allow students to be in front of the class as part of a group of students, which they may find easier than presenting alone. When several students stand together to present various parts of a report, mutual support reduces their stage fright.
- Prepare the audience before expecting students to speak formally in front of the class. Explain why good listening habits are important. Be very specific about the behaviors you expect from students as members of the audience.
- When you assign projects that students are expected to present orally, be very clear about what they are supposed to do and set a reasonable time limit for presentations.
- Allow students to have some say in the order in which they present their work. Some students genuinely prefer to be the first or the last speaker.
- Allow students to use note cards, visual aids, or other props whenever you can. Having props will lessen their fears about forgetting what they have to say.
- Allow students to narrate a PowerPoint or other type of multimedia presentation, which they may find easier than just delivering a speech.
- Teach techniques for controlling stage fright—for example, taking deep breaths before speaking to help control anxiety.
- Provide lots of different opportunities for students to speak in front of their classmates. From thirty-second round-robin responses to group presentations and debates, many different opportunities for students to speak will tend to increase their comfort level as well as their speaking skill level.
- Encourage sufficient practice before the presentation. Students who are fully prepared tend to perform better than students who are not.

A book that you may find to be a helpful resource as you work with your students to improve their speaking skills is *Well Spoken: Teaching Speaking to All Students* by Erik Palmer. This informative book, published in 2011 by Stenhouse Publishers, offers many practical strategies and activities to help students learn to speak well in front of others.

Writing Skills

Many research studies have traced the effectiveness of writing as a learning tool in all subjects and in all grade levels. The results of this work are clear: every teacher teaches writing. All teachers teach writing by modeling the language that professionals use when speaking with their students, when writing for students, and when asking them to write.

Along with modeling good language skills, you should teach writing skills and hold students accountable for their writing. You don't have to be an English teacher, a grammar expert, or a veteran teacher to teach your students to write well. Here are some effective and painless ways to help your students become effective writers:

- Encourage your students to use a dictionary and a thesaurus. If your school doesn't provide a set of these books for each teacher, then borrow a few from other teachers. If your students have ready access to the Internet, encourage them to use an electronic resource, such as Dictionary.com (http://dictionary.reference.com).

- When students ask, "Does spelling count?" say, "Yes. How can I help you spell a word?"

- Encourage students to use the writing process whenever possible. When you ask students to write even brief essays for you, encourage them to plan or prewrite their answers, write a rough draft, edit and revise that draft, and create a final copy to turn in to you.

- Encourage students to catch your errors. When you make a mistake, acknowledge it and correct yourself, showing students that correctness is not something that ends when English class is over.

- Don't be sarcastic when correcting student papers. Sometimes students will make ridiculous or very funny errors. Be kind, and save your frustration and amusement for later. The purpose of marking a paper is to help students learn.

- Circle obvious errors on papers. You don't need to circle every one or use elaborate editing marks. You should not correct the mistake yourself; instead, just make students aware of a mistake by circling it and asking them to make a correction.

- Because students tend to write the way they talk, speak Standard English around your students and expect them to speak it, too.

- Model good writing for your students. Proofread your own work.

- Offer lots of writing opportunities for your students. You can do this on tests and quizzes as well as in daily informal assignments and projects, such as reports.

Here are some resources for you to help your students with writing skills:

- **Web English Teacher (www.webenglishteacher.com).** At this site, you can access many creative K–12 resources to help your students improve their writing skills.
- **National Writing Project (www.nwp.org).** At the National Writing Project site, you can find helpful advice, books, articles, links to other sites, and many other different resources pertaining to writing instruction.
- **Teaching That Makes Sense (www.ttms.org).** At this information-packed site, teachers can access a wealth of general materials about teaching writing as well as learn about specific activities and strategies.

Vocabulary Acquisition Skills

For all students, from emergent readers to graduating seniors, vocabulary acquisition is an important skill area. In fact, it is a lifelong process for all of us. You can teach students new words and their concepts in two primary ways.

The first way that many students learn new words is through new experiences. When you take your students on a field trip, show them a video clip, sing a silly song with them, or involve them in other activities that are new and different, you expand their language skills. Such activities broaden their world and give them a real-life context in which to apply the new vocabulary words to which they are exposed.

The second significant way that students learn new words is through reading. The more reading experiences a child has, the more language he or she will acquire. However, if students are not capable or independent readers functioning at grade level, it will be very difficult for them to acquire new words from reading without help. Therefore, their teachers need to assist them in learning new words. Here are some basic actions you should take when teaching students new vocabulary words:

- Teach students to associate words with other material. Build connections between words they are studying in your class and words or concepts they have learned previously or in other contexts.
- Present vocabulary words many times and in different ways. Present the words before you teach a lesson so that students can understand them and, in turn, comprehend the text. As your students study the material, take care to go over the words again. Finally, at the end of a unit of study, review the vocabulary so that students can lock in their learning.
- Make connections with other content areas. If students can take words from your class and use them in other classes, you have been successful. Help students make this connection by asking them how they could use a word or a form of a word you are studying in other ways.

- Take the tedium out of finding meanings. Derive meanings together. When students formulate their own definitions, they tend to remember those meanings far better than the ones they look up in a dictionary. Here are some quick tips:
  - When you present a list of words before a lesson, ask students to anticipate what the words might mean in the context of the lesson.
  - Allow students to work in groups to restate textbook definitions.
  - Have students match vocabulary words to photographs that illustrate the meanings.
  - Have students brainstorm other meanings for a word under study.
  - Put a list of words in one column with a scrambled list of definitions in another column for students to try to match before they begin studying the unit.

- Because students need to hear new words, always spend time pronouncing the words under study with students. This technique is particularly helpful to auditory learners, and it assists everyone in making the words part of their spoken vocabulary.

- Show students how to use context clues. For example, you could ask students to read a passage and find three words that have the same definition. You could also have a minidiscussion in which you ask students how they figured out a word's meaning from the text.

- Expose students to a variety of words. It is not enough for poor readers to just see and hear the words in a textbook if they are going to improve their reading skills. They need to see and hear the words associated with real-life occupations, technology, academics, current events, and other aspects of everyday life. Often, students who are poor readers are not exposed to these words at home.

- Raise your students' awareness of the words around them. Use games, activities, discussions, varied readings, and other strategies to help your students pay attention to the words they encounter each day.

- Model good vocabulary acquisition skills. Let students see you looking up words in a dictionary or taking care to use the correct synonym when you write sentences on the board, setting a powerful example for all of your learners. When you teach students whose families are not well educated, whose families do not speak English as a first language, or who live in poverty, it is especially important to model good vocabulary acquisition skills often.

I've found that vocabulary is a great obstacle for students who read at low levels. When explaining content vocabulary, keep in mind that a student's vocabulary may be quite low. Don't assume that a student knows even basic concepts. Take a moment to explain.

Dawn Carroll, 17 years' experience

HOW TO MAKE YOUR CLASSROOM RICH IN VOCABULARY WORDS

If you want to enlarge your students' vocabularies, common sense will tell you that you must expose them to words. Some students do not read well because the language they are exposed to at home and away from school is not content-rich or varied enough to enable them to advance their reading skills. Fortunately, there are many ways for teachers at all grade levels to help their students learn new words. Customize some of the strategies that follow to make your classroom a place where students see and hear interesting words in a variety of ways.

- Present a word of the day. This word can be from your content area or from the academic language of school, or it can just be an interesting word from the news or daily life. Your students can learn many words painlessly in this way. Write the word on the board or use a PowerPoint; say it, post it near the clock or a window, or do whatever else it takes to make students aware of this new word.

- Have a student version of the word of the day. All but very young students can take a turn at bringing in a word for the day. Combine this word with your own word of the day, and your students can learn two new words each day with little effort.

- Use the opening and closing exercises of your lesson to make students aware of words associated with the lesson. If you hold up flash cards, write vocabulary words on the board, have students play word games, give a quick little word puzzle, or ask students to sketch the definitions of the words in the day's lesson, you are making vocabulary important to your students.

- Display large graphic organizers. Ask students to complete or create a web, chart, or other visual representation of some of the words in the lesson. Not only will students learn by completing the graphic organizer but also they will benefit again when you display them.

- Make a word wall. Although this is a popular activity with young students, it can be easily adapted to the needs of older students. Before you begin a unit of study, list the key terms that students will be learning on a large sheet of paper. Through-out the unit, the words remain on the wall, reinforcing key concepts that students should know. Variations on this idea include having students bring in words for the word wall, having students create individual word walls, and making the lists unique by adding examples and illustrations.

- Have students make personal dictionaries. The format does not have to be elaborate for students to benefit from them. A personal dictionary is a record of the words a student has learned throughout a unit of study. It can be housed in a separate folder or in a section of a student's notebook.

- Have plenty of text-rich materials on hand for students to use in class or to browse. Because many readers who are less capable have not been exposed to many forms of print media, they need to see the written word in your classroom. Newspapers, magazines, catalogues, telephone directories, cookbooks, comic books, and books are all helpful. Online resources can be especially appealing to many students. Here are some other ways to add more reading materials to your class:

- Ask students to bring in old magazines, papers, or books.
- Shop at yard sales.
- Purchase books at book sales held by public libraries.
- Ask local businesses for donations.
- Seek support and donations from your school's parent-teacher association.

- Have reference materials handy. As soon as they are able to use them, students should have access to dictionaries, thesauri, instruction booklets, atlases, old textbooks, charts and graphs of all kinds, maps, and other reference materials. Even out-of-date encyclopedias from yard sales will enrich your students' word usage. Students can use them for a variety of activities, such as browsing, reading for pleasure, looking for new words, finding facts, or writing essays and other responses.

- Have oral language materials available for students as well. Audiobooks, Library of Congress recordings, and other oral materials that allow students to hear words that they do not usually hear spoken will enrich their vocabulary. Have students read aloud to each other in small groups. Reading aloud to your students every day will also enrich their world. Here are three good resources for free e-books for your classroom:

  - **Project Gutenberg (www.gutenberg.org).** At this site, there are over forty thousand free books available for downloading. Read the copyright information on the site to make sure you can use a particular downloaded book in class.

  - **Online Books (http://onlinebooks.library.upenn.edu/lists.html).** At the University of Pennsylvania's online library, you can find over one million free e-books.

  - **Gizmo's Freeware (www.techsupportalert.com).** On the Gizmo's Freeware home page, you will be able to search for free e-books as well as free audiobooks. The site is easy to use because it has clearly defined and extensive categories of resources.

ACTIVITIES THAT MAKE LEARNING VOCABULARY WORDS ENJOYABLE AND SUCCESSFUL

Direct instruction is one of the most effective ways to increase your students' vocabulary. In the past, direct instruction meant making students look up a tedious list of words and attempt to memorize them for a weekly test. Today, educators realize that learning words out of context or from isolated lists in a textbook is not an effective method. Here are some ideas to spark interesting vocabulary activities in your classroom:

- Have students complete or create puzzles. Use one of the many online puzzle sites to create a crossword, word search, or other type of puzzle for your students to solve as they master the meanings of the vocabulary terms associated with a unit of study. Students of all ages also enjoy talking over words as they complete a puzzle as part of a team effort.

- Have students categorize words. There are many ways for students to learn to classify words. A simple one is to give students a list of words to place on a chart with column headings that you have created. For example, if your students were studying weather, you could give them a list of thirty words to place on a chart with the column headings "Cloud Types," "Types of Precipitation," and "Heat Wave Words." Another way to have students categorize words is to ask them to brainstorm as many words as they can about a certain topic. Or you can ask them to predict how words will be classified before beginning a unit of study or to classify words according to their connotation or association—positive or negative words, for example.

- Teach other forms of words. For example, if your class is studying a concept, such as *expert*, then a quick side lesson into various forms of the word itself may help readers who are less able. If they learn that *expertise* and *expertly* are related to the original word, your students have increased their vocabulary.

- Play word games with your students. A simple game that many teachers like to use is played like this: divide students into two teams. Have a representative from each team sit at the front of the room, facing the class. Write a word on the board behind them. Have team members take turns giving one-word clues until one of the students guesses the word. Or play hangman, Scrabble, or any of the hundreds of other games that can be adapted for vocabulary learning.

- Use flash cards. Students benefit from the repetition and reinforcement provided when they create flash cards. Flash cards have many other benefits, too. They offer a kinesthetic element, because students create them and then manipulate them while studying. When students study together with flash cards, they are no longer mindlessly looking over their work. To add interest to flash cards, have students use photographs or drawings, colored ink, or even mnemonic devices when making them. Many students enjoy using free online flash card sites, such as Quizlet (http://quizlet.com), Flashcard Machine (www.flashcardmachine.com), or Study Blue (www.studyblue.com).

- Discuss words with your students. After students read a passage from a textbook, ask learners each to write down a word that interests them. Have some students share their word with the class. Or find a word with an interesting history and tell students a quick anecdote about its origin. Talk about the connotations of words and why some words have the power they do.

- Appeal to students' imagination. Choose an ordinary word for an object, such as *chair* or *pencil*. Ask students to use their imagination to see how many uses the object could have other than its intended original one. Sharing their responses with their classmates can take many forms, depending on the ages and types of students you have. If your students ask for a thesaurus to look up other meanings for words associated with the object, then you will know that they are having fun and are engaged in expanding their vocabulary.

- Get students moving. Using a large font, print out the vocabulary words and meanings that your class is studying. Cut the words apart, forming individual squares, and do the same with the definitions. Pass out the squares to your students. Have them mingle until they match the words with their definitions.

- Reuse words in original sentences. Divide students into teams and give each team the same word to use in a sentence. Ask each team to have a student representative write their sentence on the board, read it aloud, or otherwise share it so that the class can decide which one is the best sentence. Or ask students to select an important sentence from the reading assignment in the lesson and rephrase it.

Some resources to improve your students' vocabulary acquisition skills include the following:

- **Marzano Research Laboratory (www.marzanoresearch.com).** On the home page of this site, you will be able to access information about various highly regarded publications devoted to vocabulary acquisition by using "vocabulary" as a search term.

- **ProTeacher (www.proteacher.com).** Here you will find many links and activities that have been tested by other teachers. Use "vocabulary" as a search term to access a wealth of materials.

- **Teachnology (www.teach-nology.com).** Use "vocabulary" as a search term to access links to other useful sites as well as strategies, activities, and lesson plans. This site is useful for teachers of students of all ages.

- **Merriam-Webster's Word Central (www.wordcentral.com).** Here students can build their own dictionary online, use a student dictionary, access a daily buzzword, and find links to other resources related to dictionaries and words.

- **Interactive Wordplays (www.wordplays.com).** At this site, your students will be able to play interactive word games, such as anagrams, puzzles, Boggle, Words with Friends, and many more.

Critical Thinking Skills

Critical thinking skills are thought processes involving such activities as logical reasoning, problem solving, and reflective thinking. To develop these skills, students need sufficient daily practice. When teachers offer opportunities for critical thinking, watching students become absorbed in their work is only one of the rewards. Critical thinking activities also promote active learning and increased retention.

When you plan lessons that involve critical thinking, students must first have some awareness of the material so that they have information to draw on. If you plan carefully, the activities that involve critical thinking will arise from the lesson itself. Offer your students games, puzzles, real-world problems, or other exercises to stimulate their thinking about a lesson. To incorporate critical thinking into your lessons, you can ask students to

- Give reasons for their answers
- Generate problems
- Generate multiple solutions
- Give extended answers
- Make predictions based on evidence
- Relate the lesson to their lives
- Solve brainteasers
- Relate the lesson to other classes
- Trace the origins of their thinking
- Compare and contrast information
- Collaborate on responses
- Determine causes and effects
- Combine ideas from widely differing sources
- Classify items in various ways
- Evaluate each other's work

Here are two excellent and well-respected resources to help you learn more about how to develop your students' critical thinking skills:

- **Critical Thinking Community (www.criticalthinking.org).** At this extensive site, you can access a wide variety of resources as well as read current articles by scholars and other experts.
- **Critical Thinking (www.criticalthinking.net).** This site provides access to a variety of articles to help guide your thinking about teaching critical thinking skills.

GIVING DIRECTIONS THAT ENCOURAGE CRITICAL THINKING

Another way to include critical thinking opportunities in your instruction is to change the language you use, giving directions that require students to examine the material in more depth. For example, if you ask students to retell a story, you are only asking them to demonstrate that they comprehend the events in the story. If you ask students to classify those same events according to whether they are causes or effects, you are requiring students not only to comprehend the story but also to analyze it. The following lists of verbs apply to the six levels of Bloom's Taxonomy. Use them to involve your students in meaningful activities.

Remembering Level

The remembering level involves the identification and recall of information. The following verbs will lead students to recall and recognize:

- Identify
- List
- Label
- Describe
- Order
- Observe
- Name
- Reproduce
- Select
- Arrange

Understanding Level

The understanding level involves the organization and selection of facts and ideas. The following verbs will lead students to interpret, explain, and demonstrate:

- Summarize
- Associate
- Clarify
- Paraphrase
- Estimate
- Infer
- Discuss
- Explain
- Distinguish
- Classify

Applying Level

The applying level involves the use of facts and principles in new situations. The following verbs will lead students to construct and solve problems:

- Modify
- Transcribe
- Change

- Solve
- Apply
- Compute
- Predict
- Customize
- Sketch
- Adapt

Analyzing Level

The analyzing level involves the separation of a whole into component parts. The following verbs will lead students to dissect, uncover, and analyze:

- Calculate
- Separate
- Inventory
- Dissect
- Infer
- Categorize
- Experiment
- Outline
- Characterize
- Test

Evaluating Level

The evaluating level involves the justification of evidence, reasons, or actions. The following verbs will lead students to discuss, relate, and generalize:

- Appraise
- Critique
- Judge
- Verify
- Select
- Assess
- Contrast
- Rate
- Compare
- Justify

Creating Level

The creating level involves the development of opinions or judgments. The following verbs will lead students to invent, create, construct, and design:

- Invent
- Construct
- Develop
- Predict
- Produce
- Devise
- Formulate
- Compose
- Revise
- Generate

USING ESSENTIAL QUESTIONS TO STIMULATE CRITICAL THINKING

In contrast to questions that ask students to just recall information by rote, essential questions ask students to develop or invent their own answers to complex, open-ended problems. They ask for insight and understanding as well as knowledge. Essential questions

- Can arise from curriculum standards
- Often lead to other questions
- Can be controversial
- Can be revisited repeatedly during the course of a term
- Can draw on personal, community, school, and technology resources
- Are relevant to students' real-life interests and concerns
- Can provide authentic motivation for learning

To begin using essential questions to help your students develop their critical thinking skills, follow these steps:

- **Step One**: Begin with a thematic unit or a strong interest your students may have. For example, your state's standards may dictate that you teach a unit on weather.
- **Step Two**: Work with students to brainstorm questions that appeal to them about this topic. Focus on general, open-ended questions rather than on detail-specific ones—for example, "How do changing weather patterns affect our lives?" Use the classic questions that expand investigations:

Who is affected by weather?

What changes are happening now?

When will the changing weather patterns improve or grow worse?

Where will citizens be safe from weather disasters?

Why are weather patterns changing?

How are we coping with these changes?

- **Step Three**: Work with your students to plan strategies for investigating answers to these questions. Help them make predictions; use planning tools; and select and evaluate materials, resources, and information.

> Don't dwell on how it has happened when students are in a higher grade than their reading level shows. Identify students with needs and address those needs.
>
> *Dawn Carroll, 17 years' experience*

- **Step Four**: As your students gather information and decide how to synthesize it, determine how you want them to present their work.

Reading Skills

Many reading experts agree on an important guideline for teaching reading skills: no single approach works for all students. Instead, instruction in reading skills tends to change as students progress in their education. Students, especially those who are beginning to learn to read, need instruction in phonics. Trained reading teachers usually perform this instruction. Older students benefit from instruction in the other aspects of reading. Any teacher, even one who works with older students in other content areas, can and should work with students to improve all areas of reading.

Even though you may teach older students or a subject, such as advanced math, in which reading is not required as frequently as it is in an elementary classroom, it is still your responsibility to work with students to help them become better readers. If reading is, indeed, the primary learning tool for all students, then working to increase your students' reading skills is a responsibility you cannot ignore. In the list that follows, you will find some easy-to-implement strategies to help students improve their reading skills regardless of their age or the content of the course.

- Be positive with struggling readers. In time, with increased instruction and support from all teachers, students can improve their reading skills.

- Try a variety of activities to teach reading skills. Appealing to students' learning style preferences is essential, regardless of their age.

- Activate any prior knowledge your students may have or provide enough background information for students to make connections between the material and their own experiences.

- Employ real-life, informational texts in your classes when appropriate.

- Read aloud to students as they follow along in a text. Poor readers often are not exposed to rich oral language at home.

- Provide time each day for students to read independently. Establishing a text-rich environment for students in every classroom does much to help them become better readers.

- Prepare students for successful reading of an assignment with activities before, during, and after the assignment.

- Work with the families of students who struggle with reading. Many times, parents, guardians, and other family members are willing to be supportive but do not know what to do. A partnership between classroom and home is an important source of support for inexperienced readers.

- Teach students how to determine the purpose of assigned reading and to adapt their rate and method of reading accordingly.

- Engage students in such strategies as reflection, questioning, and problem solving. Students who are aware of how they read are more likely to be skillful readers than students who are not aware.

- Take time for vocabulary enrichment. Many different activities can help students increase their word recognition if you take the time to build them into your lessons.

- Include activities to help students comprehend the information in the text. Using a variety of techniques, such as graphic organizers and collaboration with peers, will help students derive meaning from their assignments.

Just as important as the general strategies for helping students improve their reading skills is avoiding making mistakes that can discourage students. As you think about how to help your students become good readers, remember these guidelines:

- Don't expect other teachers to teach your students how to read. You must teach your students the skills they need to tackle the texts and language of your content area or grade level.

- Don't neglect to introduce new words before students read a passage. When students can make the connection between the words in the new material and what they already know, they can learn more quickly.

- Don't ask students to read aloud in front of other students if doing so makes them uncomfortable or if they are such poor readers that other students will ridicule them.

- Don't neglect to teach students how to pronounce words. If they are to integrate a word into their vocabulary, they need to know how to say it.

- Don't ignore the importance of rich oral language when you work to raise students' reading levels. Include such auditory experiences as having students read aloud or listen to audiobooks.

- Don't forget to include plenty of authentic reading experiences for your students. When students are reading to solve real-life problems, they read with more interest than when they are reading just to get to the end of an assignment.

Teaching reading is a complex issue, but here is one simple thing for you to remember as a first-year teacher: you must help students comprehend what they read by giving them relevant assignments and activities before they read, while they read, and after they have finished reading.

> From the math teacher: problem solving is all about interpretation and analysis. Most people think you can do math without good reading skills—not so.
>
> *Kay Stephenson, 33 years' experience*

ACTIVITIES FOR STUDENTS BEFORE THEY READ AN ASSIGNMENT

Prereading activities can benefit students of all ages and have several purposes. An important one is to activate students' prior knowledge so they can connect the new information in the text to previous learning. Another purpose is to make sure that students have the vocabulary they need to understand the concepts in the text. You should also use prereading activities to motivate students to learn more about the topic and to read independently. Finally, these activities give your students the confidence they need to read with interest, purpose, and intensity. Use the following prereading activities, or adapt them for your students and their needs:

- Show students a photograph or a video clip that is related to the content of the text. The image or images will help students engage with the reading and visualize the action or material.
- Use a Know/Want to Know/Learned (KWL) chart to help students recall what they already know and anticipate what they will learn. The benefits of a KWL chart are that it helps activate prior knowledge, engages students in the reading, and allows an opportunity for reflection.
- Create an anticipation activity in which students can predict what they will learn. Try different formats; for example,
  - A true-or-false exercise in which students respond to facts that will or will not be in the text
  - A scrambled list of events to put in order
  - A list of statements for students to agree or disagree with
  - A list of people and places to match with information about them
  - A cause-and-effect chart

- Ask students to skim the text, looking at the headings, boldface type, illustrations, and other textual elements. When they have done this, ask them to write notes on topics such as these:
  - Questions they have for you
  - Questions they want classmates to answer
  - Questions they believe the text will answer
  - Anything that appears confusing before reading
  - How long it will take them to read the selection
  - The information they already know
  - Unusual words they notice
  - Which illustrations are most interesting

- Give students a set of questions that they will answer as they read the text. Discuss the questions before they read to see what information they already have. Help them see how the questions are aligned with the text and how students should answer them.

- Discuss the best ways for students to read the text. Should they read it all at once? Read part of the way through and then answer questions? Scan for information?

- Give students a checklist of the key points to watch for so that they can check them off as they find them while reading.

- If there are questions at the end of the selection in a textbook, ask students to read them first so that they can find that information as they read.

- Give students an incomplete chart of facts or key terms from the text and ask them to predict the missing information.

- Give students a concept map, concept web, or other graphic organizer to allow them to anticipate and record what they will be learning about as they read.

- Provide students with a summary of the information they will read. This technique is surprisingly successful because it lets students read with confidence.

- Give students a summary of what they will read in which some of the information is missing. Students will read to find the missing material.

Whenever a student claimed to hate reading and refused to ask or answer questions during the assigned unit, it broke my heart. I couldn't understand why the magic I always felt when I read was missing for them, until the day a student cried and threw her book down because "who was the new person in the story and where did he come from and now nothing made sense!" So I set out to give her navigation tools. Would I have ever expected her to find her way to the new mall without a map or directions? For most students, a GPS is a wonderful thing!

Janice Dabroski, 14 years' experience

- Ask students to brainstorm what they already know about what they are going to read. If you ask them to do this by themselves for a few minutes, then to combine their information with a partner's, and then to share that information with the entire group, your students should have a good background for understanding the reading.

- Give students a problem similar to a situation in the text and ask them to solve it. Later, they can come back to this problem with new knowledge and analyze their solution.

ACTIVITIES FOR STUDENTS WHILE THEY ARE READING AN ASSIGNMENT

Activities that you ask students to complete during an assignment should motivate them to continue reading, to learn the content you want them to know, and to interact with the text in a meaningful way.

Don't hesitate to break up the reading into manageable segments so that you can monitor for comprehension early in the process. When you help students divide their reading into manageable amounts, they are less likely to be overwhelmed by the volume of information they need to master.

Other successful general strategies include making sure that students think with a pen as they read. When students read and write, they master the content much more efficiently than they do when they just read mindlessly. Students may also benefit from reading with a partner or with a group. When students work together, they can share ideas and solve problems quickly. Students can work with each other to discuss such topics as what they have learned, problems they are having, and what parts of the material they enjoy.

The following list of activities is just a brief inventory of some of the ideas that other teachers have found to be successful with their students. Consider the needs of your own students as you adapt them for your class.

- Create questions for your students to answer as they read. You can make this process pleasant for your students by building in choices or activities, such as allowing them to answer only some of the questions or to ask a friend for help when the passage is difficult.

- Have students formulate their own questions as they read. A twist on this assignment is to have students write their questions on sticky notes that they can store in their book.

- Hand students a blank strip of paper similar in shape to a bookmark. Ask them to write their notes on it as they read. Because poor readers are often uncertain about how to take notes, the limited size of this paper allows them to work with greater ease. You can vary this technique by printing key terms, an outline, or other helpful information on the bookmark.

- Have students time themselves periodically to see how fast they read. Students who read quickly tend to comprehend more than students who read and reread a passage.

- Give students a partial outline of the material and ask them to complete it. Or show students how to outline the basic parts of the text themselves.
- Have students each complete a graphic organizer similar to the one they used as a prereading assignment, filling it in with information from the text instead of their own previous knowledge. Many Web resources can be searched for graphic organizers to help your students comprehend what they read. Begin your search with these:
  - **Teachnology (www.teach-nology.com).** On the home page, click on "Teacher Tools" and then on "Graphic Organizer Makers" to access dozens of free and easy-to-use organizers for students of all ages.
  - **Scholastic (www.scholastic.com/teachers).** Scholastic's Web site has many excellent graphic organizers devoted to reading comprehension. On the "Teachers" page, use "graphic organizers for reading" as your search term.
- Ask students to find the main idea and the supporting ideas in sections of the reading.
- Have any photos or other visual representations that you presented before students began reading available for them to look at as they read.
- Have students highlight important information if the text is one they can mark.
- If the selection contains events or facts in a specific order, scramble them and ask students to put them in the correct order.
- Stop students periodically and ask, "What have you learned so far?"
- Have students read together so they can answer each other's questions as they arise.
- Have students read with a readers' checklist of suggested strategies to use to help them understand the text. For example, they can find topic sentences, look for supporting details, or formulate questions.
- Ask students to make a statement of fact from the text, and then to support their statement with evidence from the text.
- Ask students to describe what they are reading to help them visualize the material.
- Provide students with drawings or photographs of people or other items relevant to the selection and ask them to match them with items from a list of terms or other descriptors.
- If you can play appropriate music to enhance the tone of the selection, do so.
- Many students benefit from listening to an audio recording of the material. It tends to motivate them to keep reading while focusing their attention.
- Be aware that many of the activities you introduced to your students as prereading assignments can help them during the reading phase of their assignment. Work with students to continue or complete those activities as they read.

ACTIVITIES FOR STUDENTS AFTER THEY HAVE READ AN ASSIGNMENT

The third component of reading comprehension instruction involves the activities that students do after they have read a selection. The prereading activities set a purpose for reading; the activities while students are reading guide them though the assignment; and the activities afterward encourage them to use the information they have just learned.

After students have read an assignment, many of the same types of activities you have used with them earlier are still appropriate: completing concept maps, brainstorming, or working with vocabulary, for example. The difference is that after students have read, their focus should be on analyzing, synthesizing, evaluating, and reflecting on information from the content they have just studied. The following activities will help them interpret their learning in a new way so that their understanding as well as their knowledge will be broader than before they encountered the material:

- Ask students to skim the passage again, looking for specific information or details they did not look for earlier.

- Quiz students in a variety of nonthreatening ways to check their knowledge. Or have them quiz each other.

- Ask students who have made predictions as part of a prereading assignment to check the accuracy of those predictions. In fact, when students have completed any sort of anticipation activity, now is the time to check it, verify it, or complete it.

- Have students write a summary of what they have read. Or have them do their summary orally, with other students assisting them as needed.

- Have students discuss, in groups, the parts of the text that they found confusing, interesting, or significant.

- Have students interpret the material in a new, creative way by making a poster, a diorama, or some other imaginative product.

- Give students a new example, scenario, or problem to solve based on the information in the text.

- Ask students to tell you the most significant information they learned from the passage.

- Give students a provocative statement pertaining to the text and ask them to respond to it, using their new knowledge.

One of my favorite resources for developing reading literacy and comprehension skills as well as helping students find the necessary connections to integrate into the school community is the school newspaper. My goals were to motivate to read, to enhance understanding, and to place a plethora of opportunities at their fingertips. The real bonus was that virtually every aspect of school life was represented in those pages, facilitating students in finding their niche, whether it be the chess club, a community service organization, or the swim team.

Janice Dabroski, 14 years' experience

- Ask students to find quotations from the text that they find interesting, thoughtful, or confusing.

- Give students some scrambled lines from the text and ask them to put these lines in order.

- Ask students to go back through the selection and examine the textual elements again. Can they suggest changes or improvements—for example, different headings or illustrations?

Resources for teaching reading skills include the following helpful sites:

- **Federal Resources for Educational Excellence (http://free.ed.gov).** On the home page of this site, use "reading" as a search term to access hundreds of resources designed to help students improve their reading skills.

- **Scholastic (www.scholastic.com/teachers).** On the "Teachers" page, use "reading" as a search term to access thousands of practical resources for all grade levels.

- **International Reading Association (www.reading.org).** The International Reading Association is an influential organization of literacy professionals. At their Web site, you will find extensive information about literacy issues, as well as specific links to resources devoted to reading and reading issues at all grade levels.

- **Reading Is Fundamental (www.rif.org).** This organization focuses on young children. It offers advice, tips, lesson plans, book-based activities, Web resources, and daily activities for young readers.

- **ReadWriteThink (www.readwritethink .org).** At this site, the International Reading Association and the National Council of Teachers of English, two powerful organizations involved with school literacy, offer thousands of links to resources for teachers who want to help their students improve their literacy skills.

> Bumping into students a few years after graduation and hearing that they have a job will always put a smile on my face. They almost always tell me they wish they were back in school or wish they had worked harder in school to do better.
>
> *Charlene Herrala, 31 years' experience*

Best Practices Checklist

1. Don't assume that your students know the basic skills they need to be successful in your classroom. Accept responsibility for helping your students master the twenty-first-century basic skills they must acquire.

2. Use critical thinking skills to help students learn to analyze and evaluate information from the various digital media sources they encounter each day. Daily practice will quickly build competence in this area.

3. Help students improve their listening skills by offering as many practice opportunities as you can. Make good listening part of the expectations you have for your students.

4. Begin the process of having your students make presentations in front of the class by having them make brief presentations in small groups before moving on to more elaborate presentations in larger groups.

5. Model good writing for your students in a variety of different ways. Be especially careful to show them how to use the writing process whenever they have a writing assignment to complete.

6. When teaching your students new vocabulary words, make a point of using as many learning modalities as possible. Students need to see and hear the words if they are to acquire them.

7. Raise your students' awareness of the words around them by having them play games, help create word walls, maintain personal dictionaries, and discuss new and interesting words, among other strategies.

8. Take advantage of the millions of free books online to ensure that your classroom is rich in reading and vocabulary resources.

9. Provide plenty of opportunities for your students to use and develop their critical thinking skills. Bloom's Taxonomy will make this easier when you work through the various levels with your students.

10. Adopt a balanced approach to teaching reading so that all students are exposed to positive and varied strategies for learning to read proficiently. All teachers should help students learn the skills to be successful in the reading required for their content area.

Time to Reflect
Level the Playing Field by Covering Basic Skills

Use the information in this section to guide your thinking as you reflect on these questions. They are designed to encourage you to think more deeply about the issues in the text or to discuss those issues with colleagues.

1. Which of the strategies in this section are you already using in your class to help your students acquire twenty-first-century basic skills? Which can you implement right away? Which will you need help from others to implement?

2. Which of the basic skills do your students need the most immediate help with? What can you do to provide this help for them? Who can assist you in finding solutions?

3. How will you know when your efforts to improve your students' media literacy skills have been successful? What steps will you take to capitalize on this success?

4. What can you do to improve the oral presentation or listening skills of your students? What issues pertaining to your students' skills in these areas are sensitive ones? What will you need to do to manage these issues successfully?

5. How can you raise your students' awareness of the importance of improving their vocabulary and reading skills? What can you do to make your classroom a print-rich environment? What suggestions do your colleagues have concerning how to motivate students to learn to read better?

SECTION FIFTEEN

Prevent Discipline Problems

If you are like most first-year teachers, you worry about how to prevent classroom discipline issues. No teacher wants to deal with rude, out-of-control students who make learning impossible for everyone around them. Even if you don't have to deal with severe discipline issues, the constant petty disruptions, such as having to remind students to stay on task, can morph into hours of lost instructional time for the other students in the class as well as for the misbehaving ones.

By adopting a proactive approach to managing the potential discipline problems in your class, you will be able to avoid dealing with the unpleasant aftermath caused by problems that have become unmanageable. With reflection, planning, organization, practice, and skillful teaching, instead of being frustrated at your students' incessant misbehavior, you can do what you were hired to do—teach.

Punishment Is Not the Way to Prevent Problems

Punishment as a behavior management technique has been around for hundreds of years. Even though educators know that harsh punishments will not transform troublemakers into well-behaved students, threats of punishment and punishment itself are still common methods of making children of all ages behave.

There are several problems with using punishment as a means of crowd control. Punishment is a short-term solution that actually creates long-term problems. Adults cannot simply bully students into lasting good behavior. If you use punishment techniques often enough, you can expect a backlash. If you do succeed in making your students afraid of you, then you can expect to have students refuse to work, talk back to you, or worse.

Punishment is ineffective because it does not create a permanent change in your students. A class controlled by a tyrant quickly falls apart if there is a substitute teacher in the room. Students who are punished frequently do not grow into self-disciplined learners who take control of their own behavior.

Another reason not to use punishment is that, sadly, some of your students are probably accustomed to cruelty and harsh behavior. It is highly likely that at least some of your students have such a chaotic home life that a cruel teacher would be just another adult who is unkind to them. Wouldn't it be better to make an impression on your students by offering a safe haven from violence rather than inflicting more misery?

Finally, it is important not to rely on punishment to motivate students because of the effect it will have on you. Did you really become a teacher to play the part of a prison warden? Teachers who try to rule their class with an iron fist will burn out as soon as they see that this strategy does far more harm than good.

Punishment is a behavior management practice that has outlived its dubious usefulness. When you create a positive behavior management plan for your students, you minimize the role that punishment will play in your class and maximize the importance of the positive strategies at your disposal.

Self-Discipline Is the Key

If punishment is not an effective way to prevent discipline problems, then what is? The ultimate goal of spending energy to prevent discipline problems is to have students who are self-directed. Teachers strive to create self-disciplined students who are happy, cooperative, and productive. After all, who wants to teach students who behave only because the teacher is bigger or meaner than they are?

Unfortunately, just when teachers think that their disciplinary techniques have been successful, something will happen to remind them that students still need help to stay on a successful path. As a first-year teacher, you should work steadily and consistently with your students to teach them self-discipline. Even very young children can learn to control themselves when their teachers encourage them to do the right thing at the right time. Here is a brief list of some of the many ways that you can begin to teach your students to be self-disciplined learners:

- **Maintain high standards for all of your students.** If students are going to progress throughout the year, then they need to be challenged. It is especially important to maintain these high standards when students seem to struggle, or when students who are less capable are included in the class.

- **Connect effort to success.** To help students become self-disciplined, caring teachers make the effort to show students that success requires effort. Students who can see that success is the result of effort are far more likely to succeed than those who can't.

- **Model the behaviors you want your students to have.** Our own actions speak louder than our words when it comes to teaching our students the behaviors we want to see from them. One of the greatest gifts we can give our students is to be the kind of role model they need day after day.

- **Be encouraging and positive with your students.** Teachers who make it clear that they have confidence in their students' ability to succeed have students who are more apt to become self-disciplined than those whose teachers doubt their abilities. If you want to move your students toward self-discipline, encouragement and a positive approach are critical.

- **Hold your students accountable for their actions.** It isn't enough to just have high standards for your students. You also must hold them accountable for their success or lack of it in meeting those standards.

- **Motivate your students to work well.** There are many different ways to encourage your students to do their work well. If you want your students to want to become self-disciplined, it is up to you to include as many motivating techniques in each lesson as you can.

Be Aware of the Causes of Most Discipline Problems

Even the biggest troublemaker in your class does not *always* come to school with the sole intention of making your life miserable and impeding the learning of all of his or her classmates. Students are complex beings with complex reasons for acting the way they do. Your students' misbehavior can become easy to manage once you are aware of the underlying causes and can deal with those causes instead of just reacting to the misbehavior itself. Here are some of the reasons why students may misbehave in class:

- Their work is too difficult, too easy, or just not an appropriate match for their learning style preferences.
- They perceive their teacher and classmates as uncaring.
- They are distracted by someone sitting near them.
- They see no connection between the daily work they do now and a successful future.
- They live in a culture with different values from the values of the school.
- They have not learned social skills, such as classroom courtesy.
- They don't have the resources they need, such as a computer or school supplies.
- They lack the basic skills to do their work and need special help.
- Their peers mock them for any school success.
- They don't know how to manage their time, materials, or workload.
- No one at home stresses that they need to do well in school.

Easily Avoidable Mistakes Many Teachers Make

Although, as a new teacher, you may be unsure of which disciplinary techniques are effective, you should definitely avoid these harmful mistakes:

- Commanding students to comply with your directives
- Accepting excuses or being a pushover
- Making bargains with students to coerce them into obedience
- Making fun of students
- Allowing students to harass each other
- Raising your voice
- Being sarcastic
- Embarrassing students

- Being a poor role model
- Assigning work as punishment
- Nagging students
- Being confrontational
- Ignoring serious misbehavior
- Losing your temper
- Allowing students to sleep in class

> Ask other teachers of a student if the student has issues in their classes as well. Sometimes students have discipline problems caused by outside issues we have no control over.
>
> *Jane Lankford, 31 years' experience*

TEACHER WORKSHEET 15.1

How Effective Are You at Preventing Discipline Problems?

Read each of these positive management practices and grade yourself on each one. Use a traditional letter scale: A = excellent, B = very good, C = average, D = needs improvement, and F = failing.

1. _____ I have a set of positively stated rules posted in my classroom.

2. _____ I use a friendly but firm voice when I ask students to do something.

3. _____ I make sure to build relevance and interest into every lesson.

4. _____ I make sure that all my students know that I care about them.

5. _____ I have taught my students the routines, procedures, and rules that will make class run smoothly.

6. _____ I use nonverbal interventions to keep misbehavior manageable.

7. _____ I consistently enforce my classroom rules.

8. _____ I consistently enforce school rules.

9. _____ I design lessons that will engage my students throughout the class period.

10. _____ I contact students' parents or guardians to keep problems manageable.

11. _____ I praise my students more than I criticize them.

12. _____ I monitor my students constantly.

13. _____ I refuse to nag or bribe students into good behavior.

14. _____ I respect the dignity of all of my students.

15. _____ I accept responsibility for what happens in my class.

Your Role in Preventing Discipline Problems

As a classroom teacher, the responsibility for preventing discipline problems lies with you. Fortunately, preventing or minimizing discipline problems is a task that is much easier than having to cope with problems once they have occurred. In Section Seven, you can find practical advice about how to manage your classroom in such a way that all students know what is expected of them and just how to go about achieving academic and behavioral success. Although effective classroom management procedures, rules, and policies consti-tute an important component of the prevention of discipline problems, however, this aspect is only one part of your role. Teachers with smoothly running classrooms with a minimum of discipline issues to contend with also are reflective, positive, consistent, and fair, and they exhibit a high degree of "withitness" (discussed later in this section).

Teachers who take the time to reflect on how they can prevent or minimize discipline problems tend to be more successful than teachers who just react blindly when problems happen. If you find that a discipline problem is beginning to occur in your classroom, taking a deliberate and systematic approach to solving it will make it easier for you to either prevent or minimize it. Use Teacher Worksheet 15.2 to help you determine the best course of action to take to manage discipline issues in your classroom.

TEACHER WORKSHEET 15.2

Preventing or Minimizing Discipline Problems

Use this worksheet as a guide as you work to prevent or minimize discipline problems in your class.

1. What is the problem?

_____

_____

2. Who is immediately involved in the problem?

_____

3. Who is affected by the problem?

_____

4. How serious is the problem? Is it nondisruptive or disruptive?

_____

5. Does the problem involve breaking a class rule?

_____

6. How often does the problem happen?

_____

7. At what times does the problem happen?

_____

8. What seem to be the most noticeable triggers?

_____

9. What are some possible underlying causes of the problem?

_____

10. What could I be doing that may be contributing to the problem?

_____

_____

11. Who can help me work out solutions to this problem?

_____

12. What are some possible solutions that I would like to consider?

_____

_____

_____

Be Positive: Nothing Creates Success Like Success

Take a positive approach to preventing discipline problems in your class. If your students all settle down quickly after lunch, for instance, praise their maturity. When all your students turn in a homework assignment on time, be sure to tell them how much you appreciate their effort. When you catch them being good, your students not only will understand what you expect of them but also will feel encouraged to continue their good behavior. Telling students what they do right is much more effective than nagging them about their mistakes.

One of the easiest ways to increase positive behaviors and decrease negative ones is to chart your students' success. When your students see a chart of their positive behaviors, they will understand that good behavior is recognized and appreciated. Use your computer to make a pie chart, a bar graph, or another type of chart on which to record your class's positive behaviors. Display an enlarged printout for your students each day.

You will have hundreds of other opportunities to tell your students when they are successful. Don't hesitate to take advantage of those opportunities; you and your students will benefit from the positive learning environment that will result. Here are some other practical ways to increase positive behaviors:

- Be specific and sincere in your praise so that students know what they did correctly.
- Always point out how the positive behavior will benefit everyone in the class.
- Encourage students to remind each other to behave well for the good of the class.
- Photograph your students when they are working productively or being good, and display these photos as a gentle reminder.
- Periodically ask your students what they did right during class. How did it make them feel? What did they gain from this good behavior?

Become a Consistent Teacher

As a teacher, you will have to make hundreds of decisions every day. Not only will you have to make many of these decisions quickly but also you will have to make them in front of a crowd of students—all of whom have different needs. You will never have enough time to think through many of the decisions you have to make, so you will have to learn to think fast.

The number of quick decisions required of you sometimes makes it difficult to be consistent. However, consistency is one of the most important tools you have in preventing problems because it gives your students a safe framework with well-defined boundaries for their behavior. Consistent classroom management provides a predictable environment with established rules and consequences.

Consistency is crucial to successful management, but it is one of the most difficult skills to develop. You may find it challenging to be consistent if you believe that the consequences of breaking a rule are too harsh, if you believe that overlooking an infraction "just this once" will be acceptable, if the infraction occurs at an inconvenient time or place, or if you have different expectations for students whom you perceive to be less able than others. You will find it easier to be a consistent teacher if you follow these guidelines:

- Be well prepared and organized so that you will have more energy to make sound decisions under pressure.

- Teach and reteach the rules and procedures you have established for the smooth operation of your class.

- Be careful to enforce the rules for all students every day.

- Do not make idle threats. Mean what you say when you talk with your students about their behavior.

> Being fair is most important. If students know that all are on a level playing field, they respect you more.
>
> *Debbie McManaway, 19 years' experience*

Become a Fair Teacher

One of the surest ways to create discipline problems is to treat your students unfairly. Even very young students are quick to notice actions that they perceive as unfair and to react accordingly. Conversely, being regarded as a teacher who treats everyone with fairness will prevent many unpleasant discipline issues. Students will be more willing to cooperate with you and with each other if they feel that you regard them as worthy individuals with a right to be treated well. Here are some tips on how to make sure that your students will regard you as a teacher who is fair to everyone in their class:

- Allow students to explain themselves when it seems appropriate. Although you don't want to be a pushover for flimsy excuses, you do want to make it easy for students to talk to you when they experience problems.

- Keep in mind that fair does not mean equal. Not all of your students are alike, so they should not all be treated alike.

- Don't play favorites. This is one of the fastest ways to ruin relationships with all of your students.

- Don't give your students unpleasant surprises. Announce tests and quizzes in advance. Publish homework assignments and due dates in various ways so that all students know what is expected of them.

- Make your high expectations clear. Give students examples, models, and samples in advance so that they know what to do to be successful.

- Make sure that the amount of classwork and homework you assign is reasonable. Work with the other teachers on your grade level or in your content area to make sure that your expectations align with the expectations of the group.

- Expect your students to observe the same rules as the rest of the student body, as well as the classroom rules that you have established.
- Have the same high expectations for academic and behavioral success for all of your students.
- When you make a mistake, admit it. Be flexible and honest with your students.

Withitness: One of the Most Valuable Prevention Techniques

Almost everyone has had at least one teacher who was able to write notes on the board and tell students in the back of the room to stop making faces at each other at the same time. Such teachers' expertise is an inspiration for us all. As amazing and inspiring as it may be, however, no one is actually born with the trait of withitness.

Educational researcher Jacob Kounin first coined the term *withitness* in his 1977 book published by R. E. Krieger, *Discipline and Group Management in Classrooms*. What is withitness? Simply put, at all times a teacher knows what's going on in class. Teachers with withitness are said to have eyes in the back of their head. But, because they never turn their back on the class, these extra eyes are not really necessary.

As a method of preventing classroom discipline problems, withitness is crucial. Teachers who are alert to what is happening in their classroom are far more likely to be able to prevent or minimize problems; they are tuned in to their students rather than checking e-mail or dealing with just one student while ignoring nearby students who may also be misbehaving. Teachers with a high withitness quotient are vigilant and focused on what is happening in their classroom. Withitness is easy to master with just a bit of care and effort. Here are some simple tips for cultivating your own classroom withitness:

- Don't *ever* turn your back on a class.
- Be alert to signs and signals among your students.
- Be prepared so that you can focus on students instead of the lesson.
- Develop your personal multitasking skills.
- Stay on your feet and monitor your students.
- Arrange your class so that you can see and be seen.
- Pace lessons so that they flow in a businesslike manner.
- Quietly correct off-task behavior and then move on.

TEACHER WORKSHEET 15.3

What Is Your Level of Withitness?

Use the list of strategies that follows to assess your level of withitness. Rank yourself on a scale of 1 through 3 in regard to how successful you are in practicing each strategy, with 3 being as successful as possible. Any strategy for which you can't rank yourself as a 3 should be one that you continue to work to improve.

1. _____ Don't turn your back on your students for even a few seconds.

2. _____ Be alert to signs and signals among your students.

3. _____ Trust your intuition. If something seems amiss among your students during class, it probably is.

4. _____ When conducting classroom conferences, have the student sit at a desk facing away from classmates so that you can see all of your students at the same time that you are conferring with your student.

5. _____ Get to know your students as well as you can, as fast as you can.

6. _____ Greet students at the door at the start of class to scan for potential problems.

7. _____ Be prepared so that you can focus on students instead of the lesson.

8. _____ Develop your personal multitasking skills so that you can remain focused on your students during class.

9. _____ Stay on your feet and monitor your students as they work.

10. _____ When you issue a hall pass, make sure you know where the student is going and when he or she should return. Watch the clock.

11. _____ Arrange your class so that you can see all of your students and be seen by all of them.

12. _____ If you need to talk privately with a student in the hallway, keep the door open and monitor your class at the same time.

13. _____ Don't allow groups of students to congregate around your desk if you are checking work in class. Go to them instead.

14. _____ Pace lessons so that they flow in a businesslike manner. Students who have nothing to do are far more apt to misbehave than those who are engaged in learning.

15. _____ As you work with one group of students, remain aware of what the rest of the class is doing.

A Crucial Step in Preventing Discipline Problems: Monitoring

As a teacher, one of the most important skills for you to develop is monitoring—actively overseeing your students from the moment they enter the room until they leave. The reward of such vigilance, however, is a peaceful and productive classroom. By paying careful attention to your students, you will help them stay on task and be successful. Furthermore, any problems that might arise will stay small if you are actively working to facilitate instruction through monitoring.

There are several more benefits that you and your students receive when you know exactly what each one is doing at any given moment. When you successfully monitor your students, you

- Create a positive class atmosphere
- Keep problems small
- Reinforce good behavior
- Keep students on task
- Help students stay focused on learning
- Maintain a strong connection with every student

Learning to be an effective classroom monitor is not difficult, although it will require effort to become a habit. These suggestions will help you get started:

- **Circulate among your students.** You cannot monitor effectively from your desk. Your students will be far less likely to stray off task if you are moving around the room instead of just sitting at your desk.

- **Place students' desks so that you can easily move around the room.** When you arrange your classroom, make sure to avoid putting desks too close together or against walls such that you can't get around them.

- **Ask students to place book bags and other belongings underneath their desk so that you can move around the room without tripping.** After a day or two of reminders, this should become a habit. (See Section Seventeen for more suggestions on keeping aisles clear.)

- **If students are becoming distracted, stand near them for a minute or two.** Standing near restless students will often be enough to get them to settle down and focus on their work. If this does not work, then a quiet word, a glance, or a quick nod will usually suffice.

- **After your students settle down to work, wait about two minutes before you start walking around to see what they are doing.** Allow time for students to get started on the assignment and for problems to arise.

- **Maintain eye contact with your students.** Keeping eye contact lets students know that you are aware of them and discourages them from misbehaving.

- **Give all students a share of your attention.** Many teachers tend to focus on only a few students. To determine how evenly you spread your attention, carry a copy of your class roster. When you speak with a student, place a mark next to the student's name. After doing this for a day or two, you will be aware of the unconscious patterns you follow and will be able to adjust your behavior.

- **Try not to allow a large group of students to congregate around you while waiting for help.** Instead, try asking students to put their names on the board so that you can see them in order. Or you could have them take a number from a stack of note cards that you have numbered. You could ask students who have a question that others may also have to write it on the board so that you can address it for everyone.

- **Try creating a checklist for your students to follow as they work.** If they use the checklist, you will be able to check their progress as you come by their desk. You can also ask students to show you each item on their checklist as they work through it.

- **Ask students to write their name on the board when they have finished.** This not only lets you know who is finished but also lets other students know which classmates can help them if you are busy.

- **Be supportive.** Use one of these supportive statements:
  - At this moment, what are you doing that's right?
  - How may I help you?
  - When I come by your desk, please show me _____.

How Students Can Get Help Quickly

If you arrange signals to enable your students to indicate when they need help, you can prevent much of the off-task behavior that can happen when students do not know how to proceed. Try some of the these ideas to make it possible for your students to get help quickly:

- Allow students to ask other students about an assignment before they ask you. This is especially effective if students work in small groups or near study buddies.

- Offer students the opportunity to work on alternative assignments while waiting for your help. They can signal to you that they need assistance by working on the alternative assignments instead of the classwork.

- For each student, tape three note cards together to form a triangle or tent that can stand on a desk. On each side, place a signal that will let you know how a student is doing. A question mark could indicate that the student has a question; a smiling face could mean that the student has no questions; and a frowning face could mean that there is a serious problem.

Earn Your Students' Respect

One of the challenging responsibilities that novice and experienced teachers alike must take on is the task of earning their students' respect. Respect does not depend on how long you've taught or how much you know. You can plan fascinating lessons and have every procedure in place, but you will be a failure if you don't have the respect of your students.

Although respect is the touchstone of a successful relationship with students, there is no single action that can guarantee every student's respect for you. Respect lies in the small actions you take. Gaining and maintaining it require that you consistently and successfully manage a delicate balance among the many roles you have at school: disciplinarian, adviser, role model, motivator, and instructor.

When your students respect you, they see that you are not just another friendly adult; you have met their ideal of what a teacher should be. Many first-year teachers mistake affection for respect. Your students may like you for many reasons, none of which earns their respect. They may think that you do not assign too much work or that you relate well to them on a personal level. This type of affection fades when problems arise or at the end of the term, when students realize that although they enjoyed your class, they did not learn very much.

There are a number of large and small ways to earn your students' respect. Like many other aspects of your new career, earning your students' respect will require time, patience, and persistent effort on your part. You will have to work hard to earn the gift of respect from your students.

Following is a list of questions about practices that are geared toward earning students' respect. As you ask yourself these questions, judge yourself as your students would judge you.

- Do I focus my energy on preventing behavior problems instead of having to deal with the serious consequences caused by misbehavior?
- Do I make sure that my students know I care about their welfare?
- Do I know the material I am supposed to teach?
- Do I respect my students' differences and encourage them to do the same?
- Am I am a good listener who is available to my students on a regular basis?

An Unexpected Tip: Be a Good Listener

Good listening skills are among the most important you can cultivate as an effective teacher. Taking the time to listen to your students as they chatter away at various times during class, as they share opinions, as they participate in class discussions, and as they talk about the things that are important to them is an invaluable strategy for preventing or minimizing discipline problems.

Teachers who take the time to listen carefully to their students not only are aware of potential problems before they become serious but also get to know their students as individuals rather than as just members of the crowd. Once that vital connection is made, it is far easier for you to help your students be successful. They will also find it easier to behave in an acceptable manner because they will feel connected to you and to the class.

Early Intervention Strategies

Preventing misbehavior is much easier and more productive than coping with discipline problems that have already disrupted your class. Unfortunately, no single strategy will prevent behavior problems. Instead, preventing misbehavior relies on many factors that work together to create the harmonious classroom you want for your students.

Because all teachers want to prevent discipline problems from disrupting their class, thousands of Web sites address the subject. Some sites are more helpful than others; the following five offer excellent suggestions, tips, and strategies:

- **Behaviour Needs (www.behaviourneeds.com).** At this well-known British site, you can access a wealth of practical resources related to helping students behave well.

- **Intervention Central (www.interventioncentral.org).** Here you can find not only academic but also behavioral interventions. By clicking on the "Behavioral Interventions" tab, you will be able to access many different strategies and tips.

- **National Education Association (NEA) (www.nea.org).** On the NEA home page, click on the "Tools and Ideas" tab to access dozens of helpful articles about classroom behavior management.

- **Behavior Advisor (www.behavioradvisor.com).** Thousands of teachers from all over the world have visited this site, which is maintained by Tom McIntyre. Here you will find terrific advice from other teachers, thousands of practical tips, and instructions on how to manage even the toughest discipline problems.

- **ProTeacher Directory (www.proteacher.com).** Pre-K–8 teachers can access ProTeacher's archive, which contains thousands of suggestions, strategies, and tips submitted by teachers. An ongoing discussion board helps teachers find even more solutions to discipline problems.

In addition to the interventions and other strategies discussed in this section, others that teachers have found successful in preventing discipline problems are discussed in depth in other sections of this book:

- **Engage students in meaningful work throughout your entire class (Sections Ten and Eleven).** You already know that students who are busy learning will not have time to misbehave; however, it is easy to overestimate the length of time that students will need to finish an assignment. If you engage students in meaningful, interesting work from the beginning of class until the end, you will prevent many of the problems that can occur when students do not have enough to do.

- **Create a sense of community in your class (Sections Four and Five).** Students who feel that they are respected and valuable parts of the group will hesitate before letting their classmates down by misbehaving. When students are actively involved in class, they have fewer reasons to cause a disruption, and everyone benefits.

- **Reward your students when they are successful (Section Eight).** Rewarding good behavior prevents bad behavior for two reasons: it lets students know which behaviors are acceptable, and it encourages them to choose those productive behaviors.

- **Seek support from other adults in a child's life (Section Three).** Students who know that the significant adults in their lives are working together for their benefit are far less likely to misbehave than students who feel that no one cares about them. From phoning a student's home to talking with another teacher, there are many ways for you to tap into sources of support.

- **Establish and teach classroom routines (Section Seven).** Students who know how to act in predictable situations, such as a fire drill or the first few minutes of class, will behave much better than students who are waiting for their teacher to tell them what to do.

When You Should Act

Like other teachers, you may sometimes have trouble knowing at just what point you should intervene to stop a problem from becoming serious. When you should act depends on the type of problem. Behavior problems can be divided into two categories: nondisruptive and disruptive.

Nondisruptive behavior problems affect only the student with the problem. Daydreaming, sleeping, and poor work habits are common examples of nondisruptive behavior problems. Try these interventions to end a nondisruptive behavior problem:

- Move closer to the student.
- Remind the entire class to stay on task.
- Place your hand on the student's desk.
- Maintain eye contact.
- Praise the work the student has completed.
- Offer your help.
- Glance or smile at the student.
- Consider moving the student's seat.

Disruptive behavior problems involve other students and affect the learning climate. When students become disruptive, your goal must be to minimize the effect on your class. Begin by enforcing your class rules as calmly and quietly as you can. If this does not improve the situation, move the misbehaving student to the hall for a private conversation.

Most of the time, just talking quietly with a student will solve the problem. Listen to what the student has to say, and offer your help. Remind students who misbehave that they do not have the right to interfere with the right of all students to learn. If you cannot prevent the student from misbehaving again through simply talking, then you should enforce your class rules, using the necessary consequences. (See Section Sixteen for more information on how to handle disruptions once they begin.)

Harness the Power of Positive Peer Pressure

One of the greatest tools any teacher has is the power inherent in peer pressure. No child, no matter how young or old, wants to look silly in front of classmates. Too often, when students misbehave, they do so because they are not connected to the group; they feel so unattached that they have nothing to lose by failure.

With this in mind, teachers can harness the human desire to perform well in the presence of peers by working to make each child feel that he or she is a valuable, contributing member of the class. To increase the feeling of belonging that you want for your students, try some of these strategies:

- Help students learn about each other. Periodically, use icebreakers and other activities to reveal the strengths, skills, experiences, and talents your students bring to school.

- Make it easy for your students to take risks when they answer questions or try new activities in your class. Promote tolerance and courtesy to encourage this risk-taking spirit.

- Establish study buddies and other peer support opportunities. Teachers who make a consistent effort to include cooperative activities in their lessons tend to find that their students are predisposed to work well together.

- Have your students work on projects in which they interact with each other outside the classroom. This is one of the best ways to build positive peer pressure in your class.

> If this isn't fun, it's the worst job in the world. And you will do more damage than you can imagine. If you are having fun, this is the best job in the world. Enjoy learning. Enjoy watching your kids grow. Enjoy being a leader. Enjoy your tribe. Do your job well, and they will reward you with a smile, a knowing look, and a respect that can't be found in most jobs.
>
> *Matt Kissling, 20 years' experience*

Best Practices Checklist

1. Intervene early and appropriately so that you can prevent or minimize classroom discipline problems.

2. Because a classroom is a complex environment, develop wide-ranging, proactive strategies that will prevent or minimize discipline problems in your classroom.

3. Keep in mind that punishment is not an effective deterrent when it comes to discipline issues; instead, steer your students toward self-disciplined behaviors.

4. To effectively address discipline issues among your students, familiarize yourself with the underlying causes of your students' misbehavior. Make a deliberate effort to get to know your students as quickly as possible so that you can respond appropriately.

5. Be positive in your attitudes and approaches. Remember that nothing creates more success as quickly as success itself.

6. Strive to be as consistent as you can so that your students will not have to test boundaries constantly.

7. Take care to be perceived as a teacher who is fair to everyone. Being perceived as a fair-minded teacher should be one of the cornerstones of your professional reputation.

8. Cultivate your classroom withitness skills. You will prevent or minimize many potential problems with an awareness of your students' reactions and actions.

9. Implement various strategies to make sure that you are effectively monitoring all of your students all class long.

10. Listen to your students so that you can respond appropriately when a behavior issue arises. Listening carefully will help you learn a great deal about your students and enable you to prevent misbehavior.

Time to Reflect
Prevent Discipline Problems

Use the information in this section to guide your thinking as you reflect on these questions. They are designed to encourage you to think more deeply about the issues in the text or to discuss those issues with colleagues.

1. What anxieties do you feel about how well disciplined your students are? To whom can you turn for help? What plans can you make to minimize behavior problems in your classroom?

2. How can you tell whether a student is self-disciplined? What can you do to promote this trait in your students?

3. Use Teacher Worksheet 15.1 to help you assess how effective you are at preventing discipline problems. What are your strengths? What are your weaknesses? How can you improve?

4. Being a consistent teacher is not always easy. What makes it difficult for you to be consistent? What attitudes can you develop to help you be more consistent? How can your colleagues help you with this?

5. What effective monitoring techniques have you observed other teachers using in their classes? Which would work in yours?

SECTION SIXTEEN
Manage Discipline Problems

Forgotten pencils, tardiness, defiance, excessive talking—the range of discipline problems that teachers face can be more than disheartening. Part of the issue lies in the different types of behavior problems that teachers are supposed to manage successfully. A forgotten pencil can disrupt learning; so can students who openly resist even reasonable requests from their teachers. One of the challenges that all teachers face is knowing the right course of action to take when confronted with this variety of discipline problems.

The behavior issues within your classroom are not the only source of problems. Many factors outside your classroom can have a negative effect on how well you and your students are able to accomplish your goals for each term. Just a quick glance at cartoons produced for children and teens shows how negative much of what students are exposed to can be. Thousands of messages barrage your students, many of which teach them that opposition to authority is admirable and that teachers are unpleasant people who exist mainly to interfere with the fun that students could be having.

Another negative influence on the disciplinary climate in your classroom may surprise you as a beginning teacher. You will learn that not every parent or guardian will support the orderly environment you want for your students. When you call a student's home to talk over a problem and find that parents or guardians are indifferent or unable to help, you will understand why some of your students find it difficult to behave well in your class.

Your school's climate may also contribute to some of your behavior problems. If students are permitted to misbehave in common areas, such as the halls or the cafeteria, it will not be easy for you to impose order in your classroom. Furthermore, in such a chaotic climate, administrators and other teachers may be too overwhelmed to offer the support you need to manage your class effectively.

A final aspect of the disciplinary dilemma that you will have to manage successfully is your inexperience and the ways in which it may contribute to the mix of issues you have to handle. For instance, one mistake that many new teachers make is being overly lenient at first to win their students' trust; they soon find out that such permissiveness compounds the behavior problems in their classroom. When your own policies are ineffective, you will find it even more difficult to overcome the other negative influences on your students' attitudes toward authority and discipline.

Myths About Discipline

Part of the lack of confidence that many new teachers feel is due to prevalent myths about classroom discipline that may seem sound but actually are harmful to students in the end. Although these myths vary from grade level to grade level and from school to school, some appear to be universal. If a colleague advises you with one of these ideas, tactfully decline to accept the advice:

- Parents and guardians should teach values, not teachers.
- Punishment works.
- Bribing students so that they will behave well works.
- Parents and guardians need to do something about their kid's behavior.
- Teachers can remove points from a student's grade for misbehavior.
- If you are not sure who's guilty, punish the entire class until someone tattles.
- They are old enough to know better.
- A teacher's temper tantrum now and then shows that you mean business.
- Assigning punishment work will stop misbehavior.
- Don't smile until Thanksgiving.

Control Your Anxiety with Proactive Strategies

Despite your anxiety about how to manage your classroom, you can feel confident that you will soon learn how to manage all of your students' complicated discipline problems. It is understandable that you may feel anxious if you are not able to manage all of them successfully at first. As you gain experience and confidence in your ability to cope with the daily events in your classroom, however, your anxiety will lessen.

One way to control your anxiety as you learn how to control your class is to adopt proactive strategies that put you on the right track. These strategies will keep your confidence level high while your daily experiences help you learn how to handle behavior problems:

- **Put school and classroom rules to work.** If you consistently enforce school and classroom rules, your students will soon stop testing their limits. Because both sets of rules already have consequences attached, you will be able to act quickly, without having to agonize over the right course of action to take.

- **Motivate and encourage students.** If you are generous with your praise and appreciation, you will establish a strong bond with your students that will help them stay on the right track. When you motivate and encourage students, you improve their self-esteem, which in turn will eliminate many behaviors that arise when students do not feel valued by their teacher or their classmates.

- **Deliver meaningful, interesting, and well-planned lessons.** Students who are busily engaged in meaningful and interesting work will not have time to misbehave. When you plan lessons well, students will find it easier to be successful and more likely to stay on task.

- **Have confidence in yourself.** You will find it easier to control your emotions as you begin to see that you really can teach and maintain control of a group of students. Do not forget that the most important factor in every successful plan for managing classroom discipline is the teacher. You—and no one else—can control the disciplinary climate for your students.

- **Treat every day as an opportunity to add to your knowledge.** Even your setbacks will teach you something about how to manage your class. As you get to know your colleagues, you will come to have a large, supportive network of people who are willing to help you. And each successful day will make it easier for your students to trust you and for you to learn more about them.

> When handling behavior issues, try not to let the students cause you to be less than professional. Remember that you are the teacher and you are in control of every situation.
>
> *Joshua Culver, first-year teacher*

Behaviors You Should Not Accept

Before you can begin deciding how to manage discipline issues in your classroom, you should have a clear understanding of what the ideal classroom atmosphere should be. Well-disciplined classes share three important characteristics:

- The students and teacher know and understand the rules and procedures that guide the entire class.
- The focus is on learning and cooperative behavior.
- There is a persistent tone of mutual respect and even affection among students and between students and their teacher.

When you and your students are working toward establishing and maintaining a well-disciplined class, you should not have to tolerate behaviors that might destroy the fragile positive atmosphere you have established. Here are the most obvious behaviors that teachers and school districts across the nation have deemed unacceptable in any classroom:

- **Threats and intimidation.** Students are not allowed to threaten or harass each other or you. This prohibition means that no bullying, teasing, sexual harassment, or threats of physical harm can be tolerated.

- **Substance abuse.** Almost every school now has a zero-tolerance policy in regard to illegal substances at school. All medications should be administered by the school nurse or a designee; even such medications as cough drops are regulated under most zero-tolerance policies. It is against the law for students to have alcohol, tobacco, or illegal drugs on school property.

- **Interference with others' right to learn.** No student has the right to stop other students from learning. This policy is the rationale behind school dress codes that prohibit students from distracting other students. It also keeps students from making noises loud enough to interfere with the normal routines of a school day and prohibits many other seriously disruptive actions.

- **Disrespect for authority.** This behavior includes refusal to comply with a reasonable request from a teacher, administrator, or other staff member. It also includes various forms of defiance, both overt and subtle—for example, talking back, sighing, sneering, and other rude behavior directed at an authority figure.

- **Failure to complete work.** Teachers should monitor student progress closely enough so that all parents or guardians are aware of the situation if a child refuses to complete work or fails to complete it for some other reason.

- **Unsafe behavior.** Behaviors considered unsafe range from running with scissors, engaging in horseplay, or running in the halls to ignoring safe driving rules in a high school parking lot. Policies to combat unsafe behavior also prohibit students from having matches or other fire starters at school, leaving school grounds without permission, or using school equipment in an unsafe manner.

- **Dishonesty.** Students should not forge notes from home, cheat on their work, commit plagiarism, or lie to teachers or other school officials. Teachers are required to report almost all incidents of dishonesty to parents or guardians as well as administrators.

- **Tardiness.** Students are expected to be at school and in class on time. Tardiness to class is not acceptable and is part of the attendance policy in many states.

- **Truancy.** Almost every state requires local school districts to enforce attendance policies. It is the responsibility of a classroom teacher to maintain accurate attendance records.

- **Violence.** School districts in all states take violence very seriously. Students are not allowed to fight or to encourage a fight by cheering on the combatants. Regulations against violence include the prohibition of weapons and weapon look-alikes at school.

What Do Your Supervisors Expect from You?

It is not always easy to determine just how permissive or how strict you should be. Many teachers make numerous mistakes as they become skilled at managing their classes because they have not learned what their supervisors expect from them. Although expectations for student behavior can vary greatly, there are some common practices that most supervisors are likely to expect you to implement in enforcing discipline. As you work to create a safe and productive disciplinary climate, follow these suggestions:

- Prevent as many behavior problems as you can by working to contain or minimize disruptions.
- Establish, teach, and enforce reasonable class rules, including reasonable consequences for breaking them.
- Make student safety a priority; never allow any activity that could endanger your students.
- Help your students stay focused on learning instead of misbehavior.
- Handle most discipline problems on your own, but refer a student to an administrator when your school's guidelines require it.
- Although you are not expected to know every statute of school law, make it a point to know the basic laws pertaining to schools. You should be especially aware of students' rights and your responsibilities.
- Call a student's home early when behavior problems arise. Parents and guardians should be aware of behavior problems before they become serious. Be prepared to show your supervisors documentation that you contacted parents and guardians at appropriate times.
- Maintain accurate documentation of students' behavior. Your supervisors expect you to have an up-to-date file on each of your students.

Respond Instead of Just Reacting

Losing control of your emotions or relying on punishment to effect a change in your students' behavior will not solve discipline problems. What will stop students from misbehaving is a teacher who takes the stance that misbehavior is a problem with a solution.

As the adult in charge of the classroom, you have two choices when confronted with a discipline issue. You can choose to solve the problem with a calm and carefully planned response, or you can choose to vent your frustration, anger, and other emotions. Responding to solve the problem will move you and your students toward a solution; reacting emotionally will not.

Instead of just reacting to a problem, remember this: today's teachers have many constructive options when misbehavior happens in a classroom. No matter which approach you choose, you must always act decisively and avoid giving students the impression that you are unsure about the action you are taking. If you are to choose the most appropriate action to take, you will need to be aware of which options are likely to be most effective in each situation.

One way to do this is to make sure that you are aware of the management techniques you should avoid. You can use Teacher Worksheet 16.1 to help you examine what your current practices may be. Next, instead of reacting negatively, draw from this list of effectual ways to respond when students misbehave so that you can make wise choices from among the many options you have:

- **Consciously choose to ignore the misbehavior.** This is an effective option if you plan to use it, if the misbehavior is fleeting, and if other students are not seriously affected by it—for example, when a student daydreams briefly, gets a slow start on an assignment, or taps a pencil.

- **Delay taking action.** It is appropriate to delay taking action when the action you would take would cause further disruption. As an example, if a student is tardy to class, instead of stopping a presentation, you might choose to delay speaking to that student until you can do so quietly so that other students are not disturbed by your correction.

- **Use nonverbal actions.** Nonverbal actions, such as physically moving closer to a student, making eye contact, or making inquiring facial expressions are nonintrusive ways to address student misbehavior. This is often an appropriate choice for dealing with those students who seem to be momentarily off task, daydreaming, or gazing out of the window instead of engaged.

- **Praise the entire class for its good behavior.** Praising the entire group for its positive behaviors will encourage those who are doing well to stay on task and will remind those who are not behaving well of what is expected.

- **Give a quiet reprimand.** Giving a quiet verbal reprimand when a student misbehaves will usually end the trouble. Try to be positive instead of negative. "Please open your book and begin working now" will be more effective than a more negative command, such as "Stop playing around this instant."

- **Confer briefly with students.** In a brief conference, you can remind a student of the rule he or she has broken, redefine acceptable limits of behavior, encourage positive behavior, and discuss the positive and negative consequences of his or her actions.

- **Hold a longer conference with students.** Schedule a longer and more formal conference with a student when there are several issues to be resolved or when misbehavior is serious. The emphasis should be on determining the causes of misbehavior and deciding what needs to be done to resolve the problem. Here are some guidelines for a successful conference:
  - Listen sincerely and carefully as the student tells his or her side of the story.
  - Ask questions until the student has shared what he or she needs to say.

- Make sure that you have a clear understanding of what caused the misbehavior.

- Do not rush to respond. Instead, tell a student who has misbehaved that you need to think about what you have learned and that you will make a decision overnight.

- **Contact parents or guardians.** If you are having difficulty with helping students control their behavior, ask the other adults in their lives to reinforce your efforts. Too often, teachers hesitate to do this or wait until misbehavior is serious. Early intervention in the form of a request for help is always a good idea.

- **Hold students in detention.** This is a good time to hold longer conferences with students who need to resolve their behavior problems. Use detention time to work together and create a stronger relationship with a student instead of just as punishment.

- **Arrange a conference with parents or guardians.** If a student persists in misbehaving and you have tried several interventions, such as phoning a parent or guardian, with no success, then you should schedule a conference with parents or guardians. (See Section Three for more information about how to conduct successful conferences.)

- **Refer a student to an administrator.** You must make this choice when you have exhausted all other possibilities or when the misbehavior is serious. There is more information about how to handle referrals to an administrator later in this section.

From *The First-Year Teacher's Survival Guide, 3rd Edition*, by Julia G. Thompson. Copyright © 2013 by John Wiley & Sons, Inc. Reproduced by permission.

TEACHER WORKSHEET 16.1

Classroom Management Techniques to Avoid

Here are some ineffective classroom management practices to avoid. Put check marks in the appropriate boxes to indicate how you conducted your class in the past week. Then carefully consider how you can eliminate ineffective management practices from your classroom.

In the Past Week I . . .	Several Times	Once Only	Never
Failed to contact a parent or guardian when I needed to			
Assigned punishment work			
Allowed a student to sleep in class			
Raised my voice			
Accepted bad behavior from one student and not from another			
Lost my temper			
Talked over inappropriate student noise			
Used negative body language, such as pointing at students			
Nagged students			
Allowed a student to ignore me			

How to Avoid a Lawsuit: A Teacher's Legal Responsibilities

As a new teacher, you may feel particularly vulnerable to becoming embroiled in legal problems at school because you are unsure of your responsibilities under the law. Almost all of the legal policies involving teachers center on one tenet: teachers are obligated to take care of their students—to protect their safety and welfare at school. Because students don't always recognize danger even when warned of hazardous situations, teachers have a duty to anticipate and prevent hazardous situations whenever possible.

What are your responsibilities? Use the guidelines in the list that follows as a way to make sound decisions for all of your students and for yourself.

- Teachers should learn basic school law. Teachers who understand the laws, policies, and procedures governing their school conduct and duties toward students reduce the risk of legal problems. A very helpful Web site with links to many resources for teachers is maintained by the law firm Drummond Woodsum in Portland, Maine (www.schoollaw.com). An informative book is the second edition of *Legal Rights of Teachers and Students* by Martha M. McCarthy, Nelda H. Cambron-McCabe, and Stephen B. Thomas, which was published in 2008 by Allyn & Bacon.

- Once you have learned the basics of school law, you are obligated to act accordingly. Ignorance of the law is not an excuse for allowing a student under your care to come to harm.

- The rules in your classroom must have a clear educational purpose and must be governed by common sense. The consequences of breaking a rule must be appropriate to the rule. You must publish class rules and the consequences for breaking them for your students and their parents or guardians.

- Teachers are obligated to make their students aware of the risks in activities. Whether the hazard is from running with scissors or operating equipment in a vocational class, students need to be taught how to avoid danger.

- In general, younger students need to be more closely supervised than older students.

- Teachers should never embarrass a student in front of his or her peers. Some of the most violent criminal events at schools in recent years have been carried out by students who were not successful academically or socially.

- One of the best ways to prevent problems is to conduct yourself professionally at all times while you are at school. If your demeanor and dress show that you are serious about your students, your work, and how you manage a class, you will reduce the opportunities for students to act out in anger and disrespect.

- You should actively monitor your class. If a student in the front of the classroom is seriously injured while you are in the back of the classroom checking your e-mail, you could be considered negligent.

- If you have a student who is aggressive or hostile toward others and you ignore the problem, you have neglected to protect the students who may be assaulted. Be aware of potential problems and, if possible, seek administrative assistance before trouble can occur.

- A student's privacy is protected by law. Do not gossip about a student, post grades, or reveal confidential information. Be especially careful about what you transmit electronically or in writing. Keep confidential material in a secure area.

- A student's freedom of speech and expression is protected by law, as long as that speech or expression does not disrupt the learning environment. For example, if you do not appreciate a student's fashion sense, you have no legal right to enforce your personal taste.

- Students have a right to due process just as other citizens do. If you are not sure about what course of action to take when a problem arises, use your common sense first. If you are still not sure, call in a school official before you act in a way that might be in violation of a student's right to due process.

- If your students are required to submit a permission slip signed by a parent or guardian before attending a school activity, such as a field trip, that permission slip does not exonerate you from wrongdoing if a student is harmed. A permission slip is not a legal document that will protect you in court.

- You must supervise your students at all times. Special education students; young students; and those with impulsive, uncooperative, or unpredictable behavior usually require more intense supervision than others. The type of activity that students are engaging in also determines the level of supervision required. Students playing a rough-and-tumble game at recess require more direct supervision than a group of students reading in a quiet classroom. No matter how mature they are, never leave students unsupervised. *Never.*

- You should design activities with safety in mind. Consider the potential for danger to students when you design active classroom games, lab experiments, group activities, or competitive events that could quickly get out of control.

- It is not a sound practice to allow students to grade each other's final work. Although it may save you time, it is a practice that has been successfully challenged in court.

- If you suspect that a student is becoming involved in gang activity, you must report your suspicions to an administrator who will, in turn, report it to the local police. Do not attempt to confront suspected gang members on your own.

- If you suspect that a student is the victim of abuse, you are legally obligated to report it to the appropriate authorities in your school.

- You must be aware of the requirements and restrictions in a student's Individualized Education Program or 504 Plan. You are bound by law to follow those requirements.

- The decision to search students' personal property is more complicated than it first appears. Don't take it upon yourself to search student book bags or lockers. Involve an administrator instead.

- Teachers are expected to know about their students' medical needs and behavior problems as well as any other special factors that could put them in harm's way. Take time to go through students' permanent folders at the start of the term so that you have the knowledge to protect yourself and your students.

- Keep accurate records of parent or guardian conferences, interventions, student behaviors, and other pertinent information. It is especially important to document misbehavior. Use Teacher Worksheet 16.2 to keep a record that you can refer to if you are asked to give information in court.

- Teachers, parents and guardians, students, and school officials must work together to maintain a safe and orderly environment for all students. Sharing responsibility and knowledge is an important way to keep students safe.

TEACHER WORKSHEET 16.2

Behavior Incident Report

Teacher name: _____

Student name: _____

Date and time of incident: _____

Place of incident: _____

Description of incident:

_____

_____

_____

_____

Actions taken by teacher:

_____

_____

_____

_____

Results of teacher actions:

_____

_____

_____

_____

_____

Notes:

_____

_____

_____

_____

Parent or guardian contact:

_____

_____

_____

_____

Witness signature(s): _____

From *The First-Year Teacher's Survival Guide, 3rd Edition*, by Julia G. Thompson. Copyright © 2013 by John Wiley & Sons, Inc. Reproduced by permission.

Due Process Procedures

School disciplinary situations can damage the careers of teachers who are not aware of their own legal rights and the rights of their students. Although by far most of the discipline issues that you will have to handle will be minor, some of the more serious ones, such as possession of illegal substances or fighting, will require you to act decisively. When you do, it is important to keep in mind that one of the most significant rights of students involved in a disciplinary action is the right to due process. Here is a very brief explanation of the conditions for due process:

- School and classroom rules must be reasonable.
- Students must be notified of school and classroom rules and policies.
- When a student misbehaves, he or she must be made aware of the specific charge.
- Students have a right to legal counsel.
- There must be a full investigation.
- There must be documentation of the incident and the investigation.
- The disciplinary action must be fair.
- The student must have an opportunity to file a grievance.
- The student has a right to a hearing.
- The student has the right to appeal the disciplinary action.

Cultivate Grace Under Pressure

One of the worst mistakes you can make is to lose your temper in front of your students when you are upset. Not only will giving in to the emotion of the moment cause you stress and sway your good judgment but also it may do irreparable harm to your relationship with your students.

Learning to control your emotions is not an easy task. If you have had a terrible time with one class, you often may not have enough time to recover from the experience before the next class begins. However, taking out your anger or frustrations on innocent students is wrong. Although your students need to see your human side, they do not need to be subjected to your ill temper. When you are tempted to lose your cool in front of your students, restrain yourself.

Because you are a role model, your students pay attention to everything you say and do. Learning the fine art of grace under pressure is not easy, but responding with grace is a powerful tool for any caring teacher.

Students whose teacher loses control may react in various negative ways. Your outbursts may frighten some students and intimidate others. Still other students will react to your anger by losing control themselves. If you raise your voice at a student, you should not be surprised if the student shouts at you in return.

There are many things you can do to cultivate grace under pressure. Here are several strategies that other teachers have found useful:

- Remember that losing control will only make the situation worse.
- Count to ten before you speak. While you are counting, make your face appear as calm as possible.
- Instead of shouting, lower your voice to a whisper.
- If there is a great deal of noise and commotion without a threat of violence, stand quietly and wait for it to subside. Shouting at your students to settle them down will only add to the noise.
- Talk to your colleagues to vent your frustration and plan ways to manage discipline issues differently.
- Remember that you determine what happens in your class. If you lose control, you are not working to solve the problem. Channel your energy toward managing the situation in a positive way.
- Ask your students for help when you are upset. This will redirect their attention toward a productive contribution.

Great Advice: Don't Take It Personally

Sometimes, no matter what you do, students misbehave. One of the hardest attitudes for many new teachers to adopt is a refusal to take their students' misbehavior and lack of motivation personally. After a miserable day, negative student attitudes and behaviors can sometimes cause even veteran teachers to wonder why they bothered to go to school.

If you were to discuss such a day with an experienced teacher, the chances are good that you would hear, "Don't take it personally." This is excellent advice, but it is one of the hardest things for new teachers to learn to do. However, if you are to thrive in your new profession, it is an attitude that you must embrace. Recall these pointers the next time you are tempted to take it personally when your students do not live up to your expectations:

- Students will not always behave well or say the right thing. After all, they are children.
- Part of being a teacher is setting limits and establishing boundaries for your students. Although this is necessary, it isn't always easy for you or your students.
- Teaching is a very complicated task. In the course of a school week, you will have to make dozens of decisions. Not all of them will be popular with your students.
- As the adult in the classroom, you have to consider the needs of all students. When a student disagrees with a teacher, it is often because that child is only considering what he or she wants instead of what would be good for the group.
- Your students do not really know you. They see only one side of you—the teacher part. They react to that part, not to you as a person.

You May Be the Troublemaker

Your inexperience will cause you to inadvertently make many mistakes. Sometimes the mistakes you make will create discipline problems. The upside is that once you recognize that you have made a mistake, you can take steps to correct it.

Here is a list of common mistakes that many teachers have found to be sources of discipline problems. Along with each mistake, you will find suggestions for effective actions you can take instead.

- **Mistake One**: The punishment you assign for an offense is inappropriate.

Example: Students receive only a warning for getting into a loud argument in front of the rest of the class.

Suggestion: Because this is an offense that could escalate into a more serious altercation, students should be removed from the class and an administrator notified. When you create your class rules, make sure the consequences match the seriousness of the offense.

- **Mistake Two**: You are too permissive, too tentative, too easily sidetracked.

Example: You want your students to have ownership in the class and allowed them to set the class rules in a democratic fashion. Now your students are not only uncooperative but also breaking the rules they established for themselves.

Suggestion: Take the time to think through what you want from your students academically and behaviorally. Act in a decisive manner when you are with your students. You are the adult in the room. When you allow your students a voice in class decisions, never agree to rules or consequences that make you uncomfortable.

- **Mistake Three**: You are unclear in the limits you set for your students, resulting in constant testing of the boundaries and of your patience.

Example: You have allowed some mild swearing in your class by pretending not to hear it. Now students are not just swearing occasionally but also using language that is more offensive.

Suggestion: Be very specific when you set the limits for acceptable and unacceptable behavior for your students. Don't ignore behavior that makes you uncomfortable. Always directly address any student who swears around you. Teach students that swearing is not only inappropriate but disrespectful as well.

- **Mistake Four**: You do not take the time to listen to your students when they are trying to express their feelings about a problem.

Example: Your students are upset over a test question they find unfair. When they try to talk to you, the situation deteriorates until you tell them you do not want to hear more complaints.

Suggestion: Not allowing students to discuss their feelings is a serious mistake that will only worsen a situation as students grow more frustrated. Encourage students to express their concerns in an appropriate manner, and give them chances to do this.

When a large group is upset about an issue, you will save time by asking them to write you notes about the problem. You can read the notes later and decide how to respond before you face them again.

- **Mistake Five**: You are inconsistent in enforcing consequences.

Example: You are usually very strict about making students meet their deadlines for projects. However, you decide to let a star athlete have an extra day when his mother writes a note complaining that he didn't have enough time to do the work. Your other students are quick to notice this and complain that it isn't fair. Some of them don't turn in their work on time, either.

Suggestion: So that you can be consistent, make sure you are comfortable with administering the consequences for breaking a rule or failing to meet a deadline. Make it clear to all students that you intend to be consistent with rules and deadlines.

- **Mistake Six**: You punish one student while overlooking another student's offense that is more serious.

Example: You reprimand one student for leaving a book bag in the aisle during a test while failing to notice that several other students are cheating on the test.

Suggestion: Take care to assess a situation before you act. Be alert to all of your students' activity, and be consistent in how you handle their misbehavior.

Think Before You Act

Whenever you have to deal with a discipline problem, take care to understand the reason for the misbehavior before you act. If you make the effort to determine why your students act the way they do, you will benefit by having a clearer understanding of some of the times when your students are going to have trouble staying on task.

There are many ways to determine why your students act the way they do. Talk to teachers who have taught your students in the past or to parents or guardians. You can also check permanent records to find out more about each student's past, home situation, and abilities. To learn about students' behavior when you are facing a discipline problem, maintain a friendly and supportive relationship with students, listen to what they have to say, and solicit their input when appropriate. When you do make the effort to learn more about your students' behavior, several beneficial things will happen:

- Your students will feel less frustration because you will be allowing them to talk about their feelings.
- You will gain an understanding of what caused the problem.
- If there are causes other than what you first noticed, you will be able to act on them.
- You will gain insight into how your students think, feel, and react.
- You and your students will have a common ground for discussing other choices they can make in the future.

- You will probably have prevented this problem from recurring.
- Your bond with your students will be stronger because you will have shown them the courtesy of listening to and caring about what they had to say.

Don't Give Up on Your Difficult Students

Of all of the students you will teach, the difficult ones need you most, because too many other people have given up on them. All of your students, even your difficult ones, need to be confident of the following facts:

- You care about them and believe in them.
- It is the misbehavior you don't like, not the students.
- You will never give up on them.

The chief characteristic of children is that they change and grow. Even high school seniors will change dramatically between the first day of school and graduation day. Your chief purpose as an educator is to direct that change and growth so that your students can have productive and peaceful lives.

Be patient. Even though you know they will change and grow over the course of the year, it can sometimes seem almost impossible to maintain your faith in some of your difficult students. When you find your faith beginning to waver, you must resolve to give them every opportunity to overcome their difficulties.

How to Deal with a Difficult Class

Teaching a difficult class can be an unnerving and exhausting experience. A rude or disrespectful class can turn your enthusiasm into a desire to just make it through one more day. Fortunately, many strategies can be employed to turn a bunch of smart-alecky, unmanageable, or all-around indifferent students into an enjoyable class. What causes a class to be difficult? Here are just a few of the many and varied reasons a class can give you trouble:

- An unequal distribution in regard to the ability levels of students is causing frustration.
- A negative label has become a self-fulfilling prophecy.
- There is an unpleasant chemistry between you and your students.
- There is an unpleasant chemistry among students.

Perhaps the most serious reason why classes can be difficult lies in the way students regard themselves and their ability to succeed academically. Students who do not believe they can succeed have no reason to try. Teachers who achieve success with difficult classes turn the negative energy in a class into a positive force by persistently communicating their faith in their students' ability to achieve.

Here are some strategies to help you turn a difficult class into a successful one:

- Smile at your class. If you were videotaped while teaching, would your body language reveal positive or negative feelings about your students?

- Keep the expectations for your class high. Children live up to the expectations of the adults in their lives, so let them know that you expect a lot from them.

- From the first class meeting onward, establish that you control the class. Demonstrate that you will oversee the behavior in your classroom for the good of all students.

- Call parents or guardians as soon as you can when a problem arises.

- Work on the noise level every day until your students learn to govern themselves. Teach students which volumes are acceptable and which are not. Establish signals to help students learn to control the noise.

- Plan activities to fit your students' short attention spans.

- Make sure that activities offer plenty of time for practice and review.

- Never allow students to sit with nothing to do but disturb others. Keep them busy for the entire class period.

- Stay on your feet and monitor students. Learners who know that you are watching over them will hesitate before misbehaving.

- Tell your students that you expect them to do their work well and that you will help them learn to do it.

- Make sure that the work you assign is appropriate for your students' various ability levels and that you differentiate it appropriately.

- Offer incentives other than grades. Students who have never received a good grade may not be motivated by grades. Offer small, frequent rewards instead, such as stickers, computer time, or bookmarks.

- Praise good behavior as often as you can. Difficult students do not always know when they are behaving well. When you praise your class for good behavior, you are encouraging all of your students to repeat the behavior.

- Take time to teach and reteach the rules and procedures that you want your students to follow.

- Be as specific as you can when telling difficult students what you want them to do. Although you do want students to share their feelings with you, don't allow them to engage you in an argument.

- Give students opportunities to help each other. Students who are sharing their knowledge with a classmate will be so busy being productive that they will not have time to disrupt class.

- Acknowledge the rights of individuals in your class. Showing students that you are fair will ease many sensitive situations.

How to Cope with a Student's Chronic Misbehavior

Chronic misbehavior is exhausting for the teacher who tries to mitigate its negative effects on the whole class as well as on the individual student who is misbehaving. It can also make it impossible for anyone to learn. Fortunately, you can help a chronically misbehaving student learn to develop the self-control necessary to become a positive part of any class. If you have at least one student who misbehaves far too often, the guidelines that follow can help you work with this student to get him or her to assume responsibility for behaving appropriately.

- **Guideline One:** Attend to safety issues first. It is your responsibility to act decisively and quickly to keep all of your students safe. Never allow behavior that jeopardizes student health, safety, or welfare.

- **Guideline Two:** Keep disturbances as unobtrusive as possible. You'll send a strong message that the focus in your class is not on misbehavior but on learning instead.

- **Guideline Three:** Be supportive and encouraging rather than negative. With this combination of positive and supportive attitudes, you will be far more likely to change your students' misbehavior than if you just react negatively.

- **Guideline Four:** Show students how they are supposed to behave. Use plenty of models, examples, and explicit details so that your misbehaving students can have a clear idea of just how they are supposed to act.

- **Guideline Five:** Don't expect a quick fix. Chronic patterns of misbehavior usually take years to develop and a long time to change. Help your students who struggle with chronic misbehavior by setting a clearly established goal for improvement and measuring the steps in their journey toward it.

> Until students get to know you, they don't care what you know; they want to know that you care.
>
> *Edward Gardner, 36 years' experience*

How to Hold Successful Conferences with Students Who Have Misbehaved

Student conferences can be a powerful tool for teachers who want to establish a positive relationship with a student who has misbehaved. When the two of you sit down together to work out solutions to a problem, you will both benefit.

Holding a successful conference with a student who has misbehaved is not difficult. Use the strategies that follow to guarantee success by making it clear that you have given much thought to the student's concerns and to how the two of you can work together to resolve problems.

BEFORE THE CONFERENCE

- At least twenty-four hours in advance, notify the parents or guardians of any students that you intend to keep after school.

- Make sure that the conference time is workable. Younger students will have to consult their parents to coordinate their ride home. Be as cooperative about the time as you can.

- Arrange a place to meet that is as free from distractions as possible. Do not confer with students while other students are in the room.

DURING THE CONFERENCE

- Be courteous in your greeting. This will set the tone for the rest of the meeting.

- Make the area as comfortable as possible. Offer a pen and paper for taking notes, and sit side by side at student desks or at a table. Do not sit behind your desk.

- To protect yourself from charges of misconduct, when you are meeting one-on-one with a student, sit near the door to the room, and make sure the door is open. If you believe that a conference will be uncomfortable, arrange for a colleague to be in the same room with you and your student.

- Be very careful not to touch a student for any reason during a conference. Even an innocent pat on the back can be misinterpreted.

- Begin the meeting by stating that the purpose of the conference is to work together to resolve a problem between the two of you. Avoid rehashing unpleasant details, blaming the student, or showing your anger.

- Take the initiative by asking the student to tell you why you are meeting. Make sure that you each have a chance to state the problem as you see it.

- Listen to the student without interrupting.

- When you discuss the student's behavior, focus on the misdeed itself, not on your student's negative personality traits.

- After the student has spoken, restate the problem in your own words. Make sure you understand the problem and express your sincere interest in solving it.

- Be positive but firm in conveying that it is the student's responsibility to change his or her behavior.

- Brainstorm some solutions with the student. Ask questions about how the student could handle the situation differently in the future.

- Agree on a plan that satisfies both of you. Make sure that you are comfortable with implementing it.

- Calmly explain the negative consequences you will impose if the student fails to carry out his or her part of the plan.

- Once again, state that you are willing to help the student be successful.

AT THE END OF THE CONFERENCE

- Ask the student if there is anything else that needs to be said. State your willingness to listen.

- Be very clear that you consider the student's misbehavior to be in the past and that you will not hold a grudge now that a resolution has been reached.

- Thank your student for taking the time for a conference and for deciding to work with you.

Put Detentions to Good Use

If your school district allows you to detain students after school, you can use this time productively if the purpose of a detention is not to punish but to resolve problems. The following suggestions will help you make the process easy to manage:

BEFORE YOU ISSUE A DETENTION NOTICE

- Take time to learn what your district's policy on student detentions entails.
- Make sure to have plenty of detention forms on hand so that you will be able to hand out notices as students leave class.
- Before you write out a notice, try to prevent the misbehavior. Privately warn students of the rules they are breaking and of the consequences. No student should be surprised when you issue a detention for misbehavior.
- Decide what you will do if the child refuses to serve a detention. Know your district's policy on this issue before you have to address it.

WHEN YOU ISSUE A DETENTION NOTICE

- When you must issue a detention notice, do not write the notice while you are upset or in a hurry. If you do, you will appear less than professional.
- When you do write the notice, use a dark pen and write neatly. Spell the student's name correctly as well as the names of his or her parents or guardians.
- Be very specific when you write the notice so that the student and his or her parents or guardians know what has happened to cause the notice. If you assign a detention as a result of a third tardy to your class, for example, give the dates of the previous tardies and the consequences that resulted from them.
- Make it very clear to your students that their parents or guardians must sign the notice before you can allow them to serve their detention. You should never cause

parents or guardians anxiety because their child is late in coming home from school.

● Because parents and guardians often take detentions more seriously than students do, call home to let parents or guardians know that you have issued a detention notice to their child.

● Issue the detention notice quietly, matter-of-factly, and at the very end of class to avoid embarrassing students or causing a scene with an angry student.

● When you issue a detention notice, ask the student to sign a brief statement that he or she has received the notice. Be sure to date the statement and keep it in your records.

● If a student crumples the notice, tears it, or even leaves it behind, continue to be very calm. If the student does not come back for the notice and to apologize before the end of the school day, call home. You should also lengthen the time of the detention by a few minutes because you will need to discuss this issue with the student.

● Never issue detention notices to a large group of students at the same time; you will appear to have lost control of your class.

● Plan what you want to accomplish with a detained student and how you will reach that goal.

DURING THE DETENTION

● Be careful to protect yourself from being accused of misconduct by keeping the door open at all times when you are detaining a student. Do not touch the student at all.

● Establish a very businesslike atmosphere. Refuse to tolerate inappropriate behavior.

● Talk with your student about the problem and how it should be resolved. Have the student write out his or her thoughts before trying to talk with you. Such writing is not busywork but a tool to open a helpful dialogue. Try using questions such as the ones in the list that follows to get your students thinking about the changes they can make to prevent the problem from recurring.

  ● What choices can I make other than the ones I made?

  ● What are some appropriate behaviors that I have used in this class in the past?

  ● What are the reasons why I should change my behavior?

  ● How can I improve my approach to my work, my classmates, and my teacher?

  ● What are my goals for this class, and how can I achieve them?

AFTER THE DETENTION

- Make notes about what happened during the detention. Keep a record of the conversation and a copy of the student's writing.

- Do not give students a ride home. If a parent or guardian has signed the detention notice, transportation is not your responsibility.

- Do not leave a child alone at an empty school. Wait with the student until his or her ride home appears.

- Make it clear to any student you detain that you are optimistic about future behavior improvements and that you will not hold a grudge about past misbehavior.

> You cannot hold grudges. You need to remember that your students have a short memory and trust you to always do the right thing. If there is a problem, settle it, then just continue as if nothing happened.
>
> *Sarah Walski, 25 years' experience*

Manage Referrals to an Administrator with Confidence

For the discipline process to be meaningful, teachers who need assistance with students who make learning difficult for others must have some recourse. Usually, this recourse takes the form of an administrative referral.

Referring students to an administrator during your first year as a teacher is, at best, a nerve-racking experience. Consider the answers to the common questions that follow to make the referral process easier for everyone involved.

WHEN SHOULD A TEACHER SEND A STUDENT TO AN ADMINISTRATOR?

There is no question that you should refer a student to an administrator for any of these behaviors:

- Persistent defiance
- Bullying
- Stealing
- Sexual harassment
- Vandalism
- Deliberate profanity
- Bringing weapons to school
- Substance abuse
- Making threats

- Violent behavior
- Truancy
- Cheating
- Persistent disruptions
- Habitual tardiness

HOW CAN A TEACHER MAINTAIN CREDIBILITY WITH STUDENTS, PARENTS AND GUARDIANS, AND ADMINISTRATORS?

Referral to the office is a serious step and should not be taken lightly by anyone involved. To safeguard your credibility, you should follow these five guidelines:

- **Guideline One**: Don't send students to the office for minor forms of misbehavior that you are expected to handle successfully on your own, such as
  - Not doing homework
  - Scribbling on desks
  - Making rude comments
  - Infrequently being tardy
  - Not working in class
  - Engaging in nonviolent peer conflicts
  - Talking excessively
  - Chewing gum
  - Showing poor work habits
  - Not paying attention

- **Guideline Two**: Unless the misbehavior is sudden, such as a fight that requires students to be removed from the room, make sure that administrators are not surprised to receive a referral from you. When you begin to notice a pattern of misbehavior, make an appointment with an administrator to discuss the problem and to ask for help. When you finally refer a student, the administrator will then have a clear understanding of what has happened and what you have done to try to resolve the conflict. By giving administrators this background information, you not only make it easier for them to make the best decisions about how to handle problems but also present yourself as a competent educator who can handle most of your problems.

- **Guideline Three**: When you write a referral, make sure that the language you use is as professional and objective as possible. Because many different people, including the student and his or her parents or guardians, will read the referral, use behavior-oriented, factual language.

- **Guideline Four**: Call the student's parents or guardians before the end of the day to inform them of the incident and of the referral.

- **Guideline Five**: Between the time you turn in a referral and the time an administrator acts on it, speak to the administrator to discuss the problem and add any details you didn't want to write on the referral form.

> You want to make sure you are addressing the behavior, not the student. When dealing with behavior issues, trying to figure out the root problem of the behavior is where you need to start. If you can help solve that baseline issue, then there is a good chance the student may not resort to that behavior again.
>
> *Jared Sronce, first-year teacher*

HOW CAN A TEACHER AVOID MAKING THE DISRUPTION WORSE WHEN REFERRING A STUDENT?

Following are some suggestions on how to minimize disruption when referring a student:

- Have copies of the referral form on hand so that you will be able to write it quickly and with a minimum of distractions.

- Maintain a student's dignity and privacy in front of classmates. Do not tell the student that you intend to write a referral when you are in the presence of other students. Be discreet. This will also help you avoid an angry outburst that will disturb other students.

- Remain calm, and remind the student of the rules and the consequences for breaking them. Don't threaten or bully a student, even if you are angry.

- Make sure that students are not surprised when they are referred to an administrator for persistent misbehavior. By the time a student needs to be referred to an administrator, you should have intervened several times.

WHAT SHOULD A TEACHER DO IF HE OR SHE DISAGREES WITH AN ACTION THAT AN ADMINISTRATOR HAS TAKEN?

If you have been working with an administrator to prevent a student's misbehavior and to avoid writing a referral, you should know the action the administrator intends to take when you refer the student. If the administrator takes an action that turns out to be different from what you had discussed or that you are not comfortable with, speak with him or her to find out the reason for the decision. Resist the temptation to publicly criticize the decision.

HOW CAN A TEACHER PREVENT MISBEHAVIOR FROM HAPPENING AGAIN?

Here are some tips on how to keep misbehavior from recurring:

- Learn from your mistakes. Examine the actions that led to the final referral. Determine what other interventions you could have taken early in your relationship with the child to prevent the misbehavior from reaching this point.
- Help students leave the behavior and the referral behind. Make students aware that you view a referral as an end to misbehavior.
- Continue to use a variety of early interventions to prevent misbehaviors from reaching the referral point.

Handling Four Common Types of Student Misbehavior

Although it may sometimes seem as if your school days are beset with tribulations unique to a first-year teacher, experience alone will not allow you to prevent every problem. Some fall into the category of problems that all teachers have to learn to manage. Following are suggestions for handling four common problems:

1. Tardiness
2. Absenteeism
3. Substance abuse
4. Fighting

PROBLEM ONE: TARDINESS

Very few students can attend school for an entire term without being tardy at least once. Students have many reasons to delay their arrival in class, and by the end of the first few weeks of school, you will have heard many creative excuses. Expect your students to suffer from car trouble, traffic, stuck lockers, lost notebooks, arguments with friends, sleepy parents, and mysterious alarm clock failures.

The real reasons for your students' tardiness are not as colorful. Students may be late to class because they do not see an advantage to being on time. Perhaps they are late because you have not communicated the consequences of tardiness to them. Another reason for student tardiness may be that inconsistent enforcement of the consequences has led students to believe that being late to class is not a problem.

Although tardy students are the first to claim that being tardy is not a serious offense and that they are not hurting anyone else, tardy students do disrupt learning. You must raise your students' awareness of the negative effects associated with their tardiness:

- Tardy students cause a disruption, no matter how quietly they try to slip into the class. Furthermore, if students see that their classmates can be tardy with no teacher reaction, then they will believe that it is okay for them to be tardy, too. The disruptive effect will multiply if more and more students come late to your class.

- Tardy students set a negative tone in a class by tacitly sending a message that the activities you have planned for them are not important enough for them to make the effort to be on time. As a result, the focus in your class may shift from learning to a power struggle between you and the students who are testing the boundaries of your patience.

Your Responsibilities

- Make it important for your students to be on time to your class. Begin an interesting and meaningful assignment as soon as the bell rings.

- Enforce your tardiness policy consistently. Be sure that your policy is in line with your school's policy. Chronically tardy students respond particularly well to a policy with escalating consequences because it forces them to take their actions seriously.

- Involve parents or guardians if a student is tardy more than once or twice in a marking period. This is an especially important step if the tardy student is late to school and not just late from another teacher's class.

- Be aware of your school's policy for handling habitual tardiness. At some point in the process, you will be expected to refer the student to an administrator for action. Be sure to follow your school's procedures in regard to tardiness.

- Model the behavior you expect. Your students will be very quick to point out your hypocrisy if you are tardy and then reprimand them for the same offense.

Mistakes to Avoid

- Never embarrass tardy students with sarcastic remarks, such as "Glad you decided to join us." Sarcasm will not solve the problem, nor will it earn you respect; instead, it will make tardy students even more reluctant to enter the room.

- Do not delay calling a student's home. The second time a student is tardy, you should enlist support in handling the problem.

- Do not be a pushover who accepts unreasonable excuses; instead, enforce the consequences of tardiness.

- Never stop what you are doing to interrogate a tardy student in front of the rest of the class; instead, allow the student to slip into class while you continue giving instruction.

- Don't allow students to stand in the doorway before class starts. Students who block the entrance interrupt the smooth start of class because they delay their classmates from getting to their seat on time.

Strategies That Work

- Define tardiness for your students, and be reasonable in your definition. Most teachers will agree that a student who is inside the classroom but not in a seat is not tardy; others are more particular and insist that a student who is not actually sitting down is tardy. Note, however, that the second definition is difficult to justify to your students and their parents or guardians.

- Begin class quickly, with assignments that students will find enjoyable. If necessary, grade the work you assign at the start of class so that your students have a reason to be prompt. Make the first few minutes of class as meaningful as the rest.

- Establish your expectation that students will arrive promptly during the first two weeks of the term. If you make controlling tardiness a priority as the term begins, you will avoid many problems later.

- Speak with a tardy student privately to determine why he or she was late to class.

- Keep your attendance records accurate. It is sometimes confusing to stop class and change an absence mark to a tardy mark, but you must do so nevertheless. When you refer a student to an administrator or when you talk to parents or guardians, you will need to be able to give the dates.

- Move a chronically tardy student to a seat near the door to minimize disruptions. When you pass out materials and the student is not present, place materials on the desktop to prevent disruption if he or she is late.

- Find out about the backgrounds of chronically tardy students. Their tardiness is often the result of a disorganized family life in which the child has not been taught to be punctual.

- Be consistent in enforcing your procedures in regard to tardiness. If students see that you are not comfortable enforcing your policies, they will not strive to be punctual.

- Whenever you talk with your students about their tardiness, put the responsibility for their behavior where it belongs—on them. Ask tardy students what steps they plan to take to eliminate the problem. Offer support, but remain firm in your expectations.

PROBLEM TWO: ABSENTEEISM

Many factors may contribute to a child's poor attendance. A consistent pattern of poor attendance usually develops from his or her earliest days onward. For instance, when a family is in turmoil, a child finds it difficult to attend school. Frequent illness may also be a factor, especially with the rise in respiratory illness among young students.

Another factor that causes some students to miss school is having a family that does not value education and does not encourage regular attendance. Students who are parents themselves find it almost impossible to overcome the difficulties associated with having a child and attending school. Sometimes older children have to stay home to take care of younger siblings or other family members for various reasons.

Take an active role in encouraging students to attend school regardless of the reason for their absenteeism. Encouraging your students to attend school on a regular basis is one of the most important and most difficult tasks you will face in your career.

Your Responsibilities

- Be aware of the attendance patterns of your students. Find out the reasons for a student's absenteeism so that you can offer assistance.

- When you realize that a student has an attendance problem, do not ignore it. It is up to you to help that student in the most appropriate way.

- Remember that students who feel connected to their school, their classmates, and their teachers rarely miss school without good reason. Encourage regular attendance by building a strong relationship with each of your students. Children should feel that they are missed when they are absent.

- Make your classroom a place where students feel challenged and capable at the same time. If classes are too difficult or are not challenging, a student may feel that there is little reason to attend.

- Let students know that you disapprove of absence without good reason. Contact the parents or guardians of absent students so that everyone involved knows that you believe it is important for every student to attend school.

- Maintain accurate attendance records. It is not always easy to keep up with attendance records, but students and administrators need to have an accurate accounting of attendance throughout the term.

Mistakes to Avoid

- Don't assume that absent students want to miss school.

- Don't ignore attendance problems—it will only encourage students to miss more school.

- Don't make it too difficult for students to make up missing work. Give students the assignments that were missed and a reasonable length of time in which to complete them.

Strategies That Work

- Follow your school district's procedures for reporting and handling attendance, especially if you want to seek assistance for truant students.

- Consider sending a letter home with any student who misses a third day of your class. Keep a copy of the letter as documentation that you have contacted the student's parents or guardians.

- Contact the parents or guardians of students who have excessive absences to ask them to work with you on the problem. Some parents or guardians may request that you contact them any time their child is absent. Try to honor this request whenever you can.

- Encourage students and their parents or guardians to record the days that children miss school on a calendar. Some parents or guardians do not realize just how often their child is out without such a reminder.

- Ask a counselor to speak to students who are having trouble with their attendance so that the students will have a clear picture of their options. Many believe that they can drop out and then pick up a GED certificate later, not realizing how difficult the test for this certificate can be.

- Because some parents or guardians do not value school and do not encourage regular attendance, help parents or guardians of students who have excessive absences understand the importance of regular attendance and the long-term consequences for students who do not attend school.

- Talk to students about their absences. If your students are having family problems or social problems, seek help for them. Have them talk to a guidance counselor to enlist further support for maintaining regular attendance.

PROBLEM THREE: SUBSTANCE ABUSE

Students are barraged with mixed messages about cigarettes, alcohol, and drugs. On television, they see public service announcements warning them that all three substances can be deadly, yet in the same hour, they may watch programs in which substance abuse is taken lightly or, even worse, treated as a cool choice made by grown-ups. It's not surprising that so many confused students appear to be biding their time until they are old enough to experiment with illegal substances.

Many teachers do not have a clear idea about how they can help students resist the lure of drugs and alcohol. They are not sure what to do when students brag about a weekend party or reek of cigarette smoke. Many teachers want to believe that educating students about substance abuse is someone else's job. The problem with this assumption is that many families either are unable to cope with the problem or are themselves the root of the problem.

Your Responsibilities

- Know and follow your district's guidelines on substance abuse by students.

- Involve other adults to help a student as soon as you determine that a problem exists.

- Be a role model and discourage students from experimenting with illegal substances.

- Be a supportive and caring adult who will help students with substance abuse problems.

Mistakes to Avoid

- Don't assume that young students are exempt from the problem because of their age. Even young elementary students can be affected by substance abuse problems.

- Don't ignore substance abuse problems among your students; such problems do not go away by themselves.

- Don't overreact. For example, if a student makes a passing mention of a weekend party, don't lecture or notify a counselor. Instead, speak privately with the student about making sound decisions.

- Don't ignore your school's policies on students with substance abuse problems.

- Don't attempt to handle a serious substance abuse problem without involving other adults. If you have a student with a substance abuse problem, keep in mind the serious nature of the problem and recognize that it needs to be handled with support from all of the adults in a student's life.

- Don't forget that you are a role model. Teachers who talk about the fun they had at college parties do not help students make wise choices for themselves.

Strategies That Work

There are many different things that a caring teacher can do to help students who have problems with substance abuse. Here you will find advice on helping prevent substance abuse as well as on how to intervene if you notice that a student has violated school policies.

Prevention

- Do not feel the need to spend hours of instructional time teaching students about illegal substances. Instead, when the subject arises, be clear about your position on the issue.

- Give your students the facts about substance abuse, thus enabling them to make wiser choices based on real information rather than the opinions of their friends, who may be just as confused as they are.

- Remember that many students, especially younger ones, are simply not aware of the health risks and the social consequences of substance abuse. Make sure that students are aware of these risks as well as the legal penalties for substance abuse.

- Educate yourself about any programs your school district has to help students who are struggling with substance abuse. In addition, the guidance counselors at your school are good sources of information about community resources.

- Make sure that your students understand school policies concerning student use of tobacco, alcohol, and drugs, including the consequences of violating those policies.

Intervention

If you believe that a student has violated your school's policies on substance abuse, you should intervene. Follow these steps:

- Remove the student from class and quietly question him or her to determine whether there is a problem.

- Don't overlook the problem. Immediately and calmly put your school's policies into effect.

- Contact the staff member at your school who is designated to handle substance abuse problems, and explain the issue as you see it. That person will conduct a search, if necessary, and will involve the child's parents or guardians and other appropriate personnel.

- Help the student see you as a supportive and caring person. Students with substance abuse problems need support and assistance, not blame.

PROBLEM FOUR: FIGHTING

Any teacher dreads the signs that a fight is imminent. The potential for serious injury is very real when students set out to hurt each other. And because other students often gather around to encourage the participants, they are also at risk.

After a fight is over, the effects can disrupt classes for the rest of the day, if not longer. Students do not want to settle down, preferring instead to discuss the fight blow by blow. Even worse, a fight often triggers a series of other conflicts as anger and adrenaline run high throughout a school.

In the last few years, there has been a dramatic increase in the number of fights at school as students have brought in conflicts from their various neighborhoods. In recent years, conflicts have been more likely to involve the use of weapons. As an educator, you can do a great deal to reduce violence by taking a proactive stance.

Your Responsibilities

- Follow your school district's procedures for handling student fights.
- Act quickly to prevent fights by reporting student rumors about fights to administrators or security personnel. This is what your school district will expect you to do.
- Stop students from harassing each other in your presence. Encourage them to report incidents of bullying to administrators.
- Keep all of your students as safe as you can when a fight erupts.
- Take reasonable measures to stop fights without putting yourself or others in danger.
- Be prepared to provide an accurate witness report and appear in court.

Mistakes to Avoid

- Do not try to restrain violent students without help from other adults. Teachers who inadvertently hurt students while stopping them from fighting have been sued successfully. Other teachers have been injured themselves.

- Don't leave the fight area. Send students for help instead.

- Don't allow a fight to hinder the rest of the day's instruction. Settle students down quickly. A written assignment usually will focus their attention on their work.

- If you are assigned to hall duty, cafeteria duty, or any other duty, don't miss it. Be on time and be alert. A strong adult presence deters many fights.

Strategies That Work

It is important that you learn as much as you can about the strategies that can help you manage the difficult issue of students fighting at school.

Preventing Fights

- Familiarize your students with your school's policy concerning students who fight at school. Remind them of the severe penalties that they will have to pay for fighting.

- Teach students how to mediate peer conflicts. If your school has a conflict resolution program, refer students who are at risk for violent behavior.

- Make sure that your students are aware of their options in a peer conflict situation. They should not have to fight as a way of resolving problems.

- Be alert to the signs that a fight is building: rumors, a high level of excitement, and remarks about what will happen later.

- If you see that two students are beginning to square off, remind them of the serious penalties for students who fight. Often students will take this as an opportunity to back down without losing face because they can claim that they do not want to be expelled.

- Immediately contact an administrator about a possible fight. Also, contact the parents or guardians of the students who are threatening to fight.

- Make sure that all of your students are aware of the school policy on weapons and how to report weapons to an adult.

- Teach your students about bullying and sexual harassment. Make sure that they understand the limits they should observe when interacting with one another and what they should do if they are bullied or harassed.

- Encourage good behavior by refusing to allow students to insult each other, even in jest. Good-natured insults can quickly generate anger and violence.

- Teach your students that they can be punished for inciting others to fight and for blocking the area so that adults cannot get through to stop a fight.

During a Fight

- Immediately get help from other adults by sending students to fetch them. Do not try to restrain or step between students without another adult present.
- Make the safety of all students at the scene your first concern.
- Be very clear with students who are watching the fight that you want them to leave the area or, if the fight is in your classroom, to sit down.
- Be very careful about how you approach violent students so that no one, including yourself, is injured.

Fights with Weapons

- If you hear a rumor that there is a weapon in the building, contact an administrator at once. You should not attempt to handle this situation by yourself.
- When a weapon is used during a fight, do not allow other students to take it. The weapon may be used as evidence. If you can, confiscate it and turn it over to an administrator.

Fights That Result in Injuries

- Send a student for the school nurse. Deal first with any injured students and then with the other students at the scene. Do not leave the area.
- Assist the more seriously wounded students first. Be careful that the aid you offer does not injure students further.
- Protect yourself and others from contact with blood or other body fluids.
- If you are even slightly injured, seek medical attention promptly.

After a Fight

- As soon as you can, jot down the details of what happened. As a witness to the fight, you may be called on to remember these details in court, sometimes months after the incident, so be as specific as you can when you write your notes.
- If a fight took place while students were under your supervision, contact their parents or guardians so that you can work together to prevent a recurrence.
- Model the calm response you want from your students. Resume teaching immediately, without rehashing the fight or allowing students to do so.

Best Practices Checklist

1. Don't forget that consistent enforcement of classroom and school rules; clear expectations; engaging lessons; and a proactive, confident attitude will prevent many classroom discipline issues.

2. Spend time planning the most effective responses you can have to the specific types of misbehavior that are clearly unacceptable in any school situation.

3. Be aware of the expectations that your supervisors have of teachers at your school when it comes to discipline so that you have a clear idea of how to proceed when misbehavior happens.

4. Remember that responding appropriately instead of just reacting will move you and your students forward.

5. Be aware of your legal responsibilities as a classroom teacher. Consider printing out a list and reviewing it periodically.

6. Don't take student misbehavior personally. Instead, work on cultivating grace under pressure and planning appropriate responses to solve problems.

7. Use self-reflective practices to examine the different ways that you may be contributing to student misbehavior. If you are part of the problem, then you can also be part of the solution.

8. When you have a class that you consider to be a difficult one, take the time to analyze the situation so that you can act appropriately and in a purposeful, deliberate way instead of just reacting.

9. Be patient. Change takes time. Don't forget that any patterns of chronic misbehavior your students exhibit took a long time to develop and can take a long time to change.

10. Take the time to meet with a misbehaving student in a one-on-one conference. This will often help the student learn to control his or her behavior.

Time to Reflect
Manage Discipline Problems

Use the information in this section to guide your thinking as you reflect on these questions. They are designed to encourage you to think more deeply about the issues in the text or to discuss those issues with colleagues.

1. What are your skills in regard to handling students who have misbehaved? What can you improve about how you deal with misbehaving students? How can you capitalize on your strengths? How can you improve any weaknesses in handling misbehavior?

2. Why do students misbehave in your class? Can you notice a pattern or a time when misbehavior is most likely to occur? What can you do to prevent problems from happening? What can your colleagues suggest to help you prevent discipline problems?

3. What plans do you have in place for handling serious student misbehavior, such as fighting? What is your school's policy about teacher intervention in a student

fight? What can you do to keep your students and yourself safe when serious misbehavior erupts?

4. What do your supervisors expect from you in terms of discipline? How strict do they expect you to be? How can you find out what is expected of you? How will you know if you are too strict or too permissive?

5. What attitudes can you adopt to increase your confidence in your ability to cope with discipline issues? How can you improve your ability to manage the discipline concerns in your classroom?

SECTION SEVENTEEN

Learn to Solve Classroom Problems

When you experience problems while working with your students, be comforted by the knowledge that you are not alone. All teachers have to solve problems on a daily basis. Some of the problems we have to solve will be easy to manage. Others may require careful deliberation and consultation with colleagues. Still others will necessitate long-range planning, consistent adherence to the rules and procedures of the classroom, and infinite amounts of patience and humor.

Because you have hundreds of decisions to make at school each day, it is impossible to choose the best one in every situation. And because you work with unpredictable fellow humans under complex circumstances, there will not always be an absolute best choice for many of the perplexing problems you will face.

There are, however, some basic principles that can guide your thinking when you begin planning solutions to school problems:

- Solve the problem instead of punishing the child.
- Follow school rules and policies.
- Make sure that the punishment fits the crime.
- Maintain a positive relationship with each student.
- If your first attempt is not successful, try another one. Then another one . . . as many as it takes.
- Ignore as much as you can.
- Begin with small interventions. Save the office referrals for serious problems.
- Minimize disruptions by maximizing students' time on task.
- When things are not going well, try to see the problem through your students' eyes.

- Think before you act.
- If you are not sure what to do, talk to your colleagues, your mentor, and the administrators at your school.
- Involve parents or guardians while the problem is still small.
- Preserve your students' dignity. In doing so, you'll preserve your own.

In this section, you will find suggestions on how to handle some of the problems you may experience during your first year as a teacher. Because these problems are ubiquitous, there are many suggestions for dealing with each one. Only you can judge which suggestions will work best for your students.

Questions to Consider When You Are Trying to Solve Classroom Problems

As you reflect on the classroom problems that you need to solve, here are questions you can ask yourself to guide your thinking so that it is as productive as possible:

- Who is involved in the problem?
- Who is being harmed by the problem? How?
- What appears to be the underlying cause of the problem?
- What rules, procedures, or policies affect this problem?
- What will happen if I ignore the problem?
- What is the simplest solution to the problem? How workable is this solution?
- How can I treat the students involved in the problem with dignity and respect?
- Where can I find help with this problem?
- How can I enlist my students' support in such a way that they move toward self-discipline?
- What am I doing that may be having a negative impact on the problem?

Take a Problem-Solving Approach

Losing control of your emotions and relying on punishment to effect a change in your students' behavior will not solve discipline problems. What will stop students from misbehaving is a teacher who takes the approach that misbehavior is a problem with a solution.

The first step in adopting a problem-solving approach to misbehavior is to develop a proactive attitude. Refuse to take student misbehavior personally, even though you may be hurt, frustrated, and angry. Refusing to give in to your first emotional reaction will deescalate the situation to a more manageable level.

After you have forced yourself to calm down and control your reactions, you can then complete the rest of the problem-solving process. The following steps will help you not only solve problems but also prevent further ones. To apply these steps in your classroom, use Teacher Worksheet 17.1.

- **Step One**: Define the problem.
- **Step Two**: Gather information about the cause of the problem from the students who misbehaved.
- **Step Three**: Check to make sure that your students understand the pertinent rules, procedures, policies, and consequences.
- **Step Four**: Tell your students that you will need to take some time to make a decision.
- **Step Five**: Generate as many solutions as you can.
- **Step Six**: Ask an administrator, a team member, or a colleague for advice if you are not sure of the right course of action to take.
- **Step Seven**: Decide on the action that will help keep students from repeating their misbehavior.
- **Step Eight**: Decide how you will implement the solution.

In answer to the question, What skills should all teachers have?

- ▶ Patience
- ▶ Knowledge of the subject
- ▶ Patience
- ▶ Kindness
- ▶ A love of young people
- ▶ Patience
- ▶ Flexibility
- ▶ Patience

Luann Scott,
37 years' experience

TEACHER WORKSHEET 17.1
Work Through Classroom Problems

Use the step-by-step process in this worksheet to help clarify your thinking and guide your decision making as you work through the various problems that you may encounter at school.

Step One: What is the problem?

_____

_____

Step Two: According to the students involved, what appears to be the cause of the problem?

_____

_____

Step Three: Which rules, procedures, or policies apply to the situation?

_____

_____

Step Four: When should you talk with your students about the issue?

_____

_____

Step Five: What possible solutions can you suggest?

_____

_____

Step Six: What advice have you received from an administrator, a team member, or a colleague?

_____

_____

Step Seven: Which course of action will help students not repeat their misbehavior?

_____

_____

Step Eight: How will you implement the solution?

_____

_____

From *The First-Year Teacher's Survival Guide, 3rd Edition*, by Julia G. Thompson. Copyright © 2013 by John Wiley & Sons, Inc. Reproduced by permission.

Problems Associated with Individual Students

Although problems will overlap in various ways, the ten classroom problems that follow are ones that mainly affect students as individuals rather than the class as a whole. For all of the problems (here and throughout this section), a scenario is given, along with suggestions for handling that specific scenario as well as dealing with the problem in general.

PROBLEM ONE: CRYING STUDENTS

Although you are not aware of a cause, one of your students is visibly upset and crying.

Suggestions

- Spare the child's already tender feelings by showing your understanding and sympathy instead of becoming impatient.
- Allow the student to leave the room, accompanied by another student if necessary, to regain composure. This will also minimize the potential for additional class disruption.
- Talk to the student to determine the cause. Offer assistance, if appropriate.
- Be careful to work with the student even if the cause is not one you find worthwhile. Being uncaring will not end the tears.
- Contact a parent or guardian about the situation, regardless of the age of the student. There may be more to the matter than you realize.
- If the tears seem to be a chronic condition, seek advice and insight from the child's previous teachers or the school nurse in addition to parents or guardians.
- Show your concern for a student who was upset enough to cry at school by quietly checking with him or her about the incident the next day.

PROBLEM TWO: DISORGANIZED STUDENTS

At the end of class, you notice one of your students stuffing work into a backpack instead of neatly clipping it into a three-ring binder. This student also spends more time than the others at the start of class trying to find pencils, paper, and homework assignments.

Suggestions

- Make a point of checking in with disorganized students every class period to see that items are stowed away in a logical place from which they can be easily retrieved. With frequent checks, the problems with disorganization can stay small.
- Keep the requirements for paper management as simple as possible. For example, ask students to use just one folder or binder for class instead of requiring them to

keep up with several items, such as a binder, a spiral notebook, and folders with pockets.

- Help students develop routines for keeping belongings in good order. These routines should be as simple as possible so that they are easy to follow.

- Know that many students benefit from working with a study buddy so that they can check each other's folders, binders, and book bags before leaving class.

- Although creating methods of organization may seem obvious to you, be explicit in directing your students. For example, say, "Clip this handout into the assessment section of your binder," instead of "Put your papers away."

- Allow enough time at the end of class for students to pack away their belongings neatly.

PROBLEM THREE: STUDENTS EATING IN CLASS

One of your students sneaks food into your classroom as often as possible. A school rule states that students are not to have food in class, but other teachers allow it.

Suggestions

- Enforce the school rule when the situation first occurs—you have little choice but to do this. At the start of the term when you discuss class rules, be sure to tell students that you intend to honor the rule in your classroom.

- If you are uncomfortable with the rule, talk to your mentor or an administrator about how strict you should be about enforcing it. If you are the only teacher in your school who refuses to allow students to have food in class, for example, you will not be perceived as fair.

- There are many reasons for rules about food in class. Before you decide to allow it, consider the maturity of your students. Will it be a distraction? Will it cause a mess? Will students abuse the privilege? If students have food in class, are you promoting the healthy lifestyle you want for them?

- Don't eat in front of your students if they are not allowed to eat in class. It is rude, and you will be perceived as a hypocrite.

PROBLEM FOUR: STUDENTS FEIGNING ILLNESS

One of your students begins complaining that she doesn't feel well, even though you just observed her laughing and chatting with her friends moments earlier.

Suggestions

- Act as if the child is ill. Your role is not to determine whether the child is really ailing. Imagine the consequences if you were to ignore a serious medical issue because you assumed that the student was pretending. Send the child to the clinic.

- Involve the child's parents or guardians and the school nurse as soon as possible after the first instance. If this behavior is repeated, it can become a serious problem.

- As soon as you can, contact the student's parents or guardians to check on the child's well-being. If the child is really ill, you can work with the parents or guardians to manage missing work. If the child is feigning illness, the child's parents or guardians can work with you.

- Do not excuse the child totally from missed assignments; accept them late or schedule a makeup date if necessary.

- Keep in mind that students feign illness for many reasons: to gain sympathy, to get attention, to escape from work, to escape from the consequences of not completing homework, due to boredom, or because of problems at home.

- Take time to determine what is causing the child's stress. What can you do to help with the causes of this behavior?

PROBLEM FIVE: INVISIBLE STUDENTS

You have a student who appears to want to be invisible. Acutely shy and self-conscious, this student never raises a hand to volunteer an answer, seldom speaks to other students, and hurries away at the end of class.

Suggestions

- Be gently considerate in your attempts to communicate with this student. Remarks that may seem casually friendly to you may seem overwhelmingly intrusive to an extremely shy student.

- Make a point of speaking pleasantly to each one of your students every day.

- Seat the student near friendly, sensitive, and courteous students who are similar in temperament although less shy.

- Be aware that often students who appear to want to be invisible do very well when they work in pairs or triads with other students. Small-group work does not seem to overwhelm them as easily as whole-group discussions and activities.

- In class discussions, allow plenty of time for all students to think about their responses before they have to speak. Allow them to write out answers to questions before you call on them to respond.

- Be even more positive and encouraging with a shy student than you normally are with others.

- Do not give up on a very shy student. It may take a while before he or she feels comfortable enough to speak up in front of the large group.

PROBLEM SIX: STUDENTS LYING TO YOU

On the day that an important assigned project is due, several students tell you that they can't turn in their work because their printer was out of ink, there was no printer paper at home, the power went out, the dog ate it, and other obvious lies.

Suggestions

- Strive to see student falsehoods as a problem that you can cope with instead of just reacting to the issue in an emotional way. Remove as much of the negative emotion you may feel at being tricked as you can and redirect your energy in a positive way.

- When you find that a student has lied to you, privately deal with that student. Don't compound the problem by humiliating the student in front of classmates with an angry confrontation.

- Instead of accusing the student directly, ask questions that will lead him or her to admit the truth of the matter. This is especially important and effective with students who have had a momentary lapse of judgment and integrity and who will self-correct when given an opportunity.

- Contact the student's home when necessary. Sometimes it takes a united front to tackle the underlying issues that have encouraged a student to lie.

- Once you and the student have completely worked out the problem, assure the student that the matter is resolved and that you intend for both of you to move forward. Be matter of fact and friendly in your dealings so that this can really happen.

- Be a role model of integrity yourself. This is crucial if you are to be able to tackle the issue successfully.

PROBLEM SEVEN: NEW STUDENTS

It's midyear, and you receive a notice that a new student has just enrolled in your class.

Suggestions

- Make it as easy as possible for new students to adjust to your class and to their new school by keeping in mind that the transition is an extremely stressful one. Let this knowledge guide your decisions about how to help them adjust.

- Be welcoming but not effusive in your greetings. The last thing most new students want is attention called to them. They instead need reassurance that they will fit in at their new school.

- Have your students write short notes of welcome and practical advice and send the notes home with new students at the end of the day.

- Take time to go over the most important policies that new students will need to know right away to avoid embarrassment. In particular, if you teach older students, make sure they know about dress code policies and school rules governing behavior.

- Given that many students fear being lost and going to the wrong classroom by mistake, make sure that new students know how to find their classes.

- Arrange for students to accompany new students to various classes and to the lunchroom. If possible, make sure a new student has a classmate who can act as a friend all day long.

- Don't expect new students to have the school supplies they may need for your class. Provide these supplies until they have had a chance to purchase their own.

PROBLEM EIGHT: STUDENTS PASSING NOTES

Your students persist in passing notes to each other when they should be working on school assignments.

Suggestions

- Keep this problem in perspective. It is not necessarily a negative thing for students to want to write notes to each other.

- Don't take a note from a student; it was not written for you to read.

- Don't read the note. Don't display the note. In addition, think about what you would do with any knowledge you learn from the note. Are you prepared to deal with the intimate details of your students' personal lives?

- Turn an incident of note passing to your advantage by taking a creative approach. Capitalize on students' interest by providing opportunities for them to write to each other. Have a silent class day when everyone must communicate only in writing. Or allow students to write to each other at the start or end of class.

- When you see a student writing a note in class, do not overreact. Just ask the student to put the note away. Move close to the student to make sure the note has been put away. Teacher proximity is usually the best deterrent for a student who wants the contents of a note to remain private.

- If a student refuses to put the note away, remember that the problem is not with the note, but with the child's defiance. See "Problem Twenty-Three: Students Who Are Defiant" later in this section and Section Sixteen for help with handling difficult students.

PROBLEM NINE: STUDENTS FOCUSED ON TOYS, TRINKETS, AND GROOMING

One of your students seems to find new ways to distract herself during every class period. While other students settle down to work, she uses a mirror to apply lip gloss and rummages through the assortment of glitter gel pens in her book bag until she finds just the right color for each assignment, failing to produce the required work.

Suggestions

- Resist the urge to ban all personal belongings. Although it would seem an easy solution to just deny students the right to have distracting items on their desk, this is not as simple as it would appear at first. Many students with attention disorders benefit from small items that allow them to fidget productively and improve their ability to focus. An absolute ban on personal belongings during class may have a negative impact on some students with attention disorders.

- Take time to observe your students carefully to see if they are truly distracted by their belongings so that you can act accordingly. This is an issue that thoughtful teachers need to manage on an individual basis instead of as part of a whole-group policy in many cases.

- Speak privately to students who are more focused on their belongings or grooming than on working productively so that you can make your expectations for their classroom behavior clear.

- When you speak with students, tell them what you observe. Hold them accountable for learning to control their distracted behavior. Instead of demanding compliance, ask these students what their class focus should be. Once you have led students to understand the consequences of their focus on their belongings and grooming instead of on class, then you can work together to solve the problem.

PROBLEM TEN: STUDENTS SLEEPING IN CLASS

Day after day, some of your students have trouble staying awake in class. Other students notice the sleepers and expect you to react.

Suggestions

- Don't let your students miss valuable instructional time. Because sleeping students are not involved in class, they can't learn. For this reason, you must not overlook this passive misbehavior.

- Before you act, determine the cause. Speak to sleepy students in private to find out why they want to sleep. Do they stay up too late at home? Is there a medical problem? Do they have an after-school job that requires long hours? Are they bored with school?

- When you speak with a student about sleeping in class, don't be unpleasant. Instead, decide how to work with the student on the problem.

- If talking to a student does not solve the problem, contact his or her parents or guardians to elicit their support.

- Try not to disrupt the entire class by calling too much public attention to a sleeper.

- Never ask other students to wake up a sleeping classmate. Not only does this interrupt their work but also it puts them in an awkward position.

- When you see that a student is becoming sleepy, allow that child to stand up, move around, or perhaps go to the water fountain.

- Give students a reason to stay awake. When students decide that they cannot succeed in a class, they sometimes choose to sleep rather than be frustrated. Involve these students in activities in which they can be successful and that they will enjoy more than napping through class.

- If you notice that several of your students are tempted to sleep, reconsider the way you are presenting information. Few students can sleep through a lively, active class.

Problems Associated with Enforcing School Policies or Rules

The five problems in this category of classroom issues that you will have to manage all originate from students whose misbehavior goes beyond the boundaries of your classroom to violate a schoolwide rule.

PROBLEM ELEVEN: DRESS CODE VIOLATIONS

While you are monitoring homework in first period, you notice that one of your students is wearing a T-shirt with a message that promotes alcohol consumption. This is a violation of the dress code.

Suggestions

- Make sure that you are familiar with the dress code rules before you try to explain them to your students.

- Be careful not to violate the dress code yourself. It will be impossible for you to enforce it if you are also in violation.

- Make sure that your students understand the rules. If violations seem to be a problem with your students, post the dress code so that they can check it for themselves.

- Always handle dress code issues privately. If students refuse to comply with your requests, enforce your school's policy or send them to the administrator in charge of dress code issues.

- Be alert to gang activity expressed through student clothing. Speak with other staff members to learn about specific gang colors and types of clothing in your area.

- Be careful to preserve your students' dignity when enforcing the dress code. Sometimes students may not have anything else clean to wear. And if students are wearing inappropriate clothes to be defiant, you certainly do not want to give them an audience by attempting to discuss the issue where others can overhear.

PROBLEM TWELVE: STUDENTS MISBEHAVING IN THE HALLWAY

Your colleagues complain that your students are the noisiest class in the entire school when they are in the hallway. You have tried various ways to convince them to walk quietly from class to class, but nothing seems to work for long.

Suggestions

- Be proactive in your approach to this problem. To begin, make sure you know the expectations for hallway behavior at your school.

- Consider adopting the ideas that work for other teachers at your school, thereby presenting a united front to any students who may be confused about what is expected of them.

- Keep in mind that good hallway behavior, just like any other student behavior, requires explicit instructions from you, time for students to practice, and lots of praise for those students who behave well.

- If your students lapse in their good behavior after a while, take the time to calmly reteach the behaviors you expect from them while they are in the hallway.

- Get advice from your colleagues near and far about how to manage lining up students so that they can move through the hallway in an orderly fashion. In addition to consulting the other teachers in your building, you can seek advice online. Because so many teachers struggle with this issue, there is a lot of advice for you on the Internet. Try these two useful sites to learn how to line up your students so that they move quietly in the hallways:
  - **Teacher's Corner** (www.theteacherscorner.net). On the home page, use "lining up strategies" as a search term to read helpful ideas for managing this task from a variety of teachers.
  - **Pro Teacher** (www.proteacher.net). Use "walking in line" as a search term on the home page to access dozens of ideas contributed by experienced teachers.

PROBLEM THIRTEEN: STUDENTS AND PUBLIC DISPLAYS OF AFFECTION

As you greet students at the start of class, two students block the hallway with their fond farewells.

Suggestions

- Don't make the situation more troublesome by calling attention to the two students, lecturing them, embarrassing them, or mentioning their behavior in front of other students. Instead, talk calmly and privately to them about it.

- When you discuss the situation with the two students, consider using these strategies:
  - Your school probably has a policy on public displays of affection. Discuss it with them so that they will understand that you have not singled them out but are enforcing a school policy instead.
  - Sometimes students are just not sure how to express their affection in public. Be careful to explain which hallway behaviors are acceptable and which ones are not.
- If a conference with the two students does not change their behavior, contact their parents or guardians.

PROBLEM FOURTEEN: STUDENTS SEXTING

One of your students confides in you that she feels pressured to respond to a sexually suggestive text she has received from a boy in your class.

Suggestions

- Begin by educating yourself about the problem. Sexting is a widespread and extremely harmful trend among students who have access to electronic devices, such as computers and cell phones. Sexting is not just the transmission of sexually explicit photos as many suppose—it can also include text messages, social network messages, and e-mails.
- Make sure that you are familiar with your school district's policies on sexting and are aware of the steps that are required of you. Most school districts have very clear policies about how sexting should be handled.
- When you learn of a sexting incident, remain calm and follow your district's policies about how to handle the matter.
- Contact an administrator immediately to report the incident—this is your responsibility as an educator. The school administrator will report the offense to the local police.
- Do not confiscate the cell phone or device. That should only be done by an administrator or the police. Make every effort to protect yourself from criminal charges by refusing to read the message or look at any images, as they could constitute child pornography. Take care. School officials have lost their jobs by mishandling incidents of student sexting.
- For more information about sexting and how to prevent it among your students, use "sexting" as a search term on the home page of Wired Safety (www.wiredsafety.org). This national organization provides excellent information on a variety of tech safety topics.

PROBLEM FIFTEEN: STUDENTS COMMITTING THEFT

You leave the money you collected for a class trip on your desk for just a few moments while you help a student at the front of the room. When you return to your desk, you realize that the money has been stolen.

Suggestions

The suggestions for dealing with students who commit theft in your class fall into two categories: how to prevent theft and how to manage the situation once a theft has occurred.

Prevention

- Be aggressive in preventing theft. Don't leave your personal belongings in the open or on your desk. Many teachers do not carry very much cash at school and leave their credit cards at home.

- Be very careful about how you handle money you collect from your students. To avoid problems, deposit it as quickly as you can.

- Remind your students that they can prevent theft by taking good care of items that are attractive to thieves: calculators, headphones, pens, money, jewelry, electronic devices, hats, books, notes, and yearbooks.

- Always lock your classroom on leaving, and never give your keys to students. Discourage students from taking items from your personal space at school.

Dealing with a Theft

- If the stolen item belongs to you, don't threaten your students. Instead, offer a small reward for its safe return. Promise to ask no questions, and honor that promise. If the item is not returned, you may want to alert other teachers about what has happened so that they also can be on the lookout for it.

- If the stolen item belongs to a student, remain calm and follow these steps:
  - Don't use the words *steal* or *theft* because they make it difficult for students to come forward with information.
  - In a matter-of-fact manner, ask that anyone who may have picked up the item by mistake return it. Don't expect students to tell on each other, and don't expect a student to confess in front of the class.
  - Don't accuse students or continue to talk about the situation. Try to maintain as normal a class atmosphere as you can to minimize the disruption.
  - If no one returns the item, notify an administrator. Your students may need to be detained, and an administrator's help is necessary for this.

- When you catch a student stealing, keep that information as private as possible. You will have to involve an administrator and the student's parents or guardians, but try to preserve the student's dignity.

Problems Associated with Behavior During Instruction

The problems in the paragraphs that follow are ones that are most often associated with issues involving student behavior during instruction.

PROBLEM SIXTEEN: ABSENCES ON THE DAY OF AN ASSESSMENT

One of your students is frequently absent on the day of a test. According to your school's policy, students can make up missed tests without penalty if they bring in a note from home excusing the absence. Your student always has a note from home, even though it appears that the absences only happen on test days.

Suggestions

- Talk to the student to determine the cause of the problem. Show that you are concerned, but don't be so aggressive in your questioning that you back a student who already appears to be anxious about school into a corner.

- Make sure that the student understands how to prepare for tests in your class. Offer to provide extra help as the student reviews for tests.

- If possible, avoid using class time for the student to make up the missed test. Arrange for that student to meet with you before school or after school instead of missing more class.

- Assume that other students have shared details of the original test with the student who was absent and make up another test for him or her. Try to ensure that the new test is neither easier or harder than the original one.

- Contact parents or guardians if the situation appears to be chronic. Offer to help the student prepare in advance of the day of the test and encourage them to help the student feel confident about the test.

PROBLEM SEVENTEEN: BACKPACK PROBLEMS IN AND OUT OF CLASS

Your school does not have a policy concerning student backpacks. Your students carry around all of their school belongings in backpacks that sometimes seem to weigh more than they do, and their crammed backpacks block the aisles in your class.

Suggestions

This is a problem with parts that you must handle separately. First, deal with the weight of the backpacks. Then, tackle the issue of the obstructions and disruptions in your class.

Backpack Weight

- Collaborate with other teachers. When you speak with colleagues, consider staggering homework deadlines so that students can leave some of their belongings in their locker, in the classroom, or at home.

- Talk to your students to let them know how concerned you are about their health and their stress level. Ask for their suggestions on how to solve the problem.

- Consider involving parents and guardians in finding solutions.

- Find out why students feel the need to carry so much. Do they need more time to go to their locker? Do they need advice on how to manage their materials? A quick survey should yield some useful information.

Obstructions in Your Class

- When students have backpacks in class, expect them each to place their backpack under their desk or as close to them as possible to leave a safe aisle for everyone who moves around the classroom.

- Working together with students on the problem will increase the likelihood of successful resolution. If they are involved in creating the solution, students will be able to police themselves and each other.

PROBLEM EIGHTEEN: AN EMERGENCY DRILL INTERRUPTING AN ASSESSMENT

You have just handed out quiz papers to your students when the bell signaling a fire drill rings.

Suggestions

- If your students are taking a test or a quiz during an evacuation, expect that the integrity of the test or quiz has been compromised. Your students will have an opportunity to share answers during the drill. Either disregard the objective portions or allow students to use the assessment as a study guide for a retest during the next class period. You should make up a new test or quiz.

- If your students are writing essays or otherwise working on creative projects or work that is subjective rather than objective, consider allowing them to continue if you believe that sharing answers will not affect the outcome of the assessment.

- Report the interruption as a test irregularity if a drill interrupts a standardized test. Your school's testing coordinator and administrators will make the decisions about how to proceed for the entire group of students who were interrupted by the evacuation.

PROBLEM NINETEEN: EXCESSIVE NOISE DURING CLASS

Your class is too loud! You sometimes have to shout to be heard. When your students work productively in groups, you don't mind the noise as much as when your students are engaged in personal conversations and off-task activities.

Suggestions

- Never talk over noise or shout to be heard in your classroom.

- Don't allow noise to get out of control. Once students are very loud, you will have to take extreme measures to get them to stop being noisy. You'll find it easier if you begin to control noise levels as soon as class begins.

- Don't try to assume control of a noisy class without enlisting the cooperation of your students. Ask for suggestions from your students about how to manage noise.

- Make it clear that some noisy activities are just not acceptable. Teach your students that it is never acceptable to talk during a movie, talk when you are giving instructions or lecturing, shout at any time, talk during a test or other quiet activity, or talk across the room to classmates.

- When you plan activities that have the potential to be noisy, consider moving to a part of the building where you can't disturb other classes.

- Don't plan group activities without teaching students how to control the noise level of their group. One way to do this is by using distances as noise measurements. For example, students should find a one-foot voice useful for working in pairs and a three-foot voice useful for working in groups. When you give directions for an assignment, tell students the acceptable noise level for the activity.

- Model the noise level that you want from your students. If you speak softly, your students will follow your lead. If you shout, you will dramatically increase the noise level in your class because students will see this as permission for them to shout, too.

- Be consistent in enforcing the noise levels that you expect from your students. Set reasonable limits and stick to them so that students will learn to manage their own noise.

PROBLEM TWENTY: NO NAMES ON PAPERS

While you are recording the grades for a set of quiz papers, you notice that three of them do not have students' names on them. As you scrutinize the handwriting for clues, you realize that although you know the three students without recorded grades, you can't match the papers to their owners.

Suggestions

- Put a few highlighters near the area where students will turn in their paper. Place a sign there reminding students to lightly highlight their name before they turn in their work.

- Consider having study buddies check over each other's homework and classwork assignments, looking for the correct heading, a missing name, and other such small errors before they turn them in to you.

- If your class is small enough, provide permanent folders or envelopes for each student to use to turn in papers. Instead of all students using the same bin to turn in papers, each one would place completed work in his or her own folder.

- Make it a policy in your class that the first thing students write on their papers is their name. You can post reminders in conspicuous places as well as remind them verbally.

- When you give written directions for an assignment, include a directive to students to place their name on their paper.

- If you have a paper with no name on it, clip it to the board so that students who do not receive returned graded papers have a place to check for missing work.

PROBLEM TWENTY-ONE: RESTLESS STUDENTS DURING VIDEO VIEWING

You show a video that other teachers have recommended, but only a few of your students watch. Most are bored and restless.

Suggestions

- Always preview a video that you are going to show to make sure it fits the needs of your students. While you are watching, create a worksheet for students to complete as they watch. You can also plan the points at which you will stop the video for discussion.

- Talk to your students in advance about the courteous and attentive behaviors you will expect from them while they watch the video.

- Make sure that every student can see. Allow time for students to move chairs if they need to.

- Don't make the room too dark. You should avoid glare, but total darkness will make it impossible for your students to do their assignment.

- Plan a closing activity for your students in which you hold them accountable for what they should have learned during the video and during any discussions.

PROBLEM TWENTY-TWO: STUDENTS WHO DO THEIR WORK AND THEN LEAVE IT AT HOME

During a conference about a student's poor academic progress, the puzzled parents insist that their child completes the homework that you assign but then repeatedly leaves it at home.

Suggestions

- Do not rush to judgment. Many students with learning disabilities struggle not just with completing their homework but also with turning it in.

- Know that there are several different options that you can offer to make sure that students turn in the work they complete at home. Consider which of the suggestions in the list that follows would be most appropriate for your students.
  - Accept an electronic version of the work if the parents or guardians are willing to scan and send it for younger students or if older students will e-mail it to you. You could always accept a hard copy of the work later.
  - Send a checklist home so that students and their parents or guardians know exactly what work needs to be completed and returned. You could do this either electronically or on paper.
  - Consider asking parents or guardians to contact you via e-mail at night to confirm that the homework has been completed and packed into the proper binder and book bag to be turned in.
  - Be willing to think outside the box. For example, you can create a daily routine whereby the student turns in homework as soon as he or she arrives at school instead of waiting until class begins.

Problems Associated with Students' Relationship with Their Teacher

The problems in this list are ones that arise in the relationship between a teacher and students. These are not the only problems that can manifest, but they represent three common ways that students can interact negatively with a teacher.

PROBLEM TWENTY-THREE: STUDENTS WHO ARE DEFIANT

One of your students has made a mess while working on a project in class. When you ask that the mess be cleaned up, your student refuses, saying, "Why should I?"

Suggestions

- Absolutely refuse to reply to a defiant student in a rude way. Silence is better than a sarcastic retort or insisting on compliance. Do not argue or raise your voice. Stay calm and remain in control of your own emotions.

- As a first approach, try looking surprised and saying that you thought you heard wrong. This gives the student a chance to back down. If this happens, just carry on with class. Later on, meet quietly with the student and discuss the situation.

- Act decisively if the student has been defiant in front of the rest of the class. If necessary, remove the student from the room. Do not simply throw the student out of class, however. Arrange for the student to go to another classroom, a counselor, or an administrator if the situation warrants it.

- As another approach, try talking quietly and privately with the student. Begin by asking the student to tell you what is wrong and offering your help. A confrontation will only make things worse. Adopting a problem-solving approach instead of a punitive one will move the situation forward to a resolution.

- If the situation persists, involve the student's parents or guardians and an administrator. Meet with them and the student to work out a plan to solve the problem.

- Continue to work on your relationship with a defiant student. A positive relationship with this student will go far in preventing potential conflicts.

PROBLEM TWENTY-FOUR: CLASSROOM POWER STRUGGLES

One of your students seems to want to dominate every class. Although not openly rude or oppositional, this student constantly interrupts instruction with a steady flow of attention-seeking comments.

Suggestions

- To avoid power struggles with students, know when to intercede to keep a student's misbehavior as nondisruptive as possible. It is far easier to prevent a student from misbehaving than to have to deal with a full-blown power struggle. Try these guidelines to know when to act:
  - If a behavior is limited to one student, try to ignore it as much as you can.
  - If a behavior is brief in duration, try to ignore it.
  - If a behavior is distracting other students, it's time to act.

- Be as overwhelmingly positive with your class leaders as you can to avoid setting yourself up in opposition to them. Reinforcing their positive behaviors is the best strategy you can implement with students who want to engage you in a power struggle.

- Because they obviously want to lead, give power-hungry leaders plenty of opportunities to assume positive leadership roles in the class.

- Avoid sarcasm or discourteous responses when dealing with students who want to dominate the class. You will only appear foolish as the rest of the students immediately take sides sympathetically with their classmate.

- Take a sensible, long-range approach to the problem. You won't be able to win over every student, despite your obvious sincerity and very best efforts. It is unrealistic to expect otherwise.

PROBLEM TWENTY-FIVE: STUDENTS WHO TALK BACK

You tell a student who has not yet turned in a test paper that the time for the test is over and that you must have all papers. The student becomes belligerent and loudly tells the class that you don't know anything about teaching.

Suggestions

- Although it is natural that you would have something to say in your own defense, resist the temptation to argue with or reprimand the child in front of the class.

- Ask the student to step into the hall for a private conference when you are calm enough to manage the situation well. Talk with the student about the effects of disrespect on you and on the rest of the class. Take a problem-solving approach to the situation instead of escalating the confrontation and ill will.

- Make an agreement with students who feel the need to talk back; tell them that you want to hear what they have to say and are willing to listen but that they need to speak to you privately and respectfully. When you take this friendly attitude, you offer students a chance to approach you in a positive manner, a way to deal with frustrations, and an opportunity to learn how to resolve conflicts respectfully.

> Have a sense of humor. The most unexpected things are going to happen in your classroom. The key is how you react to them.
>
> *Kathleen Stankiewicz,*
> *10 years' experience*

Best Practices Checklist

1. Use reflective teaching practices and a problem-solving approach to work through the classroom problems you have to manage.

2. Adopt a deliberate approach to solving the classroom problems you will encounter on a daily basis. Think carefully before you act.

3. Don't hesitate to seek advice from other professionals when you need to find solutions to problems in your class. You can do this online through professional learning networks as well as in person at your school.

4. When things are not going well, consider your students' viewpoint. Be empathetic when you can. The chances are that they do not see things the way you do.

5. Remember that a positive relationship with each student will make it easier for you to prevent or manage classroom problems successfully. Work on your relationships with your students and discipline issues will often abate.

6. Make sure that the decisions you make to solve problems in your class are ones that will help your students move toward becoming self-disciplined learners rather than provide a temporary fix.

7. Don't be afraid to be creative in devising solutions to problems. When you use the problem-solving process, brainstorm as many solutions as you can to begin seeking solutions.

8. As often as you can, involve your students in creating solutions to classroom problems. Their insights will often allow you to have a fresh perspective.

9. Keep students busy learning interesting and worthwhile subject matter, leaving them little time to cause problems that will require solutions.

10. Don't forget that some problems will take longer than others to solve. Be patient and persistent.

Time to Reflect
Learn to Solve Classroom Problems

Use the information in this section to guide your thinking as you reflect on these questions. They are designed to encourage you to think more deeply about the issues in the text or to discuss those issues with colleagues.

1. What attitudes can you develop that will make managing problems a challenging opportunity for growth instead of a hassle?

2. How well do your students handle disruptions to the entire class, such as assemblies and fire drills? How can you manage these better?

3. What are some mistakes about discipline that you are determined to avoid? How can you make sure that you will be able to avoid them?

4. What is the best way to handle various problems with dishonesty in your classroom? What do your students tend to be dishonest about?

5. When are your students most likely to be defiant or disrespectful? How can you prevent this? What suggestions do your colleagues have about how to deal with this problem?

A Final Word

As you stand in front of your new class for the first time, you will probably have a panicky moment when you wonder how you will ever be able to manage all that you are supposed to do. Almost every teacher feels that way. Looking out at those expectant faces will fill you with a sense of awe at the seemingly impossible responsibilities that you have assumed. As a first-year teacher, you will find that you will experience many stressful moments. And you will also find that it is really a lot of fun to do the impossible—at the end of the school year, your students will be skilled, knowledgeable, and prepared for the future.

As you read through this survival guide, you probably noticed the bits of classroom wisdom from both veteran and first-year teachers. A love of teaching shines in their words, but there is also the acknowledgment of just how impossible our profession can seem to be. During your first year, when you feel overwhelmed by all of the impossible things you are asked to do, keep these three final ideas in mind:

- You are not alone! Reach out. There are lots of other teachers who feel the same way you do. Ask for help. Connect with them at your school as well as online. Let others show you the way to be the kind of teacher you want to become.

- Work with the future in mind. No matter what petty concerns may bug you in the present, the future is what is important. Be clear about your goals for your students and for yourself. Move forward.

- Never doubt that what you do is important. To some of your students, you may be the only thing that stands between them and a lifetime of poverty and misery. As a teacher, you do make a difference, and you will change lives.

Enjoy your school year! This is an exciting time for you and for your students! You will find much to make you laugh in your classroom—and much to make you glad you chose a career path as rewarding as being a classroom teacher.

Index

A

A to Z Teacher Stuff Web site, 93, 298

Abcteach Web site, 37

About.com Freebies Web site, 37

Absenteeism: on the day of an assessment, 497; mistakes to avoid when trying to manage, 475; strategies that work to manage, 475–476; understanding factors involved in, 474–476; your responsibilities regarding student, 475. *See also* Attendance; Truancy

Accommodations (504 Plan), 348

Action research: used to inform classroom decisions, 6–7; proven techniques for successful, 7

Active learning: definition and applications of, 261; differentiated instruction use of, 336

Activities: anchor, 341; used as backup plans, 297–298; for before, during, and after reading assignments, 419–424; daily plans inclusion of, 292; for differentiated classrooms, 342–345; eight-minute closing exercise, 196; first day, 115–116; introductory or warm-up, 184–185; puzzle, 298, 327, 344, 411; safety issues of, 456; "story of the day," 155; for teaching vocabulary skills, 409–410, 411–412; team-building, 160–162; tips on planning lesson, 296; unit planning by brainstorming and selection of possible, 289. *See also* Games; *specific activity*

Adaptive technologies, 157

Administrators: discipline management expectations by, 451; how to respond when you disagree with discipline action by, 471; making student referral and maintaining credibility with, 470–471; strategies for positive working relationships with, 83–84; student referrals to an, 469–471; successful collaboration with, 83–84. *See also* School community; Schools

Advanced student tiered instruction, 340–341. *See also* Gifted students

Agendas activity, 343

AllThingsPLC Web site, 75

Alphabet boxes, 342

American Federation of Teachers (AFT), 28

American Rhetoric Web site, 185

Anchor activities, 341

Animoto Web site, 273

Anxiety: over classroom management, 448; proactive strategies to control your, 448–449

Apps, 274–275

Are You a Good Role Model? worksheet, 149

Are You in Charge of Your Career? worksheet, 26

Artifact boxes activity, 343

Assessments: absences on the day of an, 497; Best Practices Checklist for, 399; daily plans inclusion of, 292; emergency drill interrupting an, 498–499; expect student challenges to grades given their, 393; grading form of, 50–55, 270, 281, 381, 386–393; interactive response systems, 385–386; journals and learning logs, 385; no names on papers used for, 499–500; open-ended questions used as, 384; performance, 385; Progress Tracking Chart worksheet for, 243; rubrics, 270, 386–388; standardized tests, 8, 20–21, 395–398; tests and quizzes forms of, 377–383, 498–499; types of authentic, 383–384; value-added, 20–21; variations on traditional tests used for, 385. *See also* Evaluation; Feedback; Formative assessments; Summative assessments

Assignment Checklist worksheet, 237

Assignment Reflection worksheet, 376

Assignments: activities for before, during, and after reading an, 419–424; Assignment Checklist worksheet, 237; chronic underachievement and, 353; chunking, 343; creating unit plans and, 289; daily plans inclusion of, 292; Format for a Unit Plan worksheet on, 290; interactive whiteboards for class editing of, 269; making sure students understand the purpose of each, 236; motivating students by offering in-depth, 225; motivating students with unusual and enjoyable, 229–230; problem of no name on, 499–500; problem of students who forget to turn in their, 501; strategies for making success attainable, 231–232. *See also* Directions; Homework assignments; Student work

Association for Middle Level Education (AMLE), 28

Association for Supervision and Curriculum Development, 28

At-risk students: description of, 348; factors contributing to, 348–349; online resources to understand, 350

Attendance: on the day of an assessment, 497; by teachers, 81. *See also* Absenteeism

Attention: command your audience's, 308–309; focused on your audience, 307–308; help students stay on track during lecture, 311–312; using toys to capture, 314–315

Attention deficit disorder (ADD), 346–347, 348

Attention deficit/hyperactivity disorder (ADHD), 346–347, 348

Audacity Web site, 273

Audience: body language to motivate your, 309–310; maintain eye contact with your, 306, 310; pay attention to your, 307–308; strategies to command attention from your, 308–309

Audio materials, 343

Auditory modes of learning, 347

Authentic assessments: description and purpose of, 383; examples of different types of, 383–384; how to decide if applicable to your students, 384

Autism Society Web site, 356

Autism spectrum disorders (ASD): resources on, 356; strategies for working with students with, 356–357; understanding issues related to, 355–356

B

Backpack problems, 497–498

Backup plans: benefits of always having a, 180, 196; strategies and activities to use as, 296–298

Backward design, 280

Ball Toss game, 161, 317

Balloon games, 161

Baseline data: description and purpose of, 370; strategies for gathering, 370

Basic skills: Best Practices Checklist on teaching, 424–425; Checklist of Social Skills All Students Should Master worksheet, 167; critical thinking, 412–417; importance of teaching, 401; listening, 94, 231, 404; media literacy, 402–403; note taking, 232, 271; reading, 417–424; reflections on teaching, 425–426; speaking, 405–406; test taking, 396–397; vocabulary acquisition, 407–412; writing, 406–407. *See also* Students

Behavior Advisor Web site, 441

Behavior Incident Report worksheet, 458

Behaviors. *See* Student behaviors; Student misbehaviors

Behaviour Needs Web site, 441

Best Practices Checklist: for assessing your students' progress, 399; for class time control, 199–200; for classroom management, 70–71, 219; for collaboration, 104; for differentiated instruction, 362–363; for discipline problem management, 480–481; for engaging instruction delivery, 328; for instruction and lesson planning and design, 300; for instructional strategies and technologies, 275–276; for motivating students, 257; for positive classroom relationships, 173; for preventing discipline problems, 444; for solving classroom problems, 503–504; for starting a successful school term, 135–136; for teaching basic skills, 424–425; for understanding how to be a twenty-first-century educator, 12–13. *See also* Teaching skills

Bingo, 317

B.J.'s Homework Helper Web site, 253

Blended learning instruction, 264

Block Posters Web site, 37

Blogs: as instructional tool, 271–272; interactive whiteboards to display, 270; photoblog type of, 271

Board games, 316

Boardgames.com, 318

Body language: maintain eye contact during presentations, 306, 310; maintain eye contact while monitoring students, 439; motivating your listeners through, 309–310

Bordessa, Kris, 161

Botbohm, Ellen, 356

Brain Bashers Web site, 185

BrainCurls Web site, 190

Bulletin boards: connecting with your students by using, 63; display of trash can and words you don't want used by students, 172; online resources for ideas on using, 63

Bullying: cyber bullying, 168, 170–171; of gay and lesbian students, 350, 351; making a referral for, 469–471; "mean girls" form of, 171; mistakes to avoid regarding, 168–169; name calling form of, 171–172; refuse to allow any form of, 363; taking a stand against, 68; teacher responsibilities related to, 168; teaching your students about, 479; what to do after an incident occurs, 169–170; what to do before an incident occurs, 169; when to seek professional help for, 156. *See also* Peer conflicts

Byrne, Richard, 274

C

Calendars, 36

Cambron-McCabe, Nelda H., 455

Carroll, Dawn: on addressing low reading levels of students, 417; on avoiding effects of negativity, 80; on having a backup plan, 297; on letting students know that you care, 151; on teaching students content vocabulary, 408

Case studies activity, 343

Cause-and-effect maps, 320

Cell phones: used as instructional tool, 268; strategies for using, 268–269

Center for Media Literacy Web site, 403

Chain Making game, 317

Chain of command, 82–83

Chalk talks activity, 343

Characteristics of Successful Teachers worksheet, 12

Charismatic teachers, 303–304

Cheating: how to manage cyber, 393–394; making referrals because of student, 470–471; as unacceptable behavior, 450; what to do when you suspect, 393. *See also* Dishonesty

Checklist for the First Day worksheet, 119

Checklist of a Teacher's Weekly Reminders worksheet, 49

Checklist of Social Skills All Students Should Master worksheet, 167

Checklist to Determine If Your Rules Will Be Successful worksheet, 215

Child abuse reporting, 456

Childhood obesity epidemic, 228

Choice boards, 342

Chronic misbehavior, 465

Chronic underachievement: description and factors of, 352; strategies for helping students to overcome, 353–354

Chunking assignments, 343

Class closing time: eight-minute closing exercise, 196; implement the two-minute dismissal, 197; Plans for Ending Class Effectively worksheet, 198; productive use of any time left at end of class, 199

Class discussions: conducting engaging, 312–314; have students reflect on, 314; including opportunities for, 225, 226; what to do before, 313; what to do during, 313–314

Class Log Page worksheet, 256

Class newsletters: description and functions of, 96; items to include in, 96–97

Class opening time: giving directions at the start of class, 212; greet each student as they enter class, 183; have students go immediately to their seats, 183–184; introductory or warm-up activity, 184–185; Plans for Starting Class Effectively worksheet, 186

Class time control: Best Practices Checklist for, 199–200; classroom time management, 179–180; the first ten minutes of class, 183–187; giving directions at start of class, 212; handling interruptions, 181–182; handling student requests to leave the classroom, 191–196; how teachers waste time, 176; how to use any time left at end of class, 199; How Well Do You Use Class Time? worksheet, 177–178; importance of, 175–176; the last ten minutes of class, 196–199; pacing instruction, 182–183; Plans for Ending Class Effectively worksheet, 198; Plans for Starting Class Effectively worksheet, 186; productive transitions used for, 187–190; raising students' awareness of class time, 180–181; reflections on your, 200. *See also* Time management

Class web page: benefits of having a, 57; online resources for creating, 58; suggestions for maintaining your, 57–58

Classroom areas: bulletin boards, 63, 172; class business, 62; for enrichment and remediation materials, 62–63; for motivating students, 62; shared supplies bank, 211, 355; take and display student photographs in, 153; for tracking progress, 62

Classroom charisma, 303–304

Classroom community building: as first-day priority for starting, 111; preventing discipline problems through, 442; removing barriers to peer acceptance and, 157–159; shared experiences and shared tasks for, 159–160; teaching and practicing courtesy to contribute to, 152, 164–165; technology used to promote, 160

Classroom environment: build a supportive class chemistry and, 157; collaborating with parents/guardians to create safe, 457; controlling negative peer pressure, 172–173; creating a bully-free, 168–171; how technology can promote a supportive, 160; "least restrictive environment" mandate of Public Law 94-142, 359; making it a risk-free, 162–163; managing name calling, 171–172; mixing collaborative and competitive activities as part of, 226; motivating students through a positive, 225; removing barriers to peer acceptance as part of, 157–159; resolving peer conflicts to build positive, 165–166; teaching and practicing courtesy to create positive, 164–165

Classroom immediacy: description of, 143; strategies for lessening emotional distance through, 143–146

Classroom management: arrange your own work area, 35–40; benefits of a well-managed classroom, 201–202; Best Practices Checklist for, 70–71, 219; Checklist of a Teacher's Weekly Reminders worksheet, 49; differentiated, 341–345; of difficult class, 463–464; the dos

Classroom management (*cont'd*) and don'ts of your school computer, 41–42; for fire, disaster, and intruder drills, 69; how to focus your class on good behavior, 202–203; how to maintain class web page, 57–58; how to maximize your time while at school, 45–49; how to save paper, 58; importance of clear expectations for, 203; Meet Your Classroom Priorities worksheet, 44; optimizing use of photocopier, 59; organize and manage student information and grading, 53–55; organizing your paper file storage, 40–41; preparing your classroom for students, 59–69; prioritizing tasks, 42–44; proactive strategies to control your anxiety over, 448–449; reflections on your, 71; rules for, 203–204, 212–218; student health concerns, 69–70; Teacher's Daily To-Do List worksheet, 47–48; teacher's legal responsibilities for discipline and, 455–457; what documents to keep and what to discard, 52–53. *See also* Discipline

Classroom Management Techniques to Avoid worksheet, 454

Classroom management tips: for managing e-mail, 56–57; for managing electronic files, 56; for managing school papers, 50–52

Classroom observation: How Observers Will Evaluate You worksheet, 19; improving your teaching skills through process of, 17; preparing for a, 17–18; turning criticism into positive experience, 20

Classroom policies: establishing your, 204; homework, 247, 254–255; Planning for Classroom Policies worksheet, 205–208; when to apply procedures, rules, and, 203–204. *See also* School policy problems

Classroom power struggles, 502–503

Classroom preparation: checklist for the start of school, 59–61; making classroom inviting on a budget, 61–63; seating arrangements, 64–66, 70; traffic flow considerations, 63–64

Classroom problem behaviors: crying students, 487; disorganized students, 487–488; invisible students, 489; new students, 490–491; students eating in class, 488; students feigning illness, 488–489; students focused on toys, trinkets, and grooming, 491–492; students lying to you, 490; students passing notes, 491; students sleeping in class, 492–493

Classroom problem solving: as approach to managing misbehavior, 484–486; basic principles for, 483–484; Best Practices Checklist for, 503–504; questions to consider when, 484; reflections on your, 504; Work Through Classroom Problems worksheet for, 486

Classroom problems: associated with behavior during instruction, 497–501; associated with enforcing school policies or rules, 493–497; associated with individual students, 487–493; associated with students' relationship with their teacher, 501–503; taking problem-solving approach to misbehaviors and, 484–485; understanding that everyone experiences, 483; Work Through Classroom Problems worksheet to work on, 486. *See also* Problems; Student misbehaviors

Classroom procedures: creating structure for students through, 304; establishing, 209; giving directions at the start of class, 212; passing out papers at the start of a lesson, 211–212; setting up a shared supplies bank, 211; for students with ADD or ADHD, 347; when to apply policies, rules, and, 203–204;

Where to Find Help with Establishing Procedures worksheet, 210

Classroom relationships: becoming a culturally responsive educator, 154–156; being a role model to students, 147–149, 203, 224, 350; Best Practices Checklist on, 173; Checklist of Social Skills All Students Should Master worksheet, 167; developing a positive relationship with students, 139–147; help students learn to relate well to each other, 157; how technology can promote a supportive class, 160; knowing how much of yourself to share with students, 150–151; letting your students know you care, 151–153; the limits of your responsibility to your students, 156–157; name calling and, 171–172; negative peer pressure and, 172–173; peer tutoring and, 163–164; the problem with being a popular teacher, 151; promoting trust, 153; protecting students from bullies, 168–171; reflections on developing positive, 174; removing barriers to peer acceptance, 157–159; resolving peer conflicts to enhance, 165–166; shared experiences and shared tasks to establish community, 159–160; supportive class chemistry for, 157; teaching courtesy to build, 164–165; teaching your students to believe in themselves, 153–154; team-building activities for the entire year, 160–162. *See also* Teacher-student relationships

Classroom routines: conduct rules for quizzes and tests, 381–382; preventing discipline problems through consistent, 442, 462; as time management strategy, 179; type of documents related to, 51

Classroom rules: Checklist to Determine If Your Rules Will Be Successful worksheet, 215; conduct rules for quizzes and tests, 381–382; creating, 213–214;

educational purpose and common sense basis of, 455; enforcing, 217–218; enlisting student support for, 218; positive versus negative consequences for breaking, 218; teach and enforce school rules, 212–213; teaching, 216–217; when to apply procedures, policies , and, 203–204. *See also* Behaviors; Discipline

Classroom seating arrangements: benefits of assigned seating, 70; creating seating charts, 65–66; issues to consider for creating the best, 64; three different types of, 64–65

Classroom Tripod Web site, 58

Classrooms: benefits of a well-managed, 201–202; building supportive class chemistry in, 157; characteristics of well-disciplined, 449; create a positive group identity in your, 133–135; creating a high performance culture in, 5–6; the differentiated, 341–342; ensuring safety in your, 66, 67–69; excessive noise during class, 499; handling student requests to leave the, 191–196; making it rich in vocabulary words, 409–410; preparing your, 59–60; preventing miscommunication with a transparent, 86–89; students eating in, 488; teacher withitness about their own, 436–437; traffic flow considerations of, 63–64

Clickers activity, 343

Coalition of Essential Schools, 28

Collaboration: with administrators, 83–84; Best Practices Checklist for, 104; chain of command issues for, 82–83; with difficult colleagues, 79–80; DVD on strategies for, 103; how to handle professional disagreements during, 78; with parents and guardians, 84–103; reflections on, 104–105; with special education teachers, 361–362; strategies for effective, 77; with the support staff, 82; what your coworkers

expect from you during, 78–79. *See also* Student collaboration; Teachers

Colleagues: managing e-mail from, 56–57; mentors from among your, 13–16; treating staff members as, 82; what they expect from you during collaboration, 78–79; working well with difficult, 79–80. *See also* Staff

Colored dot labels: description of, 326; suggestions on how to adapt for your classroom, 326

Common Core State Standards Initiative (CCSSI): how they will impact your instructional planning, 284; online resources for learning more about, 284–285; origins and scope of the, 283

Common Core State Standards Initiative Web site, 284–285

Communication: be a good listener for good, 94; be positive with parent or guardian, 92–93; class newsletters, 96–97; contact records for, 90–91; e-mail, 56–57, 101, 160; "I" messages, 147; online resources for creating positive, 93; parent conferences, 97–99; professionally interacting with parents or guardians, 93; taking care with written, 94–95; tips on teacher-parent, 86; transparent classroom to prevent miscommunications, 86–89; verbal immediacy to create positive relationships with students, 146–147; with non-English speaking parents and guardians, 93; words and phrases to avoid, 146–147; using your voice effectively during, 309. *See also* Language; Listening skills; Oral presentations

Communities of practice: description of, 74; online resources on, 75; PLC (professional learning community) type of, 74; PLN (professional learning network) type of, 74

Community: DVD on strategies for collaborating with local, 103;

reflections on collaborating with your, 104–105

Computers: arranged on your desk area, 36; interactive response systems assessment using, 385–386; providing disadvantaged students with access to, 354; students with ADD or ADHD and use of, 347

Concept maps, 319

Confidential documents, 52

Conflict: how to handle professional disagreements, 78; "mean girls," 171; name calling, 171–172; resolving peer, 165–166; student fighting, 478–480. *See also* Violence

Conflict resolution: promoting peer relations through, 165–166; strategies and online resources on, 166

Conner, Melinda: on challenges and rewards of teaching, 378; on controlling class time, 179; on creating personal connections with students, 151; on getting help from more experienced teachers, 276; on remembering every student is someone's child, 97; on setting high standards of behavior for students, 203; on teacher camaraderie, 74

Contact records: Home Contact Documentation Form, 91; importance of keeping, 90

Contract learning instruction, 265

Cooperative learning instruction, 264

Copyright laws, 59

Council for Exceptional Children Web site, 359

Course overview: determining number of units to teach, 287; Format for a Course Overview worksheet on, 288; school district curriculum guidelines to create, 287; state's standards used to begin the, 286

Courtesy: Checklist of Social Skills All Students Should Master worksheet on, 167; teaching students to practice, 164–165; use good manners when dealing with students, 152

Creativity: maintaining your teaching, 326; offering assignments that stimulate student, 230

Critical Thinking Community Web site, 413

Critical thinking levels: analyzing, 415; applying, 414–415; creating, 416; evaluating, 415; remembering, 414; understanding, 414

Critical thinking skills: description of, 412; using essential questions to stimulate, 416–417; giving directions that encourage, 413–416; online resources for teaching, 413; strategies for teaching, 412–413

Critical Thinking Web site, 413

Crying students, 487

Culturally responsive educators, 154–156

Culver, Joshua: on communicating with parents and guardians, 101; on getting acclimated to daily demands, 36; on giving students second chances, 213; on guiding your students toward success, 310; on handling behavior issues, 449

Curriculum: being familiar with state standards for, 281, 282, 283; Common Core State Standards Initiative (CCSSI) on, 283–285; debate over teaching students versus covering the, 280–281; school district guidelines for, 287; state standards for, 281–286, 292, 337. *See also* Instruction

Curriculum compacting instruction, 264–265

Cyber bullying, 168, 170–171

Cyber Bullying Research Center, 170–171

Cyber cheating: description of, 393–394; form of, 394; strategies for managing, 394

D

Dabroski, Janice: on giving students navigation tools for reading, 420; on using school newspaper to teach reading skills, 423

Daily plans: considerations for creating, 291; Easy-to-Use Format for Daily Lesson Plans worksheet, 294; list on what to include as part of, 291–293

Data analysis: action research for, 7; Data Tracking Sheet worksheet, 22–23

Data collection: action research for, 7; Data Tracking Sheet worksheet, 22–23. *See also* Grade records

Data-driven instruction: description of, 365; summative and formative assessments shaping, 365–366

Data Tracking Sheet worksheet, 22–23

Dave's ESL Cafe Web site, 318, 352

Day of Silence event, 351

Defiant behavior: how to deal with student's, 501–502; making a referral due to, 469

Description maps, 319

Desks: class location of teacher's, 36; tips for arranging teacher's items on, 36

Detention: after the, 469; how to conduct the, 468; issuing a notice for, 467–468

Detention notice: actions to take when you issue a, 467–468; what to do before you issue a, 467

Dialectical journals, 342

Dictionaries, 409

Dictionary.com, 406

Differentiated classroom: management tips for the, 341–342; strategies and activities for the, 342–345

Differentiated instruction: basic guidelines for, 336–337; Best Practices Checklist for, 362–363; challenge of accommodating needs of every learner, 333–334; description and learning benefits of, 331–332; four key strategies of, 339–341; Individualized Instruction Worksheet, 335; A Planning Tool for Differentiation worksheet, 338; reflections on, 363; resources on, 332; Response to Intervention (RTI) form of, 345–346; understanding what it is and is not, 333. *See also*

Learning styles; Students needing special care

Differentiated Instruction Made Easy: Hundreds of Multi-Level Activities for All Learners (Kaplan, Rogers, and Webster), 332

Differentiated instruction strategies: create tiered instruction, 340–341; design respectful tasks, 339; use flexible grouping, 339–340; provide anchor activities, 341

Differentiation in Action (Dodge), 332

Difficult class: reasons that you might have a, 463; strategies for turning around a, 464

Difficult colleagues, 79–80

Difficult students: coping with chronic misbehavior of, 465; don't give up on your, 463. *See also* Student misbehaviors

Direct instruction, 263

Directions: differentiated instruction and need for clear, 336–337; that encourage critical thinking, 413–416; impatient students who don't wait for, 233; provided at the start of class, 212; providing students with clear verbal, 234–235; providing students with clear written, 233–234; Simon Says game for giving, 233; to students with ADD or ADHD, 347; teach students good listening skills to follow, 231; teaching students to follow, 232–233. *See also* Assignments; Instruction

Disadvantaged students: living in poverty, 354; suggestions for helping, 354–355

Disaster drills, 69

Discipline: avoid threatening to send your students to the office, 84; challenge of learning how to, 214; detentions used for, 467–469; enforcing classroom rules, 217–218; how to response when you disagree with administrator's, 471; inconsistent application of, 432–435, 462; myths about, 448; positive versus negative consequences, 218; referrals to an administrator,

469–471; self-discipline as most effective, 428–429; think before you take action, 462–463. *See also* Classroom management; Classroom rules; Punishment

Discipline and Group Management in Classrooms (Krieger), 436

Discipline interventions: knowing when to take action, 442–443; online resources on, 441; using positive peer pressure as, 443; suggested strategies for, 441–442

Discipline problem management: acknowledging the need and dilemma of, 447–448; administrative expectations for your, 451; Behavior Incident Report worksheet, 457; Best Practices Checklist for, 480–481; Classroom Management Techniques to Avoid worksheet, 454; cultivating grace under pressure, 459–460; detentions used for, 467–468; of difficult class, 463–464; don't give up on your difficult students, 463; due process procedures, 459; managing referrals, 469–471; reflecting on your, 481–482; remember not to take it personally, 460; respond instead of just reacting, 451–454; student conferences with students who have misbehaved, 465–467; teacher mistakes in, 461–462; teacher's legal responsibilities for, 455–457; think before you take action, 462–463

Discipline problem prevention: be a good listener for, 440–441; being fair and consistent as means of, 434–436, 462; Best Practice Checklist for, 444; earn your students' respect for, 440; How Effective Are You at Preventing Discipline Problems? worksheet, 431; listening to your students for, 440–441, 461–462; monitoring students for, 438–439; Preventing or Minimizing Discipline Problems worksheet, 433; providing signals for students to use when they need help for, 439; punishment as

ineffective way for, 426–427; reflections on, 444–445; self-discipline as key to, 428–429; taking a positive approach to, 434; What Is Your Level of Withitness? worksheet for, 437; withitness as technique for, 436–437; your role in, 432–433

Discipline problems: avoidable mistakes that cause, 429–430; being consistent when dealing with, 434–435, 462; being fair when dealing with, 435–436; causes of most, 429; consulting with other teachers about, 430; teacher mistakes that can cause, 461–462. *See also* Student misbehaviors

Discovery Education Web site, 298, 318

Discussion board threat, 270

Dishonesty: lying, 490; making a referral for, 469–471; students committing theft, 495–497; as unacceptable behavior, 450. *See also* Cheating

Disorganized students, 487–488

Disrespect for authority, 450

Disruptions: making a referral and avoid making it worse, 471; making referrals due to persistent, 470

Distractions: downtime as being a, 180; ensuring that backpacks aren't an obstructions or, 498; excessive noise during class, 499; how to handle interruptions, 181–182; reducing classroom, 179; students focused on toys, trinkets, and grooming, 491–492

Diversity programs, 350

Documents: classroom routines, 51; confidential, 52; grading, 50–51; how to save paper, 58; instructional concerns, 51; to keep until the start of the next school year, 52–53; optimize your use of the photocopier, 59; professional business, 51; records of interactions with parents or guardians, 457; safely discarded at the end of each semester, 53; student information, 51–52, 53–58. *See also* Grade records

Dodge, J., 332

Door-to-door approach, 180

Dougherty, Alanna: on encouraging your students, 244; on having fun in class, 166; on managing paperwork, 50; on positive reinforcement for motivating students, 222; on stress management, 31

Dramatic/theater presentations, 311

Dress code violations, 493–494

Drummond Woodsum Web site, 455

Due process procedures, 459

DVD: directions for using the, A; managing your necessary school absences, 81; strategies for collaborating with others, 103; strategies for motivating students, 257; stress management tips on the, 31; system requirements for using the, A; troubleshooting tips on the, B

E

E-books, 270

E-mail: promoting a supportive class through class, 160; responding to negative parent or guardian, 101; tips for managing, 56–57

Easy-to-Use Format for Daily Lesson Plans worksheet, 294

Eating in class, 488

Economically disadvantaged students: living in poverty, 354; suggestions for helping, 354–355

Edublogs Web site, 273

Education Oasis Web site, 184, 320

Education Week journal, 27

Education World Web site, 184, 350

Educational Leadership journal, 27

Educational research: online resources for accessing, 260; taking advantage of the most recent, 259

Educator's Network Web site, 388

Educator's PLN Web site, 75

Edudemic Web site, 273

edWeb.net Web site, 75

Egg drop activity, 161

Eight-minute closing exercise, 196

eInstruction Corporation Web site, 386

Electronic files: maintaining class web page, 57–58; tips for managing, 56; tips for managing e-mail, 56–57

Emergency drills, 498–499

Emergency lesson plans, 45

Emotional abuse, 156

Emotional distance: classroom immediacy to lessen, 143–146; maintaining a certain, 141; verbal immediacy to lessen, 146–147

Evaluation: helping students with self-evaluation, 224, 226; How Observers Will Evaluate You worksheet, 19; impact of value-added assessments on the process of, 20–21; observation, 17–19; Progress Tracking Chart worksheet for, 243; responding to a poor, 24; turning criticism into positive experience, 20. *See also* Assessments; Teaching skills

Examples, samples, and models, 326–327

Excessive noise problem, 499

Exit slips: description of, 372; differentiated classroom activity of, 343; formative assessment using, 372–373

Explore Web site, 299

Extra credit dilemmas/solutions, 395

Extrinsic motivation: description of, 226–227; tangible rewards students enjoy for, 227–228; why you should not use food as a reward, 238

Eye contact: maintaining during presentations, 306–310; maintaining while monitoring students, 439

F

Facebook class page, 160

Faculty manual or handbook, 83

Fairness: differentiated instruction and, 336; handling discipline problems with, 435–436; as key to classroom management, 218; showing students they can count on your, 464; strategies for designing tests and quizzes with,

377–378; teacher-student relationship role of, 145; when establishing a policy for students to leave the room, 194

Fear of failure, 226

Federal Resources for Educational Excellence Web site, 299, 424

Feedback: asking your mentor to provide you with, 15; encourage students to learn from errors through, 374–375; formative assessments as opportunity to provide, 373–375; use podcasts to provide, 374; Tracking Formative Assessment Data worksheet to provide, 368. *See also* Assessments

Feigning illness, 488–489

Field trip permission slips, 456

Fighting: as common student misbehavior, 478; mistakes to avoid related to, 479; strategies that work to prevent or manage, 479–480; your responsibilities in case of student, 478

File cabinets, 36

Fire drills, 69

First-day priorities: begin to build a classroom community, 111; begin to teach the class routines, 110–111; calm your students' fears, 109–110; engage your students' minds, 110; introduce yourself, 110; take charge of your class, 109

First-day tasks: activities for the first day, 115–116; create a positive group identity, 133–135; creating student information records, 120–122; learn your students' names quickly, 123; overcoming those first-day jitters, 107, 108–109; strategies for getting to know your students, 123–133; understanding the importance for students, 107–108; welcome packet for students, 111–112; your priorities, 109–111

First-day worksheets: Checklist for the First Day, 119; Inventory: Please Tell Me About Your Child, 113; Inventory for Elementary Students, 127–128; Inventory for

High School Students, 131–132; Inventory for Middle School Students, 129–130; Letter of Introduction to Parents or Guardians sample, 114; Planning Template for the First Day of School, 117–118; Student Information Form, 121–122

First-week planning: mistakes to avoid at the start of school, 136–137; things to expect and plan for, 135–136

504 Plans: description of a, 347; students with ADD or ADHD with, 346, 348; teacher's legal responsibilities related to, 456; typical accommodations related to, 348. *See also* Individualized Education Program

Flash cards, 411

Flashcard Machine Web site, 411

Flickr Web site, 160

Flipped learning instruction, 266–267

Flyswatter Badminton, 316

Foley, Bob: on assigned seating, 70; on minimizing what you grade, 388; on prioritizing tasks, 43

Food rewards, 228

ForLessonPlans Web site, 299

Format for a Course Overview worksheet, 288

Format for a Unit Plan worksheet, 290

Formative assessments: Assignment Reflection worksheet for, 376; data-driven instruction shaped by, 365–366; exit slips used for, 372–373; gathering baseline data before beginning unit for, 370; how to effectively use, 366–367; as opportunity for teacher to offer feedback to students, 373–375; using review sessions as, 370–372; Tracking Formative Assessment Data worksheet, 368; types of, 369. *See also* Assessments

4Teachers Web site, 274, 387

A Framework for Understanding Poverty (Payne), 355

Free lunches, 355

Free Technology for Teachers Web site, 274

Freebie school supplies, 37
Freedom of speech, 456

G

Games: online resources on, 318; suggestions for managing the use of, 315–316; suggestions on adapting for class instruction, 316–318. *See also* Activities
Gang involvement, 156, 456
Gardner, Edward: on admitting you don't know the answer, 153; on being a professional at all times, 147; on connecting with students, 9; on different intelligences of different students, 333; on having top days, 25; on students wanting to know that you care, 465
Gay students: actions you can take to assist, 350–351; understanding challenges faced by, 350
GED certificate, 476
Gifted students: modifying learning process for, 357–358; modifying lesson content to challenge, 358; online resources on, 357; teaching them in a group of students with mixed abilities, 358–359; who are chronic underachievers, 352–354. *See also* Advanced student tiered instruction
Gizmo's Freeware Web sites, 410
Goal-oriented learning: motivating students through, 238; Progress Tracking Chart worksheet, 243; Setting and Achieving SMART Goals worksheet on, 239–240; teaching students to track their own mastery for, 241–242
Goal setting: Are You in Charge of Your Career? worksheet for, 26; Setting and Achieving SMART Goals worksheet, 239–240; SMART goals for professional growth, 25; Track Your Professional Goals worksheet for tracking progress, 30
Google Docs, 271
Google Images, 188
Grade records: electronic grade books, 390; general information

on management of, 389; Grade Tracking Form for Student Success worksheet, 391; how to personalize a grade report, 392; online resources on management of, 390; paper grade books, 389–390; recommendation for combination approach to, 388. *See also* Data collection; Documents
Grade Tracking Form for Student Success worksheet, 391
Grades: differentiated instruction focus on student growth instead of, 336; keeping track of, 388–391; managing electronic files related to, 56; personalizing a report on, 392; posting online, 226; what to do when students challenge, 392–393
Grading: being adequately prepared at start of, 281; extra credit dilemmas and solutions, 395; general suggestions for, 54–55; how to grade papers quickly, 54; objective questions on tests and quizzes, 381; rubrics used for, 270, 386–388; student cheating issue of, 393–394; suggestions for grading longer assignments, essays, and projects, 55; suggestions for grading quizzes and tests, 55; types of documents related to, 50–51. *See also* Student information records
Graphic organizers: cause-and-effect maps, 320; concept maps, 319; description maps, 319; learning benefits of using, 318; online resources for, 320; teaching vocabulary words using, 409; time sequence maps, 320; ways for students to use, 318–319
Grooming distractions, 491–492
Group multimedia presentations, 160
Group tests, 385
Guardians. *See* Parents/guardians
Guest speakers, 311

H

Hall Pass sample, 193
Hallway misbehavior, 494

Handouts: distributing at the start of lesson, 211–212; group work and turning in completed, 212; personalizing, 327; procedures for lost, 212. *See also* Materials
Hands-on instruction, 263
Hangman game, 317
Hatred in the Hallways report (Human Rights Watch), 350
Health concerns: avoiding classroom injuries, 66, 67–69; handling student requests to go to the nurse's office, 191; knowing your students' medical needs, 457; pay attention to your students' health, 152; protecting your student's health, 69–70; student feigning illness, 488–489; student fights that result in injuries, 480
Helicopter parents or guardians: description and problem of, 100; strategies for working with, 101–102
Herrala, Charlene: on allowing students free time, 196; on chance meetings with graduated students, 424; on communicating with parents, 86; on computer skills, 42; on giving students a chance to succeed, 346; on loving your students, 141; on planning activities, 296; on student misbehavior to mask their poor performance, 348
High performance culture: creating a, 5; hallmarks of a, 6. *See also* Professional growth
Highly effective teachers: additional strategies for becoming, 8–9; developing a reflective practice, 9–10; professional responsibility to become, 8; small but strategic steps for becoming, 8
Homelessness, 157
Homework assignments: acceptable and nonacceptable types of help on, 253–254; Class Log Page worksheet for recording, 256; creating a partnership with students and their families, 244–246; daily plans inclusion of, 292; debate over appropriate amount of, 245–246; developing

Homework assignments (*cont'd*) a homework policy, 247, 254–255; helping students make up missing work, 254–255; Homework Letter to Parents or Guardians sample, 245–246; Missing Homework Explanation Form worksheet, 252; online help for, 253; Plan Successful Homework Assignments worksheet, 248; strategies for successful management of, 249–251; surviving the debate over, 244; when students don't do their, 251. *See also* Assignments

Homework-free nights, 249

Homework Letter to Parents or Guardians sample, 245–246

Homework Spot Web site, 253

Hot Potato activity, 343

Houghton Mifflin Web site, 320

How Appropriate Are Your Relationships with Students? worksheet, 142

How Effective Are You at Creating a Transparent Classroom? worksheet, 89

How Effective Are You at Preventing Discipline Problems? worksheet, 431

How to Differentiate Instruction in Mixed Ability Classrooms (Tomlinson), 332

How Well Do You Use Class Time? worksheet, 177–178

Human Rights Watch Web site, 350

Humor: connecting with students through, 152; importance of maintaining your sense of, 503

Hunger issue, 157

I

"I" messages, 147

iLoveLanguages Web site, 93

Impatient students, 233

Independent Television Service Web site, 299

Individualized Education Program: students with ADD or ADHD in the, 346–347; teacher's legal responsibilities for, 456. *See also* 504 Plans

Individualized Instruction Worksheet, 335

Injured students, 480

Innovative Learning Web sites, 260

Inquiry methods instruction, 262–263

Instructify Web site, 274

Instruction: delivering engaging, 303–329; differentiated, 331–363; motivating students by scaffolding, 225; pacing, 182–183; reflections on effective, 301; teaching to an objective, 180; type of documents related to, 51. *See also* Curriculum; Directions; Student success

Instruction delivery: Best Practices Checklist for, 328; colored dot labels used for, 326; conduct engaging class discussions, 312–314; using games the students enjoy, 315–318; using graphic organizers to engage students, 318–320; help students stay on track during a lecture, 311–312; improving oral presentations, 305–310; improving your classroom charisma for, 303–304; learning cubes used for, 321–325; making a point students will remember, 310–311; pitfalls of, 304–305; providing models, examples, and samples for, 326–327; reflection on engaging, 328–329; strategies for appealing seatwork, 327–328; using toys to capture attention, 314–315

Instruction design: always have a backup plan, 180, 296–298; backward design approach to, 280; benefit of careful planning for, 279; Best practices Checklist on, 300; covering the curriculum versus teaching students debate, 280–281; how to adjust a lesson, 296; for nontraditional schedules, 295–296; online resources on lesson plans and, 298–300; reflections on effective, 301. *See also* Lesson plans

Instruction planning: assess your students' prior knowledge as part of, 285–286, 289; Best Practices Checklist on, 300; common problems related to, 281–282; covering the curriculum versus teaching students debate issue of, 280–281; finding the time for, 282; guidelines on being prepared, 281; how the CCSSI will impact on your, 284; reflections on effective, 301

Instruction planning process: step 1: create a course overview, 286–288; step 2: create unit plans, 289–290; step 3: create daily plans, 291–294

Instructional strategies: active learning, 261; Best Practices Checklist on, 275–276; blended learning, 264; contract learning, 265; cooperative learning, 264; curriculum compacting, 264–265; direct instruction, 263; flipped learning, 266–267; hands-on instruction, 263; inquiry methods, 262–263; interactive learning, 262; problem-based learning, 263; reciprocal teaching, 267; reflections on, 276–277; reflective discussions, 261; scaffolding, 225, 357–359, 360–361; Socratic seminars, 266; for students with special needs, 360–361; tiered instruction, 340–341; WebQuests, 265–266. *See also* Teaching; Technological classroom resources

Instructional student-related problems: absences on day of assessment, 497; backpack problems in and out of class, 497–498; emergency drill interrupting an assessment, 498–499; excessive noise during class, 499; no names on papers, 499–500; restless students during video viewing, 500; students who do their work and leave it at home, 501

Instructure magazine, 27

Integrity, 76–77

Interactive bookmarks activity, 343

Interactive learning instruction, 262

Interactive response systems, 385–386

Interactive whiteboards, 269–270
Interactive Wordplays Web site, 412
International Reading Association Web site, 424
Interruptions: minimizing negative effects by meeting three goals, 181–182; negative impact of constant, 181
Intervention Central Web site, 346, 441
Intrinsic motivation: description of, 228–229; offering novel and enjoyable assignments as, 229–230
Introductory or warm-up activities, 184–185
Intruder drills, 69
Inventory: Please Tell Me About Your Child worksheet, 113
Inventory for Elementary Students worksheets, 127–128
Inventory for High School Students worksheet, 131–132
Inventory for Middle School Students worksheet, 129–130
Invisible students, 489
iPads, 270–271

J

Jigsaws activity. *See* Puzzle activity
Journals, 385

K

Kaplan, J., 332
Kathy Schrock's Guide to Everything Web site, 63, 275, 387–388
Kelly, Megan: on disciplining students, 214; on downtime as being class distraction, 180; on first-day jitters, 109
Khan Academy Web site, 253
Kid Blog Web site, 160
Kid-cast.com, 273
Kissling, Matt: on having fun while teaching, 443; on learning to respond to student failures, 403; on motivating students by building trust, 223
Knowledge: determining essential unit, 289; Know/Want to Know/Learned (KWL) chart to gather data on, 370, 419; sharing your

knowledge with parent or guardian's, 457; taking the opportunity every day to add to your, 449. *See also* Prior knowledge
Knowmia Web site, 273
Know/Want to Know/Learned (KWL) chart, 370, 419
Krieger, R. E., 436

L

Language: display of trash can of unacceptable class, 172; "I" messages, 147; name calling, 171–172; students who are not native speakers of English, 351–352; words and phrases to avoid when speaking to students, 146–147; using your voice effectively to express your, 309. *See also* Communication
Lankford, Jane: on consulting other teachers about discipline problems, 430; on learning to effectively use technological tools, 270
Lave, Jean, 74
LD Online Web site, 359
Learn Boost Web site, 390
Learner Profile Web site, 390
Learning: modifying processes for gifted students, 357–358; nontraditional schedules and successful, 295–296; purposeful, 235–236; self-directed, 357; taking a goal-oriented approach to, 238–240
Learning Ally, 404
Learning circles activity, 344
Learning cubes: description of, 321; suggestions on how to adapt for your classroom, 321–325
Learning Disabilities Association of America (LDA) Web site, 359–360
Learning from Exemplary Teachers worksheet, 13
Learning logs, 385
Learning magazine, 27
Learning student names, 123
Learning styles: motivating students focused on their, 224; of non-English speaking students, 351; rotating lesson plan use of

three basic, 336. *See also* Differentiated instruction
Learning-Theories Web site, 260
Learning Through Listening Web site, 404
"Least restrictive environment" mandate (Public Law 94-142), 359
Lecture. *See* Oral presentations
Legal issues: accommodations (504 Plan), 348; Behavior Incident Report worksheet, 458; due process procedures, 459; IEP (Individualized Education Program) or 504 Plans, 346–348, 456; "least restrictive environment" mandate (Public Law 94-142), 359; NCLB standardized test mandate, 8; searching student property, 456; teacher responsibilities for discipline and classroom management, 455–457; teacher responsibilities related to bullying, 168. *See also* State standards
Legal Rights of Teachers and Students (McCarthy, Cambron-McCabe, and Thomas), 455
Lesbian students: actions you can take to assist, 350–351; understanding challenges faced by, 350
Lesson Planet Web site, 299
Lesson plans: benefit of careful design planning of, 279; Best Practices Checklist on, 300; emergency, 45; finding the time to write, 282; free online resources for, 298–300; having a backup, 180, 296–298; how to adjust a, 296; including multiple modes of learning in, 304; modifying content to challenge gifted students, 358; for nontraditional schedules, 295–296; proactive strategy of delivering meaningful, 449; productive transitions to use during, 187–190; reflections on designing effective, 301; rotate learning styles focus used in, 336; Shaping-Up Review activity on, 344. *See also* Instruction design

Lesson Plans Page Web site, 299

LessonPlans.com, 299

Letter of Introduction to Parents or Guardians sample, 114

Lining-up games, 161

Listening skills: as crucial for students to develop, 404; for following directions, 231; good communication by teaching students, 94; online resources on teaching, 404; preventing discipline problems by using your, 440–441, 461–462; strategies for teaching, 404. *See also* Communication

Live Binders Web site, 274

Lockers, 191

Lost papers, 213

Lunch money, 355

Lying students, 490

M

Mahoney, Stephanie Stock: on doing something fun the first day, 111; on keeping teaching creativity alive, 326; on posting grades online, 226; on scaffolding for students with special needs, 359

Making the Most of Peer Observations worksheet, 16

Making threats, 469

Manipulatives activity, 344

Many Teaching Ideas Web site, 404

Maps: cause-and-effect, 320; concept, 319; description, 319; Maps.com source of, 185; time sequence, 320

Maps.com, 185

Marzano Research Laboratory Web site, 412

Mastery Connect Web site, 274

Matching questions test, 379–380

Materials: audio, 343; bank of shared supplies for students who need, 211, 355; determining what resources are needed for, 292; Easy-to-Use Format for Daily Lesson Plans worksheet on, 294; Format for a Unit Plan worksheet on needed, 290; making reference materials available to students, 410; oral

language, 410. *See also* Handouts; Online resources

McCarthy, Martha M., 455

McManaway, Debbie: on engaging students in fun activities, 315; on importance of being prepared for class, 281; on teacher role models, 79

McTighe, Jay, 280

"Mean girls," 171

Media center, 191. *See also* Multimedia presentations

Media literacy skills: description and importance of, 402; online resources on teaching, 403; strategies for teaching, 402–403

Media Literacy.com, 403

Media Smarts Web site, 403

Meet Your Classroom Priorities worksheet, 44

Mental health issues, 156

Mentors: Learning from Exemplary Teachers worksheet, 13; Making the Most of Peer Observations worksheet, 16; seeking feedback on your professional performance from, 15; tips for working well with, 14–15. *See also* Role models

Merriam-Webster's Word Central Web site, 412

Minilessons activity, 343

Misbehaviors. *See* Student misbehaviors

Missing Homework Explanation Form worksheet, 252

Models, samples, and examples, 326–327

Monitoring students: legal obligations related to, 455; preventing discipline problems by, 438–439; as time management strategy, 179

Motivating students: Assignment Checklist worksheet to ensure, 237; Best Practices Checklist on, 257; body language used for, 309–310; chronic underachievement and, 352–354; DVD information on, 257; homework and, 244–256; how to give written directions for, 233–234; laying a solid foundation for, 223; by making

success attainable, 231–232; positive reinforcement for, 222–223; as proactive discipline strategy, 449; Progress Tracking Chart worksheet, 243; providing clear verbal directions for, 234–235; purposeful learning role in, 235–236; reflections on, 257–258; the self-fulfilling prophecy, 221–222; teaching self-efficacy purpose of, 241; teaching students to follow directions as way of, 232–233; by teaching students to track their own progress, 241–243; using a variety of methods for, 223–226. *See also* Students

Motivation: extrinsic, 226–228; intrinsic, 228–230

Multimedia presentations: interactive whiteboards for, 269–270; to make a point students will remember, 311; making group, 160; podcasting, 272. *See also* Media center

Multiple-choice question test, 380

Multnomah County Oregon Public Library Web site, 253

Music, that fits the lesson of the day, 311

Myren, Christina L.: on benefits of formative assessments, 367; on tailoring motivation approaches to different students, 223; on value of communities of practice, 75; on working with parents or guardians, 100

N

Name calling, 171–172

Name That Person game, 317

National Association for Gifted Children Web site, 357

National Association for Media Literacy Education (NAMLE) Web site, 403

National Association for the Education of Young Children, 28

National Board for Professional Teaching Standards, 27

National Center on Response to Intervention Web site, 346

National Education Association (NEA), 28, 201

National Education Association (NEA) Web site, 441

National Geographic Web site, 253, 299

National High School Association, 28

National Institute of Child Health and Human Development Web site, 356

National Writing Project Web site, 407

Negativity: avoid falling victim to, 80; dealing with, 79–80; helping students cope with peer pressure, 172–173

New students, 490–491

No Child Left Behind (NCLB): origins and impact of, 8; standardized test mandate of, 8, 20–21

Non-English-speaking parents/ guardians, 93

Non-English-speaking students, 351–352

Nontraditional schedules: description and increasing trend of, 295; strategies to master challenge of, 295–296

Note taking: developing student skills for, 232; taking electronic, 271

Notepad supply, 36

Nurse's office. *See* School nurse's office

O

Objective questions: how to quickly grade, 381; used in tests and quizzes, 379

Objectives: creative ways to help students remember the, 310–311; daily plans inclusion of, 292; Easy-to-Use Format for Daily Lesson Plans worksheet on, 294; teaching to an, 180

Observation. *See* Classroom observation

The office: making student referrals to, 469–471; student requests to go to the, 191

One-sentence summaries activity, 344

One, Two, and You're Outta Here game, 317

1001 Great Ideas for Teaching and Raising Children with Autism or Asperger's (Botbohm and Zysk), 356

Online Books Web site, 410

Online collaboration activity, 344

Online resources: on assisting gay and lesbian students, 350; on at-risk students, 350; on autism spectrum disorders (ASD), 356; Best Practices Checklist on, 275–276; on Common Core State Standards Initiative (CCSSI), 284–285; on communities of practice, 75; on conflict resolution, 166; on creating positive messages, 93; on creating puzzles, 298; on early intervention strategies for discipline problems, 441; on educational research, 260; on flash cards, 411; on games, 318; on games to adapt for class instruction, 318; on gifted students, 357; on grade management, 390; on grade reports, 392; on graphic organizers, 320; on homework help, 253; on interactive response systems, 386; on introductory or warm-up activities, 184–185; on lesson plan ideas and design, 298–300; on podcasting, 273; on productive lesson plan transitions, 188–189; on productive use of time left at end of class, 199; on promoting a supportive class, 160; on Response to Intervention (RTI), 346; on rubrics, 387–388; on "screen beans," 185; on strategies for managing hallway misbehaviors, 494; on students who are not native speakers of English, 352; on students with special needs, 359–360; on teaching critical thinking skills, 413; on teaching listening skills, 404; on teaching media literacy skills, 403; on teaching reading skills, 422, 424; on teaching vocabulary acquisition skills, 410, 412; on teaching writing skills, 407; useful Web sites for educators, 273–274; on well-managed classroom, 201–202. *See also* Materials; Technological classroom resources; Web sites

Open-book or open-note tests, 385

Open-ended problems activity, 344

Open-ended questions: used as assessment, 384; motivating through, 225

Open houses, 88

Oral language materials, 410

Oral presentations: help students stay on track during, 311–312; how to make a point students will remember, 310–311; improving your, 305–306; maintain eye contact during, 306, 310; master the art of the pause for, 306; pay attention to your audience during, 307–308; set the stage for your, 306–307; videotape yourself giving, 306. *See also* Communication; Speaking skills

Out of the Box Games Web site, 318

Oxford Dictionaries Web site, 189

P

Pacing instruction, 182–183

Pairs or triads seating, 65

Pairs test, 385

Palmer, Erik, 406

Paper clips, 36

Paper discussions activity, 344

Paperwork: general tips for managing school, 50–52; how to save paper, 58; optimize your use of the photocopier, 59; organizing your paper file storage, 40–41; student information and grades, 53–55; teacher comment on managing, 50; what to keep and what to discard, 52–53

Parent conferences: actions to take after a, 99; actions to take before a, 98; actions to take during a, 98–99; five goals for each, 97; how to conduct successful, 97

Parent/guardian–teacher communication: be a good listener, 94; be positive during, 92–93; class newsletters role in,

Parent/guardian-teacher communication (*cont'd*) 96–97; creating a transparent classroom to avoid miscommunication, 86–89; Homework Letter to Parents or Guardians sample, 245–246; keep accurate records of, 457; Letter of Introduction to Parents or Guardians sample, 114; managing e-mail, 56–57; parent conferences, 97–99; Positive Message to Parents or Guardians sample, 92; responding to negative e-mails by, 101; taking care with written, 94–95; telephone calls, 95–96; with non-English speaking parents and guardians, 93. *See also* Teachers

Parents/guardians: contact records on, 90–91; creating a homework partnership with, 244–246; creating safe classroom environment by collaborating with, 457; handling uncooperative, 102–103; handling unreasonable, 102; helicopter, 100–102; Inventory: Please Tell Me About Your Child worksheet given to, 113; Letter of Introduction to Parents or Guardians sample, 114; making student referral and maintaining credibility with, 470–471; non-English speaking, 93; objections to food rewards by, 228; preventing discipline problems by enlisting support from, 442; problems relating with, 100; professional interaction with, 93; what they expect from teachers, 85–86; working well with, 84–85. *See also* School community

Parking lot, 192

Partnership for Assessment of Readiness for College and Careers Web site, 285

Passing notes, 491

Payne, Ruby, 355

Peace Education Foundation, 166

Peer acceptance: class chemistry that supports, 157; removing barriers to, 157–159

Peer conflicts: "mean girls," 171; name calling, 171–172; resolving, 165–166. *See also* Bullying

Peer pressure: discipline management through positive, 443; help students cope with negative, 172–173; "mean girls" and, 171

Peer tutoring, 163–164, 464

Pens/pencils supply, 36

Perfect attendance, 81

Performance assessments, 385

Permission slips, 456

Persistent defiance, 469, 501–502

Personal belongings security, 36

Phi Delta Kappan journal, 27

Photoblog, 271

Photocollage, 271

Photocopier, 59

Photographs: Flickr for sharing, 160; interactive whiteboards for sharing, 269; iPads for sharing, 271; Tag Galaxy for sharing, 160; take and display student, 153

Pinterest Web site, 274

Plagiarism, 450

Plan Successful Homework Assignments worksheet, 248

Planning for Classroom Policies worksheet, 205–208

Planning Template for the First Day of School worksheet, 117–118

A Planning Tool for Differentiation worksheet, 338

Plans for Ending Class Effectively worksheet, 198

Plans for Starting Class Effectively worksheet, 186

Platt, Carole: on letting students know they are special to you, 145; on teaching as a building art form, 304; on teaching as opportunity to share love of a subject, 398

Podcasting Tools Web site, 273

Podcasts: instructional uses for, 272–273; online resources for, 273; preparing, 272

Podomatic Web site, 273

Policies. *See* Classroom policies; School policy problems

Political Cartoons Web site, 188

Poll Everywhere Web site, 274

Popular teachers, 151

Positive group identity, 133–135

Positive Message to Parents or Guardians sample, 92

Positive reinforcement: discipline through negative versus, 218; motivating students using, 222–223

Poverty: school-age students living in, 354; suggestions for supporting students living in, 354–355

Power struggles: problem of, 502; strategies for avoiding, 502–503

PowerPoint games: adapting for class instruction, 316; playing timed, 185

Practice: giving students step-by-step sequences for, 233; tiered instruction for students who need, 340

Praising students, 464

Pregnant students, 156

Preventing or Minimizing Discipline Problems worksheet, 433

Prezi Web site, 160

Print-A-Poster.com, 37

Prior knowledge: Easy-to-Use Format for Daily Lesson Plans worksheet on, 294; gathering baseline data before beginning unit of study, 370; importance of assessing students', 285; Know/Want to Know/Learned (KWL) chart to gather data on, 370, 419; strategies for assessing students', 285–286; as unit plan consideration, 289. *See also* Knowledge

Privacy laws, 456

Pro Teacher Web site, 494

Problem-based learning instruction, 263

Problems: action research for determining, 7; learning instruction based on use of, 263. *See also* Classroom problems

Procedures. *See* Classroom procedures

Profanity, 469

Professional business documents, 51

Professional conferences, 27

Professional disagreements, 78

Professional growth: evaluation process used for, 17–24; maintaining sustained, 25–30; set and work to achieve goals for, 25. *See also* High performance culture

Professional growth strategies: attend conferences, 27; Best Practices Checklist, 32–33; create a professional portfolio, 28–29; deciding to work toward national certification, 27; join professional organizations, 27–28; learn to manage your stress, 31–32; learning from role models and mentors for, 14–16; reading professional journals, 27

Professional growth worksheets: Are You in Charge of Your Career?, 26; Learning from Exemplary Teachers, 13; Making the Most of Peer Observations, 6; Track Your Professional Goals, 30

Professional journals, 27

Professional learning community (PLC): description and benefits of, 74; online resources on, 75

Professional learning network (PLN): description and benefits of, 74; online resources on, 75

Professional organizations, 27–28

Professional portfolio: artifacts to include in, 28–29; benefits of creating a, 28; reflections on your teaching practice to include in, 29

Professional responsibilities: to become a highly effective teacher, 8–9; create a culture of high performance, 5–6; for discipline and classroom management, 455–457; in regard to student testing, 397–398; use action research to inform classroom decisions, 6–7

Professionalism: description of, 4; three basic principles of, 4–5

Professionalism principles: commit yourself to establishing a productive, positive classroom environment, 5; commit yourself to actively promoting student achievement and learning, 5; commit yourself to maintaining high standards of performance, 4

Progress Tracking Chart worksheet, 243

Project Gutenberg Web site, 410

Project Look Sharp Web site, 403

ProTeacher Directory Web site, 441

ProTeacher Web site, 412

Public displays of affection, 494–495

Public Law 94-142, 359

Punishment: detentions, 467–469; history of use of, 427; using inappropriate, 461; as ineffective to prevent problems, 427–428; myth about effectiveness of, 448. *See also* Discipline

Purposeful learning, 235–236

Puzzle activity: as appealing seatwork activity, 327; building vocabulary through, 411; differentiated instruction using jigsaw activity, 344; Discovery Education's puzzle creation feature for, 298

Q

Questions: matching, 379–380; multiple-choice, 380; using objective, 379, 381; open-ended, 225, 384; short-answer, 380

Quiz Bowl game, 316

Quiz design: matching questions, 379–380; multiple-choice questions, 380; objective questions used in, 379, 381; short-answer questions, 380; true-or-false statements, 379

Quizlet Web site, 411

Quizzes: conduct rules for, 381–382; as either summative or formative assessments, 377; emergency drill interrupting, 498–499; problem of no name on, 499–500; strategies for designing fair and valid, 378–379; what to do if many students fail a, 382–383

Qwizdom Web site, 386

R

Reading Is Fundamental Web site, 424

Reading skills: activities after students have read an assignment, 423–424; activities for students before reading an assignment, 419–421; activities while students are reading an assignment, 421–423; diverse approaches to teaching, 417; guidelines for helping students with their, 418–419; online resources on teaching, 422, 424; providing students with navigation tools for reading, 420; strategies to help students improve their, 417–418

ReadWriteThink Web site, 424

Reagan, Kristin: on motivating students, 241; on paperwork management, 52; on planning to minimize stress, 61; on stress management, 32

Reciprocal teaching instruction, 267

Recycling toss activity, 162

Reference materials, 410

Referrals: avoid making disruption worse when making, 471; how to respond when you disagree with administrator's action, 471; maintaining credibility when making a, 470–471; when it is time to make a, 469–470

Reflection. *See* Student reflection; Teacher reflection

Reflective discussions instruction, 261

Reflective practice: description of, 9; questions to ask for developing a, 9–10; Template for Professional Self-Reflection worksheet, 11

Reputation, 76–77

Response to Intervention (RTI): differentiated learning application of, 345; online resources on, 346

Restroom trips, 192

Review sessions: description of, 370; used as formative assessments, 370–372

Rewards: for good behavior, 442; offering incentives through, 464

Riddles.com, 199

Risk-free environment: making your classroom a, 162; managing name calling for a, 171–172; protecting students from bullies for a, 168–171; strategies and tips for creating a, 162–163

Rogers, V., 332

Rogow, Faith, 403

Role models: of acceptance and support to gay and lesbian students, 350; Are You a Good Role Model? worksheet, 149; being a role model to students, 147–149; Learning from Exemplary Teachers worksheet, 13; Making the Most of Peer Observations worksheet, 16; motivating students by being a, 224; role modeling the good behaviors you want from students, 203; seeking feedback on your professional performance, 15; tips for finding appropriate, 14. *See also* Mentors

Roundtables activity, 344

Routines. *See* Classroom routines

Rubrics: description of, 386; how to develop your own, 386–387; interactive whiteboards to demonstrate, 270; involving students in the development of a, 388; online resources on developing and using, 387–388; sample of a simple, 387

Rules. *See* Classroom rules

S

Safety issues: activities and, 456; coping with chronic misbehavior and any, 465; electric cords and student safety, 66; fire, disaster, and intruder drills, 69; suggestions for classroom and personal safety, 67–69; when moving heavy objects, 66. *See also* Violence

Sager, Erin: on being firm and fair as key to classroom management, 218; on "story of the day" activity to build relationships, 155; on using a timer with magnet to manage class time, 187

Samples: Hall Pass, 193; Homework Letter to Parents or Guardians,

245–246; instructional use of models, examples, and, 326–327; Letter of Introduction to Parents or Guardians, 114; Positive Message to Parents or Guardians, 92; simple rubric, 387. *See also* Worksheets

Save the Last Word activity, 344

Scaffolding: for gifted students, 357–359; motivating students by, 225; for students with special needs, 359, 360–361

Scheibe, Cynthia L., 403

Scholastic Web site, 422, 424

School community: communities of practice participation by, 74–75; guidelines for using social media, 80–81; how your attendance or absence impacts the, 81; network of teams making up your, 73–74; reflections on collaborating with your, 104–105; where you fit in as a new teacher, 75; your reputation for integrity in your, 76–77. *See also* Administrators; Parents/guardians; Teachers

School computers: dos and don'ts for using, 41–42; issues to teachers, 41

School districts: basic school law followed by, 455; course overview using curriculum guidelines, 287

School newspaper, 423

School Notes Web site, 58

School nurse's office: sending student injured in fights to the, 480; student feigning illness in order to go to, 488–489; when to send a student to the, 191

School policy problems: dress code violations, 493–494; students and public displays of affection, 494–495; students committing theft, 495–497; students misbehaving in the hallway, 494; students sexting, 495. *See also* Classroom policies

School resources: easy ways to protect, 66–67; how to request repairs on equipment and other, 67

School term: being adequately prepared at start of the, 281; Best

Practice Checklist, 137–138; first-day tasks to create successful, 107–135; first-week planning for a successful, 135–137; mistakes to avoid at the start of the, 136–137; reflections on beginning a successful, 138

SchoolExpress Web site, 37

Schools: challenges facing today's, 2–3; making student referrals to the office, 469–471; problems associated with enforcing policies or rules of, 493–497; sending student to nurse's office, 191, 480; student requests to go to the office, 191. *See also* Administrators

Scissors, 36

Scott, Luann: on student's note, 3; on taking advantage of your closing time, 199; on instilling confidence in your students, 395

Searching student property, 456

Seating arrangements: benefits of assigned seating, 70; creating seating charts, 65–66, 108; issues to consider for creating the best, 64; three different types of, 64–65

Seating charts, 65–66, 108

Seatwork: creating appealing, 327–328; handouts for, 211–212, 327

Security of personal belongings, 36

Self-directed learners, 357

Self-efficacy motivation, 241–242

Self-fulfilling prophecy, 221–222

Setting and Achieving SMART Goals worksheet, 239–240

Sexting, 495

Sexual abuse, 156

Sexual harassment, 469, 479

Sexual orientation: gay and lesbian students, 350–351; when to seek professional help on issues of, 156

Shaping-Up Review activity, 344

Share My Lesson Web site, 299

Short-answer questions test, 380

Simon Says game, 233

Simulations games, 317

Situated Learning: Legitimate Peripheral Participation (Lave and Wenger), 74

Skype Web site, 273

Slate Magazine, 188

Sleeping in class, 492–493

Slide shows, 311

SlideShare Web site, 274

SMART goals: Are You in Charge of Your Career? workshop to track, 26; as best practice, 32; goal-oriented approach to learning using, 238–240; professional growth by setting, 25; Setting and Achieving SMART Goals worksheet, 239–240

Smart Tech Web site, 274

Smarter Balanced Assessment Consortium Web site, 285

Social media sites: Facebook class page, 160; Flickr, 160; guidelines for using, 80–81; Tumblr, 160, 270, 274; Twitter, 75, 160, 270, 274; You Tube, 271

Socratic seminars instruction, 266

Southern Poverty Law Center, 166

Speaking skills: importance of developing, 405; strategies for teaching, 405; *Well Spoken: Teaching Speaking to All Students* (Palmer) on, 406. *See also* Oral presentations

Special education teachers, 361–362

Spiderweb activity, 162

Sporting events game, 318

Sronce, Jared: on addressing the misbehavior and not the student, 471; on benefits of transparent classrooms, 87; on communicating common purpose with parents, 99; on first-day jitters, 107; on time management, 46

Staff: chain of command, 82–83; treating them like colleagues, 82. *See also* Colleagues

Standardized test preparation: debate over teaching to the test, 398; helping your students to succeed with, 395–396; strategies for yearlong, 396; teaching students test-taking skills, 396–397; your professional responsibilities in regard to testing, 397–398

Standardized test scores: NCLB mandate on, 8; value-added assessments of, 20–21. *See also* Summative assessments; Tests

Stankiewicz, Kathleen: on using cell phones as instructional tool, 268; on engaging students right away, 183; on having a sense of humor, 503; on writing a letter of introduction to students, 115

Stapler ("Student Use"), 36

Stapler ("Teacher Use"), 36

State standards: being familiar with your, 281, 282; Common Core State Standards Initiative (CCSSI) on, 283–285; course overview inclusion of, 286; daily plans inclusion of, 292; differentiated instruction and use of, 337; potential resources to learn about your, 283. *See also* Legal issues

Stealing, 469

Stephenson, Kay: on being a teacher and not a pal, 328; on being enthusiastic about your subject, 320; on not lecturing entire block, 289; on reading skills being important for all subjects, 419

Sticky note note-taking activity, 344

Storytellers game, 316

Stress management: good planning as, 61; importance of, 31; strategies for, 31–32

Structure building activity, 161

Struggling student tiered instruction, 340

Student behaviors: crying, 487; disadvantaged students and related, 355; disorganization, 487–488; distracted by toys, trinkets, and grooming, 491–492; eating in class, 488; feigning illness, 488–489; how to focus your class on good, 202–203; impatient students, 233; invisible students, 489; lying, 490; new students, 490–491; note passing, 491; rewarding good, 442; role modeling good, 203; sleeping in class, 492–493; unacceptable student, 449–450. *See also* Classroom management;

Classroom rules; Student misbehaviors

Student cars, 192

Student collaboration: online collaboration activity for, 344; providing opportunities for, 226. *See also* Collaboration

Student conferences: to discuss misbehavior, 465; how to conduct the, 466; what to do at end of the, 467; what to do before the, 466

Student-created board games, 317–318

Student Information Form, 121–122

Student information records: Class Log Page worksheet for recording homework, 256; confidential, 52; creating, 120; how to organize and manage, 53–54; Student Information Form, 121–122; type of documents related to, 51–52. *See also* Grading

Student inventory worksheets: Inventory for Elementary Students, 127–128; Inventory for High School Students, 131–132; Inventory for Middle School Students, 129–130; more items to fill out on your students, 133

Student misbehaviors: absenteeism, 474–476; coping with chronic, 465; disadvantaged students and related, 355; dress code violations, 493–494; fighting and violence, 36, 450, 455–456, 470–471, 478–480; in the hallway, 494; how to prevent repetitive, 472; as mask for poor performance or other problems, 348; persistent defiance, 469, 501–502; public displays of affection, 494–495; student conferences on, 465–467; substance abuse, 156, 450, 469–471, 476–478; take a problem-solving approach to, 484–486; tardiness, 450, 472–474; types of unacceptable, 449–450; violence and fighting, 36, 450, 455–456, 470–471, 478–480. *See also* Behaviors; Classroom

Student misbehaviors (*cont'd*) problems; Difficult students; Discipline problems

Student names, 123

Student observations activity, 344

Student reflection: after class discussion, 314; Assignment Reflection worksheet for, 376; daily plans inclusion of, 292; Easy-to-Use Format for Daily Lesson Plans worksheet on, 294. *See also* Teacher reflection

Student requests to leave classroom: guidelines for handling, 192–193; Hall Pass form, 193; how to establish a fair policy for, 194; keeping track of students who leave, 194; Student Sign-Out Sheet worksheet, 195; suggestions on handling specific types of, 191–192

Student Sign-Out Sheet worksheet, 195

Student-student relationships: Best Practices Checklist to promote, 173; bullying, 68, 156, 168–172; Checklist of Social Skills All Students Should Master worksheet, 167; handling requests to leave the classroom, 191–196; helping to nurture, 157; making your classroom a risk-free environment to promote, 162–163; "mean girls" and, 171; peer acceptance and, 157–159; peer conflicts and, 165–166, 171–172; peer pressure role in, 171, 172–173, 443; peer tutoring, 163–164, 464; reflections on your class, 174; removing barriers to peer acceptance, 157–159; resolving peer conflicts to promote, 165–166; shared experiences and shared tasks, 159–160; supportive class chemistry for, 157; teaching and practicing courtesy for, 152, 164–165; team-building activities to promote, 160–162; technology and online resources for promoting, 160

Student success: handling student failures experienced before, 403; motivating by facilitating

attainable, 231–232; motivating students through visible, 241; putting your students in best position for, 310, 346; with standardized tests, 395–398; taking strategic steps toward, 260. *See also* Instruction

Student theft: dealing with a, 496–497; preventing, 496

Student work: ask students to write their name on the board when finished, 439; assigning enough, 180; decorating classroom using, 61–62; distributing handouts for, 211–212; failure to complete, 450; focusing your instruction delivery on, 304; lost papers, 212; plan for quiet work days for, 336; preventing discipline problems by providing meaningful, 441; problem of students who forget to turn in their, 501; providing authentic audiences for, 225; providing signals to indicate when students need help with, 439; providing students with checklist to follow for, 439; turning in completed teamwork papers, 212. *See also* Assignments

Students: assessing prior knowledge of your, 285–286, 289; calm their first-day fears, 109–110; cheating by, 393–394; create a positive group identity among your, 133–135; creating a homework partnership with, 244–246; Data Tracking Sheet worksheet on, 22–23; don't give up on your difficult, 463; using the door-to-door approach with, 180; ensuring the safety of your, 66, 67–69; getting to know your, 123–133; health and medical needs of, 66, 67–70, 152, 191, 457; how much personal information to share with your, 150–151; impatient, 233; learning their names quickly, 123; letting them know that you care, 151–153; making referrals to administrator, 469–471; managing e-mail from, 56–57; the opportunity to make a positive difference in lives of,

2–3; personal dictionaries owned by each, 409; protecting health of your, 69–70; providing signals they can use to get help quickly, 439; raising their class time awareness, 179, 180–181; supervision of, 456; take and display photographs of your, 153; teachers as role models for, 147–149; teachers earning the respect of their, 440; teaching them to believe in themselves, 153–154; test-taking skills by, 396–397; when they challenge grades, 392–393; writing a letter introducing yourself to, 115. *See also* Basic skills; Motivating students; Teacher-student relationships

Students needing special care: at-risk students, 348–350; with attention disorders, 346–347; with autism spectrum disorders (ASD), 355–357; gay and lesbian students, 350–351; gifted students, 357–359; students who are underachievers, 352–354; students with 504 plans, 347–348; students with special needs, 359–362; who are living in poverty, 354–355; who are not native speakers, 351–352. *See also* Differentiated instruction

Students with special needs: description of, 359; instructional strategies for, 360–361; online resources on, 359–360; Public Law 94-142 mandate on, 359; strategies for teaching, 360

Study Blue Web site, 411

Substance abuse: making referrals for, 469–471; mistakes to avoid when trying to help students with, 477; strategies that work to help students with, 477–478; student issues with, 156, 450, 476; your responsibilities regarding students', 476

Suicide threats/attempts, 156

Summative assessments: data-driven instruction shaped by, 365–366; description of the, 365; Format for a Unit Plan worksheet on, 290. *See also*

Assessments; Standardized test scores

Supervision requirements, 456

Supervisors. *See* Administrators

Supplies: basic items you'll need, 37–38; online resources for freebie, 37; pens/pencils, 36; priority items to purchase for yourself, 39–40; shared supplies bank for students with need, 211, 355; useful items that may come in handy, 38–39

Supplies bank, 211, 355

Survivor activity, 161

Sweet treats, 228

Syllabus, 225

T

Tag Galaxy Web site, 160, 271, 274

Take-home tests, 385

Talk Show game, 316

Talking back, 503

Tardiness: mistakes to avoid when dealing with, 473; strategies that work to manage, 474; unacceptable behavior of habitual, 450, 472–473; your responsibilities to control, 473

Task cards activity, 343

Tasks: how to prioritize your, 42–43; Meet Your Classroom Priorities worksheet on, 44; time management for accomplishing, 46–49

Teach Net Web site, 392

Teacher reflection: on assessing your students' progress, 399–400; on class time control, 200; on collaboration and school community, 104–105; on creating a successful school term, 138; daily plan inclusion of, 293; on developing positive classroom relationships, 174; on differentiated instruction, 363; on discipline problem management, 481–482; Easy-to-Use Format for Daily Lesson Plans worksheet on, 294; on engaging instruction delivery, 328–329; on instructional strategies and technologies, 276–277; on learning to solve classroom problems, 504; on

motivating students to succeed, 257–258; on preventing discipline problems, 444–445; on teaching basic skills, 425–426; on what it means to be a twenty-first-century educator, 33; on your classroom management, 71, 219–220. *See also* Student reflection

Teacher-student relationships: becoming a culturally responsive educator for positive, 154–156; being a facilitator, guide, coach, and learning partner with students, 139–140; being a role model component of, 147–149, 203, 224, 350; characteristics of a positive, 140–141; classroom immediacy role in, 143–146; classroom power struggles, 502–503; fairness importance to, 145; How Appropriate Are Your Relationships with Students? worksheet, 142; how much of yourself to share issue of, 150–151; letting your students know you care, 151–153; limits of your responsibility to students, 156–157; maintaining a certain emotional distance from students, 141; persistent defiance, 469, 501–502; the problem with being a popular teacher, 151; problems associated with, 501–503; student expectations from their teachers, 143; students who talk back, 503; teaching students to believe in themselves, 153–154; verbal immediacy to create positive, 146–147. *See also* Classroom relationships; Students

Teachers: attendance versus absence by, 81; becoming a culturally responsive educator, 154–156; being a role model to students, 147–149; classroom charisma of, 303–304; common challenges faced by all, 3–4; conducting parent conferences, 97–99; defining traits of today's, 1–2; delivering engaging instruction, 303–329; earning the respect of their students, 440; final ideas to

keep in mind for your first year, 505; highly effective, 8–10; how much personal information to share with students issue for, 150–151; learning from role models and mentors, 14–16; learning to manage your stress, 31–32; the problem with being a popular, 151; problems relating to parents and guardians, 100; responsibilities in regard to testing, 397–398; sense of humor by, 152, 503; special education, 361–362; what parents and guardians expect from, 85–86; withitness of, 436–437. *See also* Collaboration; Parent/guardian-teacher communication; School community

Teacher's Corner Web site, 63, 494

Teacher's Daily To-Do List worksheet, 47–48

The Teacher's Guide to Media Literacy: Critical Thinking in a Multimedia World (Scheibe and Rogow), 403

Teachers Network Web site, 299, 392

TeachersFirst Web site, 356, 357

TeacherTube Web site, 199, 271

TeacherVision Web site, 201

Teaching: challenges and rewards of, 378; classroom rules, 216–217; debate over covering the curriculum versus, 280–281; debate over teaching to the test approach of, 398; maintaining creativity in your, 326; to an objective, 180; students to follow directions, 232–233; students to practice courtesy, 164–165. *See also* Instructional strategies

Teaching Channel Web site, 202, 271, 300

Teaching profession: challenges of our changing, 2–3; successful management of your, 3–4; three principles of professionalism by, 5–9

Teaching skills: ability to collaborate, 73–105; classroom management skills, 35–71; maintaining sustained professional growth in, 25–30; strategies for improving, 13–24;

Teaching skills (*cont'd*)
withitness as valuable, 436–437.
See also Best Practices Checklist;
Evaluation

Teaching That Makes Sense Web
site, 407

Teaching Tolerance Web site, 166

Teachnology Web site, 93, 412, 422

Team-building activities: list of easy
to do, 161–162; promoting
supportive class through,
160–161

*Team Challenges: 170+Group Activities
to Build Cooperation,
Communication, and Creativity*
(Bordessa), 161

Technological classroom resources:
apps, 274–275; Best Practices
Checklist on, 275–276; blogs,
271–272; cell phones, 268–269;
interactive whiteboards, 269–270;
iPads, 270–271; podcasting,
272–273; reflections on, 276–277;
useful Web sites for educators,
273–274. *See also* Instructional
strategies; Online resources; Web
sites

Technology: creating a transparent
classroom using, 87; promoting a
supportive classroom community
using, 160

TED Web site, 274

Telephone calls: strategies for
effective communication, 95–96;
when appropriate with parents
and guardians, 95

Template for Professional Self-
Reflection, 11

Test design: matching questions,
379–380; multiple-choice
questions, 380; objective
questions used in, 379, 381;
short-answer questions, 380;
true-or-false statements, 379

Test-taking skills, 396–397

Tests: conduct rules for, 381–382;
as either summative or formative
assessments, 377; emergency drill
interrupting, 498–499; problem
of no name on, 499–500;
strategies for designing fair and
valid, 377–378; variations on
traditional types of, 385; what to
do if many students fail a,

382–383. *See also* Standardized
test scores

Theater/dramatic presentations,
311

Theft. *See* Student theft

Thinkfinity Web site, 300

Thomas, Stephen B., 455

Threats: making referrals if student
has made a, 469; as unacceptable
behavior by students, 450

Tic-tac-toe, 161, 317

Tiered instruction, 340–341

Time management: Checklist of a
Teacher's Weekly Reminders
worksheet, 49; examples of
efficient, 45; Teacher's Daily
To-Do List worksheet, 47–48;
tips for effective, 45. *See also*
Class time control

Time sequence maps, 320

Timetoast Web site, 273

Tingo Tango activity, 345

Today's Cartoon by Randy
Glasbergen Web site, 188

Tomlinson, Carol Ann, 332

Toys: students who distract
themselves with, 491–492; as
teaching visuals, 314–315

Track Your Professional Goals
worksheet, 30

Tracking Formative Assessment
Data worksheet, 368

Traditional row seating, 64

Traffic flow (classroom), 63–64

Transparent classroom: How
Effective Are You at Creating a
Transparent Classroom?
worksheet, 89; prevent
miscommunication with a,
86–87; successful open house to
create a, 88; using technology to
create a, 87

Trays (teacher's desk), 36

Trinket distractions, 491–492

Truancy: making referrals because
of student, 470–471;
unacceptable behavior of
habitual, 450. *See also*
Absenteeism

Trust: motivating students by
building, 223; strategies for
building, 76–77; as vital part of
teacher-student relationship, 153

Tumblr Web site, 160, 270, 274

Twitter: building communities of
practice through, 75; iPads for
accessing, 270; microblogging
using, 274; promoting a
supportive class through, 160

Two-minute dismissal, 197

Two-minute questions activity, 345

U

Unacceptable student behaviors,
449–450

Uncooperative parents/guardians,
102–103

Underachieving students:
suggestions for working with,
353–354; understanding factors
related to, 352

Understanding by Design (Wiggins
and McTighe), 280

Unit plans: determine number and
priority of, 287; Format for a
Unit Plan worksheet, 290;
gathering baseline data before
beginning study of, 370; issues to
consider for, 289

University of Michigan's Center for
Research on Learning and
Teaching Web site, 260

Unreasonable parents/guardians,
102

Unsafe behavior, 450

V

Value-added assessment:
description of, 20; how to avoid
being adversely affected by,
20–21; impact on the evaluation
process by, 20

Vandalism: making referrals for,
469–471; strategies for
preventing, 66

Verbal abuse: name calling as type
of, 171–172; seeking professional
help with, 156; words and
phrases to avoid, 146–147

Verbal immediacy: description of,
146; "I" messages used for, 147;
words and comments to avoid,
146–147

Videos: interactive whiteboards to
show, 270; iPad for sharing, 271;
make student, 311; problem of
restless students during viewing
of, 500

Violence: making referrals because of student, 470–471; storing items that could potentially be used as weapons, 36; student fighting, 478–480; teacher responsibility to protect students from, 455–456; as unacceptable behavior, 450. *See also* Conflict; Safety issues

Vocabulary acquisition skills: activities for teaching, 409–410, 411–412; importance of developing, 407; making your classroom rich in vocabulary words, 409–410; online resources on, 410, 412; strategies for teaching, 407–408

Vocabulary charades activity, 343

Voice tone, 309

W

Warm-up or introductory activities, 184–185

Water fountain trips, 192

Weapons: fights with, 480; making referrals for, 469–471; storing items that could potentially be used as, 36; unacceptable behavior of violence and use of, 450

Web English Teacher Web site, 407

Web sites: A to Z Teacher Stuff, 93, 298; Abcteach, 37; About.com Freebies, 37; AllThingsPLC, 75; American Rhetoric, 185; Animoto, 273; Audacity, 273; Autism Society, 356; Brain Bashers, 185; Behavior Advisor, 441; Behaviour Needs, 441; B.J.'s Homework Helper, 253; Block Posters, 37; Boardgames.com, 318; BrainCurls, 190; Center for Media Literacy, 403; Classroom Tripod, 58; Common Core State Standards Initiative, 284–285; Council for Exceptional Children, 359; Critical Thinking, 413; Critical Thinking Community, 413; Cyber Bullying Research Center, 170–171; Dave's ESL Cafe, 318, 352; Day of Silence, 351; Dictionary.com, 406; Discovery Education, 298, 318; Drummond Woodsum, 455;

Edublogs, 273; Education Oasis, 184, 320; Education World, 184, 350; Educator's Network, 388; Educator's PLN, 75; Edudemic, 273; edWeb.net, 75; eInstruction Corporation, 386; Explore, 299; Facebook, 160; Federal Resources for Educational Excellence, 299, 424; Flashcard Machine, 411; Flickr, 160; ForLessonPlans, 299; 4Teachers, 274, 387; Free Technology for Teachers, 274; freebie school supplies, 37; Gizmo's Freeware, 410; Google Images, 188; Homework Spot, 253; Houghton Mifflin, 320; Human Rights Watch, 350; iLoveLanguages translator, 93; Independent Television Service, 299; Innovative Learning, 260; Instructify, 274; Interactive Wordplays, 412; International Reading Association, 424; Intervention Central, 346, 441; Kathy Schrock's Guide to Everything, 63, 275, 387–388; Khan Academy, 253; Kid Blog, 160; Kid-cast.com, 273; Knowmia, 273; LD Online, 359; Learn Boost, 390; Learner Profile, 390; Learning Disabilities Association of America (LDA), 359–360; Learning-Theories, 260; Learning Through Listening, 404; Lesson Planet, 299; Lesson Plans Page, 299; LessonPlans.com, 299; Live Binders, 274; Many Teaching Ideas, 404; Maps.com, 185; Marzano Research Laboratory, 412; Mastery Connect, 274; Media Literacy.com, 403; Media Smarts, 403; Merriam-Webster's Word Central, 412; Multnomah County Oregon Public Library, 253; National Association for Gifted Children, 357; National Association for Media Literacy Education (NAMLE), 403; National Center on Response to Intervention, 346; National Education Association (NEA), 201, 299, 441; National Geographic, 253; National

Institute of Child Health and Human Development, 356; National Writing Project, 407; Online Books, 410; Out of the Box Games, 318; Oxford Dictionaries, 189; Partnership for Assessment of Readiness for College and Careers, 285; Peace Education Foundation, 166; Pinterest, 274; Podcasting Tools, 273; Podomatic, 273; Political Cartoons, 188; Poll Everywhere, 274; Prezi, 160; Print-A-Poster.com, 37; Pro Teacher, 494; Project Gutenberg, 410; Project Look Sharp, 403; ProTeacher, 412; ProTeacher Directory, 441; Quizlet, 411; Qwizdom, 386; Reading Is Fundamental, 424; ReadWriteThink, 424; Riddles.com, 199; Scholastic, 422, 424; School Notes, 58; SchoolExpress, 37; Share My Lesson, 299; Skype, 273; SlideShare, 274; Smart Tech, 274; Smarter Balanced Assessment Consortium, 285; Study Blue, 411; Tag Galaxy, 160, 271, 274; Teach Net, 392; Teacher's Corner, 63, 494; Teachers Network, 299, 392; TeachersFirst, 356, 357; TeacherTube, 199, 271; TeacherVision, 201; Teaching Channel, 202, 271, 300; Teaching That Makes Sense, 407; Teaching Tolerance, 166; Teachnology, 93, 412, 422; TED, 274; Thinkfinity, 300; Timetoast, 273; Today's Cartoon by Randy Glasbergen, 188; Tumblr, 160, 270, 274; Twitter, 75, 160, 270, 274; University of Michigan's Center for Research on Learning and Teaching, 260; Web English Teacher, 407; Wikispaces, 273; Wired Kids, 170; World Dynamo, 188; World News, 185; You Tube, 271. *See also* Online resources; Technological classroom resources

WebQuests instruction, 265–266

Webster, R., 332

Welcome packets: create a first-day-of-school, 111; tips for managing

Welcome packets (*cont'd*)
the, 111–112; what to include in,
112
Well-managed classroom resources,
201–202
*Well Spoken: Teaching Speaking to All
Students* (Palmer), 406
Wenger, Etienne, 74
Werner, Mark, 404
What Is Your Level of Withitness?
worksheet, 437
Where to Find Help with
Establishing Procedures
worksheet, 210
Whole-group horseshoe seating, 65
Wiggins, Grant, 280
Wikis: interactive whiteboards to
display, 270; Wikispaces Web site
for creating, 273
Wired Kids, 170
Withitness: cultivating your own
classroom, 436; definition of,
436; What Is Your Level of
Withitness? worksheet, 437
Word games, 411
Word of the day activity, 409
Word splashes activity, 345
Word wall activity, 409
Work area: arranging your own, 35;
tips for your desk area, 36
Work Through Classroom
Problems worksheet, 486
Worksheets: Are You a Good Role
Model?, 149; Are You in Charge
of Your Career?, 26; Assignment
Checklist, 237; Assignment
Reflection, 376; Behavior
Incident Report, 457;
Characteristics of Successful
Teachers, 12; Checklist for the

First Day, 119; Checklist of a
Teacher's Weekly Reminders, 49;
Checklist of Social Skills All
Students Should Master, 167;
Checklist to Determine If Your
Rules Will Be Successful, 215;
Class Log Page, 256; Classroom
Management Techniques to
Avoid, 454; Contact
Documentation Form, 91; Data
Tracking Sheet, 22–23; Easy-to-
Use Format for Daily Lesson
Plans, 294; Format for a Course
Overview, 288; Format for a Unit
Plan, 290; Grade Tracking Form
for Student Success, 391; How
Appropriate Are Your
Relationships with Students?,
142; How Effective Are You at
Creating a Transparent
Classroom?, 89; How Effective
Are You at Preventing Discipline
Problems?, 431; How Well Do
You Use Class Time?, 177–178;
Individualized Instruction
Worksheet, 335; Inventory: Please
Tell Me About Your Child, 113;
Inventory for Elementary
Students, 127–128; Inventory for
High School Students, 131–132;
Inventory for Middle School
Students, 129–130; Learning
from Exemplary Teachers, 13;
Making the Most of Peer
Observations, 16; Meet Your
Classroom Priorities, 44; Missing
Homework Explanation Form,
252; Plan Successful Homework
Assignments, 248; Planning for
Classroom Policies, 205–208;

Planning Template for the First
Day of School, 117–118; A
Planning Tool for
Differentiation, 338; Plans for
Ending Class Effectively, 198;
Plans for Starting Class
Effectively, 186; Preventing or
Minimizing Discipline Problems,
433; Progress Tracking Chart,
243; Setting and Achieving
SMART Goals, 239–240; Student
Information Form, 121–122;
Student Sign-Out Sheet, 195;
Teacher's Daily To-Do List,
47–48; Template for Professional
Self-Reflection, 11; Track Your
Professional Goals, 30; Tracking
Formative Assessment Data, 368;
What Is Your Level of
Withitness?, 437; Where to Find
Help with Establishing
Procedures, 210; Work Through
Classroom Problems, 486. *See
also* Samples
World Dynamo Web site, 188
Worlds News Web site, 185
Write-pair-shares activity, 342
Writing skills: importance of
developing good, 406; online
resources on teaching, 407;
strategies for teaching, 406
Written communication: class
newsletters, 96–97; e-mail, 56–57,
101, 160; taking care with, 94–95

Y

You Tube, 271

Z

Zysk, Veronica, 356

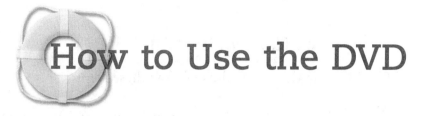

How to Use the DVD

System Requirements

PC with Microsoft Windows 2003 or later
Mac with Apple OS version 10.1 or later

Using the DVD with Windows

To view the items located on the DVD, follow these steps:

1. Insert the DVD into your computer's DVD drive.
2. A window appears with the following options:

   Contents: Allows you to view the files included on the DVD.

   Software: Allows you to install useful software from the DVD.

   Links: Displays a hyperlinked page of websites.

   Author: Displays a page with information about the author(s).

   Contact Us: Displays a page with information on contacting the publisher or author.

   Help: Displays a page with information on using the DVD.

   Exit: Closes the interface window.

If you do not have autorun enabled, or if the autorun window does not appear, follow these steps to access the DVD:

1. Click Start → Run.
2. In the dialog box that appears, type d:\start.exe, where d is the letter of your DVD drive. This brings up the autorun window described in the preceding set of steps.

3. Choose the desired option from the menu. (See Step 2 in the preceding list for a description of these options.)

In Case of Trouble

If you experience difficulty using the DVD, please follow these steps:

1. Make sure your hardware and systems configurations conform to the systems requirements noted under "System Requirements" above.

2. Review the installation procedure for your type of hardware and operating system. It is possible to reinstall the software if necessary.

To speak with someone in Product Technical Support, call 800-762-2974 or 317-572-3994 Monday through Friday from 8:30 a.m. to 5:00 p.m. EST. You can also contact Product Technical Support and get support information through our website at www.wiley.com/techsupport.

Before calling or writing, please have the following information available:

- Type of computer and operating system.
- Any error messages displayed.
- Complete description of the problem.

It is best if you are sitting at your computer when making the call.